Shame Management Through Reintegra

This ground-breaking book is a ... best-selling and influential *Crime,* ... management is becoming a centr... ...pt, in theoretical and practical terms, across a range of fields. This book makes a major contribution to the advancement of shame in a theoretical sense, and through its detailed analysis of shame management in cases of drink-driving and school bullying, it increases our understanding of reintegrative shaming in a practical sense. Criminologists have been waiting for this book, but for psychology, sociology and other areas as well, this accessible book serves as an introduction to the concepts of shame, guilt and embarrassment. It has two major theoretical outcomes: it develops an ethical-identity conception of shame, and second, a theory of reintegrative shame management which will make it a central and lasting work. Written by the key exponents of restorative justice, the book is an important re-statement of the theory and practice of shaming. It will develop important and often controversial debates about punishment, shaming and restorative justice to a new level.

ELIZA AHMED is a postdoctoral fellow in the Research School of Social Sciences at the Australian National University.

NATHAN HARRIS is a postdoctoral fellow in the Faculty of Law at the Katholieke Universiteit Leuven.

JOHN BRAITHWAITE is a Professor in the Research School of Social Sciences at the Australian National University.

VALERIE BRAITHWAITE is a senior fellow in the Research School of Social Sciences at the Australian National University (ANU). She is also the director of the ANU's Centre for Tax System Integrity.

Cambridge Studies in Criminology

Edited by
Alfred Blumstein, *H. John Heinz School of Public Policy and Management, Carnegie Mellon University*
and David Farrington, *Institute of Criminology, University of Cambridge*

The Cambridge Studies in Criminology series aims to publish the highest quality research on criminology and criminal justice topics. Typical volumes report major quantitative, qualitative, and ethnographic research, or make a substantial theoretical contribution. There is a particular emphasis on research monographs, but edited collections may also be published if they make an unusually distinctive offering to the literature. All relevant areas of criminology and criminal justice are included, for example, the causes of offending, juvenile justice, the development of offenders, measurement and analysis of crime, victimization research, policing, crime prevention, sentencing, imprisonment, probation, and parole. The series is global in outlook, with an emphasis on work that is comparative or holds significant implications for theory or policy.

Other Books in the Series:

Life in the Gang: Family, Friends, and Violence, by Scott H. Decker and Barrik Van Winkle
Delinquency and Crime: Current Theories, edited by J. David Hawkins
Recriminalizing Delinquency: Violent Juvenile Crime and Juvenile Justice Reform, by Simon I. Singer
Mean Streets: Youth Crime and Homelessness, by John Hagan and Bill McCarthy
The Framework of Judicial Sentencing: A Study in Legal Decision Making, by Austin Lovegrove
The Criminal Recidivism Process, by Edward Zamble and Vernon L. Quinsey
Violence and Childhood in the Inner City, by Joan McCord
Judicial Policy Making and the Modern State: How the Courts Reformed America's Prisons, by Malcolm M. Feeley and Edward L. Rubin
Schools and Delinquency, by Denise C. Gottfredson
The Crime Drop in America, edited by Alfred Blumstein and Joel Wallman
Delinquent-Prone Communities, by Don Weatherburn and Bronwyn Lind
White-Collar Crime and Criminal Careers, by David Weisburd and Elin Waring, with Ellen F. Chayet
Sex Differences in Antisocial Behavior: Conduct Disorder, Delinquency, and Violence in the Dunedin Longitudinal Study, by Terrie Moffitt, Avshalom Caspi, Michael Rutter, and Phil A. Silva
Delinquent Networks: Youth Co-Offending in Stockholm, by Jerzy Sarnecki
Criminality and Violence among the Mentally Disordered, by Sheilagh Hodgins and Carl-Gunnar Janson
Companions in Crime: The Social Aspects of Criminal Conduct, by Mark Warr
Corporate Crime, Law, and Social Control, by Sally S. Simpson

Shame Management Through Reintegration

Eliza Ahmed

Australian National University

Nathan Harris

Katholieke Universiteit Leuven

John Braithwaite

Australian National University

Valerie Braithwaite

Australian National University

CAMBRIDGE
UNIVERSITY PRESS

PUBLISHED BY THE PRESS SYNDICATE OF THE UNIVERSITY OF CAMBRIDGE
The Pitt Building, Trumpington Street, Cambridge, United Kingdom

CAMBRIDGE UNIVERSITY PRESS
The Edinburgh Building, Cambridge CB2 2RU, UK
40 West 20th Street, New York, NY 10011–4211, USA
10 Stamford Road, Oakleigh, VIC 3166, Australia
Ruiz de Alarcón 13, 28014 Madrid, Spain
Dock House, The Waterfront, Cape Town 8001, South Africa

http://www.cambridge.org

First published 2001

Printed in China by Everbest Printing Co.

Typeface Baskerville MT 10.7/13 pt.   *System* QuarkXPress® [PH]

A catalogue record for this book is available from the British Library

ISBN 0521 80791 3 hardback
ISBN 052100370 9 paperback

Contents

Part IV Conclusion
Valerie Braithwaite and *John Braithwaite*

Tables and figures

Tables

Figures

Preface

All of us have worked on the implications of shame in relation to different kinds of wrongdoing over a number of years during which we have accumulated many debts. Foremost, we wish to express our appreciation for the special environment at the Australian National University which has enabled us to pursue a research agenda that has been richly informed by colleagues from different disciplinary perspectives, as well as by practitioners and policy makers. In particular, we wish to acknowledge the influence that Brent Fisse, Terry O'Connell, John McDonald, David Moore, Brenda Morrison, Yvonne Pittelkow, Ros Dalziell, Stephen Mugford, Tom Scheff, Suzanne Retzinger, Tom Tyler, Gary LaFree, Lawrence Sherman, Philip Pettit and Geoffrey Brennan have had on our thinking in recent years. We also thank the numerous other colleagues who have assisted us over the years with encouragement, intellectual exchange and administrative support. They come from many different parts of the university, but especially from the Centre for Restorative Justice of the Research School of Social Sciences and the Psychology Department. Thanks are also due to the Katholieke Universiteit Leuven where Nathan Harris received support for redrafting Part II.

Thanks to several perceptive readers of the manuscript who made unusually helpful comments and to Phillipa McGuinness of Cambridge University Press for her splendid editorial advice.

We owe special debts to those who made it possible for us to draw on empirical data to advance our thinking about shame and its management. We thank Heather Strang and Lawrence Sherman for access to the Reintegrative Shaming Experiment (RISE) data which they have worked so hard to collect and to all the people who have worked on this project, especially Jamie Burton and Geoffrey Barnes for help they provided in making Part II of this book possible. The empirical work presented in Part III of the book came about through the cooperation of the Australian Capital Territory (ACT) Schools Authority and the willing participation of 32 schools, their staff, students and parents. Our thanks to all Canberrans who shared their thoughts and experiences with us in the data collection phases of our research.

The data reported in this book were very costly to collect so we owe a debt to an unusually generous set of funders. First, we must thank the Criminology Research Council, which not only contributed to the research in both Parts II and III of the book, but also funded Moore and O'Connell's preliminary research in Wagga Wagga, which laid foundations for much in this work. Other major funders were the Federal Office of Road Safety, the National Drug Crime Prevention Fund, the Australian National University (ANU) Strategic Planning Fund, the US National Institute of Justice, the Smith Richardson Foundation, and the Australian Research Council. Thanks are also extended to Malcolm Mearns for his assistance with data collection and preparation in the research reported in Parts II and III.

This book comes in four Parts. Part I summarizes the findings of the whole book and suggests how those findings might lead to revision of the explanatory and normative theory of shame and wrongdoing. Part II is an empirical study of the structure of shame and shaming in the context of the criminal processing of adult drink drivers. Part III is a study of the relationship between shame and school bullying and of the shame management of bullies and victims of bullying. While the two empirical domains are very different, convergences in what they reveal about the nature of shame are remarkable, laying foundations for the theoretical reformulation in Part I. Part IV looks back at the limitations of the research and the implications for future work.

Eliza Ahmed, Nathan Harris, John Braithwaite and Valerie Braithwaite

Shame, Shame Management and Regulation

John Braithwaite and *Valerie Braithwaite*

CHAPTER 1

Shame and Shame Management

Shame Management and the Social Sciences

Shame and guilt are related concepts, more related in light of the research presented here than we might have thought. We show in this book that shame and guilt are central concepts across the social sciences – in psychiatry, psychology, education, the new sociology of the emotions, philosophy, criminology and even in economics. If Thomas Scheff (1990a, 1991, 1994, 1996b) is right that the appeal of leaders such as Hitler and Saddam Hussein has been to transform the shame of people who have been humiliated (at Versailles in the case of Hitler, by colonialism in the case of the Arab world), then understanding shame should be more central in political science and international relations than it is. Indeed we think Scheff is right that both war between nations and war within families are often about humiliated fury. We would add hubris (pride gone wrong as a result of poor shame management). Peacemaking at all levels must be about restoring dignity and learning shame management lessons from micro arenas such as we study here – school bullying and criminal justice. These arenas seem to us to have lessons for the peace movement.

Since Darwin, the universality of blushing and shame has also been a significant topic in the biological sciences. In this book we sidestep all the biological questions about shame: Is it a human universal? Has it been essential to survival because of its capacity to regulate violence against our loved ones and provoke violence against enemies who once were a threat to our survival? Is it triggered by threats to social bonds which are necessary to our survival? While we fail to make a contribution to the biology of shame, we hope to say something to all the social sciences mentioned above and to social movements – particularly those of the peace and restorative justice movements, but also to others such as the women's movement and

movements for Indigenous rights. The shame that oppressed Indigenous minorities or women who are victims of domestic violence feel is central to understanding the persistence of their domination.

Any actor in any kind of practical affairs cannot but be ineffective by denying shame and eschewing the challenge of understanding its dynamics. This is especially so in debates around crime – from juvenile justice to genocide and Apartheid – where shame is so acute. In Part III of the book Eliza Ahmed shows that failure to acknowledge shame and discharge it is in different ways a characteristic of both school bullies and victims of bullying. Healthy shame management is important to preventing bullying on both the offender side and the victim side. This is why school principals, teachers and concerned parents are also important audiences for this book along with judges, police and others concerned about the criminal justice system.

A crucial conclusion of the book is that learning to acknowledge shame and make it work for you is important to achieving any human objective. But this is especially so when profound ethical questions challenge us as to what sort of person we want to be, what sort of politics we want to identify with. Hence, we come in Chapter 11 in Part II to favor an ethical identity conception of shame, as found in the writings of the philosopher Bernard Williams (1993). According to this conception, shame is the emotion we feel when the way we feel about ourself as an ethical person is threatened by our actions.

Shame is an emotion, like pride or hatred. In this book we make a distinction between shame as an emotion and shaming as a regulatory practice. Formal punishments and rewards are other examples of regulatory practices. Just as we find that different ways of managing shame as an emotion can make crime or bullying worse, we also conclude that there are some kinds of shaming that make crime worse and other kinds that reduce crime. On the shaming question, we are building on John Braithwaite's (1989) theory in *Crime, Shame and Reintegration*. This argues that both the empirical literatures of child development and criminology are consistent with the prediction that stigmatizing shaming (stigmatization) makes crime worse, while reintegrative shaming reduces crime. Stigmatization means shaming by which the wrongdoer is treated disrespectfully as an outcast and as a bad person. Reintegrative shaming means treating the wrongdoer respectfully and empathically as a good person who has done a bad act and making special efforts to show the wrongdoer how valued they are after the wrongful act has been confronted.

One arena in which there is a spirited debate over whether shame and shaming are useful concepts is restorative justice. Restorative justice is about the notion that because crime (or any other kind of injustice) hurts, justice should heal. This is an alternative to the view that justice must be

punitive – responding to hurt with hurt that is the wrongdoer's just deserts. So restorative justice is about hurt begetting healing as an alternative to hurt begetting hurt. Some restorative justice advocates argue that shame and shaming have no place in restorative justice because shaming is a kind of hurting and shame is a destructive kind of hurt that can make crime and injustice worse.

We conclude that they are right when shaming is stigmatizing and when shame is unacknowledged. However, to acknowledge shame and discharge it and to shame acts of injustice reintegratively are both important for preventing injustice and enabling restoration, on the analysis presented here. So our argument is that shame and shaming are indispensable conceptual tools for understanding the effects of restorative justice. This is because it is imperative to distinguish between good and bad shaming and harmful and helpful shame. This does not mean that social movement advocates should actually use the word shame as part of their reform rhetoric; with restorative justice, as Braithwaite and Mugford (1994: p. 165) have suggested, responsibility and healing are likely to supply a more politically resonant, and a more prudent neo-liberal discourse than shame and reintegration.

Still our analytic point is that no progressive social movement is likely to be effective without shaming and promoting the just acknowledgment of shame. Restorative justice cannot be effective without shaming certain punitive practices such as the death penalty and rapidly increasing imprisonment rates. The social movement against Apartheid could not have been effective without shaming Apartheid and urging its architects to acknowledge their shame for the evils they perpetrated. While social movements can never change the world for the better by sweeping shameful truths under the carpet, our argument is that they can be more effective through truth and reconciliation (through shaming that is reintegrative) than through truth and stigmatization, retribution that replaces one outcast group with another.

It follows that the kinds of research on shame and shaming in this book are vital to advancing our understanding of the conditions for the success and failure of restorative justice. It is not that we are convinced we yet have the answers on how to think about shame and shaming; indeed, this book is partly about revealing empirically some of the errors of our past thinking. But with restorative justice policy we are convinced that the shame and shaming research agenda must be out in the open as a priority. And we are convinced that restorative justice is as important a topic for the future of the world as any. We have suggested already that it is important for building world peace and domestic streets, schools and families that are freed from violence. Sherman and Strang's (2000) early reoffending results, which

became public as this book went to press, showing 38 per cent less reoffending in Canberra violence cases randomly assigned to restorative justice compared to those assigned to court, add a new edge to this view. These new results came quickly on the heels of Burford and Pennell's (1998) Canadian findings that restorative justice conferences reduced family violence, Bonta, Wallace-Capretta and Rooney's (1998) results that the Restorative Resolutions project for serious adult offenders in Manitoba reduced reoffending, Maxwell, Morris and Anderson's (1999) findings that two adult restorative programs in New Zealand reduced violent and property reoffending, and McGarrell et al.'s (2000) randomized control trial in Indianapolis finding minor juvenile property and violent offenders had 40 per cent less offending than controls after six months, decaying to 25 per cent less after 12 months.

In another volume that complements this, John Braithwaite (2001) argues that while not all the evaluations are as encouraging as the most recent results discussed in the last paragraph, restorative justice is also important to understanding how to preserve the environment, how to confront poverty and educational disadvantage, how to nurture sustainable economic development and how to transform the entire legal system. The argument is not that restorative justice is the most important thing we can do about all these problems, but that it is one of the few promising things we can do for improving the way we deal with the widest range of our biggest problems.

In Part II of this book Nathan Harris discusses restorative justice conferences which involve all the stakeholders in a criminal offence (offenders, family members, victims, police) sitting in a circle to discuss what have been the consequences of the crime and what should be done to put those consequences right. But these restorative justice conferences are just one contemporary Australian modality of restorative justice. Across the ages and across the peoples of the world, we have seen many different culturally specific modalities of restorative justice. While this book is the product of an Australian research group working on two particular kinds of restorative justice operating in Canberra (three including the nursing home regulation work referred to occasionally), the research objective of the Centre for Restorative Justice is to advance the theory and practise of restorative justice of general import. Furthermore, while the research comes out of a Centre for Restorative Justice, in this particular book our central interest is understanding the nature of shame and its management as a general question for the theory of the social sciences. We hope readers will find that dissecting the effects of restorative justice gives us an unusually strategic vantage point for advancing this general theoretical project.

Shame, Guilt, Embarrassment

In Part II, Nathan Harris tackles the way shame has been distinguished as an emotion from guilt or embarrassment. Harris explored the dimensionality of these shame-related emotions by factor analyses of the emotions surrounding 900 drink-driving cases randomly assigned to court or to a restorative justice conference.

In addition to disagreement on phenomenology and dimensionality, approaches to shame have also differed in their predictions as to why people feel shame. In particular, they dispute the effect of social disapproval, otherwise referred to as shaming. An important issue is whether shame is a response to internalized values or simply a reaction to social pressure. The way disapproval is expressed may also have important implications for the emotions felt. Reintegrative shaming theory predicts that the effect of shaming is dependent upon whether shaming is reintegrative (respectful, healing) or stigmatic (disrespectful, degrading, outcasting). According to John Braithwaite's (1989) theory, reintegrative shaming prevents crime while stigmatization makes it worse. So in Part II the analysis of the dimensionality of the emotion of shame is followed by an exploration of the dimensionality of practices of shaming. Then Harris addresses the question of whether and in what way practices of shaming engender emotions of shame.

The dimensionality of the shame-related emotions was found to be equivalent in cases randomly assigned to court versus restorative justice conferences. Harris did not find the differences expected between shame and guilt. A single Shame–Guilt factor emerged. This factor was defined by feelings of having done wrong, concern that others had been hurt, feeling ashamed of oneself and one's act, feeling anger at oneself, loss of honor among family and friends. Observed remorse was associated with this factor. Indeed this factor might have been labeled Shame–Guilt–Remorse. Shame–Guilt predicted higher empathy with victims, lower feelings of hostility and had no correlation with self-esteem or self-respect in either court or conference cases.

This Shame–Guilt factor suggests that distinctions between shame and guilt in earlier studies may be conditional on the context or methodology employed. There were, however, differences between Shame–Guilt and an Embarrassment–Exposure factor, which measured feelings of self-awareness and awkwardness. A third factor, Unresolved Shame, involving ongoing feelings that issues and emotions had been unresolved, has similarities to earlier research on unacknowledged shame. So the research in Part II shows that the distinction between shame and guilt may be less important than distinctions between Shame–Guilt (the feeling we have

when our ethics are in question), Embarrassment–Exposure (the feeling we have when our nakedness, or some other feature of ourselves we do not want displayed, is exposed) and Unresolved Shame.

Embarrassment–Exposure levels are found to be higher in court cases than in restorative justice conferences, while Shame–Guilt has higher levels in restorative justice conferences. An even more important distinction that emerges, reinforced by the results in Part III, is that between acknowledged and unacknowledged shame. These results seem to fly in the face of a remarkably sustained and coherent program of research by June Price Tangney (1990, 1991, 1992, 1993, 1995a, 1995b) and her colleagues. These studies find a clear distinction between shame-proneness and guilt-proneness as dimensions of personality (as opposed to emotion). Shame-proneness in this research is a propensity to blame or devalue the whole self in the face of failures to deal with difficult situations. Guilt-proneness is a propensity to feel responsible for specific acts over which one has control. Shame-proneness is associated in this research with a variety of pathologies, including criminality, while guilt-proneness is negatively associated with these pathologies. Braithwaite (1989) has argued strongly for the position that guilt-induction is just one form of shaming. But Tangney's research challenges this viewpoint, suggesting instead that this was a mistake – that guilt-induction in respect of serious wrongs is desirable, while shame-induction is destructive of self and therefore of law-abiding identities.

The Tangney and Braithwaite analyses actually converge at a prescriptive level. What should be avoided are degrading or disrespectful ways of communicating disapproval of wrongdoing. But conceptually, Tangney's analysis means that Braithwaite's reintegrative shaming should really be described as reintegrative guilting – induction of guilt without shame. Indeed we went into this research thinking that the resolution of Braithwaite's and Tangney's positions might be that reintegrative shaming causes what Tangney calls guilt while averting what she calls shame. Harris's work in Part II set out to explore this question among others. Contrary to Tangney, and to our own hopes for a crisp clarification, our conclusion here is that induction of Shame–Guilt together is what happens with criminal offending.

There are at least three ways of thinking about these conflicting results. One is that feeling ashamed in relation to a criminal offense is a special context where guilt about the act and being ashamed as a person are hard to separate. Tangney's findings are more generalized to proneness to shame across many different problems of living (not just crime). Second, shame-proneness as a personality trait may be a very different matter than feeling the emotion of shame. Third, it may be that our conclusion is wrong, or

more likely, partially wrong. The third possibility is suggested by the fact that the item 'During the conference/court case I felt that I was a failure' did not load on Harris's Shame–Guilt factor. Tangney might point to this item to suggest that Harris's Shame–Guilt factor excludes the very kind of item she would want to label as shame rather than guilt. If only more items like this were included (such as 'I felt a bad person') a separate shame factor might have emerged. As against this, we would say Harris's Shame–Guilt factor does include strong loadings from items about feeling 'angry with myself' and 'ashamed of myself'. Contrary to studies on shame-proneness, the Shame–Guilt factor was positively related to empathy and negatively related to anger/hostility.

In pursuing clarification and reconciliation with the Tangney results, we suspect now that we have stumbled into a more subtle ethical identity conception of Shame–Guilt that might have special explanatory and normative power with respect to crime or other serious wrongdoing. It is easiest to explain at the normative level. What we had thought we wanted offenders to feel was shame about what they had done, but not shame about themselves. Now we think this may have been a normative error. If a man rapes a child or is repeatedly convicted for serious assaults, is it enough for him to feel that he has done a bad act(s) but that there is nothing wrong with him as a person? It would seem more morally satisfactory for him to feel that he has done a bad act and therefore feels he must change the kind of person he is in some important ways (while still on the whole believing he is basically a good person). That is, we do not want the rapist to believe he is an irretrievably evil person; but we do want aspects of the self to be transformed. Harris's Shame–Guilt factor seems to capture empirically the nub of this halfway house of an ethical ideal. To a considerable extent a person cannot experience guilt about a criminal wrong without this spilling over into feeling ashamed of oneself as a person. So long as this does not go so far as to involve a total rejection of self, this now seems to us morally appropriate, at least for serious crimes.

We have noted that in some of the cultures with the strongest traditions of restoration or healing following wrongdoing there is an explicitness of commitment to the halfway house of Shame–Guilt. In Japanese culture, for example, apology can amount to dissociation of that evil part of the self that committed a wrong (Wagatsuma & Rosett, 1986). Japanese idiom sometimes accounts for wrongdoing by possession by a *mushi* (bug or worm). Criminals are hence not acting according to their true selves; they are under attack by a *mushi* which can be 'sealed off' enabling reintegration without enduring shame (Wagatsuma & Rosett, 1986: 476).

Another culture with especially rich restorative accomplishment through its peacemaking traditions is the Navajo. The Navajo concept of *nayéé'* is an

interesting part of this accomplishment (Coker, 1999: 55). Farella (1984) explains that *nayéé'* or 'monsters' are anything that gets in the way of a person enjoying their life, such as depression, obsession and jealousy. 'The benefit of naming something a *nayéé'* is that the source of one's 'illness' – one's unhappiness or dysfunctionality – once named can be cured' (Coker, 1999: 55). And healing ceremonies are about helping people to rid themselves of *nayéé'*.

There seems to be a major difference between stigmatizing cultures and cultures such as the Japanese and the Navajo in which the vague and subjective threat to a person's integrity of self is named to make it concrete, and able to be excized. Naming to excise a bad part of self creates very different action imperatives for a society from naming to label a whole self as bad (such as naming a person a junkie, criminal or schizophrenic). The former kind of shame can be discharged with the expulsion of the *mushi* or *nayéé'*. The latter kind of stigma entrenches a master status trait such as 'schizophrenic' that dominates all other identities. We suspect that we can learn from other cultures the possibility of healing a damaged part of a self that is mostly good. This is the approach to which the conception of Shame–Guilt revealed by the analyses in Part II cues us. It particularly cues us to the possibility of healing a mostly positive and redeemable self because of the finding that both Shame–Guilt and reintegration are greater when cases are randomly assigned to a restorative justice process.

Shadd Maruna's (2001) powerful study, *Making Good: How Ex-Convicts Reform and Rebuild their Lives*, showed that even though his Liverpool sample might not have had the benefit of Japanese or Navajo cultural resources, serious offenders who went straight had to find a new way of making sense of their lives. They had to restory their life histories. They defined a new ethical identity for themselves that meant that they were able to say, looking back at their former criminal selves, that they were 'not like that any more' (Maruna, 2001: 7). His persistent reoffender sample, in contrast, were locked into 'condemnation scripts' whereby they saw themselves as irrevocably condemned to their criminal self-story.

This suggests a restorative justice that is about 'rebiographing'', restorative storytelling that redefines an ethical conception of the self. Garfinkel (1956: 421–22) saw what was at issue in 'making good'': 'the former identity stands as accidental; the new identity is the basic reality. What he is now is what, after all, he was all along.' So, Maruna found repeatedly that desisters from crime reverted to an unspoiled identity. As with the *mushi* and *nayéé'*, desisters had restoried themselves to believe that their formerly criminal self 'wasn't me'. The self that committed the crime was, in William James's terms, not the I (the self-as-subject, who acts) nor the Me (the self-as-object, that is acted upon), but what Petrunik and Shearing (1988) called the It, an

alien source of action (Maruna, 2001: 93). Even without the cultural resource of a *mushi*, restorative justice might therefore help Western wrongdoers to write their It out of the story of their true ethical identity. Maruna (2001: 13) also concluded that 'redemption rituals' as communal processes were important in this sense-making because desisting offenders often narrated the way their deviance had been decertified by important others such as family members or judges – the parent or policeman who said Johnny was now his old self. Howard Zehr (2000: 10) makes the point that whether we have victimized others or been victimized ourselves, we need social support in the journey 'to re-narrate our stories so that they are no longer just about shame and humiliation but ultimately about dignity and triumph'.

The factor analyses in Part II reveal that the amount of shaming perceived by offenders was independent of the degree to which cases were perceived as reintegrative or stigmatic. However, in contrast to the predictions made by Braithwaite's (1989) reintegrative shaming theory, stigmatization and reintegration were measured as independent concepts rather than opposite poles of the same concept. As predicted, conference cases were higher in shaming and reintegration but lower in stigmatization than court cases. The findings provide evidence for the reliability and validity of these measures of reintegrative shaming.

Shaming was found to predict Shame–Guilt but only when it was by people the offender highly respected. Furthermore, Shame–Guilt was predicted by the offender's perception that the offense was wrong. Shame–Guilt was also predicted by perceptions of having been reintegrated and perceptions of not having been stigmatized. It is argued that Shame–Guilt should be understood as a product of social influence in which internalized values, normative expectations and social context have an effect. In contrast to Shame–Guilt, Embarrassment–Exposure and Unresolved Shame were predicted by perceptions of having been stigmatized and the belief that the offense was less wrong. This highlights the importance of distinguishing between the shame-related emotions. So does the finding that Shame–Guilt was greater in restorative justice conferences but that Embarrassment–Exposure was greater in court cases.

In both Part II and Part III it was found that Unresolved Shame was associated with greater anger/hostility. This finding suggests that the resolution or management of shame may be as important as whether shame is felt. The results in Part II are interpreted as highlighting the need to complement the theory of reintegrative shaming with insights from Helen Lewis (1971) and Scheff's (1990a) work on by-passed shame, the social identity theory perspective of Tajfel and Turner (1979) and the ethical conception of shame that one finds in the writing of Williams (1993). These conceptions are developed in detail in Chapter 6 which makes classificatory

sense of the complex thicket of conceptions of shame and guilt in various disciplinary literatures. A major contribution by Nathan Harris in Chapter 6 is in reducing the seemingly incomprehensible complexity in conceptions of shame to endless variations on three themes – shame as feeling disapproved by others, shame as feeling bad about oneself and shame as feeling that what one has done is wrong – and then in Chapter 8 showing that actually all three are involved in what it means to feel Shame–Guilt. Empirically what matters more than the difference between shame and guilt is the difference between Shame–Guilt and Embarrassment–Exposure and Unresolved Shame.

Unacknowledged and Acknowledged Shame

We have seen that the third dimension of shame-related emotions revealed in Part II involved ongoing feelings that issues had been unresolved, that there was uncertainty that anything wrong had occurred, but unease about it and hence impeded resolution of threat to identity. It bears strong similarities to the concept of unacknowledged shame. Obversely, Shame–Guilt in Part II is acknowledged shame. This also emerged as of central importance for Eliza Ahmed's explanation of school bullying in Part III. Bullies were more likely to suffer high levels of unacknowledged shame. Ahmed's analyses find two dimensions to be important correlates of both bullying and being a victim of bullying: Shame Acknowledgment and Shame Displacement. Shame Acknowledgment involves the discharging of shame through accepting responsibility and trying to put things right. The opposite is a resistance to accepting responsibility and making amends. Shame Displacement means displacement of shame into blame and/or anger toward others. The opposite of Shame Displacement is the control of shame feelings so that the expression of shame does not involve other-directed blame and/or anger.

Ahmed classified children into those who were neither bullies nor victims of bullying, those who were both bullies and victims of bullying, those who were just bullies without being victims and those who were victims without being bullies. Self-reported non-bully/non-victims acknowledged shame and were less likely to allow shame to be displaced into emotions like anger. Bullies in contrast were less likely to acknowledge shame and more likely to displace shame into anger. Self-reported victims acknowledged shame without displacement, but were more likely to internalize others' rejection of them. Bully/victims were less likely to acknowledge shame, were more likely to have self-critical thoughts and to displace their shame into anger. Bully/victims are thus jointly afflicted with the shame management problems of both bullies and victims (see Table 1.1).

Table 1.1 Summary Conclusions of Part III

Non-bully/non-victim	• Acknowledge shame	• Shame is discharged
	• Resist displacement of shame	
Bully	• Resist shame acknowledgment	• Shame is not discharged
	• Displace shame through externalizing blame and anger	
Victim	• Acknowledge shame	• Shame is not discharged
	• Internalize shame	
Bully/victim	• Resist shame acknowledgment	• Shame is not discharged
	• Internalize shame	
	• Displace shame through externalizing blame and anger	

Put another way, the shame problems victims have, which restorative justice might address, is internalization of the idea that I am being bullied because there is something wrong with me as a person – internalization of shame. The shame problem bullies have is a failure to acknowledge shame when they have done something wrong and a tendency to externalize their shame as anger. Restorative justice needs to help them be more like non-bully/non-victims who acknowledge shame when they do something wrong, who resist externalizing or internalizing their shame, and who thereby manage to discharge shame. Critics of confronting shame are rightly concerned that this could cause offenders, especially young or Indigenous offenders, to internalize shame. These data suggest, however, that this is much more of a problem for victims than for offenders. Managing the acknowledgment of unavoidable shame is more the offender problem, internalized rejection of self more the victim problem, while bully/victims suffer both.

If we translate this model beyond school bullying to post-Apartheid South Africa, we can construct Nelson Mandela as a survivor who discharged the shame of being a victim of 27 years' imprisonment and the shame of the violence perpetrated by his party, in the name of an armed struggle he advocated and led. While he was labeled with some justification as a 'terrorist' both for what he himself did prior to his imprisonment and for what was done in his name during that imprisonment, Mandela set up a Truth and Reconciliation Commission to acknowledge this shame and transcend it. Mandela's wife Winnie, however, remained a bully/victim who would not fully acknowledge responsibility. P. W. Botha, the former President of South Africa, remained a non-cooperative bully during the Truth and Reconciliation Commission, refusing to acknowledge wrongdoing and externalizing blame onto the Commission, black leaders and white

traitors. Many were the victims with internalized shame who were helped by the Commission to discharge it, as documented in Desmond Tutu's (1999: 107) *No Future Without Forgiveness*:

> A woman from Soweto, Thandi [had been] tortured while in detention. She was raped repeatedly. She said she survived by taking her soul and spirit out of her body and putting it in a corner of the cell in which she was being raped. She could then, disembodied in this manner, look on as they did all those awful things to her body intended to make her hate herself as they had told her would happen. She could imagine then that it was not she herself but this stranger suffering the ignominy heaped on her. She then uttered words which are filled with a deep pathos. She said with tears in her eyes that she had not yet gone back to that room to fetch her soul and that it was still sitting in the corner where she had left it.

Just as Tutu shows that many victims discharged their internalized shame through seeing clearly the evil they had suffered and forgiving it, so did many perpetrators of awful violence discharge their externalized shame by apologizing, seeking and receiving forgiveness. What Ahmed's data in Part III implies is that a nation of healed victims, bullies and bully/victims has much more prospect of going forward without new cycles of violence. Thus conceived, these data are of broader import than simply to the school context. They suggest that just as Truth (acknowledgment) and Reconciliation (the alternative to shame management with anger) can heal schoolyards, they might also heal South Africa, Northern Ireland, Palestine, Rwanda, Iraq or Yugoslavia. Apology–reparation–forgiveness sequences can give bullies and victims access to both the benefits on the victim side and on the bully side of restoration.

Here Harris's data in Part II complements Ahmed's: Harris found his Shame–Guilt factor (which incorporated acknowledgment, accepting responsibility and remorse) to be higher in restorative justice conferences than in court. And he found 'anger/hostility' to be lower in the restorative process than in court (see Harris, 1999). Restorative process in short seemed to both assist the acknowledgment and inhibit the displacement of shame. Harris also found restorative conference cases to be more reintegrative and less stigmatizing than court cases. Ahmed in turn found that stigmatizing shaming by parents was associated with self-initiated bullying on the part of their children. This is therefore another part of the case as to why the reconciliation part of the Truth and Reconciliation process ought to inhibit further cycles of bullying.

Shame and Pride

The work of Cooley (1922) and Scheff (1990b) implies that pride and shame are together the primary social emotions. For Scheff, pride is the sign of an intact bond with other human beings, shame of a severed or threatened bond. Scheff and Retzinger (1991: 175) have been critical of the original formulation of reintegrative shaming theory in *Crime, Shame and Reintegration* for its neglect of pride and praise. Parental social approval is essential to delinquency prevention (Trasler, 1972). Chapman (1985) found that young people who said that their father always 'praises me when I do my work well' engage in less delinquency than those who say they are seldom or never praised. Makkai and Braithwaite (1993) found that nursing home inspectors who use praise as a strategy for improving compliance with quality of care standards do better at increasing compliance (after controlling for the 'praiseworthiness' of the home and other control variables). This was true even though some of the praise was of a counter-productive sort – praising poor performance. Makkai and Braithwaite found that praise had some special advantages in regulating *collective* conduct, an important feature because so much bullying and other rule-breaking is collective in practice. When collectivities are praised, all involved want to share in the credit and when individual members are praised, the collectivity claims a share of the individual praise. But when collectivities are shamed, members tend to believe that it is someone other than themselves who deserve this; when individual members are shamed, collectivities disown them.

In Chapter 3, praise is more explicitly incorporated into the proposed revision of the theory of reintegrative shaming as central to the first facet of reintegration – approving persons. Brennan (1999) has made a distinction between 'weakest link' and 'best shot' regulatory contexts. Quarantine is a weakest link context: if just one traveler brings in a plant with an exotic disease, the disease will spread. Winning Nobel prizes or Olympic gold medals are best-shot contexts. What matters is not how fast the average American can run, nor the slowness of the slowest, but how fast is the fastest. Arguably shame is of most use in weakest link regulation, pride and praise in best shot accomplishment. Shame is a maximin (maximizing the minimum) regulatory mechanism (motivating people to avoid being seen by others and themselves as the weakest link), praise/pride a maximax (maximizing the maximum) mechanism (motivating new heights). One of the problems with the work criminologists do is that it has a bias against the great variety of situations where the objective is maximax; obsessed with the evil side of life, criminologists neglect the more important domains where regulatory objectives are about nurturing excellence.

Shaming and praise may also interact with identity in opposite ways. *Crime, Shame and Reintegration* argues that shaming will be most effective when it shames the act but not the person. It may be that praise is most effective when it is directed at the identity of the whole person rather than at a specific act. So when a child shows a kindness to his sister, better to say 'you are a kind brother' than 'that was a kind thing you did'. One reason is that just as the identity degradation of stigmatization destroys healthy identities, so the identity enhancement of praising the person builds healthy identity. A second is that praise of our whole character is a more profound form of praise than praise of a single act. Third, praise that is tied to specific acts risks counter productivity if it is seen as an extrinsic reward, if it nurtures a calculative approach to performances that cannot be constantly monitored.[1] The evidence is that extrinsic rewards, like extrinsic punishments, induce the belief that compliance is performed only to get those rewards rather than because the behavior is intrinsically valued (Boggiano, Barrett, Weiher, McLelland, & Lusk, 1987: Lepper & Greene, 1978). For example, Deci and Ryan's (1980) study found that children who were given rewards for performing a task that they had enjoyed came to enjoy it less as a result of giving it an instrumental meaning. Better to avert extrinsic calculativeness by recognizing good character at times other than those of bad performance (obviously recognition of good character should not be given at a time that is seen as a reward for bad performance!). Hence, regulating social conduct is more likely to be effective when the following principles are in play:

- Shaming of bad acts that averts shaming of the actor's character.
- Praise of good character that uncouples praise from specific acts.

In this way, we achieve:

- Shaming acts but not persons that repairs identity.
- Praising virtues of the person rather than just their acts that nourishes a positive identity.

Moral balance requires both processes. Hubris is the risk of unremitting praise of the person that is never balanced by shaming of specific moral failures. Shaming without praise risks a failure to develop a positive identity for the moral self.

Ahmed's data in Part III shows that Tangney's beta pride-proneness scale is associated with less bullying, though its effects were much weaker than guilt-proneness and the shame-management variables (Shame Acknowledgment and Shame Displacement). With bullying behavior at least, it seems not to be the case that pride is a more significant emotion than shame and guilt. Indeed one of the arresting things about the analyses in Part III is that in the

prediction of bullying, the shame-management variables feature as prominently as family, school and personality variables that have traditionally been the dominant explanatory variables in the delinquency literature. Moreover, the mediational analysis found that the effects of a number of variables – such as school hassles, liking for school, empathy, self-esteem and internal locus of control – were mediated through either one or both shame-management variables. Hence, our doubts that we had given too much emphasis to shame/shaming and not enough to pride/praise turned out to be misplaced in this domain. It remains the case, however, that the contexts studied here are decidedly criminological, decidedly not 'best shot' contexts where pride in excellence may be the more important motivator.

Conclusion

Notwithstanding our results, we require further convincing that shame management is a more important question than the cultivation of pride in a virtuous identity. We suspect that the best protection against bullying or crime may be having a community in which virtues like caring for others are paramount. Here we need to worry about maximin (because psychopaths with absolutely no care for others are a special danger), maximax (because saints are an inspiration to those of middling virtue) and maximode,[2] maximizing the mode, or the results most people get (because high modal levels of virtue are needed to educate all our children to virtue). All of that said, once we have reached the point where a major act of bullying has occurred or a serious crime is being processed by the justice system, it may be that shame management is more important than pride management to building a safer community, as our data indeed suggest.

Our conclusion is that the key issue with shame management is helping wrongdoers to acknowledge and discharge shame rather than displace it into anger. We also conclude that a state of being unable to make up one's mind as to whether one has done anything wrong is destructive and anger-inducing. Thus, we need institutions of justice that allow respectful moral reasoning in which the defendant is not dominated, and can think aloud with those who can help her to think. Part of the idea of this undominated dialogue is that the defendant will jump from the emotionally destructive state of Unresolved Shame to a sense of moral clarity that what she has done is either right or wrong. Sometimes we will surely think it better that a violent offender have Unresolved Shame than that he conclude the violence was right after a dialogue with friends who value toughness and a 'nasty' victim who leads the offender to conclude that she 'deserved it'. But these cases are the cost we must bear for a justice system that genuinely persuades rather than coerces a majority of offenders to accept a widely

held consensus on the evil of interpersonal violence. And they are the cost we must bear for a justice system that allows an undominated space where bad laws (or good laws badly enforced in a particular context) can be challenged by a discussion among ordinary citizens.

Finally, our data suggest that stigmatization should be jettisoned as one of the guiding principles of our criminal justice system. Reintegrative discussion of the consequences that have been suffered as a result of a wrong is suggested by the data as more productive and less destructive. So we might consider replacing the communication of stigma as a principle of sentencing in the criminal law textbooks with reintegrative dialogue to persuade the offender to a reasoned commitment to remorse and recompense. But we jump ahead of ourselves here. We cannot marry our empirical results to such a policy conclusion until we consider more carefully in the next chapter the normative foundations that might warrant them.

Notes

1 We are indebted for the ideas in this paragraph to a discussion John Braithwaite had with Jerry Lee, a successful US businessman, who explained why he did not pay bonuses to employees as a reward for doing something well, but as a kind of gift for being the dedicated kind of employee they were.
2 Our thanks to Geoffery Brennan (1999) for the concept of maximode.

CHAPTER 2

The Normative Theory of Shame

A conclusion of this book is that an ethical identity conception of shame, rather like that found among the ancient Greeks by Bernard Williams, is that which is most likely to have empirical bite. The ethical identity conception is that shame is the emotion we feel when we realize that our ethical identity is violated or threatened by our actions. Our ethical identity is defined by our commitment to a set of moral norms. Shame is what we feel when we breach these norms in some serious way.

Rediscovering Old Ideas

Williams (1993) found that the Greeks had both a conception of shame that did not involve guilt, for example when nakedness or foolishness was exposed, and of Shame–Guilt that involved implications for the morality of the self. Part of his project was to debunk the notion that because the Greeks had one word, *aidōs*, for shame and guilt, the ancients were at an earlier Piagetian stage of moral development than moderns in the sense of being other-directed to the exclusion of the internalization of shame. Williams shows that shame and guilt often went together, a critical issue being whether the shaming agent was one who shared a certain identity with the shamed person. For the ancient Greeks, shaming by disrespected or despised others seems from such literature available to us not to have induced guilt.

Williams identifies all the key concepts in this book among the ancients. In addition to Shame–Guilt and Embarrassment–Exposure, he also finds by-passed shame (Williams, 1993: 87–88) and a reflexive understanding of the acknowledgment of shame as an issue. He finds indignation or anger in response to shame – what we call Shame Displacement in Part III. He also

finds forgiveness in response to the acknowledgment of shame (Williams, 1993: 90). Finally, he argues that the ancient Greeks had both causal and intentional conceptions of personal responsibility and responsibility to put things right (even if one did not have the intention to cause the harm) (Williams, 1993: Chapter 3). While Williams does not explicitly say this, we might suggest that the ancients had a more balanced interplay than moderns between the backward-looking passive responsibility of being held responsible for a past wrong and the forward-looking active responsibility to right wrongs in which one may or may not have been personally implicated. Active responsibility is a virtue, a virtue which modern justice institutions punish: active responsibility to right wrongs today is taken as evidence of sanctionable backward-looking responsibility. If you run into another car, it is legally unwise to admit any responsibility and even more unwise to offer the other driver help to repair her car. The conception of responsibility in restorative justice, which we discuss in the next chapter as an implication of our analysis of shame, seeks to shift the balance between active and passive responsibility in our justice institutions back towards a heavier emphasis on cultivating the virtue of active responsibility (see Braithwaite & Roche, 2000).

Williams finds that even if the balance among them might have been different, the ancient Greeks had the same basic set of conceptions of freedom, responsibility and individual agency as we moderns. Our moral differences from the Greeks on so many big questions like slavery and sexual equality 'cannot best be understood in terms of a shift in basic ethical conceptions' (Williams, 1993: 7). Rather the big differences arise from the application of those more or less shared basic ethical conceptions to different values and attitudes. They had very different values from us but not very different ideas on what it means to be responsible, to be free, to be ashamed and so on.

Far from the ancients' more rudimentary conceptual foundations for morality being responsible for their beliefs on matters such as slavery, Williams sees their foundations as in some ways firmer than ours. Acknowledgment of shame and rejection of the modern preoccupation with guilt uncoupled from shame is his main illustration of basic ancient ethical conceptions being on firmer ground than our post-Kantian conceptions:

> [Guilt] can direct one towards those who have been wronged or damaged, and demand reparation in the name, simply, of what has happened to them. But it cannot by itself help one to understand one's relations to those happenings, or to rebuild the self that has done these things and the world in which that self has to live. Only shame can do that, because it embodies conceptions of what one is and how one is related to others. (Williams, 1993: 94)

If we are interested in *shame* and *acknowledgment* that motivate *transformation* of our relationships with others into more ethical and loving relationships (as Moore & McDonald (2001) suggest we should) then there is something to learn from Bernard Williams' reflections on the Greeks.

Marrying Explanatory and Normative Theory

We also show in this book that shaming is a dangerous game; shame can be a destructive emotion. Conversely, societies that lose their capacity to communicate shame risk terrible violence and disrespect of human rights because very little of the honoring of human rights is enforced by the courts. Most of us most of the time respect the fundamental human rights of others because we think it would be unconscionable (shameful, under the ethical identity conception) for us to violate their rights.

The desirability of integrating the explanatory theory of shame with the normative theory of shame follows from the theoretical position that the ethical identity conception is the most useful explanatory conception of shame. In Braithwaite's work, the explanatory theory in *Crime, Shame and Reintegration* was buttressed by the normative theory with Philip Pettit in *Not Just Deserts: A Republican Theory of Criminal Justice*. An explanatory theory is an ordered set of propositions about the way the world is; a normative theory is an ordered set of propositions about the way the world ought to be.

Pettit and Braithwaite's writing in the republican tradition suggests that shaming is a bad thing when it reduces freedom as non-domination or dominion. Shaming is a good thing when it increases freedom as non-domination. Hence, shaming of rape can be a good thing if it communicates the message that rape is wrong and as a result some men exercise their responsibility to refrain from rape; it is good because it increases the freedom of women from domination (arbitrary interference in their freedom) while restraining the freedom of men in a less profound way (and more importantly, a less arbitrary way, because the restraint is imposed by a rule of law).

Under the republican conception of freedom, domination of our choices, as opposed to interference in our choices, is the great vice to be avoided. Domination means the arbitrary exercise of power over our choices. Such domination involves a subjective belief of being under the thumb of another, of being a slave to the arbitrary power of another. Interference by a democratic rule of law designed to check domination is not arbitrary interference and therefore is not domination on this conception (Pettit, 1997). Freedom as non-domination is thus the condition of enjoying all the rights and protections against domination (e.g. social security, *habeas corpus*, freedom from rape) that the rule of law makes the due of all citizens.

Shame is a tool republican governance can use to maximize the realm of undominated choice for citizens. Shaming is morally right when it has this effect, morally wrong when it increases domination (as it often does). Similarly in the private sphere: in families shaming is desirable when it has the effect of expanding the sphere of undominated choice (e.g. respectful shaming of bullying, of refusal to attend school), undesirable when it is an exercise of the arbitrary power of a family tyrant.

Utilitarianism

In the realm of criminal justice the more influential competing theories to republicanism are utilitarianism and various deontological theories of just deserts or retribution. Utilitarianism, like republicanism, is a consequentialist theory. It seeks to maximize the good consequence of happiness as opposed to republicanism's good consequence of non-domination. Like republicanism, utilitarianism enabled Jeremy Bentham to develop in the domain of criminal justice both an explanatory and a normative theory of deterrence. Retributivism in contrast is just a normative theory; there is no retributive explanation of crime, bullying or any other wrongdoing.

Republicans think utilitarianism is a dangerous theory of criminal justice because it might allow unrestrained domination. For example, if indeterminate sentences, discretion to flog malefactors at will or dominating forms of rehabilitation were shown to reduce crime, to produce the greatest happiness for the greatest number, then utilitarians must support such policies. Republicans could not support them because in a society where such dominations are allowed, no one can feel secure from the arbitrary power of the state (see Braithwaite & Pettit, 1990). We will not press our critique of utilitarianism here, however, because utilitarianism has produced no normative theory of shame.

Retributivism

Retributivism, in contrast, has a normative theory of censure. Some retributivists are in no way interested in shame. For them retributivism is just a deontological theory of hard treatment. Wrongdoers should be punished because they have done wrong and the extent of their punishment should be proportional to the degree of their wrong. For some retributivists, punishment of wrongdoers is intrinsically good or is good because it balances benefits and burdens between lawbreakers and law-abiding members of the community. But for other theorists, censure of wrongdoing is a good in itself. These retributivists define censure in more or less the same way that we define shaming in this book – the communication of disapproval.

The most influential deontological theorists of censure in the realm of criminal justice are Andrew Von Hirsch (1993) and Anthony Duff (1986, 1996). In Duff's work there is an emphasis on deliberation in the courtroom communicating censure about the wrong involved in a crime. Through this deliberation which is given weight by an obligation to punish, Duff wishes to secure respect for the person, remorseful acceptance of guilt, self-reform, reparation and reconciliation. But our rebuttable empirical assumption as restorative justice theorists is that institutions which seek to maximize consistency of punishment are less likely to accomplish these laudable goals than restorative justice institutions which seek to minimize punishment and maximize mercy.

With Von Hirsch (1993) the emphasis is more on proportional punishments as communicating censure – stripped of any ambitions for inducing remorse, reparation and reconciliation. For Von Hirsch, the key reason crime must be responded to by punishments proportional to the seriousness of wrongdoing is to communicate censure proportionate to the wrong. We think it a fragile empirical claim that there is a strong association between the severity of punishments either imposed or written into law and the proportionate censure experienced in the community. That is, most citizens do not know what the maximum or average punishments are for armed robbery or rape, and which is higher. They have strong views about which crimes are and should be more censured by their societies, but these views, we hypothesize, are shaped by many more important variables than the quanta of sentences. Central among these is deliberative discussion of the evils of specific crimes with intimates – hence one of the appeals of the deliberative democracy of restorative justice.

So it seems irresponsible to lock one person up for two years longer than another for no better reason than to communicate to the community that the wrongdoing of the first offender was deserving of more censure to that degree. Indeed, Von Hirsch agrees. Like H. L. A. Hart, Von Hirsch makes a distinction between the general justifying aim of punishment and its distributive justification. Hard treatment would not be justified, according to Von Hirsch, if it achieved nothing more than the communication of censure. The punitive criminal justice system has the general justifying reason for its existence of preventing crime. But once it exists and that general objective has been achieved by its existence, punishments should be distributed in proportion to the censure warranted. This is an incoherent position. If criminal punishment exists because of a general justifying aim, why should we accept a distribution of punishment that defeats the very reason for the institution's existence? The evidence from meta-analyses of evaluations of changes in the level of punishment is that longer prison terms tend to increase reoffending among the punished (Gendreau, Goggin & Cullen, 1999). Hence,

if we give a person a longer prison term because she deserves more censure, we do something to this person which will increase the risk of crime. And on the Von Hirsch view, we do this in the name of an institution we only allow to exist in order to prevent crime.

The republican prescription (Braithwaite & Pettit, 1990; Pettit, 1997) is very different. It says only consider resort to punishment when there is no other way of attempting to prevent crime that poses less of a threat to freedom as non-domination. If, as in the Truth and Reconciliation Commission, adequate censure of the wrong and adequate assurance against reoffending can be secured by a process of apology and forgiveness, then proportionate punishment is not morally necessary. Censure is important in the republican prescription; it is most important that serious wrongdoing is not allowed to pass without focused communal deliberation on the evil of what has occurred. We will return later to the good consequences the republican believes flows from this communal censure. But first we must grapple with the problem of the way its position on apology-forgiveness and prevention cuts against moral intuitions that are deeply held by moderns. It seems wrong that this man who commits murder should not be punished simply because he apologizes and his victim's family forgives him, while another man who commits a lesser crime is severely punished because his victim refuses to forgive or because he continues to pose a threat to society. We think it helps to understand how the republican or restorative justice philosopher can go against this intuition by coming to an historical understanding of how retributive intuitions became so deeply held in conditions of modernity.

The moral plausibility of forgiveness defeating retribution we think comes from ancient sources. The world's great religions – Christianity, Judaism, Islam, Buddhism, Hinduism, Confucianism and most of the spiritualities of non-Western small-scale societies in Africa, the Americas, and the Pacific – involve a commitment to restorative justice that gives considerable priority to mercy over justice. That is because all these religions are pre-modern. It is these religions and contact with contemporary Indigenous communities who cling to pre-modern values which have been the primary sources of the competing intuitions supporting restorative against retributive justice.

Retributivism and the Modern Predicament

In all societies, past or present, we have visited or read about it is easy to detect the existence of both strong retributive traditions of thought and strong restorative traditions (in this context, read merciful, forgiving traditions). In some of the societies where the restorative currents are strongest

(for example New Zealand Maori and other Polynesian societies, much of Africa, Japan) these were traditionally warrior societies where retributive values had and have an unusually strong niche.

We suspect both retributive and restorative modes of thought are cultural universals because they both have had survival value. We conjecture that survival prospects have been greater when people had a capacity to heal the hurts of injustice, especially when those hurts were inflicted by loved ones who carry our genes. Communal, indeed individual survival without a capability to cooperate to heal conflicts is hard to imagine in the face of the human propensity of others to occasionally respond to our slights with deep anger. Family members one would think would be especially likely to wipe each other out if they lacked restorative capability, because they confront everyday conflicts with each other over food, resources, honor, peace and quiet and every other asset that can lead to conflict.

It is also hard to imagine how, once human beings had acquired the ability to kill each other and take each other's land, genes could have survived the millennia without being protected by warriors capable of enough anger to exact revenge on enemies. Throughout this book we speak of anger and externalization of shame as if these are pathological, as they mostly are in modern conditions. But seeing humans as hardwired to externalize an enemy as blamed other, as a focus of anger, helps us understand how they can be so irrational as to throw themselves into a battle to defend their village where the prospects of being killed are high. In the twentieth-century world of carpet bombing, nuclear and biological weapons, the retributive values manifest in a Hitler or Tojo are more a threat to survival than an assurance of it. According to the great historian Eric Hobsbawm (1996), the twentieth century has been an age of barbarism, or genocide (particularly in comparison to the century to 1914). One reason is perhaps that just when our retributive emotions have become of least use to us, certain conditions of modernity have sharpened them.

Restorative justice was the dominant way of dealing with crime, even serious crime like homicide, until about 1200 in most of Europe, according to Elmar Weitekamp (1999). Actually this was especially so with the most bloody crimes, where restorative justice was most needed to stop the shame-rage spirals of blood feuds. The dominance of restorative justice over punitive criminal justice was sustained until centuries later in parts of Europe such as Scotland where kings were weak and kin networks strong (Mackay, 1992), and in most of the non-European world. In medieval and ancient Europe, in the pre-modern worlds beyond the West until the twentieth century, restorative justice dominated within and across connected kin groups – within defensive communities – while retributive justice was more central between groups that posed threats to each other's territories. Banishment/

excommunication also seems to have been a widespread supplement to restorative justice in cases where offenders simply could not be restored.

Banishment was a decisive casualty of modernity. In the twentieth century, nation-states cannot cast out their deviants in the way medieval villages could, or in the way eighteenth-century England could cast out convicts to the United States or Australia. The state does not solve the problem by allowing one town to eject a criminal only to have them move on to cause trouble in another town. Under modern conditions, other states will not allow felons to immigrate to their shores.

The story of the demise of restorative justice is a more complex one of the division of labor in modernity. In a village or town without a complex division of labor, restorative justice is common sense. If our neighbor wrongs us, revenge risks counter-revenge and downward spiral into a blood feud. Sensible people learn how to sit down with each other and sort out their hurts and conflicts. They keep their (deeply felt) retributive emotions in check precisely because they are rational enough to know that the other has precisely those same explosive emotions.

When the king takes over criminal justice from the townfolk and the local lord, however, a different dynamic comes into play. The king can exact the most horrible retribution against the neighbor who rapes my daughter or kills my son and I have no reason to fear a blood feud. It is not me who decided to exact the horrible retribution, but the king. This changes the politics of criminal justice. The king can pander to the retributive urges of a people relieved of the backlash they had to suffer from retributive justice when justice was decided through local participation. While restorative justice made political sense for local justice, retributive justice was most politically strategic for state justice. There were other reasons why the king took over criminal justice from local lords, clans and villages. It was often profitable. Once crimes against victims were redefined as crimes against the king, the king could rake in substantial fines to right the wrong the king's peace had suffered. The church got in on the same act, selling indulgences. Just as pandering to the retributive emotions of masses decoupled from the humanity of the offender was good politics, so was it good politics to be able to grant mercy to powerful men who would return the favor by becoming part of the king's political base. This political dynamic continues to this day: social security cheats are good fodder for pandering to retributive emotions; wealthy tax cheats and major corporate criminals are good people to do favors, to make a 'low enforcement priority'.

Under the new division of criminal justice labor, not only was it a cheap political benefit for the king to fan the flames of retributive emotions, a crime control industry (Christie, 1995) was created with an interest in also doing so – sheriffs, executioners, prosecutors, police, prison administrators,

owners of galleys, convict colonies and private prison corporations. Local communities that were decoupled from any human consequences of retribution could afford to indulge this inflammation of their retributive emotions. Genocidal leaders such as Hitler simply took this modern strategy of mass appeal a big step further to creating an entire ethnic group deserving of retribution. A step too far for most decent people. Yet when criminal retributivism was clothed in a principled justification of equal punishments for equal wrongs decided dispassionately by a just state, it all seemed very right and natural to decent people.

In the face of this naturalness of retribution, hard-wired in our emotions and fanned by the division of labor in modern political-legal institutions, philosophers of punishment made two intellectual errors. First, they assumed that what people naturally want is right. Since all of us seem to have retributive urges at times, since there has never been a society that has failed to grant them some legitimacy, there must be something right about them. In fact we have suggested that the retribution people want under conditions of modernity is a result of a political separation of what people want from the adverse consequences of getting it. It is also natural for people to be born into ignorance; but this does not make it right.

Second, philosophers of punishment made the error of assuming that people want what they want – a system that punishes criminals – because it delivers what they want – freedom from crime. Law and economics professors, following in Bentham's footsteps, refined the latter error to great levels of sophistication.

Philosophers of punishment and judges refined the first error to tariffs and sentencing grids, to principles clothed in a spurious commitment to equality before the law. The universal reality of just deserts policies has been for profoundly structural reasons, just deserts for the poor and impunity for white-collar criminals (Braithwaite & Pettit, 1990: Chapter 9). Political progressives among the retributivists would call for just deserts for white-collar criminals, when practical people and serious scholars of the subject all knew that a cessation of restorative justice for white-collar criminals was neither fiscally nor politically possible, nor desirable for maximizing the protection of the community from their predations (Ayres & Braithwaite, 1992). The practical path to greater equality before the law was to extend the privilege of restorative justice from powerful to powerless criminals. But until the arrival of a nascent social movement for restorative justice in the 1990s, there was no political force arguing for this response to the glib appeal of the intellectual errors of the utilitarians and the retributive philosophers/lawyers. Instead of asking: 'How can it make political sense that we have created an institution so inhumane, costly and ineffective as the criminal justice system?' both the philosophers/lawyers

and the rational choice theorists asked 'Why is it that punitive institutions we all seem to want are good and right?' Our retributive practices (and therefore the emotions to which they pandered) seemed all the more natural when our most distinguished judges, towering intellectuals like Jeremy Bentham and Nobel laureates in economics would all provide sophisticated rationales for why the received wisdom was right. Things only got worse when a new industry, the mass entertainment industry, including the news media, found that pandering to the retributive emotions was one of the best ways of selling advertising. Print media, radio, and especially television and Hollywood, joined political leaders and the crime-control industry in having an interest in cultivating retribution while clothing it in a prosocial rhetoric of just deserts and deterrence.

The tragic thing about retributive emotions is that they feed on themselves. Yet the fact that pandering to them does not satiate them creates the political space where restorative justice can expand. Ultimately, receiving an apology one regards as sincere, some emotional and material reparation, feeling the grace of granting forgiveness, is more satisfying than the law and order auctions we get from competing politicians. The evidence is that victims, offenders, families and community members find restorative justice processes more satisfying and just than court (Braithwaite, 2001: Chapter 3). So once there are several thousand citizens who have experienced restorative justice processes in a local community there is a political constituency for restorative justice. If there is therefore no political inevitability about a continuing ascendancy of retributive shaming, what would a restorative/ republican normative theory of shame look like?

Shaming and the Curriculum of Crimes

In this book, we emphasize the productive and counterproductive effects of different kinds of shame and shaming on individual wrongdoers. We can agree with desert theorists like Von Hirsch and sociologists such as Durkheim that the functions censure performs at a macro-sociological level are of much more profound importance. For the restorative justice theorist, while serious crime can always be forgiven if that is the wish of the victim, it is not acceptable to ignore it, to sweep it under the carpet. The opportunity for deliberation of stakeholders about the hurt a serious crime or act of bullying has caused is not only about creating an opportunity for victims and offenders to discover the possibility of healing, the deliberation also educates the community as to why this particular kind of act should be shameful. The drama of the criminal process teaches citizens the curriculum of crimes. But fictional tales play an equally important part here – from children's fables to Hollywood to detective novels. Restorative justice in

its surviving Indigenous forms often brings together these two means of constituting the consciences that shame wrongdoing. In a healing circle an Indigenous elder instead of confronting an offender with the wrong she has done in this real case will tell a story, a legend with a moral lesson relevant to the real case before the community. This is a clever way of educating those present about why what has happened is wrong without confronting the offender, at least initially, in a way that might be stigmatizing.[1] Or an elder will sometimes tell a real story of the folly of her own youth to make it easier for the offender to own responsibility for what she has done.

Once the offender does own that responsibility and voluntarily apologizes for the wrong she has done, this apology is a uniquely powerful affirmation of the norm at issue. If you shame me for violating a norm, others might think you do this to put yourself above me or to even a score. But if I shame myself, such self-interested interpretations of why the shaming is happening are not in play. If even I as the wrongdoer am willing to speak out about why it was wrong, this is an especially potent affirmation of the infracted norm.

One of the appealing things about restorative justice in schools to deal with problems like bullying and theft is that it gives all children – and all are eventually touched by such wrongdoing during their school years – a chance to listen to consequences of wrongdoing for those who are hurt and to the moral reasoning of young citizens as they discover for themselves the curriculum of crimes. The messages of this moral reasoning are much more important than the messages reputedly communicated by the decisions of remote judges telling us that this kind of crime deserves twice as much punishment as that kind. Participation in discussions about why particular wrongdoers at school, in the family, in the workplace, on television or in fictional accounts, may have done wrong is the most consequential kind of shaming we engage in because cumulatively this is formative of conscience across a curriculum of crimes.

Social movement politics is especially important in shaming wrongs that are remote from our personal experience. We need an environmental movement to shame the wrong of global warming or whaling. We need a trade union movement to shame the wrong of forced child labor, a consumer movement to shame price fixing, a gay and lesbian rights movement to shame discrimination against homosexuals, a restorative justice movement to shame judges and legislators who destroy lives by needless use of imprisonment. And when a particular kind of wrong is part of our personal experience, but the domination surrounding that personal experience cuts us off from deliberative disapproval, we need social movement politics to break through that domination. Hence, the little girl who has always suffered violence from her dad, and who has been brought up to think this is normal, needs to hear the voices of the women's movement

in the public sphere. The very crimes which are least shameful in any society are those which are shielded from shame by forces of domination – the domination of business elites who insist that stock market manipulation or corruption are not shameful because they are necessary to wealth creation, the general who says his war crimes were necessary to save our country, the police chief who covers up the torturing of suspects because sometimes this is necessary to keep our streets safe, the boss who sexually harasses his staff and who successfully covers up, insisting that he was just having fun in which the girls wanted to share. Shame is structured by patterns of domination. This Braithwaite (1995) argues is what produces a reality where our biggest crime problems are those where domination has caused shame to be muted. Yet for this very reason those crime problems are quite susceptible to the mobilization of shame against them in a concerted way for the first time. Social movements are the crucial agents of shaming against forms of exploitation that traditionally have been shielded from shame.

Direct confrontation of uncontroversial wrongdoing is less important than forming consciences around a curriculum of crimes expanded to include problems that have festered through dominations that have shielded them from shame. Hence, active social movement politics in pursuit of domination is the more important implication of the theory of reintegrative shaming than is restorative justice.

Shaming by Conscience

Once we have learnt a curriculum of norms that are uncontroversial to us because they prove to be repeatedly deliberatively defensible, the most powerful form of shaming, according to the theory of reintegrative shaming, becomes shaming by our own conscience. This kind of shaming is especially powerful because it does not require detection and is therefore more certain and immediate, occurring as soon as the wrong is perpetrated, indeed during and in anticipation of its perpetration. While conscience does work according to this social learning mechanism where self-shaming can be conceived as the cost we seek to avoid, this is only part of the story of the power of conscience. When we go to visit our sick grandmother, we go because we are worried about grandmother, not simply because we are worried that if we do not go our conscience will worry us. Caring for grandma has been internalized as intrinsically motivating.

Shaming Constituting Unthinkability

The great power of a conscience that has been constituted by deliberative participation in shaming fictional or real wrongs is that it tends to put those

wrongs right off our deliberative agenda. They become unthinkable to us. Hence when someone annoys us, we refrain from killing them, not because we calculate the costs and benefits of murder, but because murder is not even considered as an option for dealing with a daily problem. Conscience-building through deliberation about past fictional and real murders makes us the kind of person for whom murder has been written out of all our scripts for daily life.

Shaming by Imagined Gossip

Once we have participated in the shaming of fictional and real wrongs of a particular sort, we know the things people say when that kind of wrong is enacted. Consequently, if we perpetrate that wrong, we imagine that others will be gossiping about us in just that way. We deter ourselves by the shame of this imagined gossip even if such gossip is not occurring.

Shaming by Actual Gossip

It follows that if actual gossip occurs about our wrongdoing and we hear of it, we may feel shame as well.

Shaming as General Deterrent

Even though we have not perpetrated a particular kind of wrong, if we see others who are being shamed by their own consciences, by imagined or real gossip, by direct confrontation with the disapproval of others or by public exposure in the media, all these forms of shaming can act as a general deterrent. 'I would hate that to happen to me.' The existence of shaming and shame in a culture that is highly deliberative about the rights and wrongs of alleged wrongdoing should deliver all these modalities of shame-based general deterrence.

Shaming as Direct Confrontation with Disapproval or Public Exposure

These are the least effective forms of shaming according to the theory of reintegrative shaming. Perhaps it is more accurate to say they are the most difficult to pull off because they bring with them the greatest risks of stigmatization. In communities that are actively deliberative about wrong-doing, it is rarely necessary to resort to direct confrontation with disapproval or public exposure. But we must resort to them when self-regulation fails in respect of serious wrongs. It is hard to directly confront a wrongdoer and

very hard to do a highly public form of exposure of their wrongdoing without being perceived by the wrongdoer as disrespectful and outcasting. When they perceive this, they will be tempted to defend their identity by rejecting their rejectors. If perceived outcasting persists, the wrongdoers may opt to forge an outcast identity collectively in a community of those who have been similarly outcast. The drug user who feels she is being stigmatized as a junkie affirms a drug-using identity in a drug subculture. When this happens, the direct confrontation has backfired, exacerbating the wrongdoing. The shame state associated with this is Eliza Ahmed's unacknowledged shame combined with externalized anger and rejection.

The data in Part II of this book affirm that encounters that are perceived as stigmatizing are less likely to induce Shame–Guilt and the data in Part III confirm that stigmatizing shaming increases self-initiated bullying. The theory of reintegrative shaming contends there are a number of things we can do to reduce the risks of stigmatization when wrongdoing is so serious that we are morally required to confront it rather than let it go. We can communicate our disapproval of the act while affirming the person as an essentially good person. We can do it in a very respectful way, avoiding any name-calling and making a point of ritually signaling when the confrontation has ended so she can put it behind her (as by a handshake, expression of forgiveness, breaking of bread, or signing of an agreement to right the wrong). The data in Part II support the contention of the theory that offenders are more likely to feel ashamed of what they have done in rituals that are reintegrative and that restorative justice conferences are more reintegrative than court processing.

We must communicate our disapproval in a way that makes special efforts to be procedurally fair, to ensure that offenders get a chance to say what they want to say in the way they want to say it, to ensure there is no bias against them on race, gender or any other grounds, to ensure that decisions can be appealed, errors corrected, rights respected and so on. At this time there is evidence showing that restorative processes are perceived as more procedurally fair than court by both offenders (Barnes, 1999) and victims (Strang & Sherman, 1997) and there are other studies linking perceptions of procedural fairness, especially process control, to compliance (Makkai & Braithwaite, 1996; Tyler, 1990).

Most powerfully, the data in Part II show that direct confrontation is most likely to induce Shame–Guilt when the confrontation is by those whom we respect very highly. Even people whom we respect fairly highly are utterly ineffective in inducing Shame–Guilt. The number one design principle for restorative justice processes is therefore that coordinators must work hard at finding out who are the particular people offenders have the highest respect for and spare no expense in getting them to attend even if

they have to be flown in for the conference. Parenthetically, these data reveal a serious empirical flaw in the contentions of retributive theorists of censure that the solemn pronouncements of judges about the relative wrongness of this offense versus that (as revealed by the severity of their sentences) will matter a jot to the most critical audience for these censuring messages – criminal offenders. In restorative justice conferences or in discussing the wrongdoing portrayed in a movie, the censuring that counts is that of those who we respect very highly. This is not restricted to intimates. In Indigenous communities, it can include elders who are remote but respected: 'Having Elders there made the difference because I was thinking about what they thought about me' (First Nations Youth from the Yukon after a restorative sentencing circle) (McCormick, 1999: 16).

Finally, we hypothesize that the genius of well-conducted restorative justice processes is that they only confront wrongdoing indirectly, implicitly inviting the wrongdoer themselves to be the one who directly confronts it, apologizes, and seeks to right the wrong. This indirectness is mostly accomplished by proceeding simply to invite stakeholders affected by the crime, especially the victim, victim supporters and loved ones of the offender, to describe how the crime has affected them. Normally this is enough. There is no need to say 'and you are responsible for this' or even that 'this is very wrong'. The simple process of just discussing the hurt that has been felt by all affected will move the offender to say those things. This is how the risk of stigmatization is minimized. But in some cultures it is appropriate to take indirectness even further: the elder talks about comparable wrongdoing in his own youth or stories from the dreamtime and waits, waits for the offender to volunteer her own confessional story.

Beyond a Retributive Theory of Censure

We now move toward a conclusion by first establishing some common ground with retributive theories of censure. Retributive theorists such as Von Hirsch are right to see the censuring of serious wrongs as one of the things a criminal justice system should accomplish. A sense of proportion about which wrongs are more serious than others may also be an important thing accomplished through communication with offenders and the community. While we agree with Von Hirsch that the maximum level of punishment for any given offense type should be set in proportion to the seriousness of harm that kind of offense can do, we should not delude ourselves into thinking that those penalty levels have much educative value in communicating proportionate censure. Most citizens do not know what they are and could not tell you if they were higher in their state than in a neighboring jurisdiction or higher for this offense than for that.

We cannot agree that censure of wrong is a good in itself, however. As Bagaric and Amarasekara (2000: p. 171) put it: 'There is no intrinsic merit in telling people that they have done the wrong thing. And even if it is felt that there is some benefit in this, it merely justifies conveying such a message; not the further step of imposing an unpleasantness.' Censure and punishment only seem good things to us when they contribute to human flourishing. That is why most people are happy to see a lot of wrongs go unpunished and uncensored. They see no point in a lot of contexts.

A republican view of how human flourishing is best accomplished is for people to enjoy maximum freedom from domination, where non-domination requires freedom from poverty, genuine access to human rights and all the other assurances necessary to enable people to enjoy the range of choices of a democratic citizen. Freedom as non-domination lacks some of the generality of utilitarianism's happiness or of harm-reduction in what it can sweep up. And this is an attractive feature – for example in better accommodating suffering to animals or harm to the environment as wrongs. Nevertheless, we think Braithwaite and Pettit (1990) have advanced some features of freedom as non-domination that make it a particularly attractive outcome for deriving some specificity of institutional guidance as to how to run domination-prone institutions such as those of criminal justice and regulation more broadly. We will not repeat those arguments here because our point is the more basic one that censure seems a bad thing when it inhibits the flourishing of human beings.

We think Anthony Duff is right that it is important that we treat offenders with respect in any regulatory activity and that it can show great disrespect to refrain from communicating to a criminal why we think what they have done is worthy of censure. Duff is also surely right that eliciting a remorseful recognition of guilt from criminals, self-reform, offers of recompense and reconciliation are desirable outcomes. Again for us they are desirable because the research program we are embarked upon demonstrates how important these things are for human flourishing. So we part company in seeing them as right in any deontological sense. It is also hard to accept Duff's argument that punishment is the best way to achieve the respectful communication and self-reform he values. Certainly the evidence is now clear that whatever the limited general deterrent benefits of imprisonment, prison actually reduces the prospects of self-reform – the longer the prison term the more so (Gendreau et al., 1999). And the reason most prisoners don't see it as very respectful to lock them up is that it isn't. It is moral reasoning with an offender that is most respectful of them. Trial and punishment where prosecutors seek to stigmatize rather than reason and defense lawyers are excuse-mongering mouthpieces that silence the heartfelt sentiments of the defendant are never likely to achieve Duff's respectful

communication of censure that induces remorse. Duff concedes this as a fact of present criminal justice arrangements, though it is not clear what his reform program would be.

Consequentialists who want a more respectful way of communicating censure that might motivate recompense, remorse, reconciliation and self-reform do have a concrete, evaluable, reform program that is in active research and development. It is called restorative justice and it will be discussed in more detail in the next chapter.

Toward a Restorative Theory of Censure

The restorative theory of censure that seems most promising to us is a republican normative theory of shame and shaming. This would have it that Shame–Guilt is a necessary emotion for any democracy that wants to make freedom from violence and respect for human rights active cultural accomplishments. Without Shame–Guilt to enforce them, rights are merely legal claims only the rich can enforce in the courts. However, Shame–Guilt is also a destructive emotion that can foster violence, domination, denial of human rights and war.

The first tenet of a republican theory would be that shame and shaming should be nurtured only when they increase freedom as non-domination. Shame and shaming that threaten freedom as non-domination should be resisted. Ironically, one of the most effective tools for such resistance will be to shame it. To illustrate: shaming gays and lesbians clearly reduces freedom in the republican sense. One way of tackling this problem is to shame homophobia and to reintegratively confront behavior that denies gay and lesbian people their human rights. The key agents of such counter-shaming are social movements with an agenda of non-domination, in this case the gay and lesbian rights movements.

This introduces the second tenet that shaming should not be stigmatizing but should be respectful, whether communicated by social movements or the state. The rest of this book is in a sense an extended development of the empirical case for why stigmatizing shaming is counter-productive. Here we simply make the normative claim that because stigma is coercive, it is, like punishment, more of a threat to freedom than a discussion of the consequences of a crime, than moral reasoning that induces a Shame–Guilt that might bring about self-reform.

Against this it might be argued that even though stigmatization might have counter-productive effects on the person who is stigmatized, because stigma is more painful than reintegration, it will better achieve the general deterrent effects of shame. Moreover, perhaps stigma makes for better gossip than reintegrative disapproval, more gripping Hollywood scripts.

Hence stigma is more likely to grab our attention to learn the curriculum of crimes and is more likely to impress upon our minds imagined gossip when we contemplate wrongdoing. So stigma might more surely render that wrongdoing unthinkable. These are actually empirical questions which we do not have the data to answer apart from knowing from Chapter 10 that stigmatization actually reduces Shame–Guilt while it increases Unresolved Shame and Embarrassment–Exposure. We don't really know if reintegrative gossip that is sad gossip has less impact than angry gossip that is stigmatizing. Nasty gossip may be thought of as the work of 'the other' and therefore be discounted in comparison with the sad gossip of our in-group. Our suspicion is that children can be and are being brought up in loving, reintegrative families that teach them the curriculum of crimes, that induce in them a concern about the ethical judgments of those they respect, without any recourse to stigmatizing tales of the Hollywood genre. In other words, at the level of general deterrence, imagined gossip and the constitution of unthinkableness, we think stigmatization is overkill. Just as punishment is normally overkill. And like punishment it can have some terrible effects on the particular individuals who suffer it.

However when praise for virtue and reintegrative shaming do fail, we would rather escalate to punishment – hard treatment imposed with explicit objectives of deterrence or incapacitation – than to stigmatization as a deterrent. Normatively, we have this preference because we think to stigmatize someone, particularly by making him or her a permanent outcast, is a very arbitrary, uncontrollable kind of power, whereas punishment can be more calibrated and therefore less arbitrary. It has an end and its end should bring an obligation for the gossip to stop. Fines and calibrated hours of community service are preferable to 'shaming penalties' (Kahan, 1996, 1998)[2] or any other attempt to control the problem by whipping up stigmatization. In those rare cases where the community needs to be directly protected from an offender, imprisonment is a form of punishment which offers an incapacitative protection that stigmatization cannot offer.

Consistent with the republican principle of parsimony in intervening in peoples' lives (also a utilitarian principle), our normative advocacy is for a preference for the reasoned dialogue of restorative justice as a first approach for dealing with wrongdoing, and a second and a third until it is clear that restorative justice has no hope of working in the particular case. Then deterrence would be attempted rather than stigmatization (partly also on the empirical grounds that if one kind of shaming fails, better to try something completely different than another kind of shaming). Then in cases where deterrent punishment failed, incapacitative punishment would be attempted. This presumptive pyramid of strategies is portrayed in Figure 2.1.

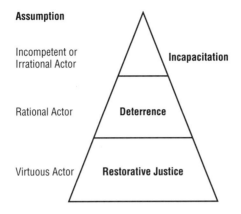

Figure 2.1 Toward an Integration of Restorative, Deterrent and Incapacitative Justice

We say it is presumptively best to start at the base of the pyramid, even with serious offenders. However, we cannot deny that in the case of a serial killer who promises to kill again, the presumption must be overridden and we must move immediately to the peak of the enforcement pyramid.

The most important point of the normative theory of restorative justice we are developing here is that it stands with Desmond Tutu and Nelson Mandela in contending that no crime is so evil that it cannot be forgiven and exempted from punishment in the cause of building a society with more freedom, more love, less poverty and less domination. Desmond Tutu is also our model for the second important point we emphasize in conclusion. This is that censure is normatively most decent when it is censure with love and by those we love. In contrast, forgiveness is maximally virtuous when it is offered by those we hate and by those we have caused most suffering.

As consequentialists, however, we must be open to empirical disconfirmation of our presumptions about when reintegration, stigmatization and punishment succeed and fail. Equally, we might get bolder about normative claims when we discover that certain normative concepts have unexpected empirical bite. For example, we have been moved to give rather more prominence to the concept of love in this normative conclusion than in previous writing by the fact that, in Part II, for restorative conference cases the reintegration item with the highest loading was 'During the conference (court case) did people suggest they loved you regardless of what you did?' In court cases, this had the lowest loading on the reintegration factor of all the reintegration items. Tina Turner's 1990s' anthem 'What's love got to do with it?' seems apt to court cases. But for conference cases, John Lennon's

'All you need is love' is closer to the mark. Imagine that. So the consequentialist must reflect on the data revealing what sustains the good consequences she wishes to promote and imagine ways of reframing her normative ideals to capture this.

Notes

1   Inuit culture is one where it is not appropriate to be direct in advice or questioning of the propriety of one's behavior. This is true even with children who must learn from their mistakes and from modeling. It is inappropriate to order a child around because the child is viewed in the culture as inhabited by a dead elder. Hence, social control relies heavily on gossip rather than confrontation (Drummond, 1999: 147–8).
2   See the critiques of shaming penalties on grounds that they are not respectful of persons (Massaro, 1997).

CHAPTER 3

Revising the Theory of Reintegrative Shaming

On Developing and Integrating Theories

Social science theories are most likely to have explanatory power if they go through many years of refinement that is responsive to strategic research and development programs. Some scholars disagree. They say it is best to put a clear statement of the theory on the bookshelves, see how it competes with other theories in explaining the phenomenon, and reject it if it does not do as well. What these competitive theory development scholars hate is theories that are moving targets.

Our preference is for a collaborative, integrative approach to theory development. That does not preclude devotees of theory competitions from taking *Crime, Shame and Reintegration* off the shelf as originally formulated and putting it in contest with other theories.[1] The basic idea of reintegrative shaming theory is that locations in space and time where shame is communicated effectively and reintegratively will be times and places where there is less predatory crime – less crime that is a threat to freedom as non-domination. Reintegrative shaming prevents such offending; stigmatization increases the risk of crime for the stigmatized. Reintegrative shaming means communicating disapproval of an *act* with respect, with special efforts to avert outcast identities and to terminate disapproval with rituals of forgiveness or reconciliation. Stigmatization means communicating disapproval of a *person* with disrespect, where offenders are labeled with outcast identities (like 'criminal', 'junkie'), where there are no rituals to terminate disapproval.

When shaming is of a stigmatizing sort, labeling theory has explanatory power; however the opposite of labeling theory predictions occur when crime is confronted in a reintegrative way. This is the contribution of the theory of reintegrative shaming: it attempts to specify the conditions

under which older theories are true and false. When persons are stigmatized the explanatory framework of subcultural theory comes into play. Criminal subcultures supply a collective solution to the status problem of people who have been similarly outcast. They define an oppositional value system that enables outcasts to reject their rejectors. In the subculture shaming works to reinforce offending because it is the law-abiding who are shamed; in a bullying subculture bullies garner pride; it is 'weaklings' who are shamed.

Opportunity theory is integrated into the framework in the following ways. Subculture formation is fostered by systematic blockage of legitimate opportunities for critical fractions of the population. For example, if a racial minority living in a slum are systematically denied economic opportunities because of the stigma of their race or neighborhood, then criminal subcultures will form in those outcast neighborhoods. Figure 3.1 shows the integrative connections forged by the theory of reintegrative shaming between labeling, opportunity and subcultural theories.

Control theory is incorporated on the reintegrative side of the theory. When interdependency is high – for example when people are strongly 'attached' (a control theory concept) to their parents, partners, school, neighbors, employer – shaming of wrongdoing will be more reintegrative and effective. The entire theory can be viewed as a social learning theory in the differential association tradition. It is a theory of differential shaming through which people learn criminal identities in criminal subcultures and law-abiding identities in interdependent communities of care. Most critically, the unthinkableness of certain crimes is learnt by the disapproval highly respected others communicate toward such crimes.

The revisions to the theory of reintegrative shaming we consider in this book will not go to the work the theory seeks to do in integrating social

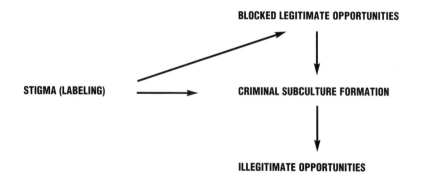

Figure 3.1 How Labeling, Opportunity and Subcultural Theories are Integrated by the Theory of Reintegrative Shaming

learning, opportunity, labeling, control and subcultural theory in criminology. Rather, our work is limited to re-examination of the foundational concepts of shame and shaming, reintegration and stigmatization, in the theory. Thanks to Sherman's (1993) development of defiance theory, nevertheless, we will later in this chapter integrate deterrence theory into our framework. Our neglect of the other integrations in this book does not mean that we doubt the need for much refinement in how they were executed in *Crime, Shame and Reintegration*. For example, why does the theory not build more seriously the hypothesis that poverty (blocked opportunity) undermines interdependency between children and their families, between children and their schools – integrating opportunity theory to the reintegration side of the theory? Some important recent works (e.g., Sampson & Laub, 1993; Weatherburn & Lind, forthcoming) suggest that such an enterprise might have value. We do not attend to these weaknesses in the integrative project of the theory here simply because they are such big questions that require a substantial further research effort.

Undertheorized Shame

From the very beginning, two weaknesses of the reintegrative shaming theory have been (a) a failure to theorize the relationship between shame and pride, shaming and praise, a question we considered in Chapter 2, and (b) a failure to concentrate on the emotion of shame that shaming practices are supposed to induce. The data in this book reveal a need for a lot of repair work to the theory in that respect.

Yet there was always the assumption that an effect of shaming on engaging with criminal subcultures would be mediated by a particular kind of shame. Part II of this book demonstrates that shaming does indeed predict shame. But the structure of shame being predicted is quite different from what was expected. As revealed earlier, we thought it a possibility that stigmatization might predict shame in the sense of feeling bad about one's self and reintegrative shaming might predict guilt in the sense of feeling that one had committed a bad act for which one was morally responsible. This would have allowed a marriage with the program of research being developed by Tangney and her associates.

Instead, however, reintegration predicted Shame–Guilt and was negatively associated with Unresolved Shame. Stigmatization was negatively associated with Shame–Guilt and positively associated with both Unresolved Shame and Embarrassment–Exposure.

The Structure of Reintegrative Shaming and Stigmatization

One of the suspicions we had in embarking on this work was that the different facets of reintegration and stigmatization might not cohere. That is, there might be no association among shaming the act (rather than the person), shaming respectfully (rather than disrespectfully), terminating rituals of disapproval (rather than leaving them open-ended) and refusing to impose a master status trait (versus labeling with a master status). This suspected problem with the theory was not realized as the facets hung together rather well in the reintegration and stigmatization scales.

However, the theoretical foundations were found to be flawed in a more fundamental way. *Crime, Shame and Reintegration* speaks of reintegrative shaming and stigmatization as opposite poles of a continuum. Hence any encounter might be observed and any shaming that occurred in it might be plotted on a continuum stretching from an extremely reintegrative to a highly stigmatizing kind of shaming. The factor analytic work in Part II suggests that while shaming is a dimension independent of how stigmatizing or reintegrative encounters were (consistent with the theory), stigmatization and reintegration were also independent dimensions rather than polar opposites. Hence, the same encounter could include both stigmatization and reintegration. Indeed we observed stigmatization and reintegration to occur in the same sentence during conferences: 'He has proved untrustworthy, but I love him.' The dangers of treating reintegration–stigmatization as a single variable is also revealed in Deng and Jou's (2000) testing of the theory in Taiwan and the US, where Taiwanese parents were found to be higher on both stigmatization and reintegration of their children compared with US parents. It may therefore be necessary to operationalize the theory by the ratio of reintegrative to stigmatizing communications or by entering the quantum of reintegration and stigmatization into regression analyses as separate variables (as we have done in this book).

The Interaction of Shaming and Reintegration

Having clarified the dimensionality of shaming, reintegration and stigmatization as independent in this way, the theory would predict that the Shaming x Reintegration interaction would be positively associated with shame, while the Shaming x Stigmatization interaction would be negatively associated with shame. In no analysis in Section II did these interactions have any effects. Shaming, reintegration and stigmatization had main effects, mostly strongly consistent with the theory, but never significant interactions. Recent results from Hay (2001) fit this pattern. In predicting

the projected delinquency of adolescents Hay found a shaming main effect and a reintegration main effect (which washed out after controlling for interdependency, another key concept in the theory), but no Shaming x Reintegration interaction. Similar results were obtained by Zhang and Zhang (2000) from a test of the theory in a US National Youth Survey reanalysis. While they found main effects for parental forgiveness (reintegration) and peer disapproval (shaming) in reducing delinquency, there was no significant Shaming x Reintegration interaction. Also consistent were results by Deng and Jou (2000) which found a significant effect of interdependence, past and projected shame in reducing delinquency and a significant stigmatization main effect in increasing delinquency, with no interaction effect being tested.[2] These results contrast with Makkai and Braithwaite's (1994) analysis of nursing home regulatory compliance where shaming and reintegration did not have significant main effects on compliance with the law, but there was a significant Shaming x Reintegration effect in the predicted direction. In this context, Braithwaite and Makkai's (1994) qualitative fieldwork suggested that a highly reintegrative regulatory encounter where there was no disapproval of failure to meet the standards was interpreted as a 'tolerant and understanding' inspection which could be interpreted as regulatory capture by the industry. Compliance with the law was in fact significantly worse following such encounters (see Figure 9.1 in Part II). Similar low-shame contexts are suggested by normal child-rearing encounters as in Baumrind's (1971, 1978) research, for example, where both laissez-faire (tolerant and understanding) parenting and authoritarian parenting were found to be less effective than authoritative parenting (firm but fair, confronting but reintegrative parenting). Gerald Patterson (1982) likewise concluded that parents who natter and whine about their children's wrongdoing, but do not confront it, are more likely to have delinquent children.

The most likely interpretation of these divergent results is that in cases where criminal liability has already been admitted and a formal state ritual convened to deal with the admission, causing the interaction to be inherently shameful, both the reintegration and stigmatization scales are already measuring interactions with shaming. In the nursing home regulation or normal child-rearing contexts, in contrast, there had been no criminal charges and regulatory encounters were normally very low on shame. It is perhaps premature to revise the theory in light of such divergent results. However, it is certainly a way to reconcile them to suggest that the theory might be revised to predict shaming, reintegration and stigmatization main effects but no interaction effects in contexts heavily laden with shame and no main effects but interaction effects for these variables in contexts where limited shame is normally experienced. There may therefore be merit in advancing explicit hypotheses to be explored in future research.

1   In high shame contexts, there will be a *shaming and reintegration* effect. This means there will be shaming and reintegration main effects on predatory crime, but no reintegrative shaming interaction effect.

2   The shaming main effect will be actually an interaction effect of high shaming and high respect for those communicating the shaming.[3] Disapproval perceived to be communicated by those who are only moderately respected will have no effect.[4] Disapproval perceived as communicated by people who are despised will increase predatory crime.[5]

3   In low shame contexts, because reintegration without disapproval will be interpreted as tolerance of predatory crime, and disapproval without reintegration will produce defiance, there will be a *reintegrative shaming* interaction effect.

Indeed, to go further, in contexts where everyone present at a restorative justice conference knows that a serious criminal transgression has already been admitted, because shame is so heavy in the atmosphere, it may be downright disrespectful even to indulge in shaming as benign as saying 'You have breached an obligation to the community here that you should not treat lightly.' Why? Because those present may know that the defendant is not taking it lightly when he has admitted criminal responsibility for it and has freely embarked upon a process in which he stands ready to do what he can to right the wrong. Better in this context to avert direct shaming altogether by saying 'John knows he has breached an obligation to the community that he does not take lightly.' It is not that shaming is not going on in this ritual, but it is going on by virtue of the very fact of the ritual itself rather than by virtue of any shaming utterances.

Contrast the regulatory inspector who says respectfully to a recalcitrant nursing home operator: 'You have breached an obligation to the community here that you should not treat lightly.' If this operator has no shame about her wrongdoing, it would show disrespect not to confront her about it because to fail to confront directly would be to treat her as a person with obligations that we are not taking seriously. Similarly, in daily child-rearing when we fail to confront a child who manifests no shame about violence against another child, we fail to show respect to that child as a human being with obligations. The moral situation only becomes different when we heap a verbal confrontation on a child who is already admitting wrong and moving at a commendable pace toward remorse, apology and recompense.

In light of our interpretation of the above results, we might add a new hypothesis to the theory of reintegrative shaming:

4   Predatory crime where remorse has not occurred will persist if left unconfronted.

Indirect methods of confrontation that seek to elicit volunteered remorse (e.g. dialogue where those who have been hurt discuss consequences of an act; others owning their share in the responsibility (Wachtel & McCold, 2001); others telling stories of their remorse for similar wrongdoing in their past) will be more effective in bringing about desistance from predatory crime than direct verbal disapproval of the act.

Where indirect methods of eliciting confession, remorse, apology and recompense fail, direct verbal confrontation with disapproval of the act (while approving of the person) will be necessary. In this situation, we suspect, though we are not aware of any evidence on this question, that a private confrontation by a highly respected other carries less risk of perceived stigmatization than overt confrontation in a public forum such as a restorative justice conference or courtroom.

Reintegration and Ethical Identity

What we are doing in propositions 1–4 above is beginning to elaborate a higher level of specificity into claims about how shaming and reintegration lead to crime. Settling on an ethical identity conception as the main conception of shame also has implications here. Tom Tyler is the scholar who has done most to work through the implications of a social identity approach for compliance with the law (see also Koh, 1997). Tyler has developed his social identity approach in the context of the social psychology of procedural justice. Tyler (1990) concludes that procedural fairness increases compliance, a view for which our own research group has found some modest support (Makkai & Braithwaite, 1996; see also Braithwaite, 2001). Barnes (1999) has used the same data set that is used in Part II of this book to show that procedural justice is higher in restorative justice conferences than in the cases randomly assigned to court.

Procedural fairness and reintegration may share a common message about respect for the offender (and indeed the victim for whom the same considerations apply). When a person is treated procedurally fairly and reintegratively by someone with whom that person has a feeling of shared identity, the shared identity is affirmed. When a person is treated unfairly and stigmatized, that person is more inclined to spurn the shared identity and search for others, such as those that might be offered by criminal subcultures. When a person is treated fairly and reintegratively by a criminal subculture, that person is more likely to take pride in membership of criminal subcultural groups. Here is a key entry point for our concern to balance shame with pride in the theory. Across four different studies, Tyler, Degoey and Smith (1996) found respectful treatment, fair treatment and trustworthiness by authorities increased pride in membership of the same

group as the authority. In one study, Tyler and Degoey (1996) found that pride in membership of one's society predicted compliance with its laws, net of other variables.

One inference from all this is that respect and fairness engender pride in oneself and in group identities shared with the respectful and fair other. Obversely, 'disrespect begets disrespect' (Zehr, 1995) and begets shame that cannot be acknowledged because to acknowledge it would imply that the shamer's judgment was worthy of some kind of respect. Part III shows that unacknowledged shame is associated with heightened risk of serious bullying. A good way of showing disrespect back to someone who disrespects us is to bully them or inflict some other kind of criminal exploitation upon them.

Sherman (1993) has woven some of the above propositions about procedural justice, the social bonds that render shaming reintegrative and unacknowledged shame into an integrated theory of defiance. It has three propositions:

(a) Sanctions provoke future *defiance* of the law (persistence, more frequent or more serious violations) to the extent that offenders experience sanctioning conduct as illegitimate, that offenders have weak bonds to the sanctioning agent and community, and that offenders deny their shame and become proud of their isolation from the sanctioning community.
(b) Sanctions produce future *deterrence* of law-breaking (desistance, less frequent or less serious violations) to the extent that offenders experience sanctioning conduct as legitimate, that offenders have strong bonds to the sanctioning agent and community, and that offenders accept their shame and remain proud of solidarity with the community.
(c) Sanctions become *irrelevant* to future law breaking (no effect) to the extent that the factors encouraging defiance or deterrence are fairly evenly counterbalanced. (Sherman, 1993: 448–49).

The special appeal of this theoretical contribution by Sherman is that it enables the integration of deterrence theory into the framework we are developing. Deterrence theory has had a bad press with criminologists, ironically similar to labeling theory. There has been a lot of research suggesting it just is not true. Sherman's defiance theory does for deterrence theory what the theory of reintegrative shaming does for labeling theory. They cause us to pause with multiple regression criminology that persists with simply placing deterrence and labeling theory measures side by side in models that guarantee zero explanatory power of both. Defiance theory saves the plausible claims of deterrence theory from oblivion by suggesting that the problem with the null returns from the research results is that they combine findings from contexts where the theory works with contexts where it not only does not work, but has counter-deterrent effects.

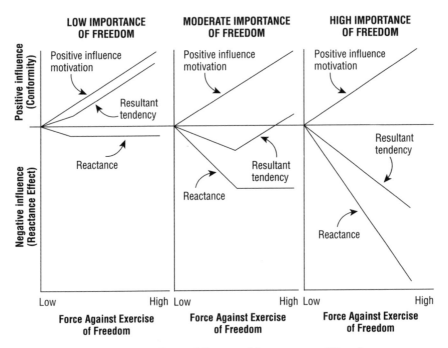

Figure 3.2 The Interactive Effects of Force and Importance of Freedom (from Brehm & Brehm, 1981: 60)

Braithwaite and Makkai (1994) have demonstrated precisely this phenomenon, and in a way that shows the emotions to hold the key to unlocking the mysteries of deterrence and counter-deterrence. Among nursing home chief executives, Braithwaite and Makkai (1994) found that the expected severity of sanctions did not predict compliance with the law. However, this null result was then decomposed into a counter-deterrent result for executives who were high on emotionality and a deterrent effect for those low on emotionality. In Sherman's terms we might say that the former were more likely to be defiant, the latter more likely to be cool, calculating rational actors.

The core defiance idea has long been subject to sophisticated development in the experimental psychology literature under the less appealing rubric of the theory of psychological reactance (Brehm & Brehm, 1981). Figure 3.2 summarizes the patterns of results from a number of experiments on the effect of force against the exercise of a freedom. More force produces more deterrence. However, it simultaneously produces more 'reactance' (read defiance). What is the net effect – the net social control – secured by a given use of force? That is given by measuring the deterrence effect and then subtracting from it the reactance effect of the intervention in question. Figure 3.2 illustrates that reactance is greatest when controlling force is used against a freedom of high importance to the citizen, as in the right-hand panel. Let

freedom of religion be involved, for example, and any law to ban the religion is likely to have an enormous reactance effect. In the left-hand panel, the freedom is of low importance to the citizen: it may be the freedom to park a car wherever one wants. As the force used against that freedom increases – as parking fines are raised, for example – reactance is low. Thus, the net social control achieved by the intervention will be mainly determined by its deterrence effect. Deterrence theory will be supported.

Figure 3.2 also shows why there are contexts where if respectful, reintegrative restorative justice fails, deterrence may succeed. Consider the middle panel of Figure 3.2 (moderate importance of freedom). Here escalating to tough deterrent sanctions may have a positive influence on compliance. The reason for this is the shape of the reactance curve when freedoms are moderately important. With an escalating threat people become more defiant until the point is reached where the coercive force confronting them becomes so severe that they give up on escalating their resistance. As deterrence effects then outstrip defiance effects, we find a context where escalating deterrence works. With the right-hand panel, we find contexts where no amount of persuasion nor any amount of deterrence will work: the man who views it as his inalienable right of fatherhood to physically abuse his children may be unpersuadable and undeterrable. Then we may need to incapacitate his criminality by taking his children away from him or even locking him up.

Hence we can see how defiance theory provides a rationale for an enforcement pyramid of the form in Figure 2.1. The idea of this pyramid is a policy presumption for trying restorative justice first, then deterrence when restorative justice persistently fails, then incapacitation when deterrence fails. The weaknesses of one regulatory strategy are covered by the strengths of the others. Normatively, the pyramid enables us to achieve the parsimony in the use of more severe sanctions that republicanism requires (for a more detailed exposition of these normative arguments, see Braithwaite and Pettit, 2000; for more detail on the explanatory theory of pyramidal regulation, see Ayres and Braithwaite, 1992).

A problem with defiance theory is that it discounts disengagement. Reactance theory does accommodate disengagement as Figure 3.2 shows. In the two left-hand panels of this figure, we see that deterrent threat up to a certain point progressively increases defiance; beyond that point, the subject of control gives up on the idea that she enjoys any control, opting out of defiance to the control. For the empirical literature that informs this aspect of the model, see Brehm and Brehm (1981: 58–97). Research derived from the 'learned helplessness' school (Seligman, 1975) led to modification of Brehm's (1966) original reactance theory to accommodate the finding that extended experience with uncontrollable outcomes leads to passivity.

While defiance (participation in a business subculture of resistance to regulation) did reduce compliance in the ANU nursing home regulation research (Makkai & Braithwaite 1991), disengagement was the bigger problem (Braithwaite, Braithwaite, Gibson, & Makkai, 1994), particularly because astute regulators found it harder to get disengagers than 'resisters' (defiers) back into compliance. Defiers play the game in some sense, whereas disengagers are in the game but not of it. Jenkins (1997), drawing Albert Bandura's (1986) social cognitive theory into the explanation, showed that sustaining the self-efficacy of managers for improving quality of care was critical to keeping them engaged with improving compliance (see also Maruna, 2001: 76–80). It follows that strategies like praise, reintegration, fairness, trust and avoidance of stigmatization (all of which have been established by this program of research as explaining compliance) have value for reducing disengagement.

Following the cues given by Charles Tittle's (1995) control balance theory, it may be that defiance increases as domination provoked by stigmatization and other modes of disrespectful control increases. However, when humiliating domination exceeds a turning point, people give up on defiance (see Braithwaite's (1997: 85–87) proposed revision and simplification of Tittle's rather complex theory in this respect). Beyond the turning point, predatory crime declines, instead submission and disengagement increase – manifested in withdrawn forms of deviance such as drug abuse, alcoholism, depressive disorders and suicide. In the terms Ahmed uses in Part III of this book, shame becomes internalized rejection of the self instead of externalized anger at others.[6]

Let us now attempt to summarize these further proposed refinements to the theory of reintegrative shaming in propositional form.

5   Predatory crime will be explained by a model that includes reintegration, stigmatization (reversed coefficient), and procedural justice, where these concepts have the following facets:

Reintegration
- Approval of the person – praise
- Respectfulness
- Rituals to terminate disapproval with forgiveness
- Sustaining pride in having the offender included as a member of communities of care (families, the school, the law abiding community at large)

Stigmatization
- Shaming the person
- Disrespect

- Ceremonies to certify deviance are not terminated by ceremonies to decertify deviance
- Labeling with an outcast identity which may be a master identity

Procedural Justice
- Consistency
- Correctability
- Process control (stakeholder empowerment)
- Impartiality
- Ethicality

6   The effect of reintegration, stigmatization and procedural justice on predatory crime will be mediated by a law-abiding identity and pride of membership in communities of care that act reintegratively toward the offender.

7   The effect of reintegration, stigmatization and procedural justice on predatory crime will be mediated by disengagement from a law-abiding identity and from membership in law-abiding communities of care.

8   The effect of reintegration, stigmatization and procedural justice on predatory crime will be mediated by defiance of respect for the law, and a defiant identification with criminal subcultures.[7]

9   Whether escalating formal and informal sanctions reduces crime depends on whether the deterrent effect of the escalation is greater than the sum of its defiance and disengagement effects.

10   Reintegrative shaming through restorative justice will be more effective when it is backed up by the possibility of subsequent deterrent enforcement when restoration fails. Not only does restorative justice have weaknesses that are complemented by the strengths of deterrence (and vice versa), but an expectation that failed restorative justice might inexorably lead to punitive escalation motivates actors to take restorative justice seriously. Moreover, deterrence is granted more legitimacy when good faith efforts for a maximally respectful restorative approach have been made first.[8]

At the macro level of the theory, Gary LaFree's (1998) work in *Losing Legitimacy: Street Crime and the Decline of Social Institutions in America*, shows that Proposition 6 probably does not go far enough. This proposition contends that stigmatization and procedural injustice increase crime by reducing the charm of law-abiding identities and undermining pride of membership in communities of care. First, LaFree translates this proposition into a more macro-sociological claim by construing the mediation that occurs as a collapse of confidence in the legitimacy of key institutions – economic, familial and political. He builds an impressive body of evidence for the

claim that when the legitimacy of these key institutions falls, crime rises. Second, LaFree builds a strong empirical case that distributive fairness (not only procedural fairness as in Proposition 6) explains trust in institutions. In particular, rises in income inequality increase crime through undermining the legitimacy of economic institutions. He also makes a case that distributive inequality (particularly based on race) can engender procedural inequality in the justice system. Elsewhere, Braithwaite (1991) has made the case that distributive inequality can engender stigmatization. Hence, there is virtue in elaborating Proposition 6 with the kind of macro-sociological move developed so eloquently in LaFree's work:

11   Inequality, procedural injustice and stigmatization at a micro level undermine law-abiding identities. At a macro level they undermine the legitimacy of economic, familial and political institutions. Crime waves result when trust in these institutions collapses.

Another effect of this theoretical move is that it gives the theory a recursive quality. One of the unfortunate consequences of crime waves, LaFree shows, is that they further erode trust in key institutions. Societies therefore spiral downwards into crises of legitimacy. Yet they can pull out of them by a combination of effective crime control and institutional renewal so that citizens return to trusting their institutions as distributively and procedurally fair as well as respectful of them as citizens. The vicious circle of institutional distrust and escalating crime can be reversed into a virtuous circle of institutional confidence-building and falling crime. Margaret Levi (1988) has demonstrated such a reversal with tax cheating in Australia and trust in the nation's economic and political institutions in the 1970s and 80s.

Acknowledged and Unacknowledged Shame

In Part II, but particularly in Part III of this book, whether shame is acknowledged or not is a decisive issue. In the early 1990s Scheff and Retzinger noted as a limitation of *Crime, Shame and Reintegration* that it failed to come to terms with the implications of whether shame was by-passed or acknowledged. They saw acknowledgment as a vital supplement to the theory given the way this had emerged as a recurrently central question in both conversational analyses and the clinical psychiatric literature on people with shame management problems, pre-eminently in the pioneering work of Lewis (1971), but also in work from a rather different perspective by Donald Nathanson (1992) and others.

Equally, this work emphasizes different kinds of displacement of shame, as in Nathanson's (1992) compass of shame. Again, our results affirm the explanatory power of Shame Displacement. These theoretical perspectives

and the results summarized in Chapter 1 (and in more detail in Parts II and III) commend the following propositional additions to the theory of reintegrative shaming.

Effect of Shame–Guilt on Crime

12 The effect of shaming by highly respected others, of reintegration, stigmatization[9] and procedural justice on predatory crime will be mediated by Shame–Guilt. Shame–Guilt will reduce crime[10] especially when it is acknowledged.[11]

13 This Shame–Guilt that will reduce crime will involve both concerns about the wrong of the criminal act and acceptance that the wrong may require repair to the self, but not total rejection of the self as a bad person.[12]

14 Shaming will only increase Shame–Guilt when the individual accepts the disapproval as correct (and this will normally require respectful moral reasoning that a shared ethical norm is at issue that is important to the individual's identity).[13]

15 Shame–Guilt, especially when it is acknowledged,[14] will increase empathy for victims and other affected persons, more so in restorative justice processes than in court cases.[15]

16 Shaming by others who are not respected and stigmatization may increase Embarrassment–Exposure, but this will not affect crime because it will not touch the ethical identity of the self.[16]

17 Apology is the most powerful and symbolically meaningful form of shaming (because it is self-shaming of the act) and of Shame Acknowledgment. Apology–reparation–forgiveness sequences accomplish a synergistic access to the benefits of restoration on both the victim and offender sides.[17]

Externalized Anger

18 The effect of stigmatization and procedural injustice on predatory crime will be mediated by externalized anger.[18]

19 Externalized anger will be higher for both offenders and victims in court cases than in restorative justice processes[19] and the externalized anger of one party will reinforce the externalized anger of the other. Put another way, externalized anger will be more likely to be in a shame–rage spiral in court, more likely to be in a condition of hurt begetting hurt, whereas in a restorative justice process, it is more likely to be in a condition of healing begetting healing.[20]

Responsibility, Empathy

20 Shame–Guilt which is acknowledged will increase willingness to take responsibility for a crime. This taking of responsibility helps restorative justice processes prevent predatory crime.[21]
21 When offenders take responsibility for crime, other participants in a restorative justice process will be more willing to take some responsibility to help with the prevention of future recurrence of crime and with the repair of past harm. This will help restorative justice processes reduce predatory crime.[22]

Restorative Justice

A final set of eight propositions (that readers can skip over) simply draws out the implications of the above propositions for the working of restorative justice.

22 Restorative justice processes will achieve higher acknowledgment of Shame–Guilt than court processing.[23]
23 Court processing will achieve higher Embarrassment–Exposure than restorative justice processes.[24]
24 When restorative justice processes achieve higher acknowledgment of Shame–Guilt, they will be more effective in reducing predatory crime than court processing.[25]
25 When the criminal process increases unacknowledged shame and externalization of shame, it will increase predatory crime.[26]
26 Restorative justice processes will deliver higher levels of reintegration than court.[27]
27 Restorative justice processes will deliver higher levels of procedural justice than court.[28]
28 Restorative justice processes will deliver lower levels of stigmatization than court.[29]
29 Stigmatization in court will induce higher unacknowledged shame and a greater increase in crime than will stigmatization in conferences. This is because stigmatization is less damaging when it comes from those we love and when it is balanced with high levels of reintegration.[30]

There is a thirtieth new proposition which we have not discussed yet, but which we will develop in the next chapter. This is:

30 The Shame–Guilt and acknowledgment engendered by a collective restorative justice process can motivate the implementation of crime prevention strategies that work. Restorative justice provides a superior framework for selection of a prevention strategy appropriate for the

context than court, police discretion or the discretion of a rehabilitative professional.

Conclusion – Back to Durkheim

Adding 30 propositions to a theory which already integrates many different theories perhaps makes it too complex. We think not when what we are doing here is just filling detail into a reasonably simple theoretical structure. Second, while the theory is rich in its harvest of explanatory propositions, when we connect it to our normative theory from Chapter 3, there is a small number of general policy prescriptions that are radically different from, for example, the punitive prescriptions of a utilitarian theory. There are nine basic prescriptions from our encompassing explanatory-normative theoretical integrations:

1 Reduce stigmatization.
2 Do not sweep crime under the carpet; seek the reintegrative way to communicate disapproval of the act.
3 Help victims and offenders acknowledge and discharge shame.
4 Reduce distributive and procedural injustice.
5 Institutionalize freedom as non-domination (republican deliberative institutions).
6 Support social movements with agendas that disapprove crimes of domination and that confront distributive and procedural injustice.
7 Support the development of individuals through loving communities of care.
8 Strengthen the justice and care of familial, economic and political institutions and thence trust in them.
9 Regulate crime responsively – restorative justice first, deterrence and incapacitation only when restorative justice fails.

Surveying both these prescriptions and our 30 new explanatory propositions, it can be seen that there is some merit in Moore and McDonald's (2001) recent suggestion that *crime, shame and reintegration* become *shame, acknowledgment and transformation*. Actually Moore and McDonald mean more than just the revised ideas captured in the 30 hypotheses above. They also want us to think about the possibilities of restorative justice for shame transformation in a more collective way.

The South African Truth and Reconciliation Commission illustrates a process where collective dialogue on a national scale led to a shared acknowledgment of a variety of deeply disturbing kinds of shame which in turn laid foundations for the possibility of a transformed South Africa (Tutu, 1999). Both reintegration and restoration are impoverished words

for these aspirations for transformation to a new social justice (which cannot be seen as the restoration of any prior status quo). This is why writers like Ruth Morris (1995) and Moore and McDonald (2001) prefer to speak of transformative justice rather than restorative justice. On the other hand, Tutu himself opts to speak of restorative justice because of the emphasis he places on healing of shattered souls. Both languages can co-exist while each side incorporates the concerns that motivate the other to use a different language.

As we, and other criminologists, set our sights on testing the above 30 hypotheses, there is a risk that we will do so in a spirit that is excessively micro-micro, and insufficiently micro-macro. The shame, acknowledgment and transformation of the Truth and Reconciliation Commission is funda-mentally collective shame, collective acknowledgment and collective transformation. It is a Durkheimian story, a story of communal moral education. One cannot understand how it seeks to prevent a continuation of the exploitative crimes of Apartheid without seeing a history of national and global social movement politics that first persuaded South Africa to conceive of a new curriculum of crimes – crimes against fundamental human rights – and then, to confront them, forgive them and heal them collectively.

Notes

1   There is the problem that this particular theory is an attempt to show how to integrate criminological theories which had previously been thought to be contradictory. So a competition between reintegrative shaming theory and control theory is a competition with a theory that is a part of itself.

2   A comparison US sample replicated the significant interdependence and projected shame effects, but in the multiple regression the effects of stigmati-zation and the frequency of past feelings of shame were not significant.

3   As reported in Chapter 1, this was what was actually found in the regression analyses in Part II.

4   Hamilton and Sanders' (1992) research suggests that when relationships of respect are strongest, sanctioning is most reintegrative: 'punishment practices are most restorative, most sensitive to rebuilding relationships of actor and victim, where relationships are highly solidary' (Hamilton & Sanders, 1992: 182). This was true in both the US and Japan, though in general sanctioning was more restorative in Japan. Hamilton and Sanders (1992: 215) speak of this phenomenon as 'the self-limiting nature of what we have called justice among friends'.

5   Recent literature suggests trust may be an important facet of respect or perhaps a separate predictor from respect (see Braithwaite, 1999b; Tyler, 1999).

6   If this analysis is correct, then the discounting of disengagement will not be a deficiency of defiance theory after all in the explanation of predatory crime.

Defiance theory will simply fail to explain distinctive forms of crimes of disengagement which are not predatory crimes (such as drug abuse and suicide). On the other hand, recent research suggests that disengagement may have effects on more predatory forms of delinquency (Bandura, Barbaranelli, Caprara, & Pastorelli, 1996; Kwak & Bandura, 1998; Bandura, 1999 (citing Elliott & Rinehart, 1995)). And an older tradition of criminological research suggests that contra-cultural defiance is a less common fact of delinquency than drift between law-supportive and law-neutralizing identities (Matza, 1964; for studies that support this view see Braithwaite, 1999a: 47–52). According to this tradition, techniques of neutralization (Sykes & Matza, 1957) are techniques of disengagement more than techniques of defiance.

7   An interesting topic for future refinement of the possibilities for theoretical integration here is between Charles Tittle's (1995) control balance theory, defiance theory and opportunity theory. According to Tittle, domination and ingratitude at the hands of actors with control surpluses (more control over others than they experience control over themselves) is humiliating for those with control deficits. This humiliation engenders defiant deviance among the powerless. Defiance in turn is reciprocated (with deviance of domination) to further extend the control of the actor with the surplus. Obversely, 'Efforts to extend control surpluses are likely to lead to efforts to overcome control deficits' (deviance of the dominated) (Tittle, 1995: 182; see also Braithwaite, 1997).

8   This is the theory of the regulatory pyramid as developed in Ayres and Braithwaite (1992). In this theory, a lot turns on whether a deterrent sword of Damocles is threatened in the foreground (thereby engendering defiance) or threatening and inexorable in the background.

9   Stigmatization will reduce Shame–Guilt, while shaming by highly respected others, reintegration and procedural justice will have positive coefficients on Shame–Guilt, acknowledgment, etc. That is, for all the propositions on this list, stigmatization will have an opposite coefficient to reintegration, procedural justice and shaming by highly respected others.

10 Many studies have reported an association between higher levels of Shame–Guilt and lower levels of law breaking. See Braithwaite (1989), Bachman, Paternoster, and Ward (1992), Makkai and Braithwaite (1994), Grasmick, Bursik and Kinsey (1991), Grasmick and Bursik (1990), Nagin and Paternoster (1993), Bandura et al. (1996), and Tibbetts (1997), Simpson (1998), Wikstrom (1998: p. 274), Brown (1999).

11 In Part II, the stigmatization scale is the strongest predictor of Unresolved Shame and reintegration has a significant negative coefficient (see Table 10.4). Reintegration shows positive coefficients whereas stigmatization shows negative coefficients for Shame–Guilt (see Table 10.2).

12 This is how the Shame–Guilt factor emerges from the factor analyses in Part II (see Table 8.3).

13 This is argued in Part II (see pp. 187–190). Shame–Guilt is less likely when the wrongness of the offense is unresolved in the mind of the perpetrator, whether that Unresolved Shame is a result of stigmatization or an absence of community consensus about the norm.

14   The data in Part II show Shame–Guilt having the strongest association with empathy (see p. 123) and the data in Part III show an association between shame acknowledgment and empathy (see p. 251).

15   The data in Part II show that empathy by offenders is higher in conference than court cases and that Shame–Guilt is a stronger predictor of empathy in conferences than in court cases (see Harris, 1999).

16   The data in Part II suggest an association between stigmatization and Embarrassment–Exposure(see Table 10.1).

17   This is a conclusion of Part III. Heather Strang's (2000) RISE research program is testing the apology-forgiveness synergy hypothesis.

18   The data in Part III show that externalized anger is associated with higher levels of bullying.

19   The data in Part II show offender anger/hostility to be higher in court than in conference cases (see Harris, 1999).

20   In her research program, Heather Strang (2000) is testing this hurt begets hurt, healing begets healing dynamic between victims and offenders.

21   The data in Part II show an association between Shame–Guilt and offender feelings of responsibility for the offense. In Part III, admitting feelings of shame and taking responsibility are positively linked; responsibility is negatively linked to bullying. Dresler-Hawke (1999) found on a German sample a measure of 'Willingness to confront the Nazi past' (items like 'Today, fifty years after the war, we should no longer talk so much about our Nazi past and the persecution of the Jews.''), which she interpreted as a measure of collective shame, positively correlated with 'Willingness to accept responsibility for the Nazi past' (items like: 'It is still Germany's moral duty to pay for the compensation of living survivors of the Nazi terror.'').

22   In Heather Strang's (2000) RISE research program she is testing the association between offenders accepting responsibility and victims being willing to help offenders.

23   The data in Part II support higher levels of Shame–Guilt in restorative justice conferences than in court (see Harris, 1999) but do not support a difference in acknowledgment.

24   The data in Part II supports this hypothesis (see Harris, 1999).

25   The data in Part III show lower levels of bullying when shame is acknowledged and discharged.

26   The data in Part III show that unacknowledged shame and externalization increases bullying.

27   The data in Part II support this hypothesis (see Table 11.1).

28   Barnes' (1999) PhD data supports this hypothesis.

29   The data in Part II support this hypothesis (see Harris, 1999).

30   For the data in Part II, stigmatization is a stronger predictor of Unresolved Shame in court cases than in conference cases (see Table 10.4).

CHAPTER 4

Just and Loving Gaze

Susan Drummond (1999: 109) in an evocative ethnography of Inuit healing and sentencing circles describes 'the just and loving gaze of the healing circle'. In another hemisphere, Trish Stewart (1993: 49) reported the discovery of the same language by a victim who said in the closing round of a New Zealand restorative justice conference: 'Today I have observed and taken part in justice administered with love.' In this book we have discovered the coming together of love, justice and the gaze of intimates with a radically different kind of data. Nathan Harris's reintegration item with the highest loading in conference but not court cases was 'During the conference (court case) did people suggest they loved you regardless of what you did?' Even the most pessimistic of us has been surprised at how far what Drummond (1999: 109) calls the 'benevolent mercy of intimacy' in the circle can go; for instance, the woman, robbed and tied up at the point of a knife, having a lost soul of a young offender live with her family after a conference.

At the same time, we have seen levels of stigmatization of young people in Canberra conferences that we have never seen in Canberra courtrooms. The Canberra program is hardly a best-practice one given the innovation that has been fostered by the social movement for restorative justice in the Northern hemisphere during the past decade. While we see a disturbing amount of stigmatization occur in these conferences, they are balanced by encouraging amounts of reintegration which come in larger measure. When stigmatization comes from those we love and is balanced by reintegrative messages from them, our data suggest it does not generate as much anger and Unresolved Shame as stigmatization that is perceived to occur in court cases. We have seen many conferences where police officers who have facilitated the process have been shockingly stigmatizing, professionally

incompetent and insensitive to restorative values. Yet some of these conferences have been movingly restorative because of the love, forgiveness and sincerity of remorse nurtured by the wisdom of the intervention of ordinary citizens in the circle.

Equally we have seen vindictive and cruel speech by citizens in conferences transformed by a wise and caring police officer asking the simple question whether others in the circle had a different view, had seen the offender's better side. The first juvenile conference any of us attended, in Wagga Wagga more than a decade ago, was just such a case. The mother of a 14-year-old girl, who had evicted the young burglary offender from their home, protested on her arrival at the conference at being asked to attend with Sergeant Terry O'Connell. He urged her to give the process a try. As she entered the room she said to her daughter: 'I'll kill you, you little bitch.' Then within minutes of the conference commencing, mum jumped up, pointing a shaking finger at the cowed girl, shouting: 'This is a load of rubbish. She should be punished.' She stormed out. The spectacle of such a stigmatizing mother transformed the emotional dynamics of the conference. Victim supporters who had arrived at the conference angry at what had been a series of major burglaries were now sorry for the girl and wanted to help, especially when they learned she was living on the street.

Researching Emotion, Healing and Justice

The genius of restorative circles is their collective emotional dynamics. At the moment, the research literature on restorative justice has not risen to the challenge of capturing these dynamics in the research reports. That limitation applies to the research reported in this book as well. The result of this failing is that even the most literate of criminologists and criminal lawyers understand restorative justice in terms of material reparation to victims rather than in terms of the symbolic reparation which all evidence to date suggests is more important.

Where we have made a start here is at least in being emotion-focused in our research. The relational victim-offender focus in Part III also involves a major advance – the simultaneous analysis of shame in victims and offenders and its management. To understand offender shame we need to understand the mutuality of victim shame. Still our methods are not relational enough, not up to tracing the historical dynamism of sequences of encounters that see shame displaced into anger or into acknowledgment and healing.

We have also made little progress on the justice part of the just and loving gaze of the circle. Justice is fundamentally about righting a wrong. The thing that crime or bullying does is to hurt, so it follows that justice should heal. Susan Drummond (1999) has inverted the traditional idea that

a court of justice might effect some healing, say by ordering compensation for a victim. Drummond suggests that in restorative justice, healing leads to justice more than justice leads to healing. What might that mean? Shame–acknowledgment–transformation sequences can lead to commitments to a more just way of living in future as a response to the injustice of a crime. Drummond's focus is family violence and the unjust world of the way men and women relate to each other beyond the circle. Desmond Tutu's just and loving gaze was on the searing truth of political violence. In effect, the Truth and Reconciliation Commission recommended redistributing resources from the retributive justice of the prison system to the restorative practices of the education system by spending money on schools named after victims of Apartheid, money that might have funded long criminal trials and punishments. Healing can foster social and commemorative justice.

> Amy Biehl was a Fulbright scholar from California attached to the University of Western Cape. Before she came to South Africa, she had been involved for a long period in the anti-apartheid student campaign at Stanford University. On 25 August 1993 she gave a lift to student friends, taking them to Gugulethu township. Youths stoned the car and when Amy and her passengers got out, the mob chased them, stoning and stabbing her. She who was so committed to justice was ironically killed by people whose cause she had espoused.
>
> Her family were obviously shattered. Yet instead of being embittered and seeking revenge, they did not oppose the amnesty applications of those who had killed their child so brutally. Mr Peter and Mrs Linda Biehl attended the amnesty application hearing and said that they supported the entire process of reconciliation and amnesty. They embraced the families of the murderers of their child.
>
> But what is more remarkable is that they have established the Amy Biehl Foundation, whose objectives are to help young people in the township where some residents could very well have been involved in the murder of their daughter. The Biehls return to South Africa regularly to oversee the operations of the Foundation and they frequently pass the spot where their child met her gruesome death. They have testified to how their daughter's death has led them to deeper insights and they have invested a great deal of their time and energy as well as their money to help develop the township community where their daughter was killed. They are passionately committed to rescuing as many as possible of Gugulethu's youth from the dead ends that might well be their lot, salvaging them from the engulfing criminal violence, and setting them on the road to responsible adulthood. (Tutu, 1999: 119)

For Tutu, if justice is an outcome of healing and forgiveness, safety is an outcome of justice:

> I was able to point out [in Jerusalem] that we had learned in South Africa that true security would never be won through the barrel of a gun. True security would come when all the inhabitants of the Middle East ... believed that their human rights and dignity were respected and upheld, when true justice prevailed. (Tutu, 1999: 216)

Justness as a psychological state that motivates justice as a political pursuit engendered by healing is a researchable topic. It is commended by work such as that of Jack Katz (1988), which finds crime motivated by feelings of injustice.

While we have ducked these deeply challenging questions, both studies here do involve results from larger samples than have been reported before and uncover some remarkably robust convergences for data from adults in one case, children in the other; criminal justice data in one case, school data in the other; and measures of the concepts which had to be radically different because of the differences in age and in the kind of wrongdoing studied. The greatest virtue of the work, we hope, is that it starts with the emotional foundations of what goes on in confrontations with wrongdoing. Because all the ethnographic work on restorative practices suggest that emotional dynamics is the key issue, this is the first priority for our work, more so than a rush to publish results on whether this program has more impact on reoffending than that, on what they cost compared to traditional processing, and other outcome-preoccupations. Our hope is for more data that will inform the refinement of our crude theories and that will enrich research and development with restorative and shame management practice.

Restorative Practices

Wachtel and McCold (2001) contend that it is naïve to think that conferences as such would have much impact on criminal offending. When rehabilitative programs that run for hundreds of hours so often fail, it takes a lot of optimism to believe that a one-hour restorative justice conference would make much difference (or indeed even six hours of conferencing). That one-hour interaction has to compete with thousands of hours of interactions with peers during the months and years after the conference. Like Tutu, Wachtel and McCold therefore want a social movement for restorative practices, not limited only to restorative justice. This means teaching children in schools how to confront any kind of wrongdoing or conflict restoratively; teaching parents how to raise children restoratively; teaching teachers how to teach restoratively; bosses how to manage restoratively; presidents how to be Nelson

Mandelas. Then, think Wachtel and McCold, we will have a social movement that really makes a difference to violence. They are right that a social movement for restorative practices broadly conceived is a more important agenda than restorative justice alone. That is why we describe in Part IV the Responsible Citizenship Program being developed by our colleague Brenda Morrison in Canberra schools, a program that helps children to discover for themselves how to confront the little and big hurts they inflict on each other in a restorative way. The Responsible Citizenship Program teaches students, rather helps students teach one another, how to REACT to hurts:

Repair the harm done
Expect the best from others
Acknowledge feelings/harm done
Care for others
Take responsibility for behaviors/feelings

But we do still think that restorative justice rituals can have a significant impact in an hour if they trigger a collective shame and acknowledgment that motivates the transformative. The hour might not be so important in itself, but important as a catalyst for what happens beyond the hour. That includes the hugs and one-on-ones that occur in the hours immediately after the conference. But we are thinking of a bigger vision for restorative justice as a motivator for crime prevention and democratic confrontation of injustice that we will consider in the next section.

Before moving on to that, however, let us not forget that the most important thing about the one hour as ritual is that it replaces what the research may reveal to be a much more destructive ritual – in terms, for example, of the anger, hostility and shame documented here. We refer to the courtroom ritual where lawyers are mouthpieces for those who need to speak about their wishes to condemn an unjust law, for vengeance, compensation, forgiveness, for a chance to put things right. We refer to the hope that restorative justice might prevent courts from sending such large numbers of criminals to prisons that demonstrably increase their odds of reoffending (Gendreau et al., 1999). We are deeply disappointed that restorative justice is not accomplishing this in our country. For this, programs are needed that target cases for conferences that prosecutors are about to argue for long prison terms (like the John Howard Society program of this kind in Manitoba (Bonta, Wallace-Capretta & Rooney, 1998)).

Restorative Justice as a Meta-Strategy for Making Prevention Happen

After decades of research we know quite a lot about how to prevent bullying and crime problems. The meta-analyses show that many types of

rehabilitation programs work (Andrews, 1995; Cullen & Gendreau, 2000; Dowden & Andrews, 1999; Lipsey, 1995) and there are a variety of other kinds of crime prevention programs that work and that are promising (Sherman, Gottfredson, MacKenzie, Eck, Reuter, & Bushway, 1997). What we seem to lack is a framework for increasing the prospects that the things we know work will actually happen. Restorative justice can be conceived as such a framework. That is, restorative justice conferences and circles might be able to have effects on crime not so much because of the large impact of the ritual itself, but because the circle is a better framework for making the effective things happen that we know ought to happen. At the moment, the mobilization of known-to-be-effective intervention fails to happen for five main reasons:

1 Lack of motivation
2 Preference for punishment over prevention
3 Lack of resources
4 Insufficiently plural and wide-ranging deliberation that prevents selection of the right intervention for the context
5 Lack of follow-through

We will discuss at length only the first of these because it is the most fundamental and the one that connects to shame. This will be done in the next section. The political *preference for punishment* inhibits prevention for a number of reasons, the most fundamental of which is that offender rehabilitation programs are shown by the meta-analyses to be less effective in correctional institutions than in the community (Andrews, 1995). Second, rehabilitation programs work better when they are embedded in networks of social support for offenders – from family and other communities of care (Cullen, 1994). Restorative justice conferences are quintessentially in the community and are designed to surround offenders and victims with social support. The social movement for restorative justice has a political strategy available to it to chip away at the contemporary preference for punishment over prevention (Braithwaite, 1999c) which is mainly about the fact that citizens who attend restorative justice processes like the justice they get more than court justice (see Chapter 2).

Lack of resources is the most difficult problem to solve, at least not without solving the political preference for punishment so that resources are diverted from prisons to crime prevention. Street enforcement by the police is the other place where resources are concentrated. Crime prevention gets few resources in police departments because it is ghettoized into specialist units. But if part of the job of arresting police officers is to attend restorative justice conferences for those they arrest, then they might be co-opted by the community into implementation of preventive measures agreed at conferences.

Meta-analyses of rehabilitation programs suggest that responsivity to the needs and risk factors evident in offenders predicts effectiveness (Andrews, 1995). More broadly, Braithwaite (1999a) has argued that bad judgments are often made about the contextual selection of crime prevention programs because *deliberation is insufficiently plural* to understand the problem. It is argued that restorative justice conferences can be designed to assemble the needed plurality of perspectives. Evaluators of rehabilitation programs often argue that professional discretion to select the right program for the right offender is a principle of correctional effectiveness (Andrews, 1995: 58), though this is a conclusion that is in no way warranted by data. On the contrary, Gendreau (1998:72) finds that only 10 to 20 per cent of rehabilitation programs in the real world satisfy the criteria for effectiveness suggested by the literature.

Professional discretion seems likely to be a principle of ineffectiveness (and plural deliberation the principle of effectiveness) because the most important choice is whether the most promising intervention will involve offender rehabilitation, environmental prevention, target hardening, advice for the victim, changes in police procedures, reconstructing power relationships between men who batter and women who are battered (Coker, 1999: 106) and so on, or rather what kind of combination of these. For example, one option for a repeat drink-driving offender is an alcohol rehabilitation program, another is to reform the habits of drinking groups who attend the conference so that there is a designated driver, another is surrender of license, surrender of the car on Friday and Saturday nights, commitments at the conference by the proprietor of the pub or club where the offender drinks to reform serving practices (join a 'responsible serving' self-regulatory program), agreement to drink at home instead of at the pub, move to low alcohol beer or some other kind of moderation commitment to be supported by drinking mates. The hypothesis is that dialogue between professionals with special competence and a community of care with special contextual wisdom, where the latter make the final choices, will result in wiser choices than professional discretion. In addition, there should be stronger collective commitment to implement the choice.

Finally, encouraging evidence of high compliance with agreements reached in restorative justice processes holds promise that follow-through may work better when conferences assign responsibility for different kinds of follow-up to its members (see Braithwaite, 1999a).

Motivating Transformation

The first and most fundamental obstacle to effective prevention is insufficient motivation. Ken Pease has argued that most prevention strategies

assume motivation, when in fact motivation is almost always what is absent (Pease, 1998). Here is where restorative justice as a meta-strategy for prevention has most to contribute. We have concluded that offender acknowledgment of Shame–Guilt as something that needs to be discharged arouses considerable collective emotion among those in a restorative justice circle, as does discussion of the ways victims and family members of offenders have suffered as a result of the offense. That individual and collective emotion is a motivational resource, albeit one that has been squandered in restorative justice practice. It can motivate mundane decisions like a long-overdue commitment by a burglary victim to install an alarm system. Or it can motivate significant structural change to South Africa (as is occurring to a degree in the aftermath of the Truth and Reconciliation Commission) or to the regulation of a major industry, as occurred as a result of the restorative justice processes about widespread insurance company fraud against Australian Aboriginal communities in the early 1990s (Braithwaite, 1999a).

Consider the drink-driver who has a serious alcohol problem. We have found that court processing has little to offer in the way of the needed motivational dynamic here. The average duration of a drink-driving case in Canberra is seven minutes of lawyer talk. Drink-driving restorative justice conferences average 87 minutes. There is time to consider the underlying problems. The data in Part II suggest there is also quite a deal of acknowledgment of Shame–Guilt (but see the qualitative qualifications in Inkpen, 1999). A ritual in which trouble with the police has to be dealt with is a unique opportunity for a family member who wishes to make an issue of an underlying alcohol problem. The seriousness and family shame of trouble with the police can motivate the confrontation of a touchy matter which has been swept under the carpet many times before. Unfortunately, the police in Canberra were somewhat discouraging of this kind of confrontation, their attitude being that the offense was drink-driving, not drinking, and 'drinking problems are not police business'.

The latter is just a special case of a general lack of interest among restorative justice advocates in harnessing the power of acknowledged shame for preventive transformation. There is a complacency that if an outcome is settled that gives a victim some comfort, prevents an offender from getting a criminal record and leaves the participants satisfied that 'something has been done", then the conference has worked out well. For serious matters, someone with professional competence could have the job of briefing the conference on some of the preventive options that are available to prevent recurrence of crimes such as this. Burford and Pennell (1998) did this in their exemplary and effective family violence conferencing program. The professional could be a social worker for say drug and

alcohol treatment programs or a problem-oriented police officer for non-therapeutic preventive measures.

It is a terribly irrational thing about the criminal justice system that police bang their heads against brick walls trying to motivate community interest in crime prevention through poorly conceived programs like Neighborhood Watch, and drug and alcohol educators spend enormous resources to persuade an uninterested community to confront their drug and alcohol problems, or their gambling problems. Yet when the wave of motivation is created to solve a gambling addiction because a robbery conference discovers that the underlying problem was gambling debts, the relevant professionals are nowhere to be seen. The famous Hollow Water holistic healing circles are an interesting case in reverse: circles established to confront drinking problems in a First Nations community in Manitoba uncovered child abuse that affected more than half their children. The community seized the wave of motivation to confront and prevent the sexual abuse of the children as well (Ross, 1996).

Our conclusion is that the great unrealized potential of restorative justice conferences and circles is harnessing of their emotional power to remove the roadblocks to contextualized selection of apposite crime prevention and offender rehabilitation programs that are known to work in reducing crime. Centuries of experience with courts tell us that they are not the meta-framework for making crime prevention happen. The deliberative democracy of the circle has much more promise in this regard, a promise that merits some priority in future research and development of restorative justice.

Training in Restorative Practices

There are important lessons from our research for the training of restorative circle facilitators or coordinators. A prior question is whether these facilitators must be trained. Not always is our answer. It is obviously inappropriate to require Western training of an Indigenous elder who conducts traditional restorative processes that have a resonance in her culture. A large proportion of people could never be good restorative justice facilitators with any amount of training. However, we hypothesize that every workplace, every church congregation, indeed every seventh-grade class, has someone with the capacity to become an effective restorative justice facilitator with days rather than weeks of training. The key idea of restorative justice is that it does not rely on the competence of a single person but on a process of sifting communal wisdom (which includes communal wisdom to seek certain kinds of professional advice).

Restorative practices can occur at many levels, all of which can benefit from some level of training:

- family disputes
- disputes in school playgrounds
- workplace disputes
- police cautioning and casual police encounters with citizens on the street
- diversion of minor juvenile offenders
- serious crime
- serious crime where there are special risks of power-imbalance (e.g. rape, corporate crime)
- major internal state crime (e.g. apartheid, genocide)
- peacemaking between warring nations

In general as one moves down this list the more training and specialized competence in the particular kind of restorative justice is needed. Also as we move down this list, training in understanding the dynamics of shame becomes more important. It seems a bad idea to try to teach school children the theory of reintegrative shaming, and indeed our group does not do this in the restorative practices programs we have been involved with in Canberra schools. The danger of half-baked training in the shame management issues traversed in this book is that people will latch onto the shame word and think it suggests that they should mobilize direct verbal disapproval against wrongdoers in shame-laden contexts where that will be counterproductive. However, for programs in which there is the luxury of training adults for a week or more, there is considerable merit in talking to them about the differences between reintegrative shaming and stigmatization. This is because you want to help them to understand that while it is sometimes necessary to mobilize disapproval, it is important to understand how not to do this, how to avoid stigmatization. Some other implications of our research for effective shaming are:

1 Work hard at finding out who are the people the offender and victim love and respect most and work hard to encourage them to participate in the circle. When there are few such people, work harder, be willing to pay for airfares to bring the right people in if necessary, adjourn and reconvene if they do not attend.
2 Don't worry about having too many respected supporters in the circle.
3 Focus discussion on the consequences of the wrong that has been committed by asking participants to describe how they have been affected. Put the problem, not the person, in the center of the circle (Melton, 1995).
4 Don't discourage people from discussing their emotions; encourage them.
5 Allow time for all the hurts to come out before a rush to heal. Adjourn and reconvene if victims in particular need more time.

6   Maneuver around demands for apology or requests for forgiveness. 'Let's come back to that.' Better to be patient and see if apology and forgiveness are offered without being solicited. Participants must come to their own acknowledgment of their own emotions in their own time.

7   Intervene to encourage participants who are being dominated by others in the circle, whose speech is being dominated. 'I really want to hear what Mary thinks about that without her having to worry about anyone jumping on her for saying what she thinks.'

8   Avert stigmatization by reframing angry, blaming outbursts into expressions of hurt (McDonald, O'Connell, Moore & Bransbury, 1994).

9   When stigmatization occurs, invite participants to speak who you believe will say something reintegrative or praiseworthy about the person.

10 If the participants frame the problem as a fundamental question of justice, understand that justice is about fairness but not about moral neutrality.

This is not, of course, even the rudiments of a list of what might be required to make restorative justice effective. It is just a list of specific implications of our analysis in this book. The last point goes to a fundamental difference between restorative justice and the ideology of mediation. Facilitators or coordinators should not seek to express their own opinions about the wrongness of the act under consideration in the circle. The data in Part II indicate that this would normally be ineffective anyhow. But restorative justice processes are processes with values, one of those being justice itself, another restoration. Being fair does not mean being morally neutral (Coker, 1999). A conference over an act of criminal violence proceeds on a clear understanding that participants know that the facilitator believes criminal violence is the kind of bad thing that something should be done about. Mediation ideology is often about reframing moral wrongs as conflicts that are stripped of any morally evaluative component. There are many arenas of human disputation where this is appropriate. Uncontroversially serious crime is not one of them. Here there is much to learn from the feminist critique of mediation as a practice that can marginalize victims by being offender-centered, that often individualizes and privatizes a communal concern and a public issue, and that demoralizes an evil of domination into a morally neutral dispute (Coker, 1999; Presser & Gaadner, 1999). The net effect of these defects of the mediation ideology in cases of violence against women is to treat victims with disrespect, without due regard to the moral seriousness of their suffering and their predicament.

In Chapter 2, we argued that non-domination should be a value of restorative justice. It follows that any crime that involves the domination of one human being by another should not be framed as a mere conflict.

Restorative justice does not prioritize settling conflicts; it prioritizes restoration with justice and there can be no justice with domination.

As a more general empirical matter, if we want to be effective in preventing crime, we must reject moral neutrality and manifest integrity of commitment to a set of anti-criminal values – anti-violence, anti-domination, pro-respect, pro-justice crucial among them. In general the evidence from the meta-analyses of the effectiveness of correctional programs is that non-directive forms of individual or group therapy that manifest no value commitment are not effective (Losel, 1995: 91). Chris Trotter's (1990, 1993, 1999) program of research shows that rehabilitation professionals who use reflective, empathic listening to reinforce prosocial anti-criminal values have clients significantly less likely to reoffend. While disapproval of predatory acts (but not of persons) is needed, we must be careful not to interpret this as commending lecturing. Confrontation of predation with disapproval in private is more likely to be effective than in a public ritual; confrontation by loved ones is more likely to be effective than confrontation by a conference facilitator. The tricky issue is that healing of victim shame may sometimes require ritual public acknowledgment that what was done to her was wrong. Even here, however, we have argued that offender apology, offender shaming of his own act, is the most morally powerful way of accomplishing this.

Conclusion: The Communal Search to Discover Ethical and Loving Identities

Far from moral neutrality, restorative practices are about helping citizens to come to terms with things that are inevitably morally charged. They are not about defusing emotion but about creating ritual spaces into which emotion can be infused, where right and wrong can be discussed by concerned and affected citizens; surely, too, where the rightness of a law can be questioned and where a group of citizens can even decide to politically challenge a law.

Processes that help people acknowledge Shame–Guilt they have over matters of right and wrong can strengthen their bonds with those they love, indeed strengthen shared identities based on love. Loving identities in turn help to shape ethical identities, a citizenry with a morally decent sense of shame. We hope in the difficult business of learning how to do this better than we have in the past, people are also learning how to be democratic citizens. These are only hopes, however. The research program in this book takes only a few of the faltering steps toward what might be needed to make something of those hopes.

Shaming and Shame: Regulating Drink-Driving

Nathan Harris

CHAPTER 5

Shaming and Shame

Crime, Shame and Reintegration presents a general theory of crime which argues that forms of social disapproval can be divided into those that are stigmatic and those that are reintegrative. The significance of this distinction, and the way it draws on previous criminological theory, is discussed in Part I. What is significant from the perspective of Part II is that the theory focuses attention on the processes of shaming. The relationship between offenders and their communities and the emotions that offenders feel are identified as central to explaining criminality. Indeed, reintegrative shaming theory argues that the process of shaming is more important to the reduction of crime than the sanctions imposed by courts. In part, this is because reputation is important to individuals. But more importantly, it is because reintegrative shaming appeals to individuals' moral values, thus developing and maintaining conscience. Yet the theory does not articulate a clear conception of what shame is or how it differs from emotions like guilt. Part II of this book addresses these issues by exploring the conceptualization of shame and its impact within criminal justice interventions. This highlights the importance of shame management that is then explored more fully in Part III. This chapter will introduce the issues to be addressed in Part II and outline the order in which they will be tackled in subsequent chapters.

Shame and Shaming in Justice

Impetus to understand the role of shaming and shame has increased with their prominence in the development of new criminal justice interventions. In particular, the emergence of restorative justice has highlighted the need to understand the process of social disapproval. Part I of this book has outlined the concept of restorative justice and its global spread.

What is most critical for the analysis in Part II of the book is that restorative justice strategies to prevent re-offending are not based upon the severity of sanctions imposed but the communication of the harm done to others and disapproval of the actions by relevant others. The way social disapproval is communicated and the circumstances that are effective in changing behavior are important in understanding the effectiveness of restorative procedures. Indeed, Braithwaite's reintegrative shaming theory is already used to explain the procedures used in restorative justice conferences and has been used in the development of conferencing techniques (Braithwaite, 1999a; Braithwaite & Mugford, 1994; Hyndman, Thorsborne & Wood, 1996; McDonald, O'Connell, Moore & Bransbury, 1994; Moore & Forsythe, 1995; O'Connell & Thorsborne, 1995; Retzinger & Scheff, 1996). It is also apparent that shaming and shame have become important concepts in other regulatory fields. For example, Grasmick and Bursik (1990) found that the expectation of feeling Shame–Guilt was a predictor of the expectation to offend and Bandura, Barbaranelli, Capara, and Pastorelli (1996) found 'guilt and restitution' to have both direct effects on delinquency and effects mediated through reduced 'aggression proneness'. There is also some evidence that expectations of feeling shame have an impact upon the perceived likelihood of committing corporate crime (Simpson, 1998).[1]

Although shaming and shame are increasingly seen as important concepts in the regulation of behavior there is also some concern about their effect on offenders. Recent use of shaming punishments by courts has emphasized stigmatizing shaming and humiliation of offenders (Kahan, 1996). For example, thieves are ordered to wear shirts or carry signs indicating to others that they stole. For many in the restorative justice movement such stigmatization contradicts the goals of restoration and is actually retributive in its philosophical basis. Certainly this type of stigmatization of offenders does not seem conducive to the restoration or reintegration of offenders into the community. Concern that shaming is inherently stigmatizing leads to questions about whether shaming should be considered relevant to restorative justice at all, and whether shame is an appropriate emotion for offenders to feel. Research by Maxwell and Morris (1999) shows that offenders who remember being made to feel bad about themselves during conferences are more likely to be persistent offenders. This research is also supported by empirical studies on shame–proneness and guilt-proneness (Tangney 1991; Tangney, Wagner, Fletcher & Gramzow, 1992a; Tangney, Wagner & Gramzow, 1992b) which suggest that offenders prone to feeling shame respond less appropriately to shameful events than guilt-prone individuals. These findings highlight the question of whether it is positive for offenders to feel shame at all. In the light of these debates, it seems important to determine whether there are

differences between the shame emotions, for example between shame and guilt.

Conceptualizing Shame

The failure to find research on shame that presents a consistent answer to questions about its role in reintegrative shaming, and more generally in restorative justice, suggests that understanding shame is also an important psychological question. Scholarly interest in the emotion of shame has increased markedly in recent years. The emotion has acquired a more central place across a range of disciplines including anthropology (Benedict, 1946; Mead, 1937), psychoanalysis (H. B. Lewis, 1971; Wurmser, 1994), sociology (Scheff & Retzinger, 1991), criminology (Grasmick & Bursik, 1990), law (Kahan, 1996), philosophy (Taylor, 1985; Williams, 1993) and psychology (Gilbert, 1997; M. Lewis, 1992; Tangney, 1991). Much of this work has attempted to define what shame is and when it occurs. However, it is also evident that within this literature there is still disagreement about some fundamental questions regarding the emotion. For example, while Wallbott and Scherer (1995) describe shame as a less moral emotion than guilt and more often accompanied by laughter, H. B. Lewis (1971) describes it as involving self-directed hostility and perceptions of being a failure. This disparity highlights some of the differences in phenomenological accounts of shame.

The relationship between shame and related emotions is another area of significant disagreement. The shame-related emotions are described by a large number of words in the English language. The distinction that has received most attention is between shame and guilt, although some attention has also been paid to the distinction between shame and embarrassment. Empirical studies have provided only limited support for the conceptual distinctions that have been drawn between the constructs (Tangney, Miller, Flicker & Barlow, 1996b; Wicker, Payne & Morgan, 1983). In particular, little factor analytical or observational work has been done to test these conceptual distinctions.

Research into shame has focused primarily upon phenomenological issues. As a result, little is known about the causal relationships that implicate the shame construct. Some approaches have described shame as a reaction to criticism or derision by others. The emotion is seen to be caused by external sources with values not necessarily shared by the individual. The primary alternative describes shame as a reaction to violation of one's own standards. In this approach the source is internal evaluation and thus requires no intervention by others. On the surface, it is reasonable to argue two quite different emotions are being described by these researchers. Shame as motivated by external sources is a non-moral, perhaps even a

valueless, response to the fear of rejection. In contrast, shame as violation of internalized goals concerns degradation of identity or loss of self-respect. These accounts of shame present very different understandings of the social context in which shame occurs. Either shame is a response to a threatening other (who may either attack or withdraw approval) or there is no social context at all. Neither of these approaches acknowledges that shame occurs in communities where values may be contentious or that shame feelings may or may not indicate an acceptance of norms. Thus, comprehending the social context in which shame occurs also seems important to developing an understanding of the emotion.

Overview of Part II

Before presenting empirical findings relating to shaming and shame, a review of the social definition of shame is presented in Chapter 6.[2] From this discussion it is possible to identify three conceptions of shame: the social threat conception, the personal failure conception and the ethical conception. These conceptions capture the primary ways of describing shame and are used to inform the questions asked in following chapters.

Chapter 7 outlines the methodology used in the Reintegrative Shaming Experiments (RISE). Measuring an emotion such as shame is not easy because it usually occurs in difficult circumstances in which researcher access is a problem. These difficulties were overcome in the research discussed in Part II by collecting data on shaming and shame through RISE. This involves four large randomized experiments conducted under the supervision of Lawrence Sherman and Heather Strang in which participants apprehended for particular offenses were observed during court cases and restorative justice conferences, and interviewed afterwards. Measures from a sample of 900 participants who were apprehended for drink-driving were analyzed.

Chapter 8 measures characteristics associated with shame as well as the emotions of guilt and embarrassment to which shame is most commonly compared. These characteristics are used in a factor analysis to determine the dimensionality of the targeted emotions.

The dimensionality of shaming, reintegration and stigmatization are examined in Chapter 9. While reintegrative shaming theory has been tested on a number of occasions (Hay, 2001; Lu, 1999; Makkai & Braithwaite, 1994; Zhang, 1995; Zhang & Zhang, 2000) there has been no evaluation of whether the structure of shaming behaviors is as predicted by the theory. In this chapter, factor analytic techniques are used to test the dimensionality of these constructs. In addition, the chapter investigates the relationship between self-report and observational measures of shaming concepts and their predictive validity in the context of court and restorative justice conferences.

Chapter 10 uses the measures developed in Chapters 8 and 9 to test various predictions regarding the relationship between shaming and shame. While it might be expected that shaming and shame are positively related, a number of other hypotheses have been proposed in the shame literature. Whether the effect of shaming is moderated by the level of respect participants have for those who are disapproving is one such hypothesis. Another is the impact of reintegrative and stigmatizing shaming on shame and shame-related emotions. These hypotheses explore the social context in which shaming and shame occur as well as the relevance of internalized standards in promoting shame.

In response to these findings a theoretical framework is proposed in Chapter 11 to account for the relationship between shaming and shame that draws heavily on the psychology of social influence. In particular, it is proposed that shame occurs as a result of the perception of violating an ethical norm and that a process of social validation mediates this perception. This approach accounts for findings that respected others' opinions and reintegrative forms of shaming are significant predictors of Shame–Guilt. It is also proposed that shame involves a perceived threat to identity that results from having acted contrary to ethical norms that in part define identity. Resolving shame involves resolving these tensions. Stigmatization and low perceptions of wrongdoing in the face of shaming inhibit the resolution of feelings of shame.

Shaming and shame have become important concepts in criminology. There is also concern regarding the stigmatizing use of shaming and whether shame itself is a healthy emotion for offenders to feel. Chapter 12 addresses these issues by arguing that the assumption that shaming within criminal justice results in shame has overlooked the importance of shame resolution. It is argued that shame will often occur as a result of criminal justice interventions regardless of whether shaming occurs actively, formally, or at all. What seems to be critical in light of our results is whether shame is resolved, an issue that Ahmed takes up in Part III of this book. Thus, Part II concludes with the proposition that shaming (conceived in the distinctively broad way advocated by Braithwaite) is not so necessary for the production of shame, but is integral to assisting the individual in the resolution of shame.

Notes

1 See further studies supporting a negative association between Shame–Guilt and crime at Chapter 3, note 10.
2 By defining shame in social terms, this approach does not attempt to incorporate the growing body of work on the physiology of shame (e.g., Tomkins, 1962, 1963).

CHAPTER 6

Three Conceptual Approaches to the Emotion of Shame

Harder (1995) describes the diverse and contradictory psychological literature on shame in terms of three basic schools of thought. The first is
comprised of clinicians who focus on the phenomenological experience of
shame and how it differs from guilt. This tradition involves theorists such as
H. B. Lewis (1971), Lindsay-Hartz (1984), Schneider (1977) and Wurmser
(1994). Tomkins' (1987) affect theory, which has been extended by theorists
such as Kaufman (1996) and Nathanson (1992), defines a second tradition
that is based upon a physiological account of the emotions as innate human
affects. Finally, the third, but much smaller, tradition involves theoretical
work on cognitive attribution and appraisal from theorists such as
Schachter and Singer (1962). While this may capture the different
approaches from within the fields of psychology and psychiatry it excludes
work from other disciplines that has contributed greatly to the study of
shame. The work of anthropologists, preeminently Margaret Mead (1937)
and Ruth Benedict (1946), in describing shame cultures as opposed to guilt
cultures has had a significant impact on theorizing in the social sciences
more broadly. Equally, shame has been of interest to moral philosophers
through the work of Williams (1993), Heller (1982) and Taylor (1985), to
sociologists as illustrated in the writings of Goffman (1959) and Scheff and
Retzinger (1991), and to legal scholars and criminologists such as Kahan
(1996), Grasmick and Bursik (1990), and Braithwaite (1989).

This chapter captures the breadth of inquiry into shame by identifying
the various theoretical traditions that have sought to explain its social and
psychological characteristics. This review does not attempt to be exhaus-
tive, but rather to capture significant theoretical themes that have occurred
across the various literatures. What becomes apparent is that debate about
the conceptualization of shame is often fragmented and disconnected.

Many of the theories put forward have not been explicitly compared or empirically tested. Partly as a result, discussion of empirical research will occur in Chapter 8 after we have identified the primary ways in which shame has been conceptualized. Also left over for later discussion is the contention that there are important differences in the way that individuals cope with shame (Lewis, 1971; Scheff & Retzinger, 1991; Nathanson, 1992). This becomes increasingly relevant to understanding the empirical analyses in Parts II and is central to analyses in Part III. A review of how these ideas on shame management have developed beyond the basic conceptions of shame presented in this chapter can be found in Chapter 14.

While diversity in the way shame is used within and between disciplines is complex, it is argued that the complexity can be reduced to these three shame issues: (a) how we feel others think of us, (b) how we feel about ourselves, and (c) the views about what is ethically shameful that are shared by us with others. Table 6.1 summarizes how the complexity of shame conceptions can be mapped as simply a diversity of positions on these three themes. Readers might like to jump to Table 6.1 at the end of the chapter to preview where our journey through the different ways of conceptualizing shame will end.

Shame Cultures

Freud's (1949/1930) influential theory of psychoanalysis hardly acknowledges shame, instead emphasizing the significance of guilt as an underlying cause of neuroticism. He does, however, identify a 'primitive guilt' which is based upon the fear of losing another's love rather than the transgression of internalized norms. This primitive guilt only occurs if one's indiscretions are discovered, or one fears their discovery. While not pursued by Freud, this primitive guilt and its obvious comparison with mature guilt describes a conceptualization of shame that has been influential. The anthropologists Benedict (1946) and Mead (1937) popularized this account of shame. Benedict compared Japanese and American society in terms of the means by which the two cultures gain conformity from individuals. Simply put, this distinction involved characterizing Japan as a shame culture, America as a guilt culture:

> True shame cultures rely on external sanctions for good behavior, not, as true guilt cultures do, on an internalized conviction of sin. Shame is a reaction to other people's criticism. (Benedict, 1946: p. 223)

Mead (1937) presents an analysis of social control among American First Nations, Maori and Samoans among others. In this she suggests that it is possible to distinguish between societies that rely predominantly on the

education of individuals to obey social standards and societies in which individuals obey standards only where forces, such as ridicule, are set in motion by others.

This way of categorizing societies by reference to the way in which they maintain social control has not been without criticism (Piers & Singer, 1953; Ausubel, 1955; Epstein, 1984). What is interesting from our perspective is that in differentiating societies in this way they define shame as a reaction to social disapproval or fear of potential disapproval. Mead does suggest that shame can become a 'relatively internalized sanction' such that it occurs without active shaming of the person. Nevertheless the disapproval, or assumed disapproval, of others is necessary. Thus, the emotion is described as one in which the individual is focused on others and their values. It is an emotion which compels the individual to submit to the values of the group or society as opposed to their own. Furthermore, as Lynd (1958) suggests, it assumes a basic separation between oneself and others, such that others are seen in relation to oneself as an audience.

Shame and the Social Self

Theoretical approaches within sociology and psychology have also proposed that shame is a central emotion in regulating the relationship between the individual and others. While Benedict and Mead were concerned with analysis at a macro level these theories focus upon explaining why shame plays an important role in the regulation of social relationships. One answer is based on the assumption that the desire to establish and maintain interpersonal relationships is a fundamental motive of human behavior (Baumeister & Leary, 1995; Leary, 2000). This is an underlying assumption of Scheff and Retzinger (1991) who build upon the sociological traditions of Goffman (1959) and Cooley (1922) to propose an explicit connection between shame and social bonds. They contend

> . . . that the degree of attunement and emotion are reciprocally interrelated: that solidarity causes and is caused by shared pride and that alienation causes and is caused by shared shame. (Scheff & Retzinger, 1991: p. 21)

Attunement describes the health of the social bond between people: Alienation is conceptualized as being equivalent to having a severed or threatened bond, while solidarity is conceptualized as having an intact bond with others. The emotions of shame and pride are seen as '. . . automatic bodily sign[s] of . . .' the health of the person's bonds with others (Scheff, 1990a: p. 15). The implication of this description is that feelings of embarrassment, shame or humiliation, which are all considered variants of shame, are the result of perceived rejection by others. Individuals

continually monitor others' reactions in order to detect social cues that indicate social exclusions (Leary, 2000). If rejection or disapproval by others is perceived it results in lower levels of self-esteem (Leary & Downs, 1995), but also negative emotions. From this perspective social ties are seen as essential to the psychological well-being of the individual. For example Scheff (1996a) suggests that there is a direct connection between shame and self-esteem.

An alternative approach is evident in Gilbert's (1997) contention that the significance of shame is based upon an innate evolutionary need to be seen as attractive by others. Within this evolutionary framework it is proposed that in order to prosper, humans and animals need attributes that give them an advantage in survival, in attracting mates so as to reproduce, and preventing competitors from reproducing. These goals are achieved in large part by having high social status and thus being dominant in the social structure. In human society the primary strategy in attaining status, and thus gaining useful relationships, is through social attractiveness. This is mediated by the individual's ability to attract positive attention from others and avoid negative attention. Gilbert argues that shame is a direct result of the perception that one is seen as unattractive and serves '. . . to *alert the self and others to detrimental changes in social status*' (Gilbert, 1997: p. 114; italics in original). Thus shame is a function of social status occurring whenever the individual sees him or herself judged badly in the eyes of others.

Finally, it is possible to identify a third explanation for shame based not on the social psychology of individuals but on the cognitive processes of self-evaluation. Drawing on Duval and Wicklund's (1972) theory of objective self-awareness, Gibbons (1990) argued that shame and guilt result from two mutually exclusive motivated states. In the first, the individual's attention is focused upon the self, and the individual is motivated to act in accordance with his or her standards and values. Gibbons conceives of their standards as unique to the individual and as relatively independent of the social context. In this state of self-awareness, violation of a personal standard is likely to produce the emotion of guilt. The second type of motivation occurs when the individual's attention is oriented towards others and their expectations. Their focus is on social norms and impression management and it is the feeling of shame or embarrassment that results when the person violates a social norm in the presence of others (Gibbons, 1990: p. 119). According to Duval and Wicklund's (1972) theory, an individual's attention, while able to oscillate between these two states of awareness (self and other), is unable to focus upon both at the same time. At any moment the individual can only be motivated by either standards of the 'self' or standards of the 'other'. Thus, the contention of this approach is that the cognitive structure of awareness causes the distinction observed between shame and guilt.

In each of these accounts shame is clearly conceptualized as a social emotion in that it only occurs as a result of social relationships, and further-more, is almost entirely dependent upon the individual's perception of others' actions or opinions. Indeed, in discussing shame as important to understanding social conformity, Scheff (1988) argues that shame is '. . . experienced by individuals as *exterior* and *constraining* . . .' (p. 395). In this respect these theories are consistent with the anthropological accounts discussed above. What they add is an explanation as to why shame might be dependent upon external evaluations: because it is a response to damaged social bonds, lost social status or occurs when attention is exter-nally focused.

The Moral Emotion

A number of perspectives within moral philosophy suggest that shame is central to regulating the relationship between individuals and their commu-nities but question whether the perception of social disapproval is sufficient to explain it. For example, Rom Harré (1990) defines shame as:

> Occasioned by the realization that others have become aware that what one has been doing has been a moral infraction, a judgment with which I, as actor, concur. (Harré, 1990: p. 199)

While the role of 'others' is central, indeed necessary, the definition also highlights the importance of other factors. One of these is that shame is a moral infraction, that should be differentiated from embarrassment, because it occurs after the intentional breach of a moral code as opposed to an unintentional breach of social convention. Furthermore, shame is dependent on individuals' acceptance that they have committed a moral infraction. Thus, shame is not only concerned about one's relationship with others but also about one's actions being wrong. In fact, acceptance of having done wrong is just as essential as exposure, with non-acceptance leading to different emotions.

> In shame, I accept the presence of the Other and the restrictions that are imposed . . . In the case of hate, I do not accept the restrictions and long for the destruction of the Other to restore my freedom. (Harré, 1990: p. 203)

While Harré gives the judgment of an 'other' a central, if not dominat-ing, place in his description, other theorists have suggested that an external audience may not be necessary at all. Taylor (1985) agrees that shame necessarily involves the feeling of public exposure but argues that the 'observer' is merely a means to an end. The 'observer' shifts the actor's attention to the role of observer of the self, as if they were another. It is, in

fact, the individual evaluation that provides adverse judgment that is critical to feeling shame. The distinction between an actual and a more important abstract 'other' is significant not just because it suggests that shame can be felt without an actual audience but also because shame is felt in reference to particular values. Bernard Williams (1993) argues that to see shame as simply a loss of face in front of any audience is a mistake:

> If everything depended on the fear of discovery, the motivations of shame would not be internalized at all. No one would have a character, in effect, . . . (Williams, 1993: p. 81)

Similar to Taylor (1985), Williams proposes that 'the other' in shame is an internalized, imagined other. But most importantly, the imagined other is not simply anyone, but rather some kind of abstracted other who incorporates one's values and attitudes. In this sense the '. . . other may be identified in ethical terms. He is conceived as one whose reactions I would respect' (Williams, 1993: p. 84). This does not mean that shame is felt only in reference to one's own views. This is because, according to Williams, one's views are not based simply upon the power of reason but are formed through an interaction with the social context.

> Whatever it is working on it requires an internalized other, who is not designated merely as a representative of an independently identified social group, and whose reactions the agent can respect. At the same time, this figure does not merely shrink into a hanger for those same values but embodies intimidation of a genuine social reality – in particular how it will be for one's life with others if one acts in one way rather than another. (Williams, 1993: p. 102)

The perspectives of Williams and Taylor, in particular, are a direct challenge to the idea that shame is a response to social disapproval. Instead shame is a response to having committed a wrongdoing. This can involve the disapproval of others but also highlights the importance of an internalized evaluation of what is right or wrong. They suggest that these things can come together because individuals share values with significant others whom they respect. Thus, the influence of others and the emotion of shame in this account are not seen as an exterior or constraining force.

Psychoanalytic Approaches to Shame and the Self

Although largely ignored by Freud, shame has become increasingly important in psychoanalytic research. In contrast to those approaches that have emphasized the social context in which shame is experienced, psychoanalytic theorizing has focused upon the internal dynamics of self-evaluation. Indeed, Piers and Singer (1953) argue that the basic structure of shame is a tension

between the ego and ego-ideal, in contrast to guilt that is thought to arise from tension between the ego and super-ego. The ego-ideal is described as containing elements of narcissistic omnipotence, positive identifications with parental images, positive identifications with other social relationships and finally goals of 'instinct mastery'. In combination, these elements represent values or principles which the individual should live up to. The emotion of shame occurs when:

> . . . a goal (presented by the Ego-Ideal) is not being reached. It thus indicates a real 'shortcoming'. (Piers & Singer, 1953: p. 11)

In essence, the individual feels shame when he or she has failed to achieve personal goals. Guilt, on the other hand, is characterized as a reaction to transgression. Both guilt and shame, however, are seen as based on the individual's evaluation of how well they live up to particular values. This key idea of Piers and Singer has had an enormous impact upon later literature.

H. B. Lewis (1971), for instance, while accepting some of the social aspects of shame, strongly rejected any suggestion that shame was a less internalized emotion than guilt. She conceptualizes shame as an evaluation of the whole self, and endorsed Piers and Singer's (1953) notion of shame as conflict between the ego and the ego-ideal.

> Identification with the beloved or admired ego-ideal stirs pride and triumph-ant feeling; failure to live up to this internalized admired imago stirs shame. (H. B. Lewis, 1971: p. 23)

In this conceptualization the self is of central importance. It is the direct focus of the emotion; it is what is being evaluated. H. B. Lewis builds on Piers and Singer's Shame–Guilt distinction by contrasting it with guilt in an additional way. While she associates guilt with a transgression, and shame with failure, she goes on to suggest that guilt is focused primarily on the act while shame encompasses the entire self. This is significant in that it describes guilt as an emotion that is not nearly as concerned with self-evaluation. The person's attention is directed outward at what they have done, and as a result, the emotion is less crippling and more attuned to acceptance of responsibility. With shame, where the emotion is fueled by a deficiency in the self, the cause for shame is seen as involuntary and the individual is left feeling helpless. The emotion is also more painful because it involves a more intense rejection of the self:

> A current of aggression, however, has been activated against the whole self, in both one's own eyes and 'others''' eyes.

and

... ashamed ideation says: ... what an *idiot I am* ... what a fool ... how *awful and worthless I am*. (H. B. Lewis, 1971: p. 36; italics in original)

Instead of simply being the result of negative self-evaluation, shame involves a hostility towards the entire self that is not present in guilt. The clinical significance of this is that shame should be associated with different types of psychopathology to guilt, a fact supported by Lewis's own clinical observations. Lewis also suggested that when shame is not acknowledged it can result in different psychological reactions. This has important implications for understanding shame management and is discussed in Part III, Chapter 14.

One of the reasons why shame is so painful, according to Wurmser (1994), is the way failure is perceived. In addition to tension between ego and ego-ideal what is required for shame to occur is

... that the inner wishful image of the self be 'betrayed' and that certain self-critical, self-punishing, and reparative processes be set in motion. (Wurmser, 1994: p. 73)

To actually feel shame, the ideal self needs to be experienced as a complete, perceptual gestalt whereby shame occurs in relation to a complex understanding of a complete image rather than simply components or aspects of the self. This involves several stages, the first of which is observation and exposure of the 'real self'. Self observation is followed by a process of evaluation and then, in shame, by criticism that involves derision and rejection of the self. Finally criticism is followed by punishment which involves a loss of self-love, contempt for oneself and ultimately a loss of self-respect.

It is important to recognize the contribution of psychoanalysis to the literature on shame through Piers and Singer (1953), H. B. Lewis (1971), Wurmser (1981) and others. This perspective began to characterize shame as an internal sanction based upon the perception of failure. A further, though less explicitly recognized contribution was to associate shame with hostility or aggression towards the self. Emphasis upon shame as self-hostility and self-derision is very much a part of the way shame is described by non-psychoanalytic theorists such as M. Lewis (1992) and Tangney (1991).

The Attribution of Failure

While psychoanalytic theorists began to define shame as an evaluation of the self, theorists outside the psychoanalytic tradition have more recently sought to describe the same evaluation but using alternative theoretical frameworks. For example, M. Lewis (1992), in his book *Shame: The Exposed Self*, presents a characterization of shame that is based upon cognitive

attribution theory. He suggests that we can identify a group of four emotions (shame, guilt, pride and hubris) that occur as a consequence of not just self-awareness but also self-evaluation. In order to feel one of these emotions the individual must evaluate whether some aspect of self is a success or failure when compared to their standards, rules and goals. Once this decision is made, the individual can either attribute the success or failure to global or specific aspects of the self, and it is this attribution that determines the emotion experienced. If we perceive ourselves as successful we can feel either pride (specific) or hubris (global). If we perceive ourselves as having failed, we can feel either guilt/regret (specific) or shame (global). In this way shame is an evaluation of our whole self whereas guilt is an evaluation of our behavior.

> I want to suggest that shame is elicited when the self orients toward the self as a whole and involves an evaluation of the total self, whereas in guilt it is orientation of the self toward the action of the self, either in terms of the actions of the self alone or in terms of the actions of the self as they have affected another. (M. Lewis, 1992: p. 71)

M. Lewis is in accord with the psychoanalytic account in two respects; that shame is focused on the whole self and that shame involves the whole self as a failure. The distinction between shame and guilt, however, is less pronounced in M. Lewis's approach. He does not develop the notion of guilt as transgression and shame as failure nor does he allow any scope for seeing shame as a more social emotion than guilt, as for example H. B. Lewis (1971) does.

While Lewis suggests that shame involves having failed to live up to personal goals, empirical work by Lindsay-Hartz (Lindsay-Hartz, 1984; Lindsay-Hartz, De Rivera & Mascolo, 1995) suggests that the attribution may be slightly different. On the basis of two phenomenological studies, she found that shame was defined by a feeling of certainty that '. . . we are not who we want to be . . .' (p. 696). This is different, according to Lindsay-Hartz, from the traditional description (H. B. Lewis, 1971; Piers & Singer, 1953) of shame as failure to live up to an ego-ideal. Shame is not failure to reach a high standard but a realization of having reached a low standard. Indeed both shame and guilt involved the perception of being a bad person, the main difference being the level of certainty.

> In summary, shame transforms our identity. We experience ourselves as being small and worthless and as being exposed. Experiences of guilt only shake up our identity. (Lindsay-Hartz, 1984: p. 696)

Despite this difference, Lindsay-Hartz conceives of shame in a way that is not dissimilar from M. Lewis. As within the psychoanalytic perspective,

shame is characterized as an internalized evaluation of the self in response to a personal failure of some kind.

Shame as a Disposition

The emphasis of research in psychology has more recently turned towards examining shame as a personality disposition. Unlike the theories already discussed, this focuses upon identifying differences in how predisposed individuals are to feel shame or guilt. The aim is to identify how these dispositions affect the individual's ability to cope with perceived failure.

Building upon the work of H. B. Lewis (1971), Tangney and her colleagues (Tangney, 1991; Tangney et al., 1992a; Tangney, Wagner, Hill-Barlow, Marschall & Gramzow, 1996c) have defined shame-proneness as the propensity to react to failure by negatively evaluating the whole self. The shameful event is seen as defining of the self because there is no distinction made between one's behavior and who one is. Thus self, and everything about it, is perceived as deficient. This is contrasted with guilt-proneness, that is, the propensity to react by negatively evaluating one's actions. In this case the self is distinguished from the act and thus remains able. In many respects this is similar to the distinction proposed by M. Lewis (1992).

It is contended by Tangney and her associates that the self-criticism associated with shame prevents the individual from feeling empathy and is more likely to result in feelings of anger that are directed towards others. It is assumed that neither of these reactions facilitate the individual's ability to constructively deal with failure. Empirical studies provide strong evidence for these hypotheses with shame-proneness, but not guilt-proneness, associated with an inability to feel other-oriented empathy (Tangney, 1991), but greater feelings of anger and hostility (Tangney et al., 1992a; Tangney et al., 1996a), and various psychopathologies (Tangney, Burggraf & Wagner, 1995).

While these findings are significant in themselves, they have also been the focus of a debate on how shame-proneness is conceptualized. A number of theorists have suggested that Tangney's definition of shame-proneness overemphasizes its negative characteristics while, conversely, her definition of guilt overemphasizes its positive characteristics (Sabini & Silver, 1997; Harder, 1995). For example, Harder argues that Tangney places too much stress upon shame, and not guilt, as a negative evaluation of the self. At the same time she ignores other dimensions upon which the emotions might be distinguished, such as whether they result from internalized disapproval or criticism by others.

> Thus, by this definition, when a person feels devalued that person is prima-
> rily ashamed, even if the basis for his or her feeling is a bad deed condemned

by an internal standard, without reference to any condemning other. (Harder, 1995: p. 381)

Harder argues that in doing so Tangney has effectively defined shame as maladaptive and guilt as adaptive. This ignores evidence from clinical experience that guilt is associated with some forms of psychopathology. The issues in this current debate reflect those that have been evident throughout the literature: first, whether shame is a result of external or internal evaluation; and second, whether shame, and not guilt, is an evaluation of the self.

Affect Theory and Shame

A distinct approach to the emotion of shame is based upon Tomkins' (1962, 1963, 1987) affect theory. This theory provides a physiological account of shame that, although fundamentally different from those theories already discussed, has since been extended and used in clinical applications (Nathanson, 1992; Kaufman, 1996). Affect theory argues that humans have nine innate affects which each have distinct patterns of neural stimulation. For example, the affect startle–surprise involves a rapid increase in stimulation while anger involves a high but constant level of stimulation. As well as having distinct patterns of neural stimulation, it is also argued that each affect is manifested through particular patterns of muscular and skin receptors in the face and the body which give each affect a particular sensation and facial expression. Within this framework shame is an auxiliary that acts to inhibit the positive affects of interest and joy. It is argued that shame occurs whenever there is an incomplete reduction of these positive affects. The reduction is incomplete in those cases in which the subject of the joy or interest remains attractive despite the perception of barriers to it. An example given is of a small child who wants to observe someone, feeling the affect of interest, but who is inhibited from doing so because the other person is a stranger. In this example the child might be said to feel embarrassment or shyness. Tomkins' definition of shame affect provides a radically different view of what shame might be. Indeed the range of situations that might elicit shame is only limited by

> . . . the innate or the learned sources of positive affect, and secondly on what are either the innate or learned sources of incomplete reduction of positive affect. Such circumstances go far beyond the questions of inferiority and guilt which have dominated the discussion of shame. (Tomkins, 1987: p. 144)

Indeed, one prediction of this theory is that the shame affect is responsible for a range of socially distinguishable emotions. This range of

emotions includes all those commonly associated with the shame family, such as guilt, embarrassment and humiliation, but also emotions which have otherwise been seen as unrelated. For example, Kaufman (1996) argues that the feeling of discouragement involves shame affect when a failure or defeat is perceived as being only temporary. Tomkins (1987) also discusses shame as present in the feelings of loss associated with the death of a loved one. In this second case, the loss of friendship as a result of death is an example of the reduction of joy or interest where the person wishes it would continue. What these examples show is that in many respects Tomkins' affect of shame does not represent, nor does it intend to, common usage of the word shame.

Although affect theory does not emphasize a 'social' definition of shame that is comparable with other approaches, more recent development of the theory in the clinical literature has resulted in a considerable effort to identify the social triggers of shame affect. In introducing the emotion of shame, Kaufman (1996) suggests that it is particularly related to transgressions, the development of conscience, and affronts to human dignity. As with the psychoanalytic approaches discussed above these themes come together because 'shame is the affect of inferiority'. Shame is again associated with the perception of failure or defeat. However, it is evident that Kaufman does not distinguish between shame and guilt in the same way as previous approaches. He argues that shame cannot be distinguished from guilt on the basis that it is more social or that it is more about the self. Rather, the word guilt has come inconsistently to represent different combinations of affects and feelings, such as shame about moral issues, the combination of disgust and anger at the self, and distress at the self.

Another theorist who builds upon affect theory is Nathanson (1992; 1997) who suggests that shame feelings become associated with the affect over time. When an individual experiences shame it involves a sequence of steps. The first is the physiological reaction which also might be called the affect of shame. The second step involves recalling memories of all previous moments in which the physiological reaction has occurred. It is in reference to these memories that the individual makes sense of the experience and associates it with feeling. Once again the concept of failure is emphasized. As Nathanson (1997) says: 'Usually it calls to consciousness that we are less than we might have liked, that we do not measure up to our best hopes for ourselves' (p. 349). The final stage of shame involves responding to the shame situation. Again the possible responses are developed over one's life and stored as scripts for possible action. Nathanson identifies four groups of responses that he describes as the compass of shame (see Figure 6.1). 'Withdrawal' involves the desire to be away from others and in some cases can be so severe that it involves complete social isolation.

'Attack self' is a second strategy in which the individual accepts shame by deprecating the self in relation to others. 'Avoidance' involves somehow distracting attention from the shame experience by focusing upon something that is positive (e.g. purchasing a prized object like a jacket). Finally, 'attack other' deflects shame from the self by reducing the self-esteem of others.

Although Nathanson and Kaufman do associate the feelings arising from shame affect with inferiority and failure to live up to ideals, it is important to note that affect theory proposes a radically different understanding of shame. Whereas many of the theories discussed above argue that failure is the cause of shame, affect theory describes these feelings as only the phenomenology of the emotion. The feelings become associated with the affect simply because, in the individual's past, impediments to the positive affects have been associated with personal failure.

Three Conceptions of Shame

Theoretical work on shame has occurred across many disciplines and in a haphazard manner, such that well-defined schools of thought have not developed systematically. In the midst of this diversity, there is no one obvious way to build a coherent typology to guide research. What is offered here is a synthesis of research that has been fundamental to our thinking about the phenomenon of shame. The three conceptions of shame described below, derived from the various theoretical traditions reviewed, provide an organizing framework rather than a neat typology. Theorists do not always fit snugly into one category. An example is the work of H. B. Lewis (1971), who presents a broad conception of shame. In such cases the theory is discussed within the conception that best describes it. A brief summary of each theory identified within the three conceptions is presented in Table 6.1.

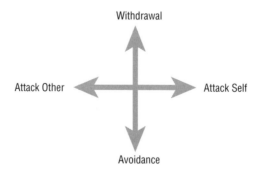

Figure 6.1 The Compass of Shame (Nathanson, 1992)

Table 6.1 Different Conceptions of Shame

Social threat conception	
Benedict (1946) & Mead (1937)	Occurs as a result of criticism/disapproval by others when one has transgressed a social norm (in contrast to guilt which involves internalized values). Mead does suggest the possibility of limited internalization.
Gibbons (1990)	Occurs as a result of the perception that one has transgressed a social norm in the presence of others. This reflects a desire to conform to social expectations.
Scheff & Retzinger (1991)	Occurs as a result of social rejection (as with embarrassment and humiliation). Individuals are motivated to maintain secure bonds with others and shame is the result of these bonds being threatened or severed. Shame results in lower perception of the individual's self-worth (i.e. self-esteem).
Leary (2000)	Occurs as a result of perceived rejection or disapproval that the individual believes weakens their relationship with others. Is accompanied by lower self-esteem. Is based upon the fundamental human motive to maintain interpersonal relationships.
Gilbert (1997)	Occurs as a result of the perception of being seen as less attractive by others. Based upon the evolutionary need to be attractive so as to maintain status.

Personal failure conception	
Piers & Singer (1953)	Occurs as the result of the perception that the perceived self (ego) has failed to live up to one's ideals (ego-ideal).
H. B. Lewis (1971)	Occurs as the result of the perception that the perceived self (ego) has failed to live up to one's ideals (ego-ideal) such that the failing leads to a condemnation of the whole self. Often occurs as the result of self-evaluation in reference to another – but one which may be an ill-defined, internalized other.
Wurmser (1981)	Occurs as the result of the perception that the perceived self (ego) has failed to live up to one's ideals (ego-ideal) and that this is a betrayal of the individual's gestalt image of self.
M. Lewis (1992)	Occurs as a result of the perception that one has failed in some respect and the attribution that this is due to one's whole self rather than simply an aspect of oneself.

Table 6.1 Different Conceptions of Shame (*cont.*)

Personal failure conception	
Lindsay-Hartz (1984)	Occurs as a result of the perception that the individual is something they don't want to be and a sense of certainty about this new negative identity.
Kaufman (1989)	Occurs as a result of an incomplete reduction of joy or interest and results in the feeling of being inadequate or inferior.
Nathanson (1992)	Occurs as the result of an incomplete reduction of joy or interest and results in feelings of failure, rejection, exposure, social embarrassment, etc.

Ethical conception	
Harré (1990)	Occurs as a result of awareness by others that one has committed a moral infraction and the actor concurs with this judgment.
Williams (1993)	Occurs as a result of having done wrong based upon the individual's ethical values as formed though an interaction between the individual and their community. Results in the question 'Who am I'?
Taylor (1985)	Occurs as a result of one's attention being focused (possibly by an audience) on oneself and the judgment by a higher order audience, with which the person identifies, that something about oneself is wrong. Results in a loss of self-respect.

The first conception that can be identified characterizes shame as a result of the individual's perception of social rejection or disapproval. We will call it the social threat conception. Scheff (1991) and Leary (2000) both describe this as the perception that one's relationships or social bonds with others have been damaged or destroyed. Gilbert (1997) hypothesizes that shame is related to the perception of being unattractive to others, while Gibbons (1990) discusses it as the result of not receiving approval. The anthropological perspectives of Benedict (1946) and Mead (1937) describe the emotion as a product of perceived disapproval. While these theories vary in their explanations of why people are sensitive to social evaluation, they all emphasize the need to be accepted by others. Leary (2000) argues that the need to have strong personal ties is a basic human motive, while Gilbert (1997) suggests that there is an evolutionary need to maintain status. Scheff (1996a) argues that shame is related to the person's perception of his or her own self-worth. An important characteristic of this conception is

that it describes shame, in the words of Scheff (1988), as exterior and constraining. The individual feels shame as a result of others' decision to reject. As a result shame, or the fear of shame, is described as a powerful motivation for individuals to continually monitor and work on personal relationships and to comply with social expectations at a broader level. This perspective can be summarized as the *social threat conception*.

The second conception that can be identified – the personal failure conception – is based upon the proposition that shame occurs when an individual perceives that they have not lived up to their standards and this leads to the perception that the whole self is a failure. For Piers and Singer (1953), H. B. Lewis (1971) and Wurmser (1994) this is defined by the perception that the ego is not as good as the ego-ideal. M. Lewis (1992) defines shame as the attribution that the whole self has failed, while Lindsay-Hartz (1984) focuses not on failure to live up to an ideal but on failure to meet a minimum standard. In Tangney's (1991) work shame-proneness is the disposition to react to failure by negatively evaluating the whole self. Finally, affect theorists Kaufman (1996) and Nathanson (1997), despite having different starting points, describe the feelings associated with shame as perceived inferiority and failure. Unlike other emotions, such as guilt, the focus of attention is the self rather than, for example, a transgression or a rule that might have been broken. Significantly, this conception does not suggest that the perception of failure results necessarily from social interaction but rather that it can occur in any context. This perspective can be summarized as the *personal failure conception*.

The third conception, which draws upon the distinctive focus of moral philosophy, incorporates the notion of wrongdoing that is recognized by the individual and society. For Harré (1990) shame is connected with serious transgression as well as the idea of fault. The individual feels shame for having intentionally committed a wrong. This is implicit in Williams's (1993) description of shame as resulting from the perception that an abstract respected other, defined in ethical terms, would think badly of us. Taylor (1985) also emphasizes the ethical nature of shame. Shame is tied to the loss of self-respect, which defines what the individual feels is tolerable and what is not. These theories take on board the personal failure conception by recognizing the violation of internalized standards as a cause of shame. At the same time, these standards are conceived of as incorporating wrongdoing and the transgression of social norms. As such, this ethical conception of shame recognizes the significance of social context. In summary, the *ethical conception* of shame acknowledges the importance that others play in feelings of shame, recognizes a shared moral code across individuals, and suggests that it is moral influence rather than rejection that is significant.

CHAPTER 7

The Reintegrative Shaming Experiments

The Reintegrative Shaming Experiments (RISE) (Sherman, Braithwaite & Strang, 1994) comprise four separate experiments that compare the effectiveness of traditional court processes and restorative justice conferences on distinct offense types. Data from the largest of these experiments are used in Part II of this book to explore the structure of the emotion of shame and the practice of shaming.

The comparison between the traditional court system and conferencing became important with the spread of conferencing from New Zealand to Australia, USA, Britain, South Africa, Canada, Singapore, Ireland and other parts of the world. This spread of conferencing has occurred, in part, because it provides a practical application of restorative justice. A movement towards restorative strategies for dealing with crime emphasizes the restoration of harm by offenders to the victims as well as restoration of the offender back into the community (Umbreit, 1985; Zehr, 1990). By attempting to achieve both these objectives, conferences provide an alternative form of justice to traditional court processes. However, their use within the criminal justice system does vary considerably across programs. In Canberra, the Australian Federal Police (AFP) has generally used conferences as an alternative to either court or to formal cautions. RISE involves the random allocation of offenders to court or conference among that population which would have normally gone to court.

Data relating to the court or conference case and participants' reactions to it were collected via observation of the treatment (i.e. the court case or conference) and an interview with the participant. Observational data were collected for 85 per cent of all assigned conference cases and 87 per cent of all assigned court cases. It is important to note that the percentage of cases for which all proceedings were observed was slightly less: 84 per cent in

both court and conference cases. This difference occurs because sometimes the proceedings for a case reconvened more than once. A number of factors prevented observers from attending all cases in the experiment. In some conference cases consent to observe could not be obtained. Lack of knowledge of treatment dates also affected observation of both conditions.

Interviews with all participants were sought between two and four weeks after final treatment of the case. However, in some cases locating and interviewing participants took much longer. On average, 40 days passed between the final treatment and the interviewing of participants. Not all cases generated interviews, either because participants could not be contacted or because participants refused to be interviewed. However, again a vast majority of participants were interviewed, 93 per cent of those assigned to conferences and 79 per cent of those assigned to court.

Participants

The data in this book are from the largest and the only completed experiment at the time of writing, the drink-driving experiment. What was special about the RISE Program is that data were systematically collected by a research team in a natural field experiment in which offenders were randomly allocated to a conference or court. The population eligible for random allocation in the drink-driving experiment was defined by the following characteristics:

(1) The individual was selected for a breathalyzer test;
(2) The individual had a blood alcohol level above .08;
(3) The individual had provided full admission of the offense committed;
(4) The individual was not involved in a collision;
(5) The individual did not have any current warrants or bonds; and
(6) The individual lived in the Australian Capital Territory (ACT).

All individuals who fitted this profile were eligible for referral to the experiment. The individuals who were referred to the research team numbered 900. Males (76%) outnumbered females and the majority were 30 years of age or younger (60%). While the ages of offenders in the experiment ranged from 17 to 74, the mean age was 30 (see Appendix 7A for a discussion of sample representativeness).

Random Assignment of Offenders and Ethical Considerations

Recruitment of participants to the experiment occurred, in most cases, at the time they were apprehended by police. The arresting constable, with

the agreement of their supervising sergeant, contacted RISE personnel if the case met a number of conditions. One set of conditions was whether the offense was consistent with the definition of the population outlined above. A second condition of entering the experiment was the officer's judgment that the offense was of a seriousness where it would be ethical to send the case either to a conference or court. Thus, offenses had to be deemed neither too serious to be conferenced nor too petty to be sent to court. In reaching this decision the police also had to indicate their own acceptance of whichever treatment was randomly assigned to the offender. The experimental procedure is described below.

Police officers with relevant cases contacted a RISE staff member by phone at the time of apprehension. Once contacted on a telephone answered 24 hours a day, seven days a week, RISE staff rechecked all the above conditions for entry into the experiment. The RISE staff opened an envelope which assigned the case to either the court or conference treatment on the basis of a pre-generated random assignment. Round-the-clock police access to RISE staff by mobile phone was particularly important for the drink-driving experiment, as many offenders were apprehended late at night or early in the morning on weekends. Twenty-four-hour contact was also important because this meant the arresting officer could make arrangements for the court or conference date at the time of arrest.

While offenders were assigned to attend a conference or court case, it is important to note that conferences were voluntary in nature. An offender could refuse to attend a conference, or at any point during a conference elect to withdraw and instead have their matter heard at court. In all these cases a summons to attend court would have been the normal option. An important issue for the experiment was whether offenders assigned to the conference condition would actually choose to accept the offer. The results show that overwhelmingly participants did choose the conference option when it was offered, with only seven (out of 900) refusing.

The voluntary nature of conferencing also had implications for the informed consent procedure that was employed. Informed consent was gained from participants at several stages of the experiment, although not obtained prior to randomization. Randomization simply involved offering some offenders the option of choosing an alternative to the normal intervention and thus did not require explicit consent to the randomization on the part of offenders. This was important because it provided some protection against knowledge of being randomly assigned affecting offenders' behavior or perceptions. However, the offender's consent to attend a conference was obtained by the police immediately after randomization had occurred. If consent was not given, the participant was treated through the normal police procedure which involved summons to court. A second

stage of consent was required for observation of conference cases. At the beginning of each conference all those in attendance were asked by the facilitator to give consent for observers to be present. This was not required for court cases as these are public hearings. Finally, informed consent was again sought for all participants prior to being interviewed. This involved mailing information and consent forms to all participants prior to their being contacted by interviewers. On making contact, interviewers received verbal consent and upon meeting participants the interviewers gained written consent to continue with the interview.

The Experiment in Action

As with all field experiments, the implementation of the study brought both expected and unexpected events and restrictions. Participant consent was respected at all times, and this affected response rates. On some other occasions, participants did unexpected things, and on a few occasions so did the police and the research team. Errors of this kind that led to imperfect implementation of the experimental design were extremely rare, however, given that the study ran over three years and involved 900 cases.

Details about the sample, sources of attrition and random allocation will not be discussed here although Appendix 7A provides details about the major methodological issues and problems and how we dealt with them. Table 7.1 provides a summary of the final sample and reports the number of individuals lost from the sample and categorizes reasons. In spite of some attrition from each group, the conference group and the court group were identical on all major social demographic variables (Barnes, 1999). For the analyses in Part II, both court and conferencing data are used, sometimes separately, sometimes together. When they are used separately, the purpose is to ensure that findings are generalizable across context, and are not peculiar to one justice context (see Appendix 7A for discussion of conference/court difference).

Of the 900 individuals referred to RISE, observational data were available for 378 offenders who attended court and for 377 offenders who attended a conference. Interview data were available for 346 offenders who went to court and for 374 offenders who attended a conference.

Measures of Court or Conference Observation

The Global Observational Ratings Instrument was designed to measure the observer's general impression of what occurred during each treatment. The instrument consisted of eight-point scales and was completed by observers at the completion of each case based upon their perceptions of the event.

Table 7.1 Sample and Participants Loss in the Drink-Driving Experiment

Sample	Court	Conference
Total sample	450	450
Treatment abandoned	*17*	*23*
Participants excluded due to multiple appearances	*2*	*2*
Participants treated other than allocated	*1*	*21*
Partial observation of treatments	*392*	*381*
Complete observation of treatments	378	377
Interview completed	346	374
Participants unable to be contacted	*34*	*19*
Interview refused by participant	*61*	*16*
Other reason for not interviewing	*9*	*17*

Questions were of a general nature, such as 'How much disapproval of the offender's act was expressed?' A list of items that measured aspects of shaming and shame are presented in Table 7.2, along with product-moment correlations of the agreement between observers.

In addition to these items, the instrument measured a range of concepts believed to be important in understanding the effectiveness of criminal justice interventions. Prominent among these were defiance by offenders (Sherman, 1993), the degree to which the process was procedurally just (Barnes, 1999; Tyler, 1990), whether offenders apologized, whether remorse was expressed, whether the offender was forgiven, the degree to which different parties were able to participate, and how outcomes or sentences were derived. The development of the measures is described in Appendix 7B.

Interview with Offenders

The offender interview underwent considerable pre-testing. This was done by interviewing recent offenders from a range of social backgrounds for a range of offenses. An important part of this process involved having interviews performed by different interviewers to identify any ambiguities in the interview.

The interview, which mostly occurred two to six weeks after the treatment, measured a range of topics. Firstly, it measured the participant's general perceptions of the case, such as whether they were treated fairly during their case (court or conference) and by the police, whether they

agreed with the outcome, and whether they felt defiant or angry as a result of the case. There were also questions regarding the deterrent effects of the treatment. A second category of questions looked at the participant's perceptions of the offense itself, for example, whether they committed the offense, how wrong they thought it was, and what others thought. A third section of the interview included questions about who was at the conference or in court, whether the participant was treated reintegratively or stigmatically, and how they felt during and after their case. A fourth series of questions addressed the participant's demographics but also included psychological measures of self-esteem, efficacy and emotionality. Finally, there were questions to measure self-reported drink-driving. The interview in the drink-driving experiment took approximately an hour and 20 minutes to administer.

The format for asking and responding to questions varied throughout the interview depending upon the topic of interest. However, all questions involved responding to set items that were read word-for-word and were answered on set scales. During some parts of the interview, particularly the early stages, the interviewer asked questions and wrote down the answers. In a number of sections the interviewer read the questions but allowed the participants to record their answers in a separate booklet. Finally, in one section participants read and answered the question themselves unless the interviewer was uncertain about their ability to do so or the participants indicated, in response to a question, that they would rather have the questions read out for them. Changing the format in this way had a number of advantages. One was to help maintain interest by preventing what was a long interview from becoming monotonous. A second was to allow participants greater privacy when answering more sensitive questions. The questions on how reintegratively the participants were treated and how they felt during the case were read out by the interviewer but answered privately by the participants.

Summary

Observational data were obtained from 755 drink-driving offenders who were randomly assigned to court or conference. Randomization was accomplished with few assignment errors. Subsequently, 720 participants were interviewed about their experiences (on average five to six weeks later). Impressive equivalence of experimental and control groups has been established through a variety of comparisons (Barnes, 1999). These data contain measures of shaming and shame that are suitable for the factor analytic and multiple regression techniques used in the following chapters.

Table 7.2 Agreement and Product-Moment Correlations between Observers

Items	% agreement	r
1 How much reintegrative shaming was expressed?	80	.79**
Respect for offender		
2 How much support was the offender given during the conference/court case?	73	.71**
3 How reintegrative was the conference/court case for this offender?	56	.58**
4 How much approval of the offender *as a person* was expressed?	53	.47**
5 How much was the offender treated by their supporters as someone they love?	55	.19 (ns)
6 How much respect for the offender was expressed?	53	.56**
Disapproval of the offender's act		
7 How much disapproval of *this type of offense* was expressed?	72	.83**
8 How much disapproval of *the offender's act* was expressed?	62	.67**
Disapproval of the offender		
9‡ How much stigmatizing shame was expressed?	87	.57**
10 How much disappointment in the offender was expressed?	69	.73**
11‡ To what extent was the offender treated as a criminal?	80	.35*
12‡ How often were stigmatizing names and labels (e.g. 'criminal', 'punk', junkie', or 'bully') used to describe the offender?	91	.38 (ns)
13‡ How much moral indignation did the victim express about the offender's action?	44	.48**
14‡ How much disapproval of the offender *as a person* was expressed?	84	.43**
Offender is forgiven		
18 To what extent was the offender forgiven for their actions?	58	.60**
19 How clearly was it communicated to the offender that they could put their actions behind them?	67	.58**
20 How much forgiveness of the offender was expressed?	50	.12 (ns)

Table 7.2 Agreement and Product-Moment Correlations between Observers *(cont.)*

Items	% agreement	r
Shame		
21 How much responsibility did the offender take for their actions?	62	.50**
22 How much did the offender retreat from and avoid the attention of others?	73	.64**
23‡ How much was the offender's speech affected by irregularities, pauses, or incoherence?	74	.53**
24 How uncomfortable (e.g. restless, anxious, fidgety) was the offender?	69	.48**
25 To what extent did the offender engage in hiding (e.g. lowering head) and concealing (e.g. hand covering parts of the face, averting gaze) behavior?	47	.51**
26 To what extent did the offender accept that they had done wrong?	69	.70**
27 How sorry/remorseful was the offender for their actions?	73	.69**

‡ The agreement scores for these variables are based upon limited variation in the sample and thus must be treated with caution. The limited variation occurred primarily due to agreement between observers on a score of 1 ('none' of the category).
See Appendix 7B for discussion of the agreement score.
*p<.05   **p<.01.

APPENDIX 7A

Details on Methodology for RISE

Differences in the Conference and Court Experiences

Conferences are a meeting of those people who have been affected by an offense. This usually includes the offender(s), their supporters, the victim(s), their supporters and a facilitator. However, in the drink-driving offenses researched in this book there was no direct victim as those cases where there was an accident causing injury or damage were excluded in the experimental pursuit of homogeneity. In the absence of a victim many of these conferences were attended by a community representative who replaced a direct victim by discussing more general fears regarding drink-driving and the risk that it poses to the whole community. Additionally, these conferences usually involved an informational component in which the police officer would provide basic information about blood alcohol levels and risks associated with drink-driving. A video was shown that documented the effect on human lives of car crashes caused by drivers who were over the legal alcohol limit. It featured interviews with victims' families designed to encourage discussion in the conference about the impact of drink-driving on victims.

This approach is obviously quite different from court cases that are shorter and involve less participation. An important aspect of the experiment is that it only includes cases where there is an admission of guilt by the offender or offenders. In court cases where there is a guilty plea there is usually a description of the facts by the prosecutor or police, submissions by the offender, or their solicitor, and finally a sentence handed down by the magistrate. Conferences are often substantially longer than court cases. For our drink-driving offenses the average length of a conferences was 87 minutes in comparison to court cases that were on average only seven minutes (Sherman, Strang, Barnes, Braithwaite, Inkpen & Teh, 1998). This difference in length has important implications for analysis of cases where measures, such as observation, are sensitive to the frequency of behavior occurring.

Representativeness of the Sample Selected

The guidelines regarding the eligibility of participants mean that the participants in the RISE experiment are not fully representative of drink-driving cases in Canberra. A large number of drink-drivers are arrested

with blood alcohol levels lower than .08. Additionally, a much smaller number of drink-driving cases are involved in collisions. Both of these groups were excluded from the experiment.

A second factor that may have affected the sample of cases collected by RISE was police discretion. Offender attitude or other factors may have impacted upon the decision made by police to enter offenders into the experiment. Indeed, analysis of all drink-driving cases in the ACT during 1997 shows that the experiment recruited only 56 percent of eligible cases (Sherman et al., 1998). It is not apparent whether the decision to include or exclude offenders occurred randomly or involved a particular bias. Some of the variation was clearly explained by the availability and commitment of police to run conferences at different times. Cases were entered into RISE at police discretion and thus it may simply have been that some cases, regardless of their characteristics, were not included because arresting officers were not supportive of the experiment.

Although the sample is clearly not representative of all drink-driving cases in the ACT, it is worth noting that in many respects the RISE cases are typical of the average drink-driving case which involves detection of the offense through random breath testing and a blood alcohol reading over .08. While only drink-driving cases that involved a blood alcohol level greater than .08 were eligible, five participants with blood alcohol levels below .08 were wrongly entered into the experiment. One of these offenders had a reading of only .01, which is illegal only for drivers on a provisional license.

Case Loss

Although 900 cases were allocated to the court or conference conditions, a number of factors affected the sample that was ultimately analyzed. Factors and their effects on the final sample are summarized in Table 7.1.

One significant factor was the abandonment of cases by the police. In total 17 cases that were allocated to the court condition and 23 that were allocated to conference resulted in no further action being taken by police. The primary reasons for abandonment of cases were either an inability to locate offenders or a loss of records by the police.

In addition to these cases, four cases (two from each condition) were excluded because the offenders were already participants in one of the RISE experiments.

A final factor that affected the final data set available for analysis was violation of the allocated treatment. One participant allocated to the court condition and 21 participants allocated to the conference condition actually received different treatments. In a small number of cases offenders were

cautioned. In most cases the allocated treatment was not received because the participant was given the opposite treatment, that is, these participants migrated from one condition to the other. The most common explanation for this event was an offender, randomly assigned to a conference, failing to attend (voluntarily), and then being summonsed to court.

These forms of treatment failure raise an important issue for analysis because they involve a violation of randomization, and threaten the comparability of the treatment groups. The decision made was to maintain the integrity of the random assignment (Gartin, 1995; Peto, Pike, Armitage, Breslow, Cox, Howard, Mantel, McPherson, Peto & Smith, 1976). Thus, all analyses involving comparisons of court and conference treatments on outcome variables were based on groups as they were randomly allocated and not according to the treatment they received.

The analyses reported in Part II of this book, however, are of a different kind. The central question that involves treatments is the following: Do the factor structures of shame and shaming, and their interrelationships generalize from the conference setting to court? Given the nature of the question, participants were analyzed on the basis of the treatment they actually received in the analyses in Part II.

APPENDIX 7B

Development of the RISE Global Observational Ratings Instrument

Development of the Global Observational Ratings Instrument occurred over a substantial period before being used in RISE. Pre-testing of the instrument involved two phases. An initial informal process occurred where Nathan Harris and a colleague attended conference and court cases with the instrument in order to evaluate how applicable the items were to each context and whether they measured important variations between cases. This process led to substantial fine-tuning and development of the instrument. The second phase of pre-testing involved a study of the inter-rater reliability of the instrument. Reliability can be measured in a number or ways, for example reliability over time (test-retest reliability), internal reliability (e.g. split-half), and scorer reliability (Anastasi, 1968). However, in a large experiment like RISE it was necessary for observations to be made by a number of different observers. Thus, a critical factor was whether it was possible to design an instrument that would be reliable between observers.

A study was performed (Harris & Burton, 1997) which evaluated inter-rater reliability across the experimental contexts. These included drink-driving conferences, property and violence related conferences and court cases of these types. The primary measure of reliability used was the agreement score. This was obtained by calculating the percentage of cases that the observers' scores were within one point of each other. Given that the items were scored on eight point scales this was considered a stringent test of agreement (Harris & Burton, 1998). Results from this study, reported in Harris and Burton (1997, 1998), demonstrate that while there was variation across items, most categories were measured reliably between observers (see Table 7.2).

Multiple Observations

Analyses of the observational measures of shaming were complicated by some cases having multiple observations of each variable. As discussed, both court and conference cases have the potential to be reconvened on a number of occasions. In fact 18 of the participants assigned to court attended more than one treatment event, while four participants assigned to a conference attended more than one treatment event. The dilemma resulting from such cases was which observation should be used or whether an average score calculated from all observations should be taken. It was decided to use the maximum score provided by any of the observations. This approach made intuitive sense because a low degree of, for example, shaming in two treatment events does not negate a high degree of shaming in a third. In this case it would still be concluded that a high degree of shaming had been expressed. This is particularly true for court cases where multiple treatment events often occur as a result of procedural issues. In fact pre-testing showed that there was little difference in the dimensionality of shaming regardless of whether the maximum or average score were used.

CHAPTER 8

Testing the Dimensionality of Shame

Three core issues have been identified as central to our efforts to understand shame – shame as a response to social threat, shame as a response to personal failure, and shame as an exposure to ethical shortcomings. Identifying these domains of interest is the first step toward clarifying our conceptualization of shame. The next step involves the measurement of these facets and an analysis of how these various aspects are interconnected. Before doing so, however, there is much to be learned in the next section from the empirical literature that has tried to untangle the three related constructs of shame, guilt and embarrassment. After operationalizing all these concepts through the RISE data, we will find in this chapter that three dimensions of shame emerge empirically – Shame–Guilt, Embarrassment–Exposure and Unresolved Shame.

Shame External, Guilt Internal

Distinguishing shame and guilt on the basis that shame is an externally induced emotion has been a popular research topic in the empirical literature. A number of studies have been conducted across different cultures and with American university students to find out if they associate the labels shame and guilt with different social contexts and different emotional states. The cross-cultural work of Wallbott and Scherer (1995: p. 56) has been inspired by Benedict and Mead's work on shame and guilt cultures. These studies support the external–internal description between shame and guilt through demonstrating that shame was more likely to be associated with situations where the social context was salient and guilt was more likely to be associated with situations involving the self. At the same time, Miyake and Yamazaki (1995) have suggested that shame and guilt cultures

camouflage a degree of complexity in the cross-cultural research that has previously been overlooked.

The study of Miyake and Yamazaki (1995) involved the analysis of Japanese participants' reports of situations they found embarrassing. In some of the situations the role of others was both important and explicit. In other situations, a second type of shame (*haji*) was identified which did not involve others' knowledge of the event. In these cases, participants simply reported that it felt like they were being watched even though they were not. Although the study provides only limited analysis of each emotion, these results suggest that there may be a more complex story to be told about the 'moral' emotions in Japan. Whereas Benedict observed that the Japanese were particularly reactive to public evaluation, it seems that feelings associated with less public evaluation also play an important role in Japanese society (also see Lebra, 1983).

Other studies with American university students have mapped memories, interpretations and feelings associated with guilt events and shame events (Baumeister, Stillwell & Heatherton, 1994, 1995; Cheek & Hogan, 1983; Jones, Kugler & Adams, 1995; Wicker et al., 1983; Tangney et al., 1996b). Sometimes the guilt and shame situations are defined by the experimenters, other times participants are allowed to recall a personal experience of their own. These studies provide, at best, mixed support for the external–internal distinction between shame and guilt. For example, the study by Wicker et al. (1983) found that participants did not clearly distinguish between the sources of disapproval. In both emotions, participants reported that they were more concerned with how others saw them than how they saw themselves. However, Wicker et al. also found that when feeling shame participants felt more submissive, inferior, and alienated from others, and a greater fear of rejection. These differences, and particularly differences regarding the fear of rejection, are consistent with the predictions of the social threat conception. Equivocal results on this comparison are also reported by Tangney et al. (1996b).

Finally, the empirical works of Baumiester and Jones draw attention to guilt as a social emotion (Baumeister et al., 1994, 1995; De Rivera, 1984; Jones et al., 1995). Both Baumeister et al. (1995) and Jones et al. (1995) report studies that show guilt is related to harming another person. In particular, Baumeister et al. found that experiences of guilt almost always involved harm done to a person in a valued relationship.

Shame as Self-focused, Guilt as Other-focused

A second distinction between shame and guilt is emphasized by the personal failure conception which is that shame involves perception of the

whole self as a failure, while guilt is limited to the act. With shame, the individual does not distinguish between the act and self (H. B. Lewis, 1971; M. Lewis, 1992; Tangney, 1991). In contrast, guilt is an emotional response to the perception of a failure or transgression that distinguishes the action from the whole self. As a result of the separation between act and the whole self, guilt is described as less painful and less introspective. Thus, when feeling guilt people are more focused on the harm done to others and ways to atone for that harm.

Again the empirical evidence on whether individuals distinguish shame and guilt experiences on the basis of self-esteem of the entire self as opposed to a specific act is mixed. Studies by Tangney et al. (1996b) and Wicker et al. (1983) failed to elicit this distinction from respondents, possibly because it is too subtle to identify with a self-report methodology. Niedenthal, Tangney & Gavanski (1994) have had some successes drawing this distinction, however with a methodology involving counterfactual thinking.

Counterfactual thinking involves reflecting '. . . on how past events might have otherwise unfolded had some aspect of the situation or their behavior been different' (Niedenthal et al., 1994: p. 585). It was hypothesized that a shameful context would result in counterfactual thinking which focused upon changes to the person's self. In contrast, it was hypothesized that guilt contexts would involve a greater focus upon aspects of the situation or the person's behavior that might have been different. These hypotheses were tested in a series of studies in which participants were either given descriptions of 'shame' or 'guilt' scenarios, or were asked to generate their own. Participants were then asked to use counterfactual thinking to identify what could be changed about the scenarios so that things might have been different or better. The results from three studies showed significant differences between the shame and guilt scenarios consistent with Niedenthal et al.'s predictions.

In a follow-up study, the procedure was reversed, with participants given scenarios and then forced to make changes to either themselves or the situation/their behavior. The results show that participants who were forced to make changes to their self were more likely to report that shame would have occurred in that context. In contrast, participants forced to make changes to their behavior or the situation were more likely to report that guilt would have been felt. These results suggest that shame is associated with deficiencies of the whole self whereas guilt is associated with deficiencies associated with behavior or the situation. However, it is worth noting that most of the characteristics of the self that were changed, even in the shame scenarios, were 'transient' characteristics.

Recent works by Tangney and her colleagues (Tangney, 1991; Tangney et al., 1992a, 1996c), have applied the whole self–act distinction between

shame and guilt to the newly developed constructs of shame-proneness and guilt-proneness. Tangney and her colleagues have been successful in distinguishing shame-proneness and guilt-proneness through their relationships with other constructs. The global denouncement of self has led Tangney to postulate and demonstrate that shame-proneness is negatively correlated with empathy and positively correlated with various expressions of hostility including resentment, irritability, and a tendency to blame others for negative events.

Although the shame-proneness and guilt-proneness scales are defined by distinguishing between a focus upon self and behavior these studies do not directly provide evidence that this is an important distinction between shame and guilt. What they do show is that shame- and guilt-proneness, defined by tendencies to attribute failure to the self or behavior, can successfully predict differences in empathy and hostility. A second important point is that these studies are based on shame and guilt as personality traits and thus it is difficult, if not impossible, to extrapolate findings to shame and guilt as discrete emotions.

Shame as Serious, Embarrassment as Trivial

While differences between shame and guilt have played an important role in the literature on shame, researchers have also attempted to distinguish shame from embarrassment. The distinction has been made on a number of grounds. The first emphasizes seriousness. Shame is a moral failure whereas embarrassment is a breach of social etiquette (Harré, 1990; Taylor, 1985). The second links seriousness with intentionality. If an individual deliberately engages in an action and is at fault, shame is the more appropriate emotional response. If the behavior is a consequence of an accident, embarrassment is more likely to ensue (Harré, 1990). A third distinction between shame and embarrassment involves the social context. For Taylor, embarrassment is more contextualized socially and temporally than is shame. This later understanding fits nicely with psychological work which understands embarrassment as a form of social anxiety (Buss, 1980) resulting from states of public self-awareness (Crozier, 1990). R. S. Miller (1995) compares this to a further explanation of embarrassment – that it can result from awkward social interaction resulting in the loss of coherent self-presentation and uncertainty as to how to behave.

The differences between shame and embarrassment have attracted much less attention in empirical studies. Sorting tasks to distinguish characteristics of shame and embarrassment (Miller & Tangney, 1994), and Likert rating scales describing personal memories (Tangney et al., 1996b) have supported the moral–trivial distinction with shame described as a more intense

emotion that results from serious transgressions, whereas embarrassment results from trivial incidents.

In summary, the literature presents a number of ways in which shame might be distinguished from guilt and embarrassment. At the same time, empirical work provides only limited evidence to support them. Nevertheless, on the basis of this literature it can be hypothesized that shame and guilt will be distinct in two ways. The first of these is that a shame dimension that includes fear of other's disapproval or rejection would be distinct from a guilt dimension that includes the individual's perception of having done wrong (see **Hypothesis: Shame 1**). The second prediction is that a shame dimension that includes negative feelings about the self would be distinct from a guilt dimension that includes negative feelings about one's actions and the consequences of those actions (see **Hypothesis: Shame 2**). Third, on the basis of the evidence available, shame and embarrassment are expected to form distinct dimensions, the latter involving feelings of social discomfort, the former feelings associated with having committed a serious moral breach (see **Hypothesis: Shame 3**).

Testing the Hypotheses

Much of the empirical work on shame and its related emotions has attempted to grasp phenomenology by asking participants to recall their own memories of the emotion and then describe that experience (Lindsay-Hartz, 1984; Tangney et al., 1996b; Wallbott & Scherer, 1995; Wicker et al., 1983). This procedure has its own limitations. Having participants recall experiences in which they felt a particular emotion requires them first to generate their own conception of the emotion and second to recall experiences consistent with it. By measuring the phenomenology of these experiences, researchers report those feelings, physiological changes, and so on that conform to participants' conceptions of emotions. Furthermore, most of these studies ask participants to recall and describe several emotions. It might be suggested that these studies simply reflect agreement among participants about labels used to describe the emotions and the conceptual differences implied by these labels.

Measurement of participants' naive theories, or conceptual frameworks, regarding the emotions is an important approach to defining the emotions. Indeed such factors may play an important role in determining which dimensions prove the most useful for distinguishing among the shame-related emotions. However, it is also evident that there has been no empirical work that has attempted to test whether conceptions of shame accurately reflect the dimensionality of feelings that occur in real-life situations like court cases.

The present study was undertaken to address this gap in the literature. RISE produced the opportunity to interview participants regarding an event that had just occurred, that was known to the experimenters, and that was assumed to involve feelings from the shame family. It is expected that this procedure is likely to provide better measures of what participants actually felt in a real-life context than procedures relying on scenarios or memories. It is also expected that this type of methodology will avoid some of the semantic issues presented by different understandings of the shame-related words. Finally, superior measurement of real-life experiences should provide a more valid database for inferring the dimensionality of these emotions through factor analytic techniques.

An important aspect of the factor analytic methodology is to sample items from the shame and shame-related emotions family comprehensively. In this study the area of interest is defined by shame and the two emotions with which it has most commonly been compared: guilt and embarrassment. As discussed earlier (see Table 6.1 in Chapter 6), descriptions of shame vary markedly. In order to represent all these facets of shame, items were constructed to reflect the different conceptions of shame uncovered in Table 6.1.

A review of the literature on guilt, with particular attention paid to those characteristics described as being contrary to shame, highlights a number of dimensions. While many conceptions stress the self-critical nature of shame, probably as many emphasize guilt as an emotion in which the individual is outward-looking (H. B. Lewis, 1971; M. Lewis, 1992; Tangney, 1991; Williams, 1993). Guilt is described as involving feelings which are focused upon the damage that one has caused, and in particular, is associated with the recognition that one has hurt others (Baumeister et al., 1995). It is also assumed to have a much more specific focus upon a particular act or omission (H. B. Lewis, 1971; M. Lewis, 1992). Again in comparison to shame, guilt is associated with the perception that one has broken rules or internalized standards. In this way it is seen as resulting from the individual's perception that they have done something wrong. The perception of having broken rules can also be associated with fear of punishment or retribution from those who have been hurt (Nathanson, 1992; Williams, 1993).

Some conceptions associate embarrassment with the knowledge that others are aware that one has breached a social convention (Harré, 1990). This view emphasizes the role of an audience, particular feelings of being the center of unwanted social attention and the fear of evaluation by others (Crozier, 1990). Related feelings are not knowing what to do in a particular situation, or simply a sense of social awkwardness (Miller, 1995). One such situation involves being in the presence of others perceived to have higher

Table 8.1 Attributes Associated with Shame and Shame-related Emotions, and Questions Developed to Measure Them

Attributes		Questions
Awareness that others know that one has acted contrary to social standards (Harré, 1990)	4	I felt bad in the conference/court case because everyone knew about the offense I had committed.
Awareness of criticism or derision by others (Benedict, 1946; Mead, 1937)	5	During the conference/court case I felt ashamed because people criticized me for what I had done.
Fear of other's evaluations of the self (Harré, 1990; Williams, 1993)	1	During the conference/court case I felt worried about what others thought of me.
Perception that one has lost honor amongst one's community (Taylor, 1985; Williams, 1993)	13	During the conference/court case I felt like I had lost respect or honor among my family.
	14	During the conference/court case I felt like I had lost respect or honor among my friends.
Perception of being a failure for not living up to ideals (H.B. Lewis, 1971; M. Lewis, 1992)	9	During the conference/court case I felt that I was a failure.
Perception that one has done something against one's moral standards (Harré, 1990; Taylor, 1985; Williams, 1993)	2	During the conference/court case I felt that the offense I committed was wrong.
Object of shame becomes the self (H.B. Lewis, 1971; M. Lewis, 1992; Tangney, 1990)	12	During the conference/court case I felt ashamed of myself.
Feelings of anger/hostility directed towards the self (H.B. Lewis, 1971; Tangney, 1991; Wurmser, 1994)	6	In the conference/court case I felt angry with myself for what I had done.

Table 8.1 Attributes Associated with Shame and Shame-related Emotions, and Questions Developed to Measure Them (*cont.*)

Attribute	No.	Question
Obsessively going over events, possible explanations, justifications, etc, after the event (H.B. Lewis, 1971; Scheff, 1990a)	20	Since the conference/court case have you found yourself continually bothered by thoughts that you were unfairly judged by people at the conference/court case?
	22	Do you feel that some of the things brought up in the conference/court case are unresolved in your mind?
	21	Since the conference/court case have you found yourself unable to decide, in your own mind, whether or not what you did was wrong?
Subject of attention is act and the harm it caused (Baumiester et al., 1995; Lewis, 1971; M. Lewis, 1992; H.B. Lewis, 1990; Williams, 1993)	3	During the conference/court case I felt bad because the offense I committed might have hurt someone.
Feeling of shame specific to the act (H.B. Lewis, 1971; M. Lewis, 1992)	19	I felt bad in the conference/court case because my actions had hurt others.
	11	During the conference / court case I felt ashamed of what I did.
Fear of the possible consequences for oneself (e.g. retribution) (Nathanson, 1992; Williams, 1993)	18	During the conference/court case I felt worried that I would have to pay in some way for the offense I committed.
Perception that one is the center of others' attention (Harré, 1990)	8	In the conference/court case I felt embarrassed because I was the center of attention.
	17	During the conference/court case I felt so exposed, I wished I could just disappear.
Feeling self-aware and awkward (Miller, 1995)	7	During the conference/court case I felt awkward and aware of myself.
Feeling uneasy because one feels of lower status (Sachdev, 1990)	16	In the conference/court case I felt uneasy because I was surrounded by people who were supposed to be more important than me.
Feeling of humiliation (Crozier, 1990)	15	I felt humiliated in the conference/court case.
Feeling that one has jeopardized future opportunities (Grasmick & Bursik, 1990)	10	During the conference/court case I felt that I had stuffed up at least some of my future opportunities.

status (Sachdev, 1990). Grasmick and Bursik (1990) suggest that an important implication of embarrassment is the feeling that one has jeopardized one's future opportunities because others know about the embarrassing event. It is also evident that the concept of humiliation is often used in conjunction with embarrassment to express a similar or stronger feeling (Crozier, 1990).

In the above section a range of attributes are identified which have been associated with the emotions of shame, embarrassment and guilt. These attributes are listed below in Table 8.1 with 23 questions that have been developed to measure them. Each question was read out as part of the offender interview and responded to by the participant on a five-point scale in a separate booklet. This scale ranged from 'Not at all' (1) to 'Felt overwhelmed by it' (5).

It is expected that self-report measures will provide the best means of testing the dimensionality of the shame-related emotions. A number of researchers, however, have suggested that shame can be measured through observation. Tomkins (1962, 1963) and Izard (1977) have argued that the emotions, including shame, can be observed from facial expressions. In particular, they emphasize the loss of tonus in the face and neck muscles (Tomkins, 1987: p. 144) apparent in the downcast face associated with shame. Retzinger (1991b) also outlines a discourse analysis for the observation of shame via paralinguistic and behavioral patterns. Shame is often associated with verbal hiding behavior that includes speaking softly, mumbling, incoherence, and hesitation. Fragmentation or confusion, for example stuttering or other irregularities, can also affect speech. Behavior associated with shame includes fidgeting and hiding behaviors such as covering of the face or looking away (Retzinger, 1991b). Other behaviors that might be associated with shame extend beyond these measures of hiding and discomfort. For example, it might be expected that participants feeling shame will acknowledge that they have done wrong, thus taking responsibility for their actions as well as expressing remorse. Seven items (see Table 8.2) developed to measure these shame-related behaviors were included in the Global Observation Rating Instrument and completed by observers at the conclusion of each court or conference case. Each item was answered on an eight-point scale ranging from 'none' (1) to 'very much' (8). Means and standard deviations of these observational shame items are reported in Appendix 8A.

Table 8.2 The Observational Shame Items

1	How much did the offender retreat from attention?
2	How much was the offender's speech affected by irregularities, pauses, or incoherence?
3	How uncomfortable (e.g. restless, anxious, fidgety) was the offender?
4	To what extent did the offender engage in hiding (e.g. lowering head) and concealing (e.g. hand covering parts of the face, averting gaze) behavior?
5	How much responsibility did the offender take for their action?
6	To what extent did the offender accept that they had done wrong?
7	How sorry/remorseful was the offender for their actions?

The Dimensionality of Shame

Three hypotheses have been proposed to distinguish shame from guilt and embarrassment. Each hypothesis predicts that key variables will be associated with certain dimensions and not others. In order to test these hypotheses principal components analyses were conducted (for court and conference cases separately) so as to partition the shame-related items into interpretable dimensions. Preliminary analyses showed that one item (no. 18) had little variance in common with other items in the analysis of conference data. Consequently it was dropped from this analysis.

Principal Component Analysis of Court Data

A principal component analysis was carried out on the responses to the questions measuring shame, guilt and embarrassment from 332 respondents interviewed after they had been to court. Three factors were extracted which explained 58 per cent of the variance. (Three criteria were used to decide on the number of factors: (a) eigenvalues > one, (b) scree test, and (c) the simple structure of the solution (Cattell, 1966; Gorsuch, 1983).) The three-factor solution was rotated using the SPSS varimax and oblimin programs. Because the factors were substantially intercorrelated, an oblimin rotation was considered most appropriate to give meaning to the factors.

A separate principal component analysis of data from participants in the conference condition (n = 367) also produced three factors, explaining 54 per cent of the variance. An oblimin rotation produced pattern matrix loadings that were very similar to those obtained using the court data. The pattern matrices for the shame-related items from court and conference data are presented in Table 8.3.

Table 8.3 Rotated Pattern Matrix* of Shame-related Items for Court (Conference) Cases

Items	Shame–Guilt	Unresolved Shame	Embarrassment–Exposure
3 Felt bad, the offense might have hurt someone.	.76 (.80)		
11 Felt ashamed of what I did.	.75 (.80)		
2 Felt the offense I committed was wrong.	.72 (.74)		
19 Felt bad because actions hurt others.	.69 (.65)		
12 Felt ashamed of myself.	.66 (.69)		.38 (ns)
14 Felt like I had lost respect or honor among my friends.	.60 (.43)	.46 (.32)	ns (.32)
13 Felt like I lost respect or honor among family.	.57 (.37)	.45 (.45)	
6 Felt angry with myself for what I had done.	.56 (.73)		.37 (ns)
5 Felt ashamed because people criticized me for what I had done.	.41 (.32)		ns (.50)
22 Some of the things brought up unresolved in my mind.		.76 (.73)	
20 Continually bothered by thoughts (of being) unfairly judged by people.	ns (−.35)	.69 (.43)	
21 Unable to decide whether or not I was in the wrong.		.58 (.70)	
10 Felt that I had stuffed up future opportunities.	.40 (.37)	.46 (.47)	
8 Felt embarrassed as the center of attention.			.92 (.73)
17 Felt so exposed, I wished to disappear.			.83 (.85)
7 Felt awkward and aware of myself.	ns (.37)		.80 (.54)
15 Felt humiliated.			.69 (.81)
16 Felt uneasy surrounded by people more important than me.			.64 (.46)
4 Felt bad, everyone knew about the offense I had committed.	.34 (.49)		.57 (.34)
1 Felt worried about what others thought of me.	.32 (.50)		.53 (.37)
18 Felt worried that I'd have to pay in some way for the offense I committed. **			.43
9 Felt I was a failure.		.30 (.33)	.39 (.41)
Per cent of variance explained	41.5 (36.7)	10.3 (9.9)	6.4 (6.9)

*Only loading .3 and above are included in this table.

**This item was only used for court cases.

Because there is such strong similarity between the court and conference solutions, the findings will be discussed together. The first factor was defined by participant reports that they felt ashamed of what they had done; felt bad because they had, or might have, hurt others; and felt that what they had done was wrong. Other significant loadings included feelings of anger at oneself, feelings of concern at others' evaluations and criticism, and concern at the loss of respect from friends. The factor is labeled Shame–Guilt though we might have labeled it Shame–Guilt–Remorse. What is particularly noteworthy is that items reflecting shame and items reflecting guilt are equally important in defining this factor.

The second factor was labeled Unresolved Shame because it was primarily defined by feelings that some of the things brought up in court or at conference had not been resolved, and participants reported being bothered by thoughts of being unfairly judged and being unable to decide whether what they had done was wrong. Respondents also reported feelings that they had lost respect or honor and that some future opportunities had probably been 'stuffed up'. The ongoing, obsessive nature of these feelings is consistent with the phenomenology of by-passed shame, identified in the work of H. B. Lewis (1971) and Scheff and Retzinger (1991).

The third factor is defined by items that measure embarrassment as a result of being the center of attention, feeling so exposed that one would like to disappear, feeling awkward and aware, feeling humiliated, and finally, feeling uneasy because one is surrounded by more important people than oneself. Other defining items expressed concern for the criticism of others. Together, the focus is upon the participant's discomfort in the situation due to unwanted social attention. Factor 3 is labeled as Embarrassment–Exposure.

We think most people can recognize very different feelings associated with these three concepts – the unsettled feeling of the second factor, the sinking feeling about doing something wrong in the first, and the more rising, blushing feeling that one gets in its most extreme form when one's nakedness is publicly exposed.

Let us now relate these findings back to our first three hypotheses.

Shame 1: *Items measuring fear of other's disapproval (Items 4, 5, 1, 13, 14, Table 8.1) would cohere and be distinct from those items that measure the individual's perception that they have done something wrong (Item 2, Table 8.1).* This hypothesis was not supported. Both fear of others' disapproval and feeling oneself that the offense was wrong defined Shame–Guilt. It was evident that many of the items measuring concern for others' reactions had moderate loadings on both the Shame–Guilt and Embarrassment–Exposure factors suggesting

that concern for the opinion of others may not always accompany feelings of wrongdoing. The important point to take away from this analysis, however, is that feelings of wrongdoing were not independent of feelings of concern about others' reactions.

Shame 2: *Items measuring negative feelings towards the self (Items 9, 12, 6, Table 8.1) would cohere and be distinct from those items that measure concern with one's actions and the consequences of them for others (Items 11, 3, 19, Table 8.1)).* Again this hypothesis was not supported. Items measuring feeling ashamed of the self, and anger at the self loaded on the Shame–Guilt factor as did items measuring feeling ashamed of one's actions, and feeling bad because others were, or might have been hurt.

Shame 3: *Items measuring the perception that one has committed a serious moral breach (i.e. acted in a way that is morally wrong (2), hurt others (3, 19) and behaved without honor (13, 14)) would cohere and be distinct from those items that measure social discomfort (i.e. feelings of self-consciousness (7, 8, 17)).* This hypothesis was supported. Feelings that the offense was wrong, concern for having hurt others and compromising one's own honor loaded on the Shame–Guilt factor, whereas feelings of social awkwardness form a separate factor of Embarrassment–Exposure.

Developing Scales to Measure Shame–Guilt, Unresolved Shame and Embarrassment–Exposure

Individuals were given scale scores on Shame–Guilt, Unresolved Shame and Embarrassment–Exposure by summing their responses to those items that loaded cleanly on each factor (i.e. that had a high loading on the factor of interest but low loadings on the other two factors). The items comprising the Shame–Guilt, Unresolved Shame and Embarrassment–Exposure scales appear in Table 8.4.

The scale produced for the Shame–Guilt factor consisted of six items (2, 3, 6, 11, 12, and 19) and had a Cronbach's alpha coefficient of .88 for court cases and .86 for conference cases. A scale for the Embarrassment–Exposure factor consisted of five items (7, 8, 15, 16, and 17) and had a Cronbach's alpha coefficient of .88 for court cases and .80 for conference cases. Finally, the Unresolved Shame factor was represented by three items (20, 21, and 22) and had a Cronbach's alpha coefficient of .66 for court cases and .55 for conference cases.

As was expected on the basis of the principal component analysis, the scales were correlated with each other. Most notable is the strong

correlation between the Shame–Guilt and the Embarrassment–Exposure scales in both the court and conference settings (see Table 8.5). This outcome provides some insight into why discussions concerning the internal and external components of shame have failed to produce consensus. The internal and the external are difficult to disentangle.

Do the Observational Data Support the Findings based on Self-Reports?

It was predicted that the self-report measures of the shame-related emotions would be positively related to the observation of shame. To test

Table 8.4 Items Comprising the Shame–Guilt, Embarrassment–Exposure and Unresolved Shame Scales

Shame–Guilt

2	Felt the offense I committed was wrong.
3	Felt bad, the offense might have hurt someone.
6	Felt angry with myself for what I had done.
11	Felt ashamed of what I did.
12	Felt ashamed of myself.
19	Felt bad because actions hurt others.

Embarrassment–Exposure

7	Felt awkward and aware of myself.
8	Felt embarrassed as the center of attention.
15	Felt humiliated.
16	Felt uneasy surrounded by people who more important than me.
17	Felt so exposed, I wished to disappear.

Unresolved Shame

20	Continually bothered by thoughts (of being) unfairly judged by people.
21	Unable to decide whether or not I was in the wrong.
22	Some of the things brought up unresolved in mind.

Table 8.5 Product-moment Correlations between Factor Scores for Court (Conference) Cases

Scales	Shame–Guilt	Embarrassment–Exposure
Embarrassment–Exposure	.60** (.52**)	
Unresolved Shame	.11 [ns] (.00)[ns]	.34** (.15**)

** p<.01

this hypothesis, product-moment correlation coefficients were calculated between the observational items and the shame-related emotion scales. The results appear in Table 8.6. Findings differ for court and conference. In conference cases, the first four observational ratings which are measures of social awkwardness, did not correlate with any of the self-report scales. However, the last three observational ratings, which measure observations that the offender took responsibility for their actions, accepted that what they had done was wrong and felt sorry and remorseful, were positively associated with Shame–Guilt and Embarrassment–Exposure, and negatively correlated with Unresolved Shame.

For court cases, the pattern of relationships was weaker. Observational ratings of participants trying to avoid attention were positively correlated with Shame–Guilt and Embarrassment–Exposure. Observational ratings of offenders taking responsibility for their actions and accepting that what they had done was wrong were most likely to accompany low scores on Unresolved Shame as indicated by the negative correlation in Table 8.6. The fact that stronger linkages between observational and self-reported ratings were obtained in the conference setting than the court setting is not surprising. Court cases were much shorter and involved participants far less than conferences. Thus, observations in court were constrained by a short time-frame and high levels of inaction (and therefore non-responsiveness) to proceedings.

A second issue to note in relation to the observational data arises in relation to the conference findings. Potentially, the setting provided a good opportunity to observe social awkwardness and responsibility and remorse. Convergence of findings only emerged for the responsibility and remorse settings, however. We have yet to understand why the observational data on social awkwardness did not concur with participants' self-reports. At this stage, we are not ruling out the possibility that how people present themselves in a public, formal and novel forum tells us little about their feelings.

On the basis of these findings, only partial support can be claimed for the hypothesis:

Shame 4: *Observational measures of shame would be associated with the self-report measures.* The observation of social awkwardness is a weaker measure of the shame-related emotions than observation of responsibility and remorse.

The Meaning of Shame and Shame-related Emotions

Another approach to validating the shame-related constructs is through examining their empirical relations to other standard measures. For instance, some theorists have suggested that shame is less likely to be

associated with empathy but positively associated with anger and hostility. For example, Tangney (1991) argues that the emotion of shame is likely to prevent the individual from feeling empathy for others because of its inward focus. Phenomenological studies (Lindsay-Hartz, 1984; Wicker et al., 1983) report that the experience of shame is both a painful emotion and involves negative evaluation of the self. Neither of these features, it is argued by Tangney (1991), are consistent with empathy. The intense focus on oneself is incompatible with the outward attention required to take another's perspective and understand what emotions they are feeling, both central to feeling empathy (Eisenberg & Strayer, 1987; Feshbach, 1975; Mehrabian & Epstein, 1972). There is some evidence that in order to deflect or avoid the emotion, individuals sometimes use defensive mechanisms (H. B. Lewis,

Table 8.6 Product-moment Correlations between Observation and Self-reported Data on Shame-related Emotions for Court (Conference) Cases

Items	Shame–Guilt	Embarrassment–Exposure	Unresolved Shame
1 How much did the offender retreat from and avoid the attention of others?	0.14* (.01)[ns]	0.14* (.04) [ns]	0.00 [ns] (.01) [ns]
2 How much was the offender's speech affected by irregularities, pauses or incoherence?	.03 [ns] (.07)	.06 [ns] (.01) [ns]	.05 [ns] (.01) [ns]
3 How uncomfortable (e.g. restless, anxious, fidgety) was the offender?	.05 [ns] (.04) [ns]	.08 [ns] (.04) [ns]	.09 [ns] (.03) [ns]
4 To what extent did the offender engage in hiding (e.g. lowering head) and concealing (e.g. hand covering parts of the face, averting gaze) behavior?	.05 [ns] (.08) [ns]	.03 [ns] (.08) [ns]	.07 [ns] (.08) [ns]
5 How much responsibility did the offender take for their actions?	−.08 [ns] (.18**)	.03 [ns] (.05) [ns]	−.14* (−.12*)
6 To what extent did the offender accept that they had done wrong?	−.04 [ns] (.26**)	.03 [ns] (.12*)	−.14* (−.11*)
7 How sorry/remorseful was the offender for their actions?	.09 [ns] (.27**)	.10 [ns] (.18**)	−.07 [ns] (−.11*)

*p<.05   **p<.01

1971; Nathanson, 1992; Scheff & Retzinger, 1991). It is suggested that defensive mechanisms such as attacking others, withdrawal, and avoidance of the situation will act to prevent the individual from feeling empathy. Tangney (1991) finds empirical support for her theory: shame-proneness was negatively associated with empathic responsiveness, but guilt-proneness was positively associated with empathic responsiveness. Tangney suggests that the positive association between guilt-proneness and empathic responsiveness is a result of guilt being a far less painful emotion that is focused upon one's action rather than oneself.

Just as shame has been described as inhibiting empathy, shame is postulated as being positively associated with anger and hostility (Tangney et al., 1992a, 1996a). Again, it was hypothesized that it is the intense focus upon the self in shame that results in a positive relationship between shame and hostility. Most notably H. B. Lewis (1971) suggests that shame involves a sense of anger directed at the self, but when unacknowledged it can become redirected at others. Scheff (1994) and Retzinger (1991b) claim that unacknowledged shame can result in shame–rage spirals. A shame–rage spiral is a loop in which unacknowledged shame leads to hostility and anger towards others which in turn leads to increased shame and so on. Tangney et al. (1992a) have tested the relationships been shame, guilt and hostility, and have found that shame-proneness was associated with the disposition to feel anger and hostility, but on the whole guilt was not.

Previous research suggests that shame should be positively associated with hostility and negatively associated with empathy; guilt should be positively associated with empathy and not correlated with hostility. Given that the factor analysis failed to distinguish shame and guilt, the central question is whether the obtained dimensions of Shame–Guilt, Embarrassment–Exposure and Unresolved Shame relate to hostility and empathy in a theoretically interpretable manner.

In order to measure participants' empathy for others during the case, a scale consisting of two items was developed. The items were: 'During the conference/court case I found myself really affected by the emotions of those who had been hurt in some way' and 'In the conference/court case I began to understand what it actually felt like for those who had been affected by my actions.' The Cronbach's alpha for this scale was .68 for court cases and .68 for conference cases.

Another scale was developed to measure participants' feelings of anger/hostility after the case. The scale consisted of four items: 'You feel bitter about the way you were treated in the case', 'The conference/court case just made you angry', 'You feel that the people who accused you in the conference/court case were more wrong than you were' and 'You wish

you could get back at the people who were accusing you in the conference/court case.' The Cronbach's alpha for this scale was .69 for court cases and .69 for conference cases. These empathy and hostility scales were used to predict the set of self-reported emotions of Shame–Guilt, Unresolved Shame and Embarrassment–Exposure (Harris, 1999). Shame–Guilt was positively related to empathy but inversely related to anger/hostility. Unresolved Shame was linked to greater empathy as well as greater anger/hostility toward others. Embarrassment–Exposure was positively related to anger/hostility and not related to empathy.

Differentiating Shame from Guilt and Embarrassment

The emergence of three factors representing Shame–Guilt, Unresolved Shame and Embarrassment–Exposure has implications for a theoretical discussion of the relationship between shame and guilt, the relationship between shame and embarrassment and the conceptualization of shame.

The Relationship Between Shame and Guilt

One feature of the present analyses which are at odds with much of the empirical and theoretical work on shame is the failure to distinguish shame from guilt. Importantly, it appears unlikely that this is the result of a failure to represent the domain sufficiently well. Particular care was taken to ensure that all dimensions traditionally used to distinguish shame from guilt were included. Equally, it is difficult to explain this result simply by suggesting that the context was peculiar. The situation participants were asked about was one in which both emotions might have been expected. In both court and conference conditions the individual is in a situation where they publicly face up to having violated a law and are possibly aware of having violated their own moral standards. In both situations, but particularly conferences, the harm done to others is discussed, as is disapproval of the offense and the need for reparation.

One possible explanation for the finding that guilt and shame are not differentiated by the factor analysis lies in the methodology. Previous empirical approaches to differentiating shame and guilt have asked participants to report the phenomenology of previous shame and guilt experiences (Lindsay-Hartz, 1984; Tangney et al., 1996b; Wicker et al., 1983) or to report what they could have done differently to avoid such experiences (Niedenthal et al., 1994). As argued in the introduction, these studies effectively measure the characteristics participants associate with their conceptions of the emotions being measured. In some cases it is explicitly or implicitly communicated to participants that the goal of these studies is to

differentiate between guilt and shame. Thus, there is a degree to which previous methodologies have forced a distinction between the constructs that is not a feature of the factor analytic method. What past studies have demonstrated is that participants are able to conceptually distinguish shame from guilt on a number of dimensions. In contrast, this study measures the dimensionality of feeling states in a specific situation. Participants are not told that shame or guilt is of interest but simply respond to the degree to which they experienced certain feelings. This explanation would suggest that while there are widely recognized conceptual distinctions between shame and guilt, these distinctions do not necessarily reflect the way in which the emotions are experienced in a context in which wrongdoing has occurred.

If, as these results suggest, there is no empirical reason to distinguish shame from guilt, the findings reported have important implications for theoretical approaches to these emotions. One implication is that defining the differences between them may deserve less attention than it has traditionally received. Importantly, these results suggest that the feelings associated with shame and guilt are not incompatible. Some research has suggested that shame may be such a painful emotion that it prevents the individual from focusing on harm to the other (Tangney, 1991). This analysis is more supportive of the position taken by Bernard Williams (1993) who argues that guilt and shame almost always occur together and thus are complementary rather than alternative responses. From our data, where an individual is affected by the harm they have caused others, they are also likely to experience feelings of global self-evaluation. This finding makes intuitive sense. If someone feels guilt about having hurt another person it would seem odd if they did not also feel some shame because their actions had threatened their perception of the kind of person they are and their perception of how others judge them. In conclusion, these results suggest that in the context of criminal offending the distinction between guilt and shame may not be as important as has been suggested.

The Relationship Between Shame and Embarrassment

One distinction supported by the factor analysis is that between Shame–Guilt and Embarrassment–Exposure. While both the Shame–Guilt and Embarrassment–Exposure factors correlated highly and included items that signal concern for others' opinions or evaluations, there are important differences between them on the basis of other attributes. Most noticeably, the items that load exclusively on the Embarrassment–Exposure factor focus solely on feelings of self-consciousness. In contrast, Shame–Guilt is associated with feelings of a more ethical nature, such as how ethically one

has acted, whether others have been hurt, what others think of oneself and that one has lost honor in one's community. Thus, while Shame–Guilt involves feelings of concern regarding others' reactions to the shameful act, it is not characterized by feelings of social awkwardness.

This finding contradicts several previous empirical studies on shame. For example, Wicker et al. (1983) found that shame was highly associated with wanting to hide, feeling self-conscious and feeling exposed. Similarly, Lindsay-Hartz (1984) found that the examples which participants discussed when asked to report an incident of shame included feelings of being exposed, wanting to hide and feeling small. The cross-cultural literature also suggests that similar feelings are associated with shame (Wallbott & Scherer, 1995). Thus, a considerable amount of systematic research on shame has emphasized links with social awkwardness.

Differences between the current and previous studies regarding the distinctiveness of social awkwardness may be partly due to the fact that many previous studies have sought to distinguish shame from guilt without seeking to clarify the relationship with embarrassment (for an exception, see Tangney et al., 1996b). One study that has explicitly addressed this distinction, that of Tangney et al. (1996b), supports our claim that embarrassment is associated with greater feelings of self-awareness.

Another possible explanation for the differences between this research and other investigations of the shame and embarrassment link is that differentiating between these emotions is difficult for individuals. This hypothesis is consistent with the substantial relationship between shame and embarrassment found in this study (a correlation of .5 (conferences), .6 (court)) which demonstrates that the two emotions are often felt in conjunction with each other. Indeed, the strong association between these two emotions makes intuitive sense. If someone feels Shame–Guilt because they have been drink-driving, then they should also feel Embarrassment–Exposure when the incident is discussed with others or in front of an audience. This would imply that in many contexts the feelings of Shame–Guilt will be intimately tied to feelings of Embarrassment–Exposure and thus difficult to separate. It might be speculated that Embarrassment–Exposure is distinct from Shame–Guilt in this analysis because while Shame–Guilt is likely to trigger social awkwardness in a criminal justice setting, the relationship is not reciprocal. Embarrassment–Exposure does not imply remorse or internal sanctioning of oneself for one's actions (Shame–Guilt). For example, a committed participant in a criminal subculture might feel pride in their crime rather than shame, but they still might feel awkward and exposed while in court.

Despite the high correlation between Shame–Guilt and Embarrassment–Exposure, this analysis suggests that it is important to distinguish them.

The factor analysis shows that Shame–Guilt is associated with concern that one has hurt others, feeling that the offense was wrong, concern with substantive evaluations by others, anger directed at oneself, and loss of honor. In comparison, embarrassment is focused upon the social discomfort or self-consciousness resulting from a social situation. However, the substantial correlation between these factors suggests that this conclusion needs to be tested in other contexts to further validate the distinctiveness of these emotions.

Conceptualizing Shame

The factor analysis indicates that shame and guilt are not empirically distinct in these data. Although surprising, given the emphasis that has been placed upon distinguishing shame from guilt, this finding is consistent with aspects of the literature. For example, some theoretical perspectives such as affect theory (Nathanson, 1997; Tomkins, 1987) argue that a single shame affect is the basis for each of these socially constructed emotions. It is also evident that the dimensions upon which shame and guilt have been distinguished are sometimes confused in conceptions of shame and guilt. For example, the social threat conception of guilt and the personal failure conception of shame are similar in that both predict that the emotions occur in reference to internalized standards. Thus, it is not surprising that these two different conceptions of shame and guilt might refer to the same emotion. One conclusion from the empirical results reported in this chapter might be that shame and guilt should be conceptualized as a single emotion, or as two facets of a single emotion, that are closely related and complementary. The results here certainly question the distinctiveness that has been claimed for them at an empirical level.

Although the social threat, personal failure and ethical conceptions did not define distinctive dimensions, all three conceptions contribute to the phenomenology of Shame–Guilt. As predicted by the social threat conception, the Shame–Guilt factor involves a consciousness or fear of disapproval or rejection by others. Consistent with the personal failure conception, Shame–Guilt was represented by items that were clearly focused upon evaluation of the self. Finally, it was evident that Shame–Guilt also measured the feeling of having done something wrong, as predicted by the ethical conception. Thus, each of the primary predictions of each of the conceptions of shame is evident in the phenomenology of Shame–Guilt. This suggests that perhaps, in the past, different conceptualizations of shame and guilt have simply identified different facets of a single phenomenon.

Recent work in the field of criminal justice has highlighted the importance of another related emotion: remorse. Indeed, the expression of

remorse has for a long time been accepted as a reason for reducing the severity of punishments applied by judges to defendants (Costanzo & Costanzo, 1992; Taylor & Kleinke, 1992). Recent research on restorative justice conferences in New Zealand (Maxwell & Morris, 1999) has also suggested that feelings of remorse reported by offenders who attended conferences are associated with lower levels of persistent reconviction, a result confirmed on South Australian conferences by Daly (2000: p. 10). Interestingly, there are a number of similarities between the concept of remorse and the Shame–Guilt factor. In Maxwell and Morris's (1999) study, remorse was measured by the participants remembering the conference, feeling sorry for what they had done, expressing that they were sorry, feeling that they had repaired the damage they had caused, and completing the outcomes of the conference. Others have suggested that central to the concept of remorse are ideas of being responsible for a wrong and the wish that it had not occurred (Landman, 1993). It can be seen that the concept of remorse from both perspectives shares a number of similarities with Shame–Guilt. Indeed, Webster's dictionary defines remorse as a '. . . gnawing distress arising from a sense of guilt for past wrongs . . .'. This definition suggests that remorse might be conceptualized as a reparative response emerging from the sense of wrongdoing and concern for others, which is evident in Shame–Guilt. These suggestions are given some support by the finding that observation of feeling sorry or remorseful in conferences was correlated with self-reports of Shame–Guilt. It would seem important for future research to explore further the way remorse is related to or is part of Shame–Guilt.

Summary

This chapter provides insight into the structure of the shame-related emotions experienced by individuals who have attended either conferences or court cases after a drink-driving offense. Three shame-related emotions were identified in the factor analysis, one was a co-assembly of items measuring Shame–Guilt, the second measured feelings associated with non-resolution of the shameful situation, while the third was Embarrassment–Exposure. The Shame–Guilt factor suggests that a single emotion is associated with feelings of having done the wrong thing, fear of others' disapproval, concern that one has hurt others, feeling ashamed of one's actions, feeling ashamed of oneself, feeling anger at the self and loss of honor amongst one's community. This chapter has sought to provide a description of the emotion of shame. While answering some questions that are important to developing an understanding of the emotion, the chapter raises others. In particular, the role of Unresolved Shame has yet to be understood and integrated into our

conceptualization. Furthermore, the interaction between and causal sequencing of concern about the opinion of others and feelings of disappointment in oneself need much more research. Later chapters will attempt to answer some of these questions by exploring the association between shaming and the shame-related emotions.

APPENDIX 8A

Means (standard deviations) of RISE Observational Shame Items

Items		Conference cases	Court cases
1	How much did the offender retreat from attention?	2.68(1.71)	2.47(1.37)
2	How much was the offender's speech affected by irregularities, pauses, or incoherence?	2.77(1.74)	2.60(1.60)
3	How uncomfortable (e.g. restless, anxious, fidgety) was the offender?	4.26(1.85)	3.46(1.45)
4	To what extent did the offender engage in hiding (e.g. lowering head) and concealing (e.g. hand covering parts of the face, averting gaze) behavior?	2.94(1.92)	2.45(1.48)
5	How much responsibility did the offender take for their action?	6.94(1.46)	6.30(1.87)
6	To what extent did the offender accept that they had done wrong?	6.61(1.69)	6.03(1.97)
7	How sorry/remorseful was the offender for their actions?	5.21(2.05)	3.87(2.3)

Means (standard deviations) of RISE Interview Shaming Items across Contexts

Items		Conference cases	Court cases
Respect			
1	Did you learn from the conference/court case that there are people who care about you?	3.47 (0.81)	2.12 (1.13)
2	During the conference/court case did people suggest that they loved you regardless of what you did?	2.71 (1.15)	2.13 (1.26)
3	Were you treated as a trustworthy person in the conference/court?	3.11 (0.87)	2.47 (1.02)
4	During the conference/court case did people talk about aspects of yourself which they like?	2.73 (1.00)	1.75 (1.06)
Forgiveness			
5	At the end of the conference/court case, or since then, have people made it clear to you that you can put the whole thing behind you?	2.51 (1.12)	2.37 (1.11)

Means (standard deviations) of RISE Interview Shaming Items across Contexts (*cont*)

Items	Conference cases	Court cases
Forgiveness		
6 At the end of the conference/court case did people indicate that you were forgiven?	2.51 (1.00)	1.88 (1.05)
7 Did others at the conference/court case say that you had learnt your lesson and now deserve a second chance?	2.83 (1.03)	1.96 (1.13)
8 Even though the conference/court case is over do you still feel that others will not let you forget what you have done?	2.15 (1.11)	2.08 (1.05)
9 During the conference/court case did any of the people who are important to you reject you because of the offense?	1.16 (0.49)	1.16 (0.70)
10 Offender's mean perception of forgiveness expressed by those who were present at the case? #	0.73 (0.67)	0.19 (0.70)
Labeling		
11 Were you treated in the conference/court as though you were likely to commit another offense.	1.58 (0.84)	1.69 (0.88)
12 Did people during the conference/court case make negative judgements about what kind of person you are?	1.45 (0.79)	1.53 (0.89)
13 Did people in the conference/court case say that it was not like you to do something wrong?	2.92 (1.16)	1.81 (1.12)
14 During the conference/court case did people indicate that they accepted you as basically law abiding?	3.36 (0.81)	2.59 (1.02)
Master Status Trait		
15 During the conference/court case were you treated as though you were a criminal?	1.74 (0.85)	2.00 (0.97)
16 During the conference/court case were you treated as though you were a bad person?	1.70 (0.79)	1.76 (0.86)
Shaming		
17 Offenders mean perception of disapproval by those who were present at the case. #	1.51 (0.63)	1.23 (0.70)

These items were measured on a 5-point scale ranging from −2 to 2. All other items were measured on a 4-point scale from 1 to 4.

CHAPTER 9

Testing the Dimensionality of Shaming

While the last chapter was about the affect structure of shame, this chapter is about the behavioral structure of shaming. Understanding the effects of social disapproval, otherwise referred to as shaming, is essential to developing a more complete knowledge of shame. In the previous chapter a factor analysis of the shame-related emotions identified three distinct factors: Shame–Guilt, Embarrassment–Exposure and Unresolved Shame. Both the Shame–Guilt and Embarrassment–Exposure factors consisted of items that measured the individual's concern with disapproval by others. This finding is consistent with the social threat and ethical conceptions of shame identified in Chapter 6, which suggest that shaming plays an important causal role in the occurrence of shame. While the factor analysis in Chapter 8 provides insight into the phenomenology of Shame–Guilt, it cannot provide an adequate analysis of why people feel Shame–Guilt. This chapter will begin to tackle these issues by examining the process of shaming. Reintegrative shaming theory (Braithwaite, 1989) provides one way of analyzing shaming. It suggests that social disapproval can be reintegrative or stigmatic. Having in Part I provided the wider context in which reintegrative shaming was developed, this chapter focuses in much greater detail on the elements central to the theory. In particular, whether the concepts of reintegration, stigmatization and shaming can be operationalized as predicted.

Defining Important Components of Reintegrative Shaming Theory

A central tenet of reintegrative shaming theory is that shaming plays an important role in the regulation of behavior. The theory argues that the importance of informal processes of social disapproval have generally been

underestimated by criminal justice systems as well as by criminological theory. Furthermore, it is hypothesized that shaming is not uniform in the effect it has on behavior. Shaming varies along a continuum in the degree to which it is either stigmatizing or reintegrative of the individual. It is argued that shaming that is more reintegrative will have a more positive influence on behavior. Shaming that is stigmatizing, on the other hand, will have a negative influence (Makkai & Braithwaite, 1994). This brief description of the central hypotheses of reintegrative shaming theory identifies the three concepts that are essential to operationalize the theory: shaming, reintegration and stigmatization. Below we elaborate on the meaning of these constructs and their operationalizations in the RISE experiments.

Shaming as Disapproval

In *Crime, Shame and Reintegration*, Braithwaite (1989) defines shaming as:

> . . . all societal processes of expressing disapproval which have the intention or effect of invoking remorse in the person being shamed and/or condemnation by others who become aware of the shaming. (Braithwaite, 1989: p. 100)

An important aspect of this definition is that the concept of shaming covers a broad range of behaviors. Shaming is not described as necessarily public, humiliating or directed at demeaning the person being shamed. It might, for example, involve a discussion between parents and a child of how an act impacted upon others. In many of his writings Braithwaite has described the self-shaming of apology as the most effective form of shaming in shaping behavior.

A second aspect of this definition is that shaming is defined as '. . . having the intention or effect . . .' of invoking certain outcomes and thus is not necessarily intentional. For example, the intention of the parents in discussing how an act impacted upon others may not be to make the child feel shame. Nevertheless, reintegrative shaming theory suggests that we can describe what they are doing as communicating social disapproval, i.e. shaming. Finally, it is worth noting that shaming is not described as an extraordinary event but rather as a social process occurring in everyday life. Thus, shaming can also be thought of as expressions of disapproval that occur in many different social contexts.

Stigmatization as Rejection and Labeling of the Whole Self

The concept of disintegrative shaming is largely informed by the literature on labeling theory. This perspective argues that deviance is not a static phenomenon but rather is defined by the societal reaction to any given

behavior. In this way the community is described as defining both what and whom is deviant. It is this second aspect, the labeling of individuals as deviant, which is relevant to the concept of stigmatization. The action of labeling or classifying the person as having a deviant identity has important social and psychological significance. Erikson (1962) argues that the process involved in being charged with a crime, found guilty of it in a court and then sanctioned is particularly destructive because it ceremonially changes the position of the person in society to that of a deviant. Because such ceremonies in modern society are not followed by ceremonies that decertify this label of deviance, the individual remains marginalized. Labeling is described as a social process that impacts upon the individual in a number of ways. One impact involves a psychological process in which the individual's sense of identity is changed. Social validation that the individual is a criminal, thug, drug-pusher, results in the individual thinking of the self in this way. Labeling the individual also changes his or her status within society such that the community treats them as deviant, which can diminish their opportunities within society. It is also predicted that where labeling occurs, the individual can come to attain a master status trait in which the new deviant identity comes to dominate all other identities.

This characterization of the effect of the criminal justice system on offenders is the basis for Braithwaite's concept of stigmatization.

> Stigmatizing is disintegrative shaming in which no effort is made to reconcile the offender with the community. The offender is outcast, her deviance is allowed to become a master status, degradation ceremonies are not followed by ceremonies to decertify deviance. (Braithwaite, 1989: p. 101)

Reintegration as Forgiveness and Respectful Treatment

While stigmatization, based upon the concept of labeling, anchors one end of the shaming continuum, reintegration anchors the other. Unlike labeling theory, which proposes 'radical non-intervention' (Schur, 1973), reintegrative shaming theory argues that some forms of shaming produce positive influence. Indeed, reintegrative shaming is in many respects the expression of social disapproval without stigmatization. The theory argues that the key to this is focusing upon disapproval of the offender's act without denigrating the offender.

> Reintegrative shaming is shaming followed by efforts to reintegrate the offender back into the community of law-abiding or respectable citizens through words or gestures of forgivingness or ceremonies to decertify the offender as deviant. Shaming and reintegration do not occur simultaneously but sequentially, with reintegration occurring before deviance becomes a

master status. It is shaming which labels the act as evil while striving to preserve the identity of the offender as essentially good. It is directed at signifying evil deeds rather than evil persons in the Christian tradition of 'hate the sin and love the sinner'. Specific disapproval is expressed within relationships characterized by general social approval. (Braithwaite, 1989: p. 100–101)

The above definition identifies two central aspects of reintegration. The first of these is that for shaming to be reintegrative it must involve forgiveness or some form of decertification of deviance. While many criminal justice procedures act to certify the offender's deviance, reintegration places an emphasis on the expression of forgiveness once shaming is finished.

A second component of reintegrative shaming is that the shaming occurs in such a way that it is respectful of the person. It avoids labeling the offender as bad, so that shaming occurs within a continuum of approval of the person. While Braithwaite argues that shaming and reintegration are sequential, another important feature of the concept of reintegrative shaming is the (respectful) way shaming is conducted.

Relationships Among Shaming, Stigmatization, and Reintegration

As already discussed, the concepts of reintegration and stigmatization are conceptualized as two poles of a continuum upon which behavior towards an individual (or collectivity) can be described (Makkai & Braithwaite, 1994). It is also evident that the reintegration–stigmatization continuum is always paired with the concept of shaming. Thus, all shaming can be evaluated on the degree to which it is reintegrative–stigmatic. This structure identifies two dimensions upon which shaming can be measured: (1) the extent of shaming that occurs, and (2) the type of shaming expressed, i.e. reintegrative shaming, stigmatizing shaming. In this way a small degree of shaming, for example mild disapproval, could be either reintegrative or stigmatic, as could a profoundly sweeping act of shaming.

Two predictions regarding the dimensionality of reintegrative shaming can be made. The first of these is that reintegration and stigmatization are bipolar opposites and as such will form a single dimension. The second prediction is that shaming will form a separate dimension to reintegration and stigmatization.

Shaming 1: *Reintegration and stigmatization would form opposite poles of a single dimension.*

Shaming 2: *Shaming would form a dimension independent of reintegration and stigmatization.*

Braithwaite describes reintegration and stigmatization as if they are unidimensional constructs, albeit with component features. Makkai and Braithwaite (1994) provided the first empirical test of the theory and represented the components of reintegration and stigmatization using a facet structure. This facet structure is in most part an extension of the original definitions of reintegration and stigmatization quoted above. Stigmatizing shaming is defined as lacking forgiveness, labeling of the offender and allowing the offender to develop a deviant master status trait. Reintegration is described as involving forgiveness and an attitude of respect towards the offender. Makkai and Braithwaite (1994) use these characteristics to propose four facets that define the continuum between reintegration and stigmatization (see Table 9.1).

A facet structure such as the one described here does not necessarily imply that the facets are independent. In many cases facets simply outline those characteristics which describe a single concept. However, it is also possible that these facets may define dimensions that are empirically distinct. In order to test this possibility it is hypothesized that:

Shaming 3: *The facets of reintegration and stigmatization defined by Makkai and Braithwaite (1994) would form distinct dimensions.*

Previous Tests of Reintegrative Shaming Theory

Many studies have found reintegrative shaming theory useful for post hoc interpretation of results (Chamlin & Cochrane, 1997; Hagan & McCarthy, 1997; Sampson & Laub, 1993: p. 122; Sherman, 1992, 1993; Zhang et al., 1996), but relatively few empirical studies have operationalized and tested

Table 9.1 Four Facets of Reintegration and Stigmatization

Facets	Reintegration	Stigmatization
Respect	• Disapproval while sustaining a relationship of respect;	• Disrespectful disapproval, humiliation;
Forgiveness	• Ceremonies to certify deviance terminated by ceremonies to decertify deviance;	• Ceremonies to certify deviance *not* terminated by ceremonies to decertify deviance;
Labeling	• Disapproval of the evil of the deed without labeling the person as not evil;	• Labeling the person, not only the deed, as evil;
Master status trait	• Not allowing deviance to become a master status trait	• Allowing deviance to become a master status trait

reintegrative shaming theory (Hay, 2001; Lu, 1998, 1999; Zhang, 1995; Zhang and Zhang, 2000).

One empirical study by Makkai and Braithwaite (1994) used reintegrative shaming to explain levels of compliance by nursing homes to a newly introduced set of 31 regulatory standards. Compliance data were collected from inspectors' reports for two consecutive years. Reintegrative shaming was measured through asking inspection teams about the regulatory strategies they employed on the job. Shaming was measured using a two-item scale that asked inspectors their attitude towards expressing disapproval. Reintegration was measured by a further six questions representing the facets of forgiveness and respect. Neither of the facets, labeling nor master status trait, were operationalized by Makkai and Braithwaite (1994) because the offender in this particular regulatory domain was the organization rather than an individual.

The results from this study provide strong support for the hypothesis that reintegrative shaming leads to higher rates of compliance. A significant interaction between shaming and reintegration–stigmatization showed that high levels of shaming combined with high levels of reintegration produced a greater increase in compliance than low levels of shaming that were reintegrative or high levels of shaming that were stigmatizing (see Figure 9.1). While reintegrative shaming produced a 39 per cent increase in compliance, stigmatizing shaming produced a 39 per cent decrease in compliance.

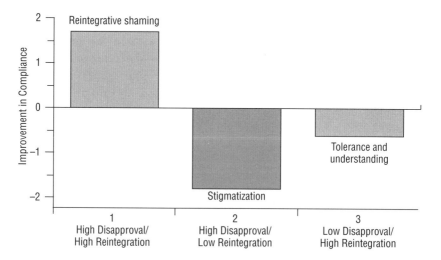

Figure 9.1 Mean Improvement in Compliance for Nursing Homes Where Inspectors Used High Disapproval and High Reintegration Styles; High Disapproval and Low Reintegration Styles; Low Disapproval and High Reintegration Styles (N=129; F-Value=3.58; p=.03) (From Makkai & Braithwaite, 1994)

Tolerance of non-compliance (low shaming and high reintegration) also produced a decrease in compliance, but not as great as that for stigmatizing shaming. This pattern of results is consistent with the predictions made by reintegrative shaming theory that shaming is important in changing compliance and also that reintegrative shaming is more effective than stigmatizing shaming.

These results have received some support from a recent study by Maxwell and Morris (1999), although these authors did not set out to operationalize and test the theory of reintegrative shaming. The object of this study was to survey all the factors that predicted variation in offending six and a half years after a restorative justice conference. As it happened, the Maxwell and Morris 'shame' measure was operationalized consistently with stigmatization, as it focused upon denigration of the offender. The results show that those offenders who recall being made to feel bad about the self during the conference were more likely to be persistent offenders. Thus, as with the Makkai and Braithwaite (1994) nursing home study, stigmatizing shaming was related to increased offending. Maxwell and Morris (1999) also found 'remorse' closer to the Shame–Guilt factor in Chapter 6 (and therefore a dimension of shame as an emotion rather than a dimension of shaming as a practice) to explain reduced reoffending.

A recent study by Hay (2001) of US adolescents' perceptions of how much reintegration and shaming was used by their parents in their upbringing found that both shaming and reintegration predicted projected delinquency, though the reintegration effect disappeared after controlling for interdependency (which according to the theory is causally prior to reintegration). And there was no Shaming x Reintegration interaction as in Makkai and Braithwaite (1994). Also in the US Zhang and Zhang (2000) found main effects for parental forgiveness (reintegration) and peer disapproval (shaming) in reducing delinquency, but again there was no significant Shaming x Reintegration interaction.

An earlier test of the theory focuses on juvenile offending and the use of reintegrative shaming in families from different ethnic backgrounds (Zhang, 1995). The study interviewed the parents of male delinquents, of either African-American or Asian-American ethnicity, who were sentenced by a court to 'home on probation' for the first time. The study hypothesized a cultural difference in how parents supervized and managed their children. Asian-American parents were expected to use more reintegrative shaming than African-American parents. The concepts of shaming and reintegration were measured through an interview with the boy's parents after the court case. Shaming was broken into a number of types: non-verbal (e.g. angry looks), verbal, physical (e.g. spanking in front of others) and communitarian (e.g. talking to others about the offense). These different categories of

disapproval were measured using 22 items that were summed to form a shaming scale. Reintegration was operationalized using a series of questions measuring the parents' interdependency with the delinquent boy, a question asking whether the parents forgave their child for the offense and another question which asked their opinion regarding their child's 'goodness'. These items were summed to form a single measure of reintegration. Contrary to expectations, very few differences were found between African-Americans and Asian-Americans in either their use of shaming or reintegration.

The non-significant result found by Zhang (1995) may have occurred because of a number of factors. Zhang's study is based on the assumption that Asian-American families have a lower offending rate than African-Americans because of different shaming practices. Yet the sample used was not representative of African-American and Asian-American communities. The sample comprised families in which the child had already offended. If shaming practices are related to offending rates, a key prediction of reintegrative shaming theory, one would not expect cultural differences between those segments of the African-American and Asian-American populations where an offense had already taken place.

The second reason for Zhang's (1995) non-significant result may involve the use of interdependency as a proxy for reintegration. Braithwaite suggests that reintegrative shaming is facilitated by interdependency, but the two should not be equated. Interdependency refers to a reciprocal positive relationship, in this case between the parent and child, and is a much broader concept than reintegration. Furthermore, interdependency is a measure of an ongoing relationship, whereas reintegration-stigmatization is a measure of how an individual or group reacts in a specific context. So while the measurement of shaming is consistent with the theory, the measurement of reintegration may lack adequate focus.

Both the studies by Makkai and Braithwaite (1994) and Zhang (1995) highlight a number of important issues for operationalization of the theory. Although Zhang identified four categories of shaming behavior and measured them using 22 items, he nevertheless reports reservations about whether the measures were sensitive to subtle forms of shaming. For example, interviewers reported that parents behaved as if they were ashamed of their children's behavior, but the behavioral response was not always captured by the items. Furthermore, spontaneous facial expressions indicating disapproval were not always deliberate behaviors open for discussions with the interviewer:

> The problem is how to translate these subtle and involuntary non-verbal cues into measurable variables; and more important, whether parents can remember or are aware of ever using them. (Zhang, 1995: p. 259)

While Zhang tried to capture specific and discrete behavioral measures of shaming through his self-report scale (e.g. 'Did you . . . say to him something like, "you are such a disgrace to your family"?'), Makkai and Braithwaite used much more subjective questions which required the shamer to report their general approach or attitude in their role as a nursing home regulation inspector (e.g. 'After I have had a battle with a nursing home, whether I win or lose, I like to forgive and forget.'). It would seem, on the basis of these studies, that shaming may be more successfully measured by questions which allow the participant to report their inter-pretation of their behavior rather than identifying discrete behaviors. However, while Makkai and Braithwaite's operationalization of the theory through general questions produced more encouraging results, it is also apparent that their research did not measure what actually happened, but rather how inspectors perceived themselves behaving at inspection events. How well such an indirect measure predicts actual behavior is uncertain, making this a less satisfactory method of operationalization. Measures such as Zhang's, that ask participants about what actually occurred in the specific situation have greater face validity. Both the studies outlined above have limitations in their operationalization of the theory of reintegrative shaming. Furthermore, they proceed from the assumption that the facets are inter-correlated. Whether or not the facets are highly related and whether reintegration and stigmatization represent opposite poles of one dimension is yet to be empirically tested.

On the basis of these early studies, a number of approaches might be employed to improve measurement of shaming and reintegration. One approach might involve observation. Measuring shaming and reintegrative behavior through observing the shamer would be consistent with reinte-grative shaming theory because the theory focuses on the behavior directed towards an individual rather than on the individual's attitude towards that behavior or its end result.

At the same time, arguments for a self-report approach can be made using, as a base, research findings on stressful events (see Lazarus, DeLongis, Folkman & Gruen, 1985) and their consequences for well-being. This substantial body of research has moved toward recognizing perception and appraisal of events as more important predictors of adaptation than the events themselves. Psychological factors have been shown to affect the way in which events are understood by individuals, and it is this understanding that is the critical factor in shaping well-being, not the severity of the event itself. These findings have implications for the measurement of reintegrative shaming. While reintegrative shaming can be seen as a set of objective behaviors, it is also true that they usually occur in the context of long-held relationships. The individual's interpretation of others' behavior as

disapproving, reintegrative or stigmatizing is based on a multitude of factors relating to the individual's relationship with these individuals. Considerations such as past conflicts, knowledge of others' expectations and moral standards, suggest that a measure of reintegrative shaming based upon the shamed person's perceptions may be a more critical measure in shaping future offending than the objective and contextualized measures of behavior made by an impartial observer.

Given the strengths and weaknesses of both the observational and self-report measures, a useful approach is to test both kinds of measures in the empirical context. The use of multiple methods, based upon the principle of triangulation (see Denzin, 1988), employs a range of measures with different sources of error; the expectation is that weaknesses of one method will be counter-balanced by strengths of the other and that conclusions will be stronger if they are based on findings that are robust across methods. It is expected that although observational and self-report measures will differ in significant ways, they will also provide evidence of triangulation. The following hypothesis will be tested in this regard:

Shaming 4: *Observational and self-report measures of reintegrative shaming would demonstrate evidence of triangulation.*

Reintegration, Stigmatization and Shaming in Court and Conference Cases

Conferences should be characterized by more reintegrative shaming and thus less stigmatizing shaming than court cases. Conferences are believed to be potentially more reintegrative than traditional court procedures for a number of reasons. One of the main reasons is that a significant number of the people invited to the conference are those who care for and are respected by the offender. The role of these people is to support and help the offender through the conference. This is quite different from court where there is much less involvement by the offender's community and where witnesses are sometimes used to harm the offender's case. A second but related factor is the focus of the conference procedure on the offense and its consequences rather than on the character of the offender. Both these factors mean that conferences are intended to involve offenders in a ritual where people care for and respect them and where they are less likely to be labeled as deviant.

Another important aspect of conferencing is the role of victims and the emphasis on resolving outstanding issues between the offender and victim. As part of the conferencing process victims are able to relate the impact of the offense upon them and ask for reparation from the offender. In many

cases this provides the opportunity for the offender to apologize and make reparation to all those affected, which in turn facilitates the forgiveness of the offender. In most cases forgiveness at an informal and formal level is structured into the conferencing procedure. In comparison, court cases rarely involve victims and so rarely provide the opportunity for the victim to relate the consequences of the offense or for the offender to make direct reparations to the victim. These factors, as well as the rational, impersonal nature of court, provide much less opportunity for the expression of forgiveness at court.

Here we report on data collected from drink-driving conferences. As pointed out in Chapter 7, these conferences are different from many others because they do not involve a direct victim. In the Australian Capital Territory program this role is replaced by a community representative whose role is to discuss the consequences of drink-driving from the perspective of the whole community. Despite this difference there is no reason to expect these conferences to be less respectful and caring of the offender, less forgiving of the offender, less focused on the evil of the incident rather than the evil of the offender, or more likely to allow the offender to develop a deviant master status trait than other conferences. Indeed, drink-driving conference design and facilitator training were oriented towards sustaining these objectives. Our next hypothesis is:

Shaming 5: *Conference cases would be more reintegrative than court cases.*

The Dimensionality of Shaming

The dimensionality of shaming was examined using responses to the items in the offender interview from the RISE data (see Chapter 7). Shaming was operationalized using offenders' perceptions of how much others disapproved of what they had done. Participants were asked about the disapproval of each person whom they felt played a significant role at the conference or court case: 'Next, I would like to get some idea about what each of these people thought of the offense you committed. Again starting with . . . [Mary] . . . would you say that s/he: strongly approved, approved . . .' Responses were recorded on a five-point scale ranging from 'strongly approved' to 'strongly disapproved'. The mean score for all participants was calculated and this provided a single shaming measure.

Reintegration–stigmatization was measured by a series of 16 questions that assessed the four facets outlined by Makkai and Braithwaite: respect, forgiveness, labeling and master status trait. Four respect items (see items 1 to 4, Table 9.2) asked the offender to indicate the degree to which they were treated as a person who was trusted, cared for and loved. Responses

were recorded on a four-point scale ranging from 'not at all' to 'a lot'.

Three of the six forgiveness questions (items 5 to 10, Table 9.2) asked if others present at the case had made it clear to the offender that they could put the offense behind them (item 5), indicated that they were forgiven (item 6), and said that they deserved a second chance (item 7). Two questions (item 8 and 9) were reverse scored as they were negatively worded, measuring the absence of forgiveness. One item (item 10) asked specifically about each person whom the subject remembered as being present at the case: 'Next, I would like to get some idea of how much each of these people forgave you at the end of the conference/court case? Starting with . . . [Mary] . . . would you say s/he was . . .' Responses were recorded on a five-point scale ranging from 'very unforgiving' (–2) to 'very forgiving' (2). The mean score for all those at the case was calculated to provide a single measure.

Labeling was measured using four questions (items 11 to 14, Table 9.2). Two of the questions (items 11 and 12) asked if the participant was treated as though they were likely to commit the offense again and if negative judgments were made about that person. The remaining two questions (items 13 and 14) were reverse scored: participants were asked if others treated them as though they were basically law-abiding and if others said that it was not like them to do something wrong. Responses were again recorded on a four-point scale.

The final facet, master status trait, was measured by two items (items 15 and 16, Table 9.2) which asked participants first if they were treated like a criminal and second if they were treated like a bad person. Again, responses to these questions were recorded on a four-point scale ranging from 'not at all' to 'a lot'.

The shaming, reintegration and stigmatization questions were asked with the interviewer reading out each question and the participant recording the answer in a separate booklet. Means and standard deviations of shaming, reintegration and stigmatization items are reported in Appendix 8A.

The responses to the 17 shaming, reintegration and stigmatization questions were used to test some of the assumptions of reintegrative shaming theory. The self-report measures developed for this purpose had not previously been used so that their validity and reliability were unknown. Questions about reliability and validity of the measures were made more acute by the fact that relatively few other researchers have attempted to operationalize these variables. Thus, in order to explore the measures prior to testing the hypotheses, the sample was randomly divided into two parts. One half of the sample was used for two exploratory factor analyses (one for court cases and one for conference cases) in order to examine how the items behaved as measures of shaming, reintegration and stigmatization in

Table 9.2 The Interview Items Across Contexts

Respect

---

1   Did you learn from the conference/court case that there are people who care about you?
2   During the conference/court case did people suggest that they loved you regardless of what you did?
3   Were you treated as a trustworthy person in the conference/court case?
4   During the conference/court case did people talk about aspects of yourself which they like?

Forgiveness

---

5   At the end of the conference/court case, or since then, have people made it clear to you that you can put the whole thing behind you?
6   At the end of the conference/court case did people indicate that you were forgiven?
7   Did others at the conference/court case say that you had learnt your lesson and now deserve a second chance?
8   Even though the conference/court case is over do you still feel that others will not let you forget what you have done?
9   During the conference/court case did any of the people who are important to you reject you because of the offense?
10 Offender's mean perception of forgiveness expressed by those who were present at the case. #

Labeling

---

11 Were you treated in the conference/court case as though you were likely to commit another offense?
12 Did people during the conference/court case make negative judgments about what kind of person you are?
13 Did people in the conference/court case say that it was not like you to do something wrong?
14 During the conference/court case did people indicate that they accepted you as basically law abiding?

Master Status Trait

---

15 During the conference/court case were you treated as though you were a criminal?
16 During the conference/court case were you treated as though you were a bad person?

Shaming

---

17 Offenders *mean* perception of disapproval by those who were present at the case. #

These items were measured on a 5-point scale ranging from -2 to 2. All other items were measured on a 4-point scale from 1 to 4.

the court and conference contexts. The data from the second half of the sample were subjected to a confirmatory factor analysis in order to test the central hypotheses concerned with the structure of reintegration, stigmatization and shaming: Shaming 1, Shaming 2 and Shaming 3.

An Exploratory Analysis of the Self-Report Data

A preliminary analysis of the 17 variables measuring reintegration, stigmatization and shaming in court and conference contexts revealed that a number of items (5, 8, 9 and 17) had low squared multiple correlations (SMCs). When included in the factor analysis these items had low loadings on all factors. One other item (item 10) posed a similar problem in the analysis of the conference data, although it was highly correlated with items in the court data. Accordingly, these variables were considered outliers (Tabachnick & Fidell, 1989) and were excluded from the respective factor analyses.

Exclusion of item 17 is most significant, as this is the only item measuring shaming. A low SMC does not necessarily mean that the item is a poor measure but might alternatively indicate that the item measures a distinct dimension. Thus, although removed from the factor analyses, the relationship between shaming and the other items can be and should be assessed separately.

Factor analyses of the remaining items from the court (13 items) and conference (12 items) data sets produced solutions that were rotated using the varimax procedure. This produced highly similar results in the two data sets (see Appendix 9A for rotated factor structures). Using eigenvalues greater than 1 and the scree test as the number of factors criteria (Cattell, 1966; Gorsuch, 1983), two factors were extracted in each context, accounting for 51 per cent (court) and 35 per cent (conference) of the variance.

The first factor represented reintegration. The items that defined the factor reflected the offenders' belief that they were respected, liked, cared for and forgiven, and that others believed in them. The primary difference between court and conference cases concerning this factor (reintegration) is the importance of the item measuring the expression of love by others (item 2). While this is the most marginal item in the court factor analysis it has the highest loading on reintegration in the conference factor analysis. This difference is not surprising in light of our extensive observations of court and conference cases. Expressions of love might be expected to have more shared variance with reintegration in conferences because it is a behavior that is encouraged in this context. In contrast, the behavior, while remaining an expression of reintegration, may be suppressed as inappropriate in court cases.

The second factor represented stigmatization. The items represented the offenders' perception that they were bad, that others considered them as a criminal, and as someone who would offend again. The overall theme of the factor was perceiving the self in negative terms. Thus the factor captures the concept of negative image of the whole self that is at the heart of stigmatization.

As is evident from the factor analysis with court cases (see Appendix 9A), items 3, 10 and 14 had moderate loadings on both factors. The factor analysis for conference cases also showed that two of these three items (items 3 and 14) had moderate loadings on both factors. All three items represented the opposite pole of the labeling facet (positive labeling in effect). As such, they capture some of the meaning associated with respect for the offender, which may explain why they load on the reintegration factor as well as the stigmatization factor.

Apart from providing a two-factor model for testing in a confirmatory factor analysis, these preliminary analyses allowed for an evaluation of which items proved best as measures of the factors. It was evident from the communalities that a number of items did not measure factors equally well in both contexts. The perception that others expressed love for the offender (item 2) was a poor measure in court cases but not in conference cases, while the mean perception of others' forgiveness (item 10) was a poorer measure in conferences than in court. In addition to variation between contexts it was also evident that a number of items (items 3 and 14) were relatively poor measures in both contexts because they measured both factors with only moderate success. Items that were not strong measures in both contexts were omitted in the confirmatory analysis.

Testing the Dimensionality Hypotheses

Having used an exploratory factor analysis on half of the sample to develop measures of reintegration and stigmatization, a confirmatory analysis was performed on the other half to test whether this structure provided a sound description of the data. Court and conference data were combined for this analysis. The model tested is depicted in Figure 9.2 and involved nine items. Items 1, 4, 6, 7 and 13 were predicted by the model to load on one factor called reintegration, while items 11, 12, 15 and 16 were predicted to load on a stigmatization factor. The variance of the factors was constrained to equal one, while the factor loadings of variables and the correlation between factors were unconstrained. This model is depicted in Figure 9.2.

This model was estimated using the maximum likelihood estimation procedure in EQS version 4 (Bentler, 1993). The goodness-of-fit chi-square

of 35.39 (*df*, 26, *p* = 0.1) indicated that the model fitted the data fairly well. The high Comparative Fit Index score of .989 supported this conclusion. Although such statistics are said to be fairly robust both in terms of non-normal data and categorical variables (Bollen, 1989), the model was also tested using the Satorra-Bentler scaled chi-square with the resulting score of 34.14 (*df* 26, *p* = .13), which shows little variation from the unscaled score.

This procedure was repeated using polychoric correlations, which are correlations calculated on the assumption of normally distributed categorical data. It should be noted that the sample size is less than ideal for this methodology. The results should therefore be treated with some caution. The resulting chi-square was 82.08 (*df* 26, p< .00) which implies that the model does not adequately describe the data. However, the parameter estimates did not differ substantially between the polychoric and initial model. It was also evident that the Comparative Fit Index also calculated using the polychoric correlations was .96, indicating a good fit between model and data. The combined analyses suggest that the

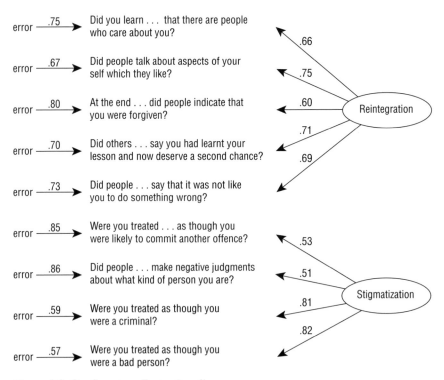

Figure 9.2 Confirmatory Factor Loadings

two-factor model is an adequate description of the data analyzed.

The exploratory factor analyses and the confirmatory analysis define reintegration and stigmatization as separate and uncorrelated factors, an outcome inconsistent with hypothesis Shaming 1. To test if reintegration and stigmatization are opposite poles of a single dimension the correlation between reintegration and stigmatization was constrained to -1. The chi-square for this nested model ($\chi^2 (27) = 399.23$) indicated that it was a poor fit of the data. Furthermore, a chi-square significance test indicates that the nested model was significantly worse ($\chi^2 (1) = 363.84$, $p > .01$) than the unconstrained model. This suggests that stigmatizing and reintegrative shaming should be conceptualized as separate dimensions and not as opposite poles of one dimension. It was not possible to test a confirmatory model that defined separate factors representing the respect, forgiveness, labeling and master status trait facets outlined by Makkai and Braithwaite, as the limited number of items would prevent identification of the model. However, the high degree of fit found for the non-facet model together with the low standardized residuals between the forgiveness and respect items and the labeling and master status trait items, provides evidence that the facets are not separate dimensions.

Is shaming independent of reintegration and stigmatization? To answer this question, scales measuring reintegration and stigmatization were created based on the confirmatory factor structure. The reintegration scale had a Cronbach's alpha coefficients of .70 for conference cases and .76 for court cases. The stigmatization scale had a Cronbach's alpha coefficient of .70 for conference cases and .81 for court cases. These reliability coefficients demonstrate the scales' reliability in both contexts. Product-moment correlation coefficients between these scales and the shaming measure were calculated and are presented in Table 9.3. The correlations show no significant relationship between shaming and either reintegration or stigmatization for conference cases and only a very low correlation between stigmatization and shaming for court cases. This suggests that both reintegration and stigmatization are distinct from shaming.

Table 9.3 Product-moment Correlations between Reintegration, Stigmatization and Shaming for Court (Conference) Cases

Scales	Shaming	Stigmatization
Stigmatization	$-.03$ [ns] (.12*)	
Reintegration	.03 [ns] (.00) [ns]	$-.05$ [ns] (-.12*)

*p<.05

Do the Observational Data Support the Findings Based on Self-Reports?

Observational measures of reintegration, stigmatization and shaming formed part of the Global Observational Rating Instrument completed by observers after each conference or court case. Having been present during the case, observers were required to answer questions on the basis of their general impression of events. All sources of information, including the duration, quality, and source of interactions, non-verbal behaviors, and paralinguistic cues were to be taken into account.

Initial analyses of the observational data showed that there were marked differences between the court and conference cases. The observed scores for court cases were so low that most of the items were severely skewed. This was particularly evident for the stigmatization items, a number of which involved distributions so severely skewed that more than 90 per cent of cases recorded the same score. Observations of the conference cases produced more normal distributions. However, even here it was evident that the stigmatization items involved extreme distributions such that most of the cases recorded the lowest possible score. This finding is consistent with Harris and Burton (1998) who reported that the inter-rater reliability of many of the stigmatization items could not be assessed in their small sample due to the truncated nature of the data. The addition of more cases has not altered this situation. As a result, it was decided that factor analysis of these data would be futile. Thus, in order to test the hypothesis regarding triangulation between the interview and observation data (Shaming 4), individual items from the Global Observational Rating Instrument that measured reintegration, stigmatization and shaming were correlated with the self-report scales. The correlations show that in both conference and court cases, self-report and observational measures of reintegration correlate significantly, with the exception of one forgiveness item in the court cases.

Efforts to achieve triangulation among measures of stigmatization were less successful overall. For conference cases, two of the three observational items were significantly correlated with the self-report stigmatization scale. Only one of the three observational items was significantly correlated with self-reports for the court cases. Of interest, however, is the finding that in court cases, observation of low forgiveness is associated with self-reported stigmatization. This suggests that in court cases, it may be an observable lack of forgiveness that best captures the expression of stigmatization.

The results provide no evidence of triangulation between the observational and self-report measures of shaming in either court or conference. However, from Table 9.4 it is evident that observation of shaming in court cases is linked with perceptions of being stigmatized. In contrast, the

Table 9.4 Product-moment Correlations between Self-report and Observational Measures of Shaming for Court (Conference) Cases

Items	Reintegration	Stigmatization	Shaming
Reintegration items			
How much support was the offender given during the conference/court case?	.34** (.29**)	-.03 [ns] (.01) [ns]	.03 [ns] (-.05) [ns]
How much approval of the offender as a person was expressed?	.45** (.40**)	-.10 [ns] (.04) [ns]	.04 [ns] (-.04) [ns]
How much respect for the offender was expressed?	.37** (.34**)	-.10 [ns] (.06) [ns]	-.01 [ns] (.01) [ns]
To what extent was the offender forgiven for their actions?	.09 [ns] (.29**)	-.19** (.01) [ns]	-.09 [ns] (-.02) [ns]
How clearly was it communicated to the offender that they could put their actions behind them?	.18** (.19**)	-.15** (-.09) [ns]	.00 [ns] (.03) [ns]
Stigmatization items			
How much stigmatizing shaming was expressed?	-.06 [ns] (-.08) [ns]	.06 [ns] (.14**)	.08 [ns] (-.10) [ns]
To what extent was the offender treated as a criminal?	-.14 [ns] (-.03) [ns]	.05 [ns] (.16**)	.05 [ns] (-.07) [ns]
How much disapproval of the offender as a person was expressed?	-.02 [ns] (-.04) [ns]	.15** (.08) [ns]	.12 [ns] (-.02) [ns]
Shaming items			
How much disapproval of this type of offense was expressed?	.00 [ns] (.02) [ns]	.18** (.09) [ns]	.04 [ns] (.01) [ns]
How much disapproval of the offender's act was expressed?	-.03 [ns] (-.04) [ns]	.21** (.08) [ns]	.08 [ns] (.08) [ns]

* p <.05   **p<.01

observation of shaming in conference cases was not significantly correlated with participants' perceptions of stigmatization. This result implies that the context in which shaming was communicated, i.e. court or conference, affects the way it is perceived.

The results provided mixed support for triangulation across methods. There are a number of reasons why the relationships of self-report with observational data are variable. One explanation is that the observational measures were not sensitive enough to detect subtle forms of stigmatization. Indeed, as discussed, observational measures of stigmatization had extremely low means and skewed distributions.

Another explanation is that the temporal framing used for collecting observational and self-report data is different. Observational data were drawn from the time spent in the courtroom. In contrast, self-report data also included what occurred before and after the case. For example, the self-report measure of shaming was not restricted to disapproval expressed in the case but a more general evaluation of how much particular individuals disapproved of the offense. These issues will be addressed later in the discussion.

Comparing Court and Conference Cases

To test the hypothesis that conferences are more reintegrative and less stigmatizing than court, mean scores for the self-report and observational measures were calculated (see Table 9.5). Differences between the two groups were tested using independent samples t-tests and the Type 1 error rate was protected using Dunn's multiple comparison procedure (Kirk, 1982). As can be seen from Table 9.5, the self-report measures show that conference participants perceived more reintegration and less stigmatization than court participants. However, the difference between court and conference for stigmatization was quite small.

Comparative analyses using the observational indices suggest a similar pattern to the self-report scales. Conference cases were significantly higher than court cases for each of the measures of reintegration. However, the stigmatization items present conflicting results. The offender was observed as being treated more like a criminal in court, as hypothesized, but in conflict with expectations, the offender was observed as being more strongly disapproved of as a person in the conference. The more general item measuring stigmatizing shaming was not significantly different for court and conference cases. With regard to the shaming measures, the self-report and observational data pointed to the same conclusion. Shaming, that is, the act of disapproving of the offender's behavior (not the person) was higher in conferences than in court. Overall, the results from the observational data are largely supportive of the hypothesis:

Shaming 5: *Conference cases would be more reintegrative than court cases.*

Table 9.5 Means and standard deviation for the Self-report and Observational Scales for Court and Conference Cases

	Court mean (SD)	Conference mean (SD)	t-value (df)
Self-report scales			
Reintegration scale	1.9 (0.8)	2.9 (0.7)	18.0** (711)
Stigmatization scale	1.7 (0.7)	1.6 (0.6)	2.63* (711)
Shaming item	1.2 (0.7)	1.5 (0.6)	5.62** (707)
Observational scales			
Reintegration items			
How much support was the offender given during the conference / court case?	2.4 (1.6)	5.8 (1.6)	29.17** (764)
How much approval of the offender as a person was expressed?	2.2 (1.6)	4.8 (2.0)	19.46** (761)
How much respect for the offender was expressed?	2.6 (1.6)	4.6 (2.0)	17.20** (764)
To what extent was the offender forgiven for their actions?	1.2 (0.8)	3.8 (2.5)	18.89** (762)
How clearly was it communicated to the offender that they could put their actions behind them?	1.5 (1.3)	4.1 (2.3)	19.59** (761)
Stigmatization items			
How much stigmatizing shaming was expressed?	1.4 (1.2)	1.6 (.96)	1.83 (763)
To what extent was the offender treated as a criminal?	1.6 (1.2)	1.3 (0.7)	4.07** (764)
How much disapproval of the offender as a person was expressed?	1.2 (0.6)	2.1 (1.2)	12.07** (765)
Shaming items			
How much disapproval of this type of offense was expressed?	2.3 (1.8)	6.0 (1.9)	27.91** (742)
How much disapproval of the offender's act was expressed?	2.6 (1.7)	4.9 (1.9)	17.25** (765)

Note. Self-report scales range from 1 to 4, except shaming which ranges from −2 to 2.
*p<.05, **p <.01

Summary of Findings

The results provide mixed support for the dimensionality predicted by reintegrative shaming theory. The hypothesis that shaming would be independent of both reintegration and stigmatization was supported in both the court and conference settings. The idea that the four facets of reintegration and stigmatization would form separate dimensions, however, was not supported. No support was found for the notion that reintegration and stigmatization were opposite poles of the same continuum. Both the exploratory and confirmatory factor analyses pointed to the conclusion that reintegration and stigmatization are discrete concepts.

This chapter sets out to demonstrate triangulation between the observational and self-report measures of the three concepts, reintegration, stigmatization and shaming. It does so with limited success. Observational measures were significantly and consistently correlated with the self-report reintegration scales, and were moderately well associated with the stigmatization scales. Self-report and observational shaming measures, however, did not converge.

Attempts to validate the measures through a comparison of court and conference cases were moderately successful. Both reintegration and shaming in the self-report and observation scales where significantly higher for conference cases. Stigmatization was significantly higher for court cases based on the self-report measure. The observational measures of stigmatization suggested no consistent differences between court and conference cases.

Conclusions on the Dimensionality of Reintegrative Shaming

Despite providing general support for reintegrative shaming theory, some important questions are raised by the rejection of the hypothesis that reintegration and stigmatization are the opposite poles of the same dimension. Reintegrative shaming theory states that while reintegration involves forgiveness of, and respect for, the offender, stigmatization does not. Furthermore, while stigmatization labels the offender and allows him or her to develop a master status trait, reintegration does not. This suggests a structure in which reintegration and stigmatization must be a continuum because low reintegration also implies high stigmatization. The results, however, strongly contradict this structure, instead they suggest that reintegration and stigmatization are distinct concepts.

While surprising, this finding is consistent with research into other concepts that have previously been assumed bipolar. Indeed, a recent review of studies on attitudes (Cacioppo, Gardner & Berntson, 1997)

argues that many positive and negative attitudes should be considered as having a bivariate relationship rather than a bipolar one. The studies reviewed suggest that the positive and negative affects resulting from academic success or failure (Goldstein & Strube, 1994) and medical donations (Cacioppo & Gardner, 1993) have bivariate structures. More specifically the study into medical donations showed that participants could be split into four groups on the basis of their positive and negative attitudes. The four groups were characterized by (1) high negativity and low positivity (negative attitude), (2) high positivity and low negativity (positive attitude), (3) high positivity and high negativity (ambivalence), and (4) low positivity and low negativity (indifference). The implication of this review is that in many cases positive and negative reactions are not reciprocally controlled and thus should not be treated as bipolar.

A similar argument has been put forward by Diener and Emmons (1984). These researchers argued that within a period of time, people's experience of positive and negative affect could take the following forms: they could experience both, neither, or one but not the other. The longer the measurement period, the more likely that both positive and negative affect will be experienced. Thus, measures that tapped positive and negative affect over longer periods, the past week for instance, are more likely to be two-dimensional than bipolar.

Time-frame may be a factor in relation to stigmatization and reintegration because it is possible that court or conference cases change in how reintegrative or stigmatizing they are over the course of the case, or that participants in court and conference cases vary in how reintegrative or stigmatizing they are. Equally, because reintegrative shaming can be split into different facets, it may even be possible that single interactions between people are both reintegrative and stigmatizing. One such example is reported by Braithwaite and Mugford (1994), who quote a Maori man at a New Zealand conference as saying to a young car thief 'You've got no brains, boy . . . But I've got respect for you' (p. 146). The first part labels the offender as stupid, but the second part communicates respect. Such examples suggest that independence between stigmatization and reintegration may be a result of the summing of numerous shaming communications.

An important prediction of reintegrative shaming theory is that the measurement of shaming would be independent from reintegration and stigmatization. This is central to the theory as it predicts that shaming can be of either type. A strong association between shaming and reintegration or stigmatization would refute this basic claim. The results supported the prediction that shaming is independent, with almost no correlation between the measures. In summary, these results provide strong evidence for the construct validity of the reintegrative shaming measures, while also

showing that reintegration and stigmatization are not bipolar as predicted by Braithwaite (1989).

Conclusions on the External Validity of the Reintegrative Shaming Measures

Comparison of the observational and self-report measures provides important information about the measurement of reintegrative shaming. The observation of court cases presented particular difficulties because very little shaming behavior of any type was observed in that context. This highlights an important difference between self-report and observation. Self-report measures include information regarding perceptions resulting from simply turning up to a case, the impact of communication with others present at the case which could not be observed, and the impact of communications with others before and after the formal case. None of this information was captured by the observational analysis. These factors not only presented difficulties in analysis of the data but also may have affected the strength of the relationship between the self-report and observational measures.

An extremely low level of stigmatization in both conference and court cases made assessing this category particularly difficult, although there was some evidence of triangulation on findings using different measuring procedures. An important implication of the low levels of observable stigmatization, particularly in court cases, may be that stigmatization is not overtly communicated in the way expected. Rather than openly disapproving of the person it may be that stigmatization is expressed in private or through more subtle gestures, such as a failure to shake hands or smile. Consistent with this possibility was the finding that observations of disapproval (shaming) and non-forgiveness in court cases were correlated with the perception of stigmatization. It might be speculated that overt disapproval in a public forum is in itself stigmatizing. This highlights an important difference between court cases and conferences. In conferences, observed shaming did not result in perceived stigmatization. Reasons for the difference between contexts may be that conferences are much less public, that those present are primarily supporters of the participant, that the disapproval was more likely to be expressed by a supporter of the participant and that conferences may be perceived as less threatening or hostile than court cases. These factors may affect the way in which disapproval is interpreted. Importantly, this also highlights one process by which court cases may be inherently more stigmatizing than conferences. It may be more difficult for courts to communicate shaming without it being perceived as stigmatizing. Given this relationship it may be worthwhile

exploring ways in which shaming is communicated other than through the expression of overt disapproval.

The correlations between the observational and self-report measures were not exactly as predicted by the **Shaming 4** hypothesis. In particular, the different measures of shaming were not significantly correlated in either context. However, there was evidence of triangulation among some of the other measures. In both conferences and court cases, the observational items measuring reintegration were strongly correlated with self-report measure obtained from offender interviews. Observational measures of stigmatization were less consistent but some items did correlate significantly with the self-report measures. These results are significant given the differences between the observational and self-report measures discussed above. It is also worth noting that in court cases the negative correlation of observed forgiveness with perceived stigmatization provides some further support for the validity of these measures.

A second measure of the external validity of reintegrative shaming is provided by the distinction between conference and court cases. It was predicted that conferences would be more reintegrative because of their format. Conferences were attended primarily by supporters of the participant, they focused upon the consequences of the offense rather than the offender, and both informal and formal processes of forgiveness were structured into proceedings. The results confirm this expectation, showing that both observational and self-report measures of reintegration and shaming were higher at conferences. In addition, the self-report measure of stigmatization was higher for court cases. These findings provide evidence for the validity of these measures. In summary, the results presented in this chapter provide an adequate basis for the operationalization and testing of a revized reintegrative shaming theory.

APPENDIX 9A

Rotated Factor Matrix of the Court Cases (Conference Cases) RISE Interview Data

Items		Reintegration	Stigmatization
1	Did you learn from the conference/ court case that there are people who care about you?	.65 (.55)	
4	During the conference/court case did people talk about aspects of yourself which they like?	.64 (.64)	
7	Did others at the conference/court case say that you had learnt your lesson and now deserve a second chance?	.64 (.58)	
6	At the end of the conference/court case did people indicate that you were forgiven?	.61 (.58)	
13	Did people in the conference/court case say that it was not like you to do something wrong?	.57 (.45)	
14	During the conference/court case did people indicate that they accepted you as basically law abiding?	.54 (.43)	−.35 (-.33)
3	Were you treated as a trustworthy person in the conference/court case?	.51 (.50)	−.47 (-.37)
10	Offenders *mean* perception of forgiveness expressed by those who were present at the conference/court case.**	.47	−.32
2	During the conference/court case did people suggest that they loved you regardless of what you did?	.40 (.65)	
15	During the conference/court case were you treated as though you were a criminal?		.85 (.71)
16	During the conference/court case were you treated as though you were a bad person?		.78 (.61)
11	Were you treated in the conference/court case as though you were likely to commit another offense.		.64 (.56)
12	Did people during the conference/court case make negative judgements about what kind of person you are?		.62 (.48)
Percent of variance explained		34.4 (23.2)	16.8 (11.7)

* Table includes only loadings equal to or greater than .3.
** This item had low Squared Multiple Correlation in conference case and hence was excluded from the analyses with conference data.

CHAPTER 10

The Relationship between Shame and Shaming

This chapter seeks to explore the relationship between shaming and shame. It is assumed that shaming of an offender's act is positively associated with feelings of Shame–Guilt. However, there is evidence that other factors may affect this relationship. One such factor is the way shaming is expressed. As seen in Chapter 9, shaming behaviors can be qualified by the degree to which they are reintegrative or stigmatizing. Reintegrative shaming theory predicts that offenders will react differently depending upon which of these types of shaming occurs. Another factor which may affect shame is the social relationship between the offender and those who are doing the 'shaming'. A number of conceptions of shame predict that individuals will only be responsive to shaming by those they respect. Others argue that shame is dependent upon the individual's own ethical judgment.

Chapters 8 and 9 provided the empirical bases for testing these ideas. Chapter 8 did this by exploring the empirical dimensionality of the shame-related emotions. The first type was a Shame–Guilt emotion which involves feelings that what one has done is wrong, fear that others will disapprove of oneself, feeling bad that one has (or might have) hurt others, anger at oneself, and feelings of loss of honor. The second type of emotion was Embarrassment–Exposure, and the third, Unresolved Shame capturing a sense of uncertainty about one's wrongdoing, a sense of unfairness about the proceedings.

Chapter 9 explored the dimensionality of reintegrative shaming and found three distinct factors: shaming, reintegration and stigmatization. This chapter brings these concepts together and searches for empirically verifiable associations between shame and shaming. In the present chapter we find that, contrary to the theory of reintegrative shaming, the Reintegration *x* Shaming and Stigmatization *x* Shaming interactions have no effect on any

kind of shame. However there are main effects consistent with the theory. Stigmatization reduces Shame–Guilt and reintegration increases it. Shaming, at least when by highly respected others, also increases Shame–Guilt.

However, it is the results that go beyond the original formulation in *Crime, Shame and Reintegration* that are more interesting. Given the importance of Unacknowledged Shame in Ahmed's analysis (Part III), it is notable that we find in the present chapter that stigmatization has the opposite effect on Unresolved Shame to its effect on Shame–Guilt. Stigmatization increases Unresolved Shame as it reduces Shame–Guilt. Because we will find that stigmatization also increases Embarrassment–Exposure, we might say that stigmatization has some deterrent effects that work through the shame emotions. But stigmatization does not win hearts and minds because there may be a defiance effect revealed here in the reduction of Shame–Guilt. The data in this chapter reveals Shame–Guilt to be importantly about offenders sharing a belief that the conduct shamed is morally wrong.

Theoretical Expectations about Shaming and Shame

Awareness of an 'other' and particularly their critical judgment of oneself is evident in at least two of the shame conceptions (social threat and ethical conceptions) identified in Chapter 6. The third conception of shame, personal failure, excludes the social context in which shame occurs by emphasizing the perception of failure. However, even within this conception, H. B. Lewis (1971) acknowledges the role of others and the Tangney, Wagner and Gramzow (1989) measure of shame-proneness (TOSCA) suggests the presence of others as an important component.

While the relevance of the disapproval of others, or shaming, is acknowledged throughout the literature, the social threat conception argues that there is a direct causal relationship between shaming and shame. This conception can be summarized as defining shame as a response to the perception of rejection by others (Scheff, 1988), or their judgment that one is unattractive (Gilbert, 1997). Many theorists of this type make the assumption that shame is felt in reference to an actual other and that the other plays an active role (shaming). This may involve something like rejection, criticism or abuse of the person. This is particularly relevant in the anthropological literature, which is interested in shame and guilt as the emotional counterparts of social control (Benedict, 1946; Mead, 1937). Shame is seen as a sanction that the community uses to deter or punish those who step outside social norms. As a result the cause or reason for the emotion is characterized as external to the individual because the emotion is about the loss of others' respect rather than the loss of self-respect. The implication of this theoretical perspective is that whenever the individual

perceives that they are disapproved of, raising the prospect of rejection or lower attractiveness, then shame will inevitably result. Thus, the expectation was that:

Shaming – Shame–Guilt 1: *Perceived shaming would predict Shame–Guilt.*

The argument that shame occurs as a direct response to criticism or derision by others is rejected by a number of theorists. Piers and Singer (1953) were perhaps the first to argue against the assumption that shame only occurs as a result of an actively disapproving other. They suggest that instances of shame occur when individuals are alone, which provides a clear indication that others are not necessary. Along with others, personal failure theorists (H. B. Lewis, 1971; M. Lewis, 1992; Wurmser, 1994) argue that shame is a direct result of the individual's perception that they have failed to live up to an ideal. This suggests that shame results from not living up to internalized standards. Whether or not this perception occurs as a result of scrutiny and disapproval by others, or in private, is not important from this viewpoint.

The ethical conceptions of shame, with the exception of Harré (1990), also reject the idea that shame is necessarily a reaction to an actual other. Ethical concept theorists argue that shame occurs as a response to the realization of having done wrong. Williams (1993), like Braithwaite (1989), suggests that although the basic shame experience is one of exposure to another, that other might be an imagined other. Similarly Taylor (1985) argues that the basic shame experience involves two audiences, one which draws attention to the self and a second abstract other from which an ethical judgment is made. The first audience, which is comparable with criticism from an actual other, is not necessary, as it is only a mechanism for shifting one's attention. Thus, as with the personal failure conception, this approach emphasizes the importance of an internal attribution in reference to the individual's own standards. Even though Harré does suggest the importance of an actual observer, he too argues that a critical factor is the individual's agreement that what they have done is wrong. If the individual does not agree, Harré suggests that the restrictions imposed on the individual by others' disapproval actually result in feelings of hate rather than shame.

Thus, in contrast to the social threat conception, both the ethical and personal failure conceptions point to the hypothesis that shame occurs as a result of violating the individual's standards, not necessarily as a result of shaming by others. Drawing from the ethical and personal failure conceptions, the second hypothesis was that:

Shaming – Shame–Guilt 2: *Participants' perceptions of how wrong the offense was, before their court or conference case, would predict the extent to which they felt Shame–Guilt.*

While rejecting the argument that shaming directly predicts shame, the ethical conception argues that disapproval does play an important role in ethical decision-making. Indeed, Williams (1993) argues that the social threat conception involves an overstated distinction between guilt as the individual's independent judgment of wrongdoing and shame as a reaction to other people's judgment. The distinction is overstated because internalized values cannot exist in social isolation but rather are dependent upon social approval. For example, Williams (1993) argues that if someone held an ethical belief which was refuted by everyone else it would be difficult to distinguish between that individual as '. . . a solitary bearer of true justice or a deluded crank' (p. 99). Thus, it is questionable whether a sense of guilt can exist simply on the basis of values derived through rational thought or religious illumination, and in relative independence from the person's social world. Rather, it is argued that the individual's own values are strongly tied to their communities which means that disapproval by those communities is of significance.

However, a critical aspect of disapproval according to both Taylor and Williams is from whom it comes. Taylor (1985) argues that the relationship between the person and the audience is critical to whether shame is felt because this determines how the person interprets the audience's reaction. For example, a man looked upon critically by an audience that is not respected is unlikely to feel shame, and may even feel pride. However, if the observer's opinion is respected then their critical judgment is much more likely to result in feelings of shame. Williams (1993) who places more emphasis upon the 'other' as an abstract entity makes a similar argument. He argues that rather than simply representing an actual person or group the 'other' is identifiable in ethical terms and more particularly as someone whose ethical reactions the person would respect. However, the internalized other does not simply represent the individual's own ethical beliefs but represents a genuine social perspective.

While the ethical conception suggests that Shame–Guilt is related to internalized values it also suggests that shaming by respected others will influence that judgment. Thus, it was hypothesized that:

Shaming – Shame–Guilt 3: *Shaming would result in feelings of Shame–Guilt, but only when the shaming was by respected others.*

Reintegrative Shaming Theory and Shame

Shaming is conceptualized as the expression of social disapproval, not necessarily intentional. Shaming might simply be others' knowledge of an act, which in turn results in the individual feeling ashamed. This broad

definition is consistent with the notions of shaming and exposure discussed by different conceptions of shame.

In contrast to the shame conceptions that do acknowledge the role of shaming, reintegrative shaming theory provides little analysis of the impact of shaming on individuals' emotional responses. While acknowledging the theoretical distinctions between shame and guilt identified by Benedict (1946) and distinctions between shaming and guilt induction in child development, Braithwaite argues that neither distinction is important from the perspective of a theory of shaming.

> In other words, from the perspective of the offender, guilt and shame may be distinguishable, but guilt *induction* and sham*ing* are both criticism by others. (Braithwaite, 1989: p. 57)

Braithwaite argues that the effectiveness of shaming depends upon a number of factors. The first of these is that individuals are motivated to be accepted by others whom they find attractive, and thus are motivated to be attractive to them. Shaming by these people is a clear threat to this relationship and thus proves an effective deterrent. A considerable amount of research on deterrence demonstrates that the informal consequences of being caught for a crime are considered by people as important, and in some cases as more important, than the formal consequences (Grasmick & Bursik, 1990; Paternoster & Iovanni, 1986). It is evident that this function of shaming is consistent with aspects of the social threat conception, which argues that fear of disapproval by others is the basis of shame.

A second result of shaming is its relationship to the development and maintenance of internal controls by individuals, conceived of as conscience or super-ego. Shaming is seen as having an effect upon individuals through appealing to their sense of right or wrong. It is this aspect of shaming which Braithwaite argues is most important to preventing serious crimes:

> People comply with the law most of the time not through fear of punishment, or even fear of shaming, but because criminal behavior is abhorrent to them. (Braithwaite, 1989: p. 71)

The process of shaming also acts to prevent crime by reinforcing the social norms that make committing crime abhorrent not just for the individual but for the broader community. These aspects of shaming are most consistent with the ethical conception which describes shame as a response to having violated norms which one accepts. From these descriptions of how shaming is effective it is clear that reintegrative shaming theory assumes an emotional response similar to that identified by a number of conceptions of shame. This is the emotion of Shame–Guilt empirically defined in Chapter 8.

Like many other theories of shame, various factors are assumed to affect the shaming–shame relationship. The central notion in reintegrative shaming theory is that shaming can be evaluated not just in terms of how strong it is but also in the degree to which it is stigmatizing or reintegrative. Research on reintegrative shaming theory focuses upon the effect these different types of shaming have on offending and recidivism. However, it is also consistent with the theory that the form shaming takes will have different effects upon the individual's emotional response and that this may provide an explanation for the link between shaming and recidivism.

Stigmatization is shaming that identifies the individual as evil and creates a deviant identity. This rejection of the individual is associated, in both labeling theory and reintegrative shaming theory, with a tendency for the individual to reject their shamers. This occurs because the act of labeling the offender as deviant, particularly through socially significant ceremonies, has the potential to change the individual's identity such that they come to see themselves as deviant, which in turn informs their behavior. In this respect the stigmatizing ceremony comes to be a self-fulfilling prophecy. The theory also argues that deviant identities can be supported or enhanced through the association of the individual with others who share similar identities. Subcultural theory (see Braithwaite, 1989: p. 24) argues that deviant groups provide individuals with alternative status systems which allow, or perhaps in some cases actively encourage, delinquency.

The marginalization of offenders in the way described seems unlikely to result in greater feelings of Shame–Guilt. This is firstly because individuals who are rejected and disrespected by the social group are less likely to be concerned with maintaining respectability in the eyes of those people who have stigmatized them. They have already lost that respect. Secondly, the loss of ties with law-abiding communities and the development of ties with subcultural groups will shift the individual's moral values away from those held by the law-abiding. Rather than feeling shame for an offense the individual may even feel pride. Thus it can be hypothesized:

Shaming – Shame–Guilt 4: _Shame–Guilt would be predicted by higher reintegrative shaming and lower stigmatizing shaming._

Offenders' perceptions of having been unfairly judged and being unsure about the 'wrongness' of their offense were identified in Chapter 8 as a factor that was called 'Unresolved Shame'. This response may be a reaction to the process of stigmatization, in which individuals react to judgments that they are bad by rejecting or neutralizing claims that the act was wrong. Although Unresolved Shame as an alternative emotion to shame is explicitly discussed by Braithwaite (1989), in Retzinger and Scheff's (1996) various commentaries on Braithwaite's theory they hypothesize that

stigmatization will be associated with an unresolved or unacknowledged shame they refer to as by-passed shame. The third emotion discussed in Chapter 8, Embarrassment–Exposure, involved feelings of social awkwardness due to being the center of attention and feelings of being humiliated. Thus, it is reasonable to hypothesize:

Shaming – Shame–Guilt 5: *Embarrassment–Exposure would be predicted by higher stigmatizing shaming because of its negative focus upon the individual.*

Reintegrative shaming is shaming which is respectful and forgiving of the individual. It can be hypothesized that reintegration should be different from stigmatization in two ways. The process of labeling the offender draws attention away from the offense and the harm it has caused and instead focuses on judgments about the offender's person. Reintegration avoids focusing on the offender's person and is thus less likely to result in the offender developing a deviant identity or feeling the need to reject the shamers. A second characteristic of reintegration is that it attempts to reinforce ethical norms in a way that is inclusive of the offender. In this respect reintegration is an appeal to ethical values that are shared by both the offender and the broader community. Thus, the theory predicts that reintegrative shaming will result in greater feelings of Shame–Guilt. As a result of this orientation, it is also predicted that

Shaming – Shame–Guilt 6: *Unresolved Shame would be predicted by higher stigmatizing shaming and lower reintegrative shaming.*

Testing the Relationship between Shame and Shaming

This chapter looks at the empirical relationship between the following variables of shame and shaming. The shame-related emotions are (1) Shame–Guilt; (2) Embarrassment–Exposure; and (3) Unresolved Shame. The shaming variables are (1) shaming; (2) stigmatization; and (3) reintegration.

Other measures included to test the hypotheses outlined above were:

(1)   Participants' respect for others at the conference: This was measured by obtaining the mean score for a self-report item that asked how much the participant respected each significant person at their case. The question asked: 'To start, I would like to find out what you think of these people. For each person on the list, could you circle the words which best describe how much you respect them.' Participants responded on a five-point scale, ranging from 'strongly disrespect' to 'strongly respect' ($M = 1.2$; $SD = .76$).

(2)   Participants' attitudes towards the offense. This was measured by asking 'Did you feel, before the conference/court case, that the offense you

committed was . . .'. Responses were given on a five point scale ranging from 'totally right' to 'totally wrong' ($M = 4.68$; $SD = .68$).

Design and Explanations of the Analyses

The first group of analyses tested the relationship between shaming and the shame-related emotions. Product-moment correlations (see Table 10.1) were calculated among the dependent variables (the shame-related emotions) and independent variables (the shaming variables). These provide an initial look at the association between the variables as well as addressing the hypotheses. Three hierarchical regression analyses were performed to predict Shame–Guilt, Embarrassment–Exposure and Unresolved Shame. The hierarchical regression analytic technique allows assessment of whether each block of variables, and in particular the interaction terms, adds significantly to the variance accounted for by the control variables and the main effects. The same set of independent variables was used in the prediction of Shame–Guilt, Embarrassment–Exposure and Unresolved Shame. A standard set of predictor variables is desirable to understand differences and similarities among the predictors of the shame-related emotions.

The analyses used centered variables (variable scores minus their mean). This technique protects against multicollinearity among interaction terms (A x B) and their main effects (A, B) (Aiken & West, 1991). Testing for interactions was important for understanding the way shaming, reintegration, stigmatization and respect were related to Shame–Guilt, Embarrassment–Exposure and Unresolved Shame. Tests for interactions were also used to ascertain whether the independent variables had different effects in the two contexts.

Accounting for differences between the two contexts was an important issue for the analyses. In part this was achieved by including treatment type as a control variable. In addition, the interactions between treatment type and the independent variables were also included as control variables. These interactions test whether the relationship between the dependent and independent variables is different between the treatment types. An example of this is the significant 'treatment x reintegration' interaction in the Shame–Guilt regression analysis (see Table 10.2), which indicates that reintegration is a stronger predictor of Shame–Guilt in conference cases than in court cases. The advantage of controlling for differences between treatments in this way is that all cases are included in a single analysis, which simplifies the results as well as allowing for statistical testing of differences between treatments.

The Analyses

The shaming and shame-related emotions were intercorrelated using product-moment correlations (see Table 10.1). As expected, shaming is significantly correlated with Shame–Guilt for court and conference cases. The results also show support for the view that perceptions of having done wrong are important. Perceived wrongness was significantly and positively correlated with Shame–Guilt for both court and conference cases.

Predicting Shame–Guilt

To find out which variables were doing most of the work in predicting Shame–Guilt, a hierarchical regression analysis was used in which variables were entered in four steps. In step one, variables were entered to control for the potential effects of Embarrassment–Exposure, Unresolved Shame and treatment type (court or conference). The shaming measure was included in the equation at step two. In step three measures of reintegration, stigmatization, respect for others present, and perceived wrongness of the offense were entered into the equation. Finally, interactions between shaming and respect, shaming and reintegration, and shaming and stigmatization were entered. These interactions test two hypotheses:

Shaming – Shame–Guilt 3: *Shaming would result in feelings of Shame–Guilt, but only when the shaming was by respected others.*

Shaming – Shame–Guilt 4: *Shame–Guilt would be predicted by higher reintegrative shaming and lower stigmatizing shaming.*

The regression analysis predicting Shame–Guilt is presented in Table 10.2. The shaming variable proved to have a small but significant positive effect on Shame–Guilt. Reintegration, respect for others present, and the perception that the offense was wrong all predicted higher levels of Shame–Guilt. Stigmatization predicted significantly lower levels of Shame–Guilt. The shaming interaction terms did not contribute significantly to the model.

The absence of significant findings in relation to the interaction terms was disappointing. Theoretically, these were of central importance. It was suspected, on the basis of the variables' distributions, that some of the hypothesized interactions might involve a threshold effect with the interaction only occurring at the extreme ends of the scales. For example, because most participants reported a high level of 'respect for others at the case', it was suspected that only those participants who reported very high respect would be different from the other participants. Equally, because most participants perceived a high degree of shaming, there was added interest in cases where participants reported very high shaming. To test this,

Table 10.1 Product-moment Correlations among the Shame and Shaming Variables for Court (above diagonal) and Conference (below diagonal) Cases

Variables	1	2	3	4	5	6	7	8
1 Shame–Guilt		.60**	.11 (ns)	.19**	.28**	.06 (ns)	.27**	.37**
2 Embarrassment–Exposure	.52**		.34**	.10 (ns)	.13*	.29**	.08 (ns)	.09 (ns)
3 Unresolved Shame	.00 (ns)	.15**		−.03 (ns)	−.12*	.51**	−.21**	−.17**
4 Shaming	.27**	.07 (ns)	−.07 (ns)		.01 (ns)	.07 (ns)	.03 (ns)	.14*
5 Reintegration	.41**	.23**	−.11*	.05 (ns)		−.12*	.32**	.04 (ns)
6 Stigmatization	−.07 (ns)	.22**	.33**	.01 (ns)	−.07 (ns)		−.29**	−.05 (ns)
7 Respect	.17**	.05 (ns)	−.07 (ns)	.14**	.13*	−.14**		.06 (ns)
8 Perceived wrongness		.23**	.02 (ns)	−.15**	.28**	.01 (ns)	−.04 (ns)	.04 (ns)

*p<.05 **p<.01

Table 10.2 Beta Weights and R^2 for the Hierarchical Regression Analysis Predicting Shame–Guilt

Variables	Model 1	Model 2	Model 3	Model 4	Model 5
1 Controls					
Treatment type	.30**	.27**	.08**	.08*	.07*
Embarrassment–Exposure scale	.55**	.53**	.48**	.48**	.47**
Unresolved Shame scale	–.08*	–.06 (ns)	.07*	.07*	.07*
Treatment x Reintegration	.05 (ns)	.05 (ns)	.07**	.07**	.07*
Treatment x Stigmatization	–.05 (ns)	–.05 (ns)	–.05 (ns)	–.05 (ns)	–.04 (ns)
Treatment x Shaming	.08*	.08**	.04 (ns)	.04 (ns)	.02 (ns)
Treatment x Respect for others present	–.07*	–.08*	–.04 (ns)	–.05 (ns)	–.04 (ns)
Treatment x perceived 'wrongness'	–.08*	–.09**	–.04 (ns)	–.05 (ns)	–.04 (ns)
2 Shaming					
Shaming measure		.18**	.13**	.13**	.05 (ns)
3 Other main effects					
Reintegration scale			.24**	.25**	.24**
Stigmatization scale			–.11**	–.11**	–.10**
Perceived 'wrongness' of offense			.23**	.23**	.22**
Mean respect for others present			.11**	.12**	.07*
4 Shaming interactions					
Reintegration x Shaming				–.00 (ns)	.00 (ns)
Stigmatizing x Shaming				.00 (ns)	–.01 (ns)
Respect x Shaming				.05 (ns)	
5 High-shaming high-respect					.14**
Adjusted R^2	.37**	.40**	.52**	.52**	.52**
R^2 change	.38**	.03**	.12**	.00	.01**

*p<.05 **p<.01

dummy variables were produced that measured those cases where a high score was recorded for both main effects. For example, the dummy variable equaled one in those cases where the participant reported very high respect for others present at the case *and* reported that others were very highly shaming. Analyses revealed that the addition of these dummy variables had a significant impact on only the Shame–Guilt regression and only for the 'respect' by shaming interaction. This is presented in the Shame–Guilt regression analysis as a fifth model in which the shaming by respect interaction was replaced by a dichotomous variable called 'high-shaming high-respect'. This model significantly added to the main effects models with the high-shaming high-respect item predicting significantly more Shame–Guilt.

Summary of the Findings

The findings from this set of analyses predicting shame and guilt can be summarized as follows:

Shaming – Shame–Guilt 1: *Perceived shaming would predict Shame–Guilt.*

The significant correlations between shaming and Shame–Guilt, for conference and court cases, demonstrate a positive relationship between these variables. However, the hierarchical regression analysis shows that with the addition of the high-shaming high-respect variable, shaming is no longer a significant predictor. This suggests that shaming only predicts Shame–Guilt when there is strong disapproval coming from those who are highly respected as specified in Shaming – Shame–Guilt (3).

Shaming – Shame–Guilt 2: *Participants' perceptions of how wrong the offense was, before their court or conference case, would be an important predictor of whether they feel Shame–Guilt.*

It is evident in Table 10.2 that perceived wrongness of the offense is a strong positive predictor of Shame–Guilt. This conclusion is supported by the hierarchical regression analysis in which the perception of wrongdoing predicts greater Shame–Guilt.

Shaming – Shame–Guilt 3: *Shaming would result in feelings of Shame–Guilt, but only when it is by respected others.*

The significance of the high-shaming high-respect variable demonstrates that respect for others present at the case is a significant moderator of shaming. Furthermore, the addition of this variable to the analysis resulted in shaming no longer being a significant predictor. This suggests that the effect of shaming is conditional on respect.

Shaming – Shame–Guilt 4: *Shame–Guilt would be predicted by higher reintegrative shaming and lower stigmatizing shaming.*

The Reintegration x Shaming and Stigmatization x Shaming interactions tested this hypothesis. Neither was significant and thus the hypothesis should be rejected. It was evident, however, that the main effects for reintegration and stigmatization did predict Shame–Guilt in the expected direction. Reintegration was associated with greater Shame–Guilt while stigmatization was associated with lower Shame–Guilt.

Predicting Embarrassment–Exposure

The regression analyses predicting Embarrassment–Exposure, presented in Table 10.3, are somewhat disappointing in what they reveal about this shame-related emotion. Only the control variables and main effects entered in model three contributed significantly to the prediction of Embarrassment–Exposure. Treatment type was a significant predictor with participants who went to court reporting significantly more than those who attended a conference. This is an interesting finding given that conferences are thought to be more emotional and shaming than court cases.

We had hypothesized that *Embarrassment–Exposure would increase with higher stigmatizing shaming because of its negative focus upon the individual* (**Shaming – Shame–Guilt 5**). Contrary to this hypothesis, the Stigmatization x Shaming interaction term was not a significant predictor of Embarrassment–Exposure. The Stigmatization main effect, however, was a strong predictor of Embarrassment–Exposure. Also significant were prior perceptions of wrongdoing. The less wrong the person thought the offense to be, the more he/she was inclined to be embarrassed.

Predicting Unresolved Shame

As with the previous set of analyses, the control variables explained a considerable proportion of the variance in Unresolved Shame (see Table 10.4). Treatment type did not predict the degree of Unresolved Shame. However, the interaction between treatment type and stigmatization was significant. Stigmatization was a stronger predictor of Unresolved Shame in court cases than in conference cases. This suggests that the court context may act to augment the impact of any stigmatization expressed or perhaps that conferences act to dampen the impact of stigmatization.

In this analysis, we had hypothesized that *Unresolved Shame would be predicted by higher stigmatizing shaming and lower reintegrative shaming*

(Shaming – Shame–Guilt 6). This was not the case. The shaming by reintegration and shaming by stigmatization interactions were not significant. Reintegration and stigmatization main effects, however, were significant in predicting Unresolved Shame. Reintegration was associated with a decrease in Unresolved Shame, while stigmatization was associated with an increase.

Table 10.3 Beta Weights and R^2 for the Hierarchical Regression Analysis Predicting Embarrassment–Exposure

Variable	Model 1	Model 2	Model 3	Model 4
1 Controls				
Treatment type	–.22**	–.21**	–.22**	–.22**
Shame–Guilt scale	.56**	.57**	.59**	.59**
Unresolved Shame scale	.23**	.23**	.12**	.12**
Treatment x Reintegration	.01 (ns)	.01 (ns)	.00 (ns)	.01 (ns)
Treatment x Stigmatization	.01 (ns)	.01 (ns)	.01 (ns)	.01 (ns)
Treatment x Shaming	–.04 (ns)	–.04 (ns)	–.03 (ns)	–.00 (ns)
Treatment x Respect for others present	–.00 (ns)	.00 (ns)	–.01 (ns)	–.01 (ns)
Treatment x Perceived 'wrongness'	.01 (ns)	.01 (ns)	–.00 (ns)	–.00 (ns)
2 Shaming				
Shaming measure		–.03 (ns)	–.03 (ns)	–.03 (ns)
3 Other main effects				
Reintegration scale			.02 (ns)	.02 (ns)
Stigmatization scale			.21**	.21**
Perceived 'wrongness' of offense			–.08*	–.08*
Mean respect for others present			.00 (ns)	.00 (ns)
4 Shaming interactions				
Reintegration x Shaming				–.06 (ns)
Stigmatizing x Shaming				.01 (ns)
Respect x Shaming				–.00 (ns)
Adjusted R^2	.36**	.36**	.40**	.40**
R^2 change	.37**	.00	.04**	.00

*p<.05   **p<.01

Table 10.4 Beta Weights and R^2 for the Hierarchical Regression Analysis Predicting Unresolved Shame

Variable	Model 1	Model 2	Model 3	Model 4
1 Controls				
Treatment type	−.07 (ns)	−.07 (ns)	.01 (ns)	.01 (ns)
Embarrassment–Exposure scale	.32**	.31**	.15**	.15**
Shame–Guilt scale	−.11*	−.10*	.10*	.10*
Treatment x Reintegration	−.02 (ns)	−.02 (ns)	−.04 (ns)	−.03 (ns)
Treatment x Stigmatization	−.11**	−.11**	−.08*	−.08*
Treatment x Shaming	−.01 (ns)	−.01 (ns)	.01 (ns)	.02 (ns)
Treatment x Respect for others present	.07 (ns)	.08*	.04 (ns)	.04 (ns)
Treatment x Perceived 'wrongness'	.04 (ns)	.04 (ns)	.02 (ns)	.02 (ns)
2 Shaming				
Shaming measure		−.06 (ns)	−.06 (ns)	−.05 (ns)
3 Other main effects				
Reintegration scale			−.13**	−.13**
Stigmatization scale			.35**	.35**
Perceived 'wrongness' of offense			−.17**	−.17**
Mean respect for others present			−.06 (ns)	−.06 (ns)
4 Shaming interactions				
Reintegration x Shaming				−.03 (ns)
Stigmatizing x Shaming				.03 (ns)
Respect x Shaming				−.01 (ns)
Adjusted R^2	.11**	.11**	.26**	.26**
R^2 change	.12**	.00	.16**	.00

*p<.05   **p <.01

Summary of Research Findings

The results do not provide support for the hypothesis (**Shaming – Shame–Guilt 1**) that shaming independently predicts the emotion of Shame–Guilt. Rather, the results suggest that the relationship between shaming and shame is dependent upon the amount of respect the participant has for those who disapprove of their actions. However, the results also

showed that the prediction of Shame–Guilt by shaming was not driven by either the interaction between shaming and reintegration or the interaction between shaming and stigmatization (**Shaming – Shame–Guilt 4**). This is despite the findings that the main effects for reintegration and stigmatization were significant.

Shame–Guilt was independently predicted by the degree to which participants reported feeling that the offense was wrong prior to the case (**Shaming – Shame–Guilt 2**). The results also found no support for the hypotheses that Embarrassment–Exposure would be predicted by the Stigmatization *x* Shaming interaction (**Shaming – Shame–Guilt 5**), even though there was a strong stigmatization main effect in increasing Embarrassment–Exposure. Unresolved Shame was not predicted by higher Stigmatization *x* Shaming and lower Reintegration *x* Shaming (**Shaming – Shame–Guilt 6**), though the stigmatization main effect significantly increased Unresolved Shame and reintegration significantly reduced it.

Reintegrative Shaming and Shame

The relationship between the shaming variables and the shame-related emotions is inconsistent with the hypotheses informed by reintegrative shaming theory. Indeed, neither Shaming *x* Reintegration nor Shaming *x* Stigmatization (interaction terms) was a significant predictor of any of the shame-related emotions. Reintegrative shaming does not appear to play the role expected of it in shaping shame-related emotions. Most notably, the relationship between the shaming measure and feeling the emotion of Shame–Guilt was the same regardless of whether shaming was reintegrative or stigmatic. Reintegration and stigmatization were strong predictors of the shame-related emotions in their own right, but their effects are not linked to those of shaming as we expected from the reintegrative shaming theory framework. As discussed earlier, in a criminal justice context stigmatization and reintegration main effects may in reality be the interactions predicted by reintegrative shaming theory because shaming may be inherently laden in any criminal justice process.

An important factor in determining how much Unresolved Shame occurs is the degree to which people report feeling that the offense was wrong prior to the case. The less wrong it was perceived to be the more Unresolved Shame that was felt. This implies that Unresolved Shame may have less to do with repression and denial of responsibility than with uncertainty or rejection of the shaming. While the concept of denial has received considerable attention in the shame literature, few perspectives acknowledge the possibility that individuals might reject or question the validity of shaming. Whereas denial suggests that the individual should feel shame, or

is in some sense dysfunctional for not acknowledging what they feel, the concept of rejecting shame implies that the individual might legitimately reject shame because they do not agree with the 'shamers'. What is interesting is that while there was an association between Unresolved Shame and hostility, there was also a moderate relationship between Unresolved Shame and empathy (see Chapter 8). Unresolved Shame is not just the response of defiance. One hypothesis as to why this pattern of results might occur is that Unresolved Shame is associated with uncertainty regarding the offense and the legitimacy of shaming. Where the individual believes that the offense is less than 'totally wrong' in a shaming context, uncertainty is increased. However, where the person believes that the offense was 'totally wrong', shaming confirms the person's view and decreases uncertainty.

The third shame-related emotion, Embarrassment–Exposure, involves feelings of humiliation and awkwardness due to unwanted attention. Consistent with this description, the emotion was not predicted by shaming and was negatively related to perceptions that the offense was wrong. The response would seem to originate from feelings of exposure in the social context rather than bad feelings about the offense. Stigmatization makes it worse but reintegration does not sooth it.

From Shaming to Shame

The conceptions of shame reviewed in Chapter 6 made different predictions regarding the role of shaming. An important difference between conceptions was whether shame occurs as a result of perceived disapproval, or whether it results from acting contrary to one's own standards. The results presented in this chapter have shown that on its own shaming does not significantly predict how much Shame–Guilt is felt by the participant. However, in cases where those present strongly disapproved of the offense and were highly respected by the participant, self-reported Shame–Guilt was greater. These results are consistent with Makkai and Braithwaite's (1994) finding that when nursing homes had no personal relationship with inspectors, reintegrative shaming had no effect on subsequent compliance with the law. However, the reintegrative shaming by personal relationship interaction substantially increased the positive main effect of reintegrative shaming. Chief executives of nursing homes knowing the inspector personally made reintegrative shaming quite powerful in this study.

It was also evident in the RISE data that the offender's perception of how wrong they thought the offense was prior to the conference or court case was a strong predictor of Shame–Guilt. This result suggests that perceptions that the offense was wrong play an important role, and may even be a prerequisite to the emotion. Thus, it would seem that there is

more to the emotion than simply fear of rejection. In addition to the apparent importance of internalized values, the roles of reintegration and stigmatization also question the relationship between Shame–Guilt and fear of rejection. The regression analyses have shown that stigmatization, which involves outcasting or rejection of the offender, is actually associated with lower perceptions of Shame–Guilt. On the other hand reintegration, which was positively associated with Shame–Guilt, involves acceptance and forgiveness of the individual. Not only does a social threat analysis not fully explain these results, but it also seems to contradict the relationships of Shame–Guilt with reintegration and stigmatization.

Although social rejection does not fully account for these results, it is evident that the regression analyses also imply that Shame–Guilt was not simply a reaction to one's own perceptions of the offense. Shaming by those who the subject highly respected did predict Shame–Guilt, suggesting that the individual was reactive to the social context. Significantly, this result suggests that the effect of shaming is not homogeneous, that it is not simply disapproval that predicts shame but who is disapproving. Although not surprising, this relationship has not received much attention outside philosophical discussions (Taylor, 1985; Williams, 1993). Indeed it has been assumed that shame can occur as a result of any audience. For example, Scheff and Retzinger (1991) observed shame in the responses of people appearing on game shows where the audience was largely anonymous. Given the results in Chapter 8, it might be speculated that the emotion observed by Scheff and Retzinger was Embarrassment–Exposure. This emotion describes feelings of awkwardness due to exposure, or unwanted attention, and was predicted by stigmatization in the regression analyses. Scheff and Retzinger did not empirically distinguish between shame and embarrassment and in many respects do not distinguish between them theoretically.

The finding that only shaming by respected others predicts Shame–Guilt can be explained in a number of ways. If shame is a response to rejection, as argued by the social threat conception, then this finding suggests that individuals are only concerned with rejection by particular people. This explanation has some intuitive appeal because there is little reason to think that people will care what disrespected others think. However, an alternative explanation is provided by the ethical conception of shame. From this perspective, shaming causes shame because others' disapproval convinces the person of wrongdoing. In this case the opinion of respected others is considered more valid and their shaming is therefore more influential in convincing the person that what they have done is wrong. This explanation is consistent with the strong relationship between the perception that the offense was wrong and Shame–Guilt, which suggests the individual's

internalized values are important. It is not possible, using the data collected for this study, to test either explanation of why shaming increases Shame–Guilt, whether it is through the threat of rejection, through persuasion, or some interaction between these motivations. However, this is an important question for future research.

A number of issues relating to the relationship between shaming and shame have parallels in social psychological theories of influence and conformity. A central issue in conformity research is why individuals conform to particular beliefs or behaviors. One answer is that others' behavior provides important information, particularly in contexts where there is ambiguity. Deutsch and Gerard (1955) identify this form of influence, which is also seen in Sherif's (1936) autokinetic experiments, as informational influence. An alternative approach, identified by Deutsch and Gerard as normative influence, is that individuals conform to maintain acceptance or approval. Indeed, discussion of these two processes of conformity have dominated work on social influence (Asch, 1956; Festinger, 1950; Kelley, 1952; Kelman, 1958; Moscovichi, 1976; Tajfel, 1972; Turner, 1991). The concept of normative influence has an obvious parallel with the conception of shame as a response to social rejection. Conformity to a norm occurs so as to maintain approval, but when compliance with the norm does not occur social rejection results in feelings of shame.

Parallels can also be drawn between the ethical and personal failure conceptions of shame and informational influence. In these conceptions, shame can occur without influence at all because it is a response to internalized values. However, the ethical conception explicitly suggests that others who the individual respects play a role in shaming the individual (the personal failure conception does not argue against this). In this case the individual accepts that the normative values held by others are valid and shame is a response to having violated these accepted values.

The importance of particular people is also evident in the development of ideas regarding reference groups and the role they play in regulating social behavior (Festinger, 1950; Kelley, 1952; Newcomb, 1943). A reference group refers to a group to which individuals compare themselves and with which they share norms and values (Turner, 1991). Reference groups have been hypothesized to exercise both normative and informational influence. Kelley describes a reference group as:

> . . . denote[ing] a group in which the individual is motivated to gain or maintain *acceptance*. To promote this acceptance, he holds his attitudes in conformity with what he perceives to be the consensus among group members. Implicit here is the idea that the members of the group observe the person and evaluate him. (Kelley, 1952: p. 411)

This definition clearly emphasizes the role of normative influence. Others suggest that reference groups satisfy informational needs or a combination of needs. For example, Festinger (1950) argued that the need to socially validate beliefs leads people to seek consensual support for their beliefs with others who they see as similar (i.e. a reference group). Whether the process of influence is informational or normative, the concept of reference groups may explain why individuals only feel shame if shamed by people they respect. Respect may be a function of perceiving others to be part of one's reference group.

A number of parallels between the concept of shame (and the results on Shame–Guilt) and the process of conformity have been drawn. Shame–Guilt is a response to having violated norms, whether they are internalized or imposed by others. Understanding how norms are formed, maintained or changed is important to understanding shame and its relationship to shaming. Indeed, it might also be argued that understanding the emotion of shame would improve understandings of conformity. These issues will be discussed in greater length in the next chapter.

Summary

Shame–Guilt varies according to the person's beliefs about the wrongness of the offense, others' beliefs about the wrongness of the offense (communicated through shaming), the relationship between the person and those who felt the offense was wrong (measured by high respect), and finally how others communicate to the person that the offense was wrong (either reintegratively or stigmatically). These results suggest that the link between shaming and Shame–Guilt may be a dynamic process in which both the shamers and the person being shamed play an active role. The individual is active in the decision to accept others' opinions as valid, based upon the respect they have for those people. The shamers are active participants in the process by deciding both that the offense was wrong and by choosing how they communicate their disapproval. Importantly, these findings suggest that Shame–Guilt needs to be seen as an ethical emotion and that as such it needs to be understood in the context of decisions, both individual and social, about what is right and wrong.

CHAPTER 11

An Ethical-Identity Conception of Shame–Guilt

In Part II we have tested the dimensionality of the shame-related emotions and the relationship between these emotions and shaming by others. The aim of this chapter will be to develop a theoretical framework for understanding shame in light of these results. A summary of the results along with the hypotheses are outlined in Table 11.1. Following this, a new theoretical framework is presented that builds upon previous conceptions of shame as well as drawing upon recent work on social influence and cognitive dissonance. We move to this ethical identity interpretation of our results by arguing in the first section that Shame–Guilt is felt in reference to values that are perceived as ethical, then by contending that research on social validation provides evidence that individuals conform with social norms when they are given evidence that these norms are held by a valid reference group. Both Shame–Guilt and Unresolved Shame are then interpreted as a threat to an individual's identity. How quickly this threat is resolved has profound implications and this, it is argued, depends on how reintegrative the shaming is and who communicates it.

An Ethical-Identity Theory of Shame–Guilt

Analysis of how offenders felt during criminal justice cases (see Chapter 8) suggested that there was no need to distinguish between emotions of shame and guilt. Feelings assumed to be characteristic of one or other emotion were measured by the same factor. Thus, what we found in conferences and court cases was an emotional reaction that involved internalized perceptions of wrongdoing, concern for others' disapproval, negative evaluation of the self and concern at having hurt others. This chapter presents a theoretical conception that attempts to explain this emotional reaction

177

Table 11.1 Summary of Outcomes for Hypotheses Tested

Hypotheses		Support for hypothesis
Shame 1	Items measuring fear of other's disapproval (Items 4, 5, 1, 13, 14, Table 8.1) will cohere and be distinct from those items that measure the individual's perception that they have done something wrong (Item 2, Table 8.1).	*Rejected* (all items loaded on Shame–Guilt factor).
Shame 2	Items measuring negative feelings towards the self (Items 9, 12, 6, Table 8.1) will cohere and be distinct from those items that measure concern with one's actions and the consequences of them for others (Items 11, 3, 19, Table 8.1).	*Rejected* (all items loaded on Shame–Guilt factor.
Shame 3	Items measuring the perception that one has committed a serious moral breach (i.e. acted in a way that is morally wrong (2), hurt others (3, 19) and behaved without honor (13, 14)) will cohere and be distinct from those items that measure social discomfort (i.e. feelings of self-consciousness (7, 8, 17)).	*Supported* (an Embarrassment–Exposure factor measuring social discomfort was distinct from Shame–Guilt).
Shame 4	Observational measures of shame will be associated with the self-report measures.	*Partially supported* (observational items correlated with Shame–Guilt, but less strongly in court cases).
Shaming 1	Reintegration and stigmatization will form opposite poles of a single dimension.	*Rejected* (reintegration and stigmatization are independent).
Shaming 2	Shaming will form a dimension independent from reintegration and stigmatization.	*Supported* (low correlations between shaming and reintegration and stigmatization).
Shaming 3	The facets of reintegration and stigmatization defined by Makkai and Braithwaite (1994) will form distinct dimensions.	*Rejected* (The dimensions measure reintegration and stigmatization)
Shaming 4	Observational and self-report measures of reintegrative shaming will demonstrate evidence of triangulation.	*Partially supported* (evident for measures of reintegration, weaker for measures of stigmatization, and not evident for measures of shaming).

Table 11.1 Summary of Outcomes for Hypotheses Tested (*cont.*)

Hypotheses		Support for hypothesis
Shaming 5	Conference cases will be more reintegrative than court cases.	*Supported* (reintegration and shaming significantly higher in conferences).
Shaming–Shame–Guilt 1)	Perceived shaming will predict Shame–Guilt.	*Rejected* (not a significant predictor of Shame–Guilt)
Shaming Shame–Guilt 2	The participant's perception of how wrong the offense was will predict Shame–Guilt.	*Supported* (perceived wrongdoing predicted Shame–Guilt).
Shaming–Shame–Guilt 3	The effect of perceived shaming on Shame–Guilt is conditional on the level of respect for others at the case.	*Supported* (high shaming by high respect predicted Shame–Guilt).
Shaming–Shame–Guilt 4	Shame–Guilt will be predicted by higher reintegrative shaming but lower stigmatizing shaming.	*Rejected* (predicted by main effects for reintegration and stigmatization but not interactions with shaming).
Shaming–Shame–Guilt 5	Embarrassment–Exposure will be predicted by higher stigmatizing shaming.	*Rejected.* (predicted by the main effect for stigmatization but not the interaction with shaming).
Shaming–Shame–Guilt 6	Unresolved Shame will be predicted by higher stigmatizing shaming but lower reintegrative shaming.	*Rejected* (predicted by main effects for reintegration and stigmatization but not interactions with shaming).

which we will refer to as Shame–Guilt. This conception will pay particular attention to a number of characteristics that seem essential to understanding this reaction. First, Shame–Guilt is as an ethical emotion concerning issues of right and wrong. Second, Shame–Guilt is associated with regulating the relationship between the individual and others. Third, Shame–Guilt is not only felt about a particular act, but relates to the person's identity.

Shame–Guilt is Felt in Reference to Values that are Perceived as Ethical

The term 'ethical values' has been used to describe the beliefs people draw on to make judgments about wrongdoing. This is consistent with the ethical conception of shame (Harré, 1990; Taylor, 1985; Williams, 1993) which draws primarily on contributions from moral philosophy. However, it is important to specify what, at a psychological level, is meant by the term ethical value. Rokeach (1973) has suggested that beliefs can be descriptive, evaluative or prescriptive, and that beliefs constitute the building blocks of attitudes and values. While attitudes comprise clusters of beliefs that focus on an object or a specific situation, values are:

> . . . single prescriptive beliefs about end-states (e.g. peace) and modes of conduct (e.g. justice) that transcend specific objects and situations and that are held to be personally and socially preferable to opposite end-states of existence (e.g. war) and modes of conduct (Rokeach, 1973). (V. Braithwaite, 1998: p. 224)

Using an expanded list of Rokeach's values, Braithwaite (1998) has shown their almost universal acceptability in Australian society. Schwartz (1977) has demonstrated universality across cultures. Research on conformity, however, has more often employed the concept of norms than values. In large part, norms have been used to describe beliefs occurring at a group level which define how members of a group should and should not act (see Brown, 1990). But it is also evident that they have been operationalized at an individual level where they are seen as a result of the idiosyncratic learning of values and rules (Schwartz, 1977). An important characteristic of norms is that they express a belief about how people should behave, and thus, like values, are prescriptive. This is evident in both personal norms, where Schwartz (1977) describes them as generating feelings of moral obligation, and social norms where they are defined by Turner, Hogg, Oakes, Reicher and Wetherell (1987) as '. . . any shared standard or rule that specifies appropriate, 'correct', desirable, expected, etc., attitudes and conduct' (p. 13).

The prescriptive and evaluative elements of normative beliefs are consistent with the emphasis upon right and wrong in our use of the term ethical

values. However, it is also evident that while shame is associated with 'serious transgressions' (see Harré, 1990), norms are not restricted in this way. For example, social norms might relate to clothing fashions, the attractiveness of colors, or to the shape of cars. Sherif and Sherif (1969) suggest that norms vary in their degree of importance to the individual and social groups. They argue that norms that are peripheral to group life will have wide latitude of acceptability, making deviations from the norm more tolerable. In contrast, norms that are central to the group's existence or to the definition of the group will have limited latitude of acceptability, which limits the scope for deviation. The operation of different latitudes of acceptability might be seen in a comparison of judgments made regarding fashion or theft. In most circumstances, wearing unfashionable clothing, no matter how unfashionable, will be tolerated by society. The individual might be laughed at but not banished. In contrast, stealing money from other people, even the 'borrowing' of only moderate amounts, is met by much stronger disapproval and the possibility of social sanctions such as fines or prison sentences. Thus, almost no level of stealing is acceptable but almost all levels of bad fashion are. Ethical norms can be defined as beliefs about what is wrong and right and in particular what is considered morally acceptable or good. Non-compliance with an ethical norm is considered not only undesirable but also wrong, the latitude of acceptance being very small. In line with Sherif and Sherif (1969) it might also be hypothesized that moral norms are central to the way individuals or groups conceive of themselves, for example, having certain moral values is important to being a member of society or to being human.

In summary, we argue that Shame–Guilt is only felt when the norms violated are perceived as central to defining the individual, that their violation is thought of as wrong and thus are ethical norms.

The Shaming–Shame Relationship is Mediated by Social Validation

It is hypothesized that a precondition to feeling Shame–Guilt is the perception that one has violated an ethical norm. Implicit in this is the assumption that the ethical norm is held or is shared by the individual. If the individual did not accept the norm then the cause of Shame–Guilt would not be the perception of having violated a norm but rather others' reaction to that violation, or fear of their reaction. Thus, an important assumption is that Shame–Guilt is felt in reference to internalized norms. At the same time, however, shame has often been seen as a social emotion because it is assumed to mediate between the individual and society (Lynd, 1958). Indeed, a number of approaches (Barbalet, 1998; Benedict, 1946; Epstein,

1984; Mead, 1937; Scheff, 1988) are based upon the assumption that shame plays a central role in social conformity and should be understood within that context. The finding that perceptions of shaming by highly respected others predict Shame–Guilt (see Chapter 10) supports these perspectives. The ethical-identity conception proposes that the impact of shaming by others is mediated by processes of social influence and in particular of social validation (Festinger, 1950; Hogg & Turner, 1987). Shaming leads to Shame–Guilt when it is perceived to provide valid information about ethical norms. This explains how Shame–Guilt occurs in reference to internalized ethical values while at the same time is responsive to the shaming of others. Furthermore, it explains why distinctions between shame and guilt on the basis of whether disapproval is internal or external (see Chapter 6) may not be so important.

The concept of social validation assumes that the need to hold valid beliefs is an important motivation (Festinger, 1950). Beliefs, however, vary in the degree to which they are based upon physical reality, in other words the degree to which they can be confirmed via a physical test. For example, it is easy to test whether glass breaks but difficult to test if God exists. Festinger argues that beliefs not easily subject to physical reality testing are confirmed via social reality testing. This form of belief testing is based upon the degree to which others have the same opinion or belief and is said to provide social validation.

Subsequently a number of researchers have suggested that social validation may play an even greater role than that proposed by Festinger (1950). Tajfel (1972), Moscovici (1976) and Hogg and Turner (1987) argue that, even where it is possible, physical reality-testing does not by itself provide the individual with certainty. They argue that even the most basic forms of physical reality testing rely on social validation because they require the individual to place an interpretation on the physical facts.

> It is true, of course, that technical instruments permit an individual to make decisions about the environment by himself; but even these instruments conceal a consensus, since the mode of action of a tool or the appropriateness of a measuring device must be agreed upon by all if the result of such operations is to carry any information. (Moscovici, 1976: p. 70)

Thus, it is argued that individuals rely on social validity testing to validate all kinds of beliefs. Even where reality would appear to be fairly straightforward, people are sensitive to others' opinions, especially where there is a consensus that one is wrong.[1] To the extent that shaming is a form of social validation it can either confirm for individuals that what they have done is wrong or it can undermine the belief of not having done anything wrong.

An important characteristic of social validation, especially given our interest in Shame–Guilt, is that social validation can only come from others who are seen as adequate reference points. According to Festinger these reference groups are comprised of people who are similar to oneself, and it is their similarity on significant dimensions that gives their opinions validity. A recent approach has defined reference groups on the basis of shared social identity (Tajfel & Turner, 1979; Turner, 1991). This theory proposes that individuals' identities are partially composed of their social group memberships (social identities). When membership of a particular social group is salient, the individual will 'categorize' the self according to this identity, perceiving him or her self similar to others with the same social identity. For example, if someone has a social identity of 'mother' they might think of themselves and other mothers as similar in that they are caring, nurturing people. This perceived similarity in social identity should result in others being perceived as a relevant reference group in some contexts and thus as appropriate people to provide social validation. For example, if discussing the disciplining of children another mother is more likely to be seen as having a valid opinion.

The role of reference groups in the development and maintenance of norms has been investigated on a number of occasions. One example is Newcomb's (1943; Newcomb, Koenig, Flacks & Warwick, 1967) longitudinal study of attitudes in an American college. In this research the effects of an apparent reference group on compliance with norms were still measurable after 25 years. These results are supported by studies showing that shared social identity results in greater compliance with group norms. For example, using a polarization paradigm, Mackie (1986) found that when participants' attention was focused upon their group membership, conformity to the group norm, and thus polarization, was greater. The perception of having a similar identity to others has also been shown to increase conformity in the Asch (1956) paradigm.[2] Abrams, Wetherell, Cochrane, Hogg, and Turner (1990) found that if in the standard Asch paradigm participants perceived the confederates to be in-group members (sharing the same social identity) rather than out-group members, then conformity was significantly greater. These studies appear to demonstrate that we are influenced by our reference groups.

Hogg and Turner (1987) summarize the effects of social validation with a theory of referent informational influence. This proposes that individuals expect that others whom they perceive as similar (having the same social identity) will have the same beliefs and will act in the same way as themselves. When this expectation is fulfilled, it provides social validation: the individual's belief is confirmed. However, when the individual's beliefs are inconsistent with those whom they expect to agree with them, the belief is undermined. This increases the individual's uncertainty, making influence more likely.

Applied to Shame–Guilt, this research provides an explanation for the effect of shaming. While Shame–Guilt is felt in relation to the individual's own ethical norms, these are often norms shared with others, and particularly reference groups, that act to confirm and shape them. So while Shame–Guilt might occur in social isolation, because the individual has ethical values that are internalized, they can also be responsive to the shaming of others. As a result it is not necessary to distinguish between a shame that is based upon external criticism and a guilt based upon internalized values. In this model we predict that shaming by reference groups would validate an individual's belief that their actions were wrong. Equally, shaming by reference groups would produce uncertainty and influence in the event that the individual believes that his or her actions were not wrong. Most critical to this process is whether the individual perceives the shamers as a valid reference point. This highlights the importance of the interaction between the individual and their social context.

In summary, we argue that shaming results in Shame–Guilt to the extent that it socially validates the individual's belief that they have violated an ethical norm. Whether or not shaming provides social validation depends upon the degree to which individuals perceive the shamers as valid reference points.

Shame–Guilt Involves Threat to an Individual's Identity

Shame–Guilt has just been described as occurring when the individual perceives that they have acted in a way that they believe is wrong, and that this perception is based upon ethical norms that are formed and maintained in part through social validation with reference groups. Indeed it is argued by social identity theorists that the values an individual accepts, and thus will feel ashamed for violating, are determined by their identity. This is because social identities entail beliefs that provide the individual with a framework in which to understand the world and their place in it. However, this also highlights the importance of values to identity and the reciprocity of this relationship. This is particularly evident in social identity theory, which predicts that the identity of an individual will be, in part, determined by the similarity they perceive between self and others on particular values. Thus, having certain values is essential to having a particular identity.

> If shared social identity is the basis of mutual influence between people (Turner, 1991), it is also a central object of influence: the construction and validation of people's definition of who they are (and are not) are basic to the task of developing shared norms, values and goals. (Turner & Onorato, 1999: p. 27)

Having argued that there is a reciprocal relationship between normative beliefs and identity, it follows that when one becomes aware that one has acted contrary to norms, one's identity is called into question. It is proposed that a defining feature of Shame–Guilt is that it involves a threat to the individual's identity. Threat to identity occurs because the contradiction between the individual's ethical norms and their behavior[3] cannot be easily reconciled. In contrast, the violation of non-ethical norms – not fitting in by dressing badly, not concentrating and dropping the ball at a sporting contest, saying something stupid at work – might engender Embarrassment–Exposure when they occur in public, but will not result in Shame–Guilt. The experience of Shame–Guilt involves an inconsistency between a global sense of the self, based upon ethical values, and evidence to the contrary. This state is accompanied by a need to resolve this tension. In some respects this is similar to Wurmser's (1994) description of shame as betrayal of a global or gestalt image of the self because it is a threat to the whole framework of one's identity.

An important aspect of threat to identity, because of the reciprocal relationship between identity and belief, is that it undermines certainty. Shame–Guilt involves a loss of confidence regarding who one is and how one fits into broader social structures. It calls into question values and normative beliefs much broader than the ethical norm that was violated. Identity, and particularly social identity, is viewed by many as a regulator of social interaction. Social identities provide frameworks for interpreting the actions of others as well as defining the relationship between the self and others. If Shame–Guilt involves uncertainty regarding identity then it restricts the individual's ability to interpret others' behavior, thus inhibiting social interactions. We think that it is this uncertainty that explains why shame is associated with feelings of social isolation (or withdrawal), difficulties in interpersonal communication, feelings of helplessness and depression (Epstein, 1984; H. B. Lewis, 1971; Nathanson, 1992; Sachdev, 1990).

The potential effects of shame highlight the importance of its resolution since this can have a profound impact upon the well-being of individuals. Threat to identity stems from an inconsistency between one's behavior and ethical norms that challenges one's understanding of the world. Thus it is proposed that resolution occurs via a process of remaking sense of what has occurred. This might involve changes in one's identity as a result of re-evaluating and changing one's ethical norms. Alternatively it might involve the justification of one's actions in relation to one's current ethical norms. For example, actions might be justified as simply a lapse that is put right by apology or reparation. In some cases this process will occur very quickly. At the other extreme, shame may persist over long periods because the individual is unable to decide whether their actions were wrong, or are

unable to find a way to discharge shame which they have acknowledged. So while we recognize one response as Shame–Guilt we can also identify an Unresolved Shame which might be similar to H. Lewis's (1971) unacknowledged shame or a number of alternatives identified by Nathanson's compass of shame (1992). Even though Unresolved Shame may involve uncertainty regarding how shameful one's actions are, we can hypothesize that it also involves threat to identity. Not being able to decide what is right is indicative of not knowing who one is. Indeed, being unable to decide whether one has violated ethical norms, but yet thinking this likely, makes resolution of shame more difficult.

Social validation can also play a significant role in the resolution of Shame–Guilt by confirming particular ethical norms and validating efforts to make right any wrongdoing. This might, for example, occur when an individual's behavior is shamed but there is also acceptance of an apology and compensation. The importance of this process is highlighted in Sachdev's discussion of *whakama*, a Maori concept that incorporates ideas of shame, guilt, embarrassment and humiliation. For some individuals, *whakama* becomes a severely debilitating experience in which individuals report symptoms including difficulty communicating with others, withdrawal from the community, depression, self-exile, and sometimes suicide. According to Sachdev, Maori apply two primary treatments. These either involve building up the individual's esteem or, if the reason for *whakama* is a transgression, applying a suitable punishment followed by reintegrating the individual back into the community (Sachdev, 1990). This second approach might be interpreted as assisting an individual resolve Shame–Guilt by providing a mechanism to validate their actions as wrong and allowing the person to resolve internal tension through repentance.

In summary, we argue that Shame–Guilt involves a threat to the individual's identity. The emotion is diminished when the threat to identity is resolved through the realignment of behaviors and ethical values. Unresolved Shame occurs when threat to identity cannot be resolved.

Behavioral Integrity and Cognitive Dissonance Theory

The conception of Shame–Guilt outlined in this chapter emphasizes the importance of consistency between individuals' ethical values and behavior. Consistency between beliefs is also central to cognitive dissonance theory (Festinger and Carlsmith, 1959) which argues that when individuals' cognitions are inconsistent they experience psychological discomfort and are motivated to alter their cognitions so as to make them consistent. More recent extensions of the theory have emphasized the importance of consistency, particularly when beliefs are about the self. One variation on the

theory is that of Aronson (1969, 1997) who argues that cognitive dissonance occurs primarily when an element of the self-concept is threatened. Individuals try to maintain a self-concept that is both consistent and positive, which means that engaging in actions that threaten the self-concept are particularly powerful in producing dissonance. The result, as in the original Festinger formulation, is a process of self-justification that involves changing the dissonant cognitions so that they are no longer dissonant. Another alternative proposed by Steele (Steele, 1988; Steele & Liu, 1983) argues that the individual's need for self-affirmation is the motivation responsible for the effect found by Festinger and Carlsmith (1959), rather than the need for cognitive consistency. Steele (1988) argues that this is distinct from cognitive dissonance because it focuses upon global integrity of the self rather than consistency between specific cognitions. Thus, resolving specific dissonance between cognitions is not as important as maintaining a perception of overall esteem.

While the debate between dissonance theorists cannot be adequately addressed here, research into these theories demonstrates that when people act contrary to normative beliefs, feelings of dissonance are produced. Furthermore, these feelings of psychological discomfort motivate the individual to find a 'dissonance reducing strategy' to dampen their discomfort (Elliot & Devine, 1994). In one study reported by Elliot and Devine (1994), participants who experienced dissonance also reported feeling greater levels of discomfort, which involved feelings of being uncomfortable, uneasy and feeling bothered, as well as feeling greater negative feelings towards the self, which involved anger, dissatisfaction, disgust and annoyance with the self. While participants did not report differences in embarrassment or shame both discomfort and negative evaluation are associated with shame. This would appear to suggest that cognitive dissonance involves feelings similar to those experienced in Shame–Guilt and in turn that Shame–Guilt may involve a process similar to dissonance reduction. By the same token, Shame–Guilt can not simply be understood as dissonance between cognitions because Shame–Guilt involves an undermining of the individual's identity, their whole framework of beliefs. Shame–Guilt also involves a strong ethical content that is not necessary evident in cognitive dissonance.

Explaining Shame and Shaming Within Justice Cases

So far we have outlined a new conception of Shame–Guilt. In this section we will explore how this conception can be applied to the criminal justice cases that we observed. Even though the theoretical propositions in this chapter are not tested by our empirical work, we will begin by showing that they provide a coherent explanation for the relationship found between

shaming and Shame–Guilt. The analyses of this relationship, found in Chapter 10, showed that offenders who remember thinking the offence wrong before the conference or court case also reported greater feelings of Shame–Guilt. This is consistent with the proposition that Shame–Guilt is a reaction to ethical norms that are internalized. The theory also proposes, however, that shaming by reference groups will validate the individual's perception of having violated an ethical norm. While the analysis cannot test whether social validation is responsible the analyses do show that shaming only predicted Shame–Guilt when it was perceived to come from highly respected others. While respect is not equivalent to the concept of similarity or shared social identity on which membership of reference groups is based, respect for others should be a function of reference group membership.

The regression analysis predicting Shame–Guilt also highlighted reintegration and stigmatization as significant predictors. While reintegration was associated with greater Shame–Guilt, stigmatization predicted less of this emotion. Reintegrative shaming is where others disapprove of the offender's act but also attempt to integrate the offender into the community by treating him or her with respect and forgiveness. This type of shaming communicates to the person that they are part of the same community as the shamers and emphasizes the individual's similarity and belongingness to the group. It is suggested that this results in greater feelings of Shame–Guilt because it strengthens (or maintains) the individual's perception that the shamers are a reference group, giving their view greater validity. In contrast to this process, stigmatization involves out-casting the offender by labeling him or her with a deviant identity. In a fairly direct way this identifies the offender as being different, as not sharing the same social identity. Referent informational influence hypothesizes that an out-group cannot influence an individual because the beliefs of such a group are not valid for someone who is by definition different. Indeed, there is evidence (David & Turner, 1996) that where attempts to influence are made by an out-group, the influence actually exerted is counter-normative: the individual's attitudes move in the opposite direction to those of the out-group. This may be the same phenomenon that criminological theorists such as Cohen (1955) identify when they speak of rejecting one's rejecters. Thus, the theory would predict that stigmatization is less likely to result in Shame–Guilt because it undermine the shames as a valid reference point.

While Shame–Guilt signifies an acceptance of wrongdoing, a second form of shame identified in the analysis was Unresolved Shame. This response was stronger in those offenders who thought that the offence was less wrong (although almost none reported thinking that the offence was right), offenders who reported less reintegration by others and those who reported greater stigmatization. Unresolved Shame is conceived here as

occurring where threat to identity cannot be resolved, often because of uncertainty about how wrong the behavior was. This uncertainty threatens identity in the same way that perceived wrongdoing can because it involves doubt about one's behavior and raises questions about one's ethical identity.[4] Unlike Shame–Guilt, Unresolved Shame is more difficult to manage because uncertainty over having done wrong prevents the individual from acting to resolve it. The relationships between Unresolved Shame and reintegration and stigmatization (Chapter 10) are also consistent with this conceptualization. Reintegration reduces Unresolved Shame by validating ethical norms and helping the individual to resolve shame. In contrast, stigmatization presents a hurdle for resolution because it alienates the individual from those who think what they did was wrong. In doing so, it legitimizes or encourages rejection of the group norm, thus enhancing conflict within the individual. This is particularly so in those cases where stigmatization comes from those the individual would normally rely on for social validation or where the norm is one the individual would normally accept. Stigmatization impedes resolution for those already unsure and introduces uncertainty for those who initially felt Shame–Guilt.

The explanation of how reintegration and stigmatization mediate the effect of shaming highlights the way in which groups choose to identify themselves and those they seek to influence. An interesting parallel can be found in research by Reicher and Hopkins (1996) which examines how social identity is determined in part by negotiation and argument between social actors. The study reported by Reicher and Hopkins uses discourse analysis to document the way an anti-abortionist campaigner attempts to influence medical practitioners. In an attempt to be persuasive, the anti-abortionist uses his speech to define anti-abortionists and medical practitioners as similar (in-group members) on the basis of a relevant dimension, that is they are both life savers. The importance of this point is that it suggests that the social identities that occur in a conference or court case are not determined simply by structural features of the case but are negotiated by the participants. Those present in a case work to define one another's social relationships (i.e. social identities) through the way they choose to disapprove of the offense, i.e. reintegratively or stigmatically, and how they react to disapproval. By doing this participants engage in a process of defining their own identity.[5]

The analysis by Reicher and Hopkins (1996) also raises a point regarding the nature of identities that shaming appeals to. Social identity theory (Turner et al., 1987) suggests that individuals can have many different identities (mother, teacher, soccer player) but also that identities can be more or less specific, such that some can be described as subordinate (e.g. being a member of a particular soccer team) while others are superordinate (e.g.

Australian, human). This suggests that shaming could appeal to competing identities like 'family member' over 'gang member', or to superordinate identities like 'life savers' as in Reicher and Hopkins' example involving doctors and an anti-abortionist. Although both may result in Shame–Guilt, we might speculate that it is an appeal to superordinate identities that is more significant. This is because we think that ethical norms are precisely those beliefs that do transcend other identities. As research by V. Braithwaite (1998) shows, broader social values such as not hurting others intentionally are almost universally held. This suggests that Shame–Guilt will be stronger in contexts where common values and identities are salient, as opposed to differences in values and identities among those present.

Summary of Propositions

The theoretical framework outlined in this chapter can be summarized by a number of key propositions regarding the three shame-related emotions and their relationship to shaming.

The Shame-related Emotions

1 Shame–Guilt occurs as a result of the realization that one has acted contrary to an ethical norm and this realization threatens one's identity. Such a threat to identity can possibly be well managed because of this realization.
2 Unresolved Shame occurs as a result of uncertainty regarding whether one has acted contrary to an ethical norm *and* this uncertainty threatens one's identity. Such a threat becomes difficult to resolve because violation of an ethical norm in neither accepted nor rejected.
3 Feelings of Embarrassment–Exposure occur when one is exposed, or believes that one may be exposed, in public as non-normative.

Shaming and Shame

4 Shaming will produce Shame–Guilt to the extent that it validates offenders' belief, or influences them to believe, that they acted contrary to an ethical norm and that this threatens their identity.
5 Shaming will produce Unresolved Shame to the extent that it creates uncertainty as to whether the individual acted contrary to their ethical norms and this uncertainty threatens his/her identity.
6 Shaming will result in Shame–Guilt only when shaming is by a relevant reference group.
7 The degree to which shaming is reintegrative or stigmatic will affect whether those who shame the individual are seen as a valid reference group. Reintegrative or inclusive disapproval will reinforce the status of the reference group as a source of influence while stigmatization or

out-casting will diminish the status of the reference group as a source of influence.

While the empirical studies we have reported in this book are consistent with these propositions, this research did not set out to test them. A significant limitation of the correlational analyses reported here is that they are unable to determine causality. Greater understanding of the causal connections between the key concepts will provide greater insight into what psychological mechanisms account for the emotions.

The ethical identity framework suggests that a precondition for feeling Shame–Guilt is the perception that one has violated an ethical norm. Significant others influence what is perceived as right and wrong through the process of social validation. However, while the perception of wrongdoing may result in Shame–Guilt, it is the fact that this is inconsistent with one's identity, and thus threatens identity, that defines the experience of Shame–Guilt. It is this uncertainty regarding identity from which the feelings of Shame–Guilt emerge, including those of self-consciousness, uncertainty regarding values, discomfort and anger at the self.

Notes

1 This same point is made in reference to shame by Bernard Williams (see Williams, 1993) in his book *Shame and Necessity*.

2 The Asch paradigm involved participants estimating the length of lines with a group they believed to be other participants, but who were confederates of the experimenter. The responses of the confederates were manipulated to be obviously incorrect in some of the trials. The variable of interest was the frequency that participants conformed to this incorrect response.

3 This discussion focused upon behaviors which are violations of ethical norms. It is worthwhile noting, however, that it may be possible in some circumstances to see our experiences or even our self as a violation of our ethical norms. This may explain why shame and guilt are experienced by victims (Zehr, 2000) or those who have suffered trauma (Herman, 1992). Such events may result in these emotions because they directly change our identity but also because they can raise ethical questions. For example, a victims of rape might unfortunately feel Shame–Guilt because even to be raped is perceived as normatively wrong. This may explain why restorative justice processes, which allow victims to participate in a process that focuses upon the harmful behaviors of offenders, appear to play an important role in the recovery process of victims (Strang, 2000). The importance of shame in understanding victimization is further explored in Part III.

4 Of course certainty that what one did is not wrong will not result in Shame–Guilt or Unresolved Shame.

5 Negotiation of identity is also applied to broader explanations of delinquency by Emler and Reicher (1995).

CHAPTER 12

Ethical Identity, Shame Management and Criminal Justice

One motivation for studying the emotion of shame was to test the theory of reintegrative shaming by exploring what emotion or emotions are experienced as a reaction to shaming. This chapter will discuss the implications of our results for the application of reintegrative shaming theory and, more broadly, the roles that shaming and shame play in criminal justice interventions. While the negative self-evaluation associated with the emotion of shame has caused concern (Maxwell and Morris, 1999; Tangney, 1991), this chapter argues that shame management is possibly a more important issue. Placing greater emphasis upon shame management also has implications for how shaming is conceptualized within criminal justice settings. Particular attention will be paid to the relevance of shaming and shame to restorative justice as well as more specific implications for how restorative justice conferences are facilitated. Whereas the previous chapter provided a theoretical framework for understanding shame, this chapter will focus on policy implications.

The Rediscovery of Shame in Criminology

The relevance of shaming to the regulation of behavior is not new. Shaming has been identified as playing an important role in social control by anthropological studies of Polynesian (Mead, 1937) and Asian (Benedict, 1946) societies, as well as analyses of European criminal justice practices in earlier centuries (Braithwaite, 1989). Equally well documented is a move away from stigmatizing practices in European-based criminal justice systems during the century-and-a-half until the 1970s (Braithwaite, 1989). However, in the 1980s and 1990s, a number of developments have re-emphasized the role of shaming. Criminologists (Grasmick & Bursik, 1990)

have begun to explore the effect that the emotions have in criminal justice interventions. In particular, Braithwaite's (1989) theory of reintegrative shaming argues that informal shaming that occurs as part of criminal justice practices is of central importance in understanding the effectiveness of such procedures.

A second development is a movement in some criminal justice systems around the world towards restorative justice. Unlike traditional court procedures that emphasize the importance of just sentences, these approaches place considerable importance upon resolution of conflict and reparation of harm. In doing so, restorative justice emphasizes the importance of the relationships among offenders, victims and the rest of the affected community. Reconciliation is emphasized with genuine apologies from offenders, often considered by victims and restorative justice practitioners as more important than material reparation (Retzinger & Scheff, 1996). As well as emphasizing reparation over retribution (but see Barton, 1999; Daly, 1999), it is also apparent that this approach aims to convince offenders of their wrongdoing by exposing the offender to the consequences of what they have done. Both of these aims place a much greater focus on understanding the way communities express disapproval of offenses. Reintegrative shaming is consistent with this approach because implicit in restoration is reintegration of the offender back into the community. Stigmatization or outcasting offenders is clearly not restorative.

Finally, it is worth noting that the explicit use of shaming by courts has also become popular again in a way that is quite distinct from, indeed contradictory to, restorative justice. Recent examples have occurred, particularly in American criminal justice, where shaming has been used in the court system as a deterrent or punishment for convicted offenders. Offenders are ordered to complete 'shame sentences' relevant to the crime they commit instead of spending time in jail. Shoplifters have been ordered to stand outside shops holding signs declaring that they stole. Drink-drivers are ordered to attach 'DUI' stickers to their cars, while those convicted of soliciting sex are ordered to sweep the streets (see Kahan, 1996, 1998). Another area of American criminal justice which reputedly incorporates shaming are boot camps where offenders are subject to military-style discipline but are also publicly confronted with their offense, a form of intervention that seems rather ineffective. While these approaches to crime have become more popular, there is also concern that humiliation of this type is a regressive step which simply demeans offenders' dignity (Massaro, 1997) while failing to protect basic human rights or allow rehabilitation. This type of shaming, and criticism of it, has highlighted the question of whether shaming can play a constructive role in the criminal justice system.

Questions are also directed at more private offender–victim recon-ciliation processes, such as restorative justice conferences. One concern is that shaming a young offender, who potentially has low self-esteem, may actually exacerbate problems rather than prevent re-offending. If offenses are committed in part due to low self-esteem, gained through lack of emotional support or a difficult past, damaging the offender's esteem further is only going to exacerbate problems. Concerns are given some support by studies that have differentiated between shame and guilt, casting doubt on whether shame is actually a desirable emotion for offenders to feel (Zhang, 1995). Tangney (1991; Tangney et al., 1992a) has argued that shame can be differentiated from guilt because its negative focus is inward upon the individual rather than outward upon the act. Because of this, shame is characterized as not only a much more painful emotion but also as a less productive emotion because it is unlikely to facilitate empathy and reparation and is more likely to result in hostility and anger. As discussed in Chapter 10, Tangney and others (Tangney, 1991; Tangney et al., 1992a; Tangney, Hill-Barlow, Wagner, Marschall, Bornstein, Sanftner & Gramzow, 1996a) have demonstrated an empirical relationship between measures of shame-proneness and the dispositions to feel anger and lower empathy. Thus, an important question to address is whether shame is a constructive emotion for offenders to feel.

Such concerns regarding the emotion of shame are also supported by the results of a recent study which examines long-term re-offending by offenders who attended restorative justice programs in New Zealand (Maxwell & Morris, 1999). In an evaluation of new youth justice legislation introduced in New Zealand in 1989, Maxwell and Morris (1993) followed 211 offenders who had been referred to restorative justice conferences (or, as they are called in New Zealand, family group conferences). In a follow-up to this research, 67 per cent of the original sample of offenders were re-interviewed regarding a broad range of factors believed to predict re-offending, including a number of questions regarding the restorative justice conference. Results from discriminant function analysis show that feelings of 'shame: being made to feel a bad person' (Maxwell and Morris, 1999: p. 6) in the conference were related to persistent reconviction by participants. In contrast, feelings of remorse occurring as a result of the conference were negatively related to persistent reconviction.

Redefining the Role of Shame

The results reported by Tangney and Maxwell and Morris suggest that when offenders feel shame during court or conference cases it is likely to be harmful. Both argue that emotions focused upon the offense will be more

productive. For Tangney this emotion is guilt, while for Maxwell and Morris the healthy response is remorse. As was discussed in Chapter 8, both these emotions have been described as involving recognition of wrongdoing, concern for the consequences of one's actions and a desire to make amends. The implication of their findings is that to avoid damaging offenders' self-esteem the criminal justice system needs to avoid focusing upon the offender's identity. This is consistent with Braithwaite's (1989) reintegrative shaming theory which argues that shaming that involves disapproval of the offender's person will lead to re-offending. Braithwaite, however, also argues that these forms of shaming can be separated from reintegrative shaming which focuses on the offense and its consequences, leading to reduced levels of re-offending. Results in Chapter 9 provided support for this distinction. Factor analysis of items measuring reintegration, stigmatization and shaming showed that the perception that others' disapproved of what one did was not associated with perceptions that others were either reintegrative or stigmatic. Thus, in practice it would seem that court and conference processing is able to disapprove of the offense without having a negative focus on the offender's identity.

However, the results question whether this distinction carries over to the emotions felt by offenders. In particular, the factor analyses in Chapter 8 suggest that participants who felt guilty about what they had done also felt shame. Items that operationalized feelings of anger at oneself, feelings of having lost honor and respect and feeling ashamed of oneself were measured by the same factor (Shame–Guilt) as items which measured feeling ashamed of one's actions and concern that others had been hurt by one's actions. Thus, it would seem that when participants feel remorse or guilt about what they have done, these feelings flow on to feelings of shame.

In some respects this finding is intuitive. Surely someone who recognizes that they have done something wrong would also be concerned about what their actions say about the self. An example might be someone who has knocked down and robbed an elderly person. If this individual accepted that their actions were wrong, understood the consequences for the elderly person, and empathized with the victim's feelings, then it seems likely that they would also feel bad about themselves because they were responsible for what has occurred. Indeed, it might be argued that something would be wrong if they did not. It seems unhealthy and undesirable that individuals could behave in ways they regarded as wrong, yet not see their behavior as directly related to who they are. In a significant sense we might interpret this as a denial of responsibility for their actions. Thus, the healthy response might not be to think 'I have done a bad act, but in no way am I other than a good person.' The healthiest response might be, 'I have done a bad act.

While this tells me something bad about myself that I want to change, I am still basically a good person."

Although intuitive, the finding that shame and guilt co-occur raises questions from the perspective of criminal justice policy. While the studies by Tangney and Maxwell and Morris suggest that feelings of shame should be avoided, our data suggest that shame will accompany feelings of guilt or remorse. However, the results in this book also question how destructive shame feelings are for individuals' self-respect. While the Shame–Guilt factor identified in Chapter 8 measured the feeling of being ashamed of oneself, it was not defined by feelings of being a failure nor of being humiliated, both of which are indicative of a threat to self-esteem. Post-hoc tests also reveal that the Shame–Guilt factor did not correlate significantly with Rosenberg's (1965) self-esteem scale (court cases $r = .05$, conference cases $r = -.04$) nor with a question asking if their 'self-respect' had increased or decreased as a result of the conference or court case (court cases $r = -.1$, conference cases $r = .05$). These findings suggest that Shame–Guilt was neither associated with perceptions of a debased self nor with lower self-esteem. It was also apparent in that in contrast to Tangney's shame-proneness scale, Shame–Guilt predicted lower feelings of hostility and predicted greater empathy with victims. Thus, in some important respects, the feeling of Shame–Guilt that emerged in this book is not nearly as worrying as might have been assumed, even though it is partially measured by anger and shame towards the self.

Disparities between the empirical results on the emotion of shame may be explained by differences in the way it has been measured. While negative feelings directed towards the self are evident in Shame–Guilt, they are not a generalized loss of esteem in oneself nor a feeling that one is a bad person; it is feeling ashamed of oneself as a result of a criminal offense. Maxwell and Morris's (1999) measure, in contrast, is completely about feeling one is a bad person: 'Did the way [the conference] was dealt with make you feel that you were a bad person?' Tangney's measure also focuses upon shame as a negative evaluation of the whole self. Indeed, Harder (1995) argues that the '. . . tendency to consider almost all negative self-evaluations as shame . . . is also evident in the wording of the TOSCA [Test of Self-Conscious Affect] scale items.' (p. 382). Harder's criticism is that measurement of shame by Tangney's scale is limited to one dimension of the emotion: negative self-evaluation. In contrast, the Shame–Guilt factor in this book measures a range of feelings not evident in these other measures. In particular, Shame–Guilt also involves feeling that what one had done was wrong, concern that others had been hurt, the feeling that one had lost respect or honor in one's community, and fear of other's reactions. It might be speculated that when experienced as part of this broader

emotion in the context of having done a serious wrong, the negative self-evaluation associated with shame is not nearly so toxic.

Another important difference is that Shame–Guilt measures a discrete emotional experience while Tangney's measure of shame-proneness (TOSCA) is a personality disposition. It was argued above that it was intuitive that individuals would make negative evaluations about themselves as a result of recognizing that they had done serious wrong. However, what the TOSCA measures in extreme cases is a disposition to make negative self-evaluations in response to a much greater range of situations. An example might be of a person who trips over at a party and as a result feels that they are worthless. Thus, it might be speculated that shame-proneness measures a tendency to see negative implications for one's self-image in inappropriate situations. The reasons for this tendency might have to do with low self-esteem or with developmental issues. However, it is this conception of shame as an underlying personality trait that resonates with some concerns regarding the emotion of shame occurring in criminology and other contexts. In particular, there is fear that shaming of vulnerable (shame-prone) individuals may simply make them feel worse about themselves. However, given the apparent differences between results of studies on shame-proneness and the present results, it is important to distinguish between the discrete emotion on the one hand and the personality disposition on the other.

Beyond Shame

Much interest has been focused upon shame. In the work presented in Part II, the importance of other shame-related emotions is highlighted. The factor analysis in Chapter 8 identified Embarrassment–Exposure and Unresolved Shame factors. It seems likely that these emotions have a number of implications for conceptions of shame within the justice system. The Embarrassment–Exposure emotion, which measured feelings of unwanted attention and humiliation, is significant because it is a shame-related response that participants report experiencing more in court than in conference cases (see Chapter 8). The impact this emotion has on offenders is not clear, but it appears more concerned with discomfort due to public exposure than remorse for the offense. Perhaps more important is Unresolved Shame, which leaves offenders unable to put the case, or the offense, behind them. Participants feeling Unresolved Shame reported ongoing uncertainty about how wrong the offense was, were 'continually bothered' by thoughts that they were unfairly treated, and were more likely to be feeling anger and hostility towards others present at the case. The elements of uncertainty and non-resolution suggest that this emotional

reaction is not simply one of defiance in which the participant is rejecting the entire process. Rather, these participants seem unable to decide whether or not they should feel Shame–Guilt. In this respect, the emotion seems to represent a sense of possible shame which the person is unable to dispel.

While acknowledgment of wrongdoing in Shame–Guilt is associated with empathy and low hostility, the results suggest that Unresolved Shame may be destructive for both the offender and the criminal justice system. The critical factor for criminal justice interventions may not be whether they produce shame, but how well they assist offenders in the resolution of shame. It was argued above that it seemed necessary in some contexts for people to feel shame, because it acknowledged that they are responsible for their behavior. It might further be argued, in light of these results, that acknowledgment of shame may be important for the well-being of offenders. This is because acknowledgment of shame provides certainty that what they did was wrong, which appears to be psychologically important. Furthermore, acknowledgment of wrongdoing allows offenders to remedy what they have done. Neither of these are possible if shame is unresolved, because in such circumstances, offenders are hampered in being forgiven by others or in rebuilding their social standing in their community. It is important to point out that this is discussed in the context of criminal cases where it is generally assumed that what the person has done is wrong. In Part III we move down to bullying, which is not necessarily criminal, and explore in more detail the implications of irresolution and the absence of acknowledgment of shame. Finally, it might also be argued that in some cases Unresolved Shame should be resolved by not feeling shame at all.

In many respects our findings on acknowledgment are consistent with a considerable body of qualitative research on shame. In her clinical work, H. B. Lewis (1971) identified a form of shame which although unacknowledged by the person experiencing it had a number of identifiable characteristics. The emotion was different to acknowledged shame because it only involved consciousness of a 'wince' or 'shock' in feeling associated with doubt about how others see the self. Most identifiably by-passed shame involves an element of cognitive confusion. H.B. Lewis describes this:

> The back and forth ideation about guilt leaves the patient in an insoluble, plaguing dilemma of guilt thought which will not be solved. (H. B. Lewis, 1971: p. 234)

Thus, like the Unresolved Shame factor, the experience involves an ongoing inability to make sense of the 'shameful' event. H. B. Lewis also noted that this form of shame was particularly associated with feelings of hostility. Scheff (1990a) extends H. B. Lewis's analysis by arguing that unacknowledged shame results in shame–rage spirals. In Scheff's analysis

shame is a signal that the bond between the individual and others is threatened. When the feelings of hurt (shame) associated with this rejection are not acknowledged by the individual then this emotion can become redirected as further shame and anger at the self and others (Scheff, 1990a: p. 171). Scheff argues that this form of unacknowledged shame is often the cause of humiliated fury and can potentially explain not just individual anger but also conflict between nations (Scheff, 1994). In both H. B. Lewis's and Scheff's accounts of shame it is evident that when shame is not acknowledged it manifests itself in an unhealthy reaction. Although Nathanson (1992, 1997) does not discuss by-passed shame, he also argues that individuals cope with or avoid shameful experiences in a number of different ways. Nathanson identifies four reactions that are manifestations of shame: withdrawal, attack self, attack other, and avoidance. Each of these behavioral scripts can be expressed to varying degrees that are either more or less healthy. In each case extreme manifestations of these reactions are potentially harmful to the individual and/or others. For example, while attack self might involve gentle self-derision, at the extreme it might also include masochistic behavior. The shame management implications of these concepts, especially the issue of acknowledgment, will be explored in Part III.

Shaming and Resolution

It has been argued on the basis of our results and other research that a critical factor for criminal justice is the way individuals cope with, or manage, shame. If attention is focused not on whether individuals feel shame but how they resolve it then this also has implications for how shaming is conceptualized. It suggests that avoiding shaming will not help insulate individuals from shame but may actually make it more difficult for offenders to resolve shame. It was argued above that it would be natural for an offender to feel shame for having attacked an elderly person. In such an example it would be difficult to imagine how a community could insulate that offender from their own sense of shame or repress their own feeling of disapproval. Rather, it would seem that shaming, or disapproval by relevant others, plays an important role in enabling the resolution of shame – averting the adverse implications of Unresolved Shame such as externalized anger. First, because it validates that a particular behavior is wrong and second, when reintegrative, it helps identify what the individual needs to do in order to reclaim respectability. Not addressing the issue at a community level denies the individual the chance of acknowledging what they have done and rebuilding their self-respect. It might even be argued that the avoidance of shaming is a naive goal because disapproval and

anger will be felt as a result of offenses and thus will be expressed even if in very subtle ways. This suggests that shaming needs to be understood in terms of the way it helps resolve shame as much as the degree to which it results in shame.

Before addressing this further, it is important to discuss a number of conceptual issues regarding the concept of shaming. The extreme nature of 'shaming punishments' has highlighted a particular definition of what shaming is. In particular, these forms of punishment suggest that shaming involves public humiliation of the individual, an explicit or implicit evaluation of the offender, and ongoing implications for the social standing of offenders. However, a substantially different use of the term shaming is employed by reintegrative shaming theory which defines shaming as a broad spectrum of disapproving behaviors ranging from those that are highly respectful of the offender (reintegrative) to those that are disrespectful (stigmatizing). The stigmatizing shaming evident in the public humiliation of offenders is captured by this definition, but so too are more subtle and positive forms of disapproval. The breadth of this definition is central to Braithwaite's theory because it allows the theory to distinguish between forms of social disapproval. It is by seeking to classify a broad range of social behavior on this single dimension that the theory acquires its explanatory power.

An important implication of differences between these definitions of shaming is that criticisms of 'shaming' in the criminal justice system envisage a substantially different concept to the one defined by Braithwaite. Indeed a possible criticism of Braithwaite's use of the word 'shaming' is that it is not consistent with common usage. It might be argued that because of cultural values attached to the word 'shaming' it should only be applied to what he terms 'stigmatizing shaming' and that an alternative label is needed for reintegrative forms of disapproval. Indeed it might even be argued that the term 'social disapproval' better represents the breadth of meaning intended. Braithwaite intended to provoke twentieth-century sensibilities by suggesting that nineteenth-century Victorians, contemporary Asians, and Polynesians among others, had more healthy ways of thinking about shame and shaming. Highlighting, as Scheff (1990a) puts it, that we have '. . . become ashamed to be ashamed . . .' (p. 16; also see Scheff, 1990b). Given that acknowledgment is believed by writers such as Scheff to be fundamental to healthy negotiation of shame, twentieth-century sweeping of shame and shaming under the carpet is unhealthy. The important point made by this discussion is that the use of the term 'shaming' throughout this book, based upon reintegrative shaming theory, refers to a much broader concept than simply public humiliation, or even private denigration of the individual.

The importance of differentiating between conceptions of shaming is evident in discussion of restorative justice conferences, which have been explained using reintegrative shaming theory. 'Shaming' intuitively implies an active, intentional process. It suggests that the other participants at a conference act with the intention to make the offender feel the emotion of shame. Moreover, this in turn has been taken as implying that this is done through a format which is explicitly focused upon making the offender feel bad about themselves or their act. However, this picture is far from accurate. Conferences are not structured in a way that encourages participants to intentionally shame offenders, even if in some cases this is what occurs. The structure of conferences, as well as the style of questions asked by facilitators (McDonald et al., 1994) focuses participants upon discussing the consequences of an offense as well as finding solutions to any harms that have occurred. Braithwaite's (1989: p. 100) definition of shaming includes all behavior with the *intent or result* of causing remorse in the offender and/or condemnation by others. An attractive aspect of this definition is that it is inclusive of behavior, such as discussion of consequences, even where those involved are not aware of shame or shaming. Defined this way shaming is a much more appropriate description of what occurs at conferences and much more analytically useful for dissecting the differences in what happens at different conferences. Indeed, our research findings suggest that shaming at court and conference cases is not exhaustively measured through offenders' perceptions of others' disapproval. Social disapproval, or shaming, can be expressed by simply attending a conference or court case, or simply by hearing the consequences of one's action. In fact one important feature of conferences might be that they are able to communicate disapproval without necessarily expressing it directly. Given Braithwaite's definition, shaming is an important theoretical tool for understanding this social process. However, it is also worthwhile noting that it is not, and nor does it claim to be, a description of how people understand their own behavior.

Shaming was measured here as the perception of others' disapproval of the act. The results in Chapter 10 show that in cases where the offender had a high degree of respect for those present, the perception of strong disapproval was associated with greater feelings of Shame–Guilt. It was also apparent that shaming did not predict either Embarrassment–Exposure or Unresolved Shame. Thus, disapproval was not associated with feeling that things had not been resolved or things were unfair. However, these results do suggest that shaming may play an important role in the acknowledgment that behavior was wrong.

The offender's perception of reintegration or stigmatization was also related to whether Shame–Guilt was acknowledged in the case and whether

Unresolved Shame occurred afterwards. It was evident that when the shaming context labeled the offender as evil and applied a master status trait the offender was more likely to feel Unresolved Shame and Embarrassment–Exposure. It might be speculated that this type of shaming discourages resolution for a number of reasons. It was hypothesized in the previous chapter that stigmatization may communicate to offenders that they are different to the shaming community, in turn undermining the validity of that community's beliefs and engendering in the offender a desire to distance themselves. While this explanation was drawn from social influence perspectives (Turner et al., 1987) a similar argument is evident in labeling theory (Erikson, 1962) and reintegrative shaming theory (Braithwaite, 1989). It could also be speculated that stigmatization may be used by offenders to neutralize Shame–Guilt about the offense on the basis that others' behavior towards them had been worse.

The regression analyses also show that stigmatizing shaming predicts lower amounts of Shame–Guilt. Stigmatization may prevent individuals from acknowledging wrongdoing because it creates a context in which the individual's attention is focused upon defending the self. The offender may be fearful of admitting wrongdoing for fear that the response will elicit further stigmatization. Of course an alternative hypothesis, because causal direction cannot be tested, might be that denial of Shame–Guilt is justified by perceptions of stigmatization. Nevertheless, at this stage we can say that the results are consistent with the argument that stigmatization reduces acknowledgement of Shame–Guilt and increases Unresolved Shame.

The reverse pattern of results was evident for the measure of reintegration. Where shaming of an act is respectful of the offender and is accompanied by attempts to forgive, lower levels of Unresolved Shame and greater feelings of Shame–Guilt are evident. This is also supportive of the argument that reintegration and shaming assist offenders in the acknowledgment of shame. Just as stigmatization was hypothesized to alienate the offender from the values of the shaming community, reintegration may help validate the community's disapproval. Reintegration communicates to the offender that they are a respected member of the community, thus enhancing the strength of this social identity and the validity of its values. Equally, reintegration might allow greater acknowledgment of wrongdoing because the context is not threatening to the offender, thus allowing greater disclosure on the offender's part.

In the above discussion it has been suggested that reintegration and stigmatization may have different effects upon the shame-related emotions experienced by offenders. This is not intended to imply that influence is only occurring in that direction. As mentioned above, the results reported in this book are correlational and thus do not provide information

regarding the causal direction of effects. Thus it might be that the emotions of Shame–Guilt and Unresolved Shame actually cause the perceptions of reintegration and stigmatization. It is perhaps more likely that the relationship between shaming and Shame–Guilt is recursive, with for example, reintegration leading to Shame–Guilt but this also allowing greater reintegration, and so on. It might also be that lower feelings of Shame–Guilt result in greater stigmatization, due to perceptions by participants that the offender is not remorseful, leading to less Shame–Guilt and greater Unresolved Shame. Although the causal direction is not known, it is significant that shaming that is reintegrative of the offender is associated with greater acknowledgment of Shame–Guilt while stigmatization is associated with Unresolved Shame.

It has been argued that within criminal justice the distinction that may be of greatest importance is not whether shame or guilt is felt but rather whether feelings of shame are resolved. Furthermore, shaming would appear to play an important role in how shame is dealt with in criminal justice cases. Overt shaming of the individual may result in the ongoing negative self-evaluation identified by Tangney (1991) and Maxwell and Morris (1999). Citizens who perceive that they have been stigmatized leave conference or court cases with the feeling that matters are not resolved and feeling angry with others. However, reintegrative shaming of the offense by respected others is associated with greater acknowledgment of wrongdoing and remorse during cases and less ongoing negative emotion. Thus, concern that shaming damages offenders' self-esteem and alienates them from the community seems to be restricted to stigmatizing forms of shaming. There is also some evidence that shaming plays an important role in allowing offenders to resolve issues arising from an offense and may even be crucial in resolving feelings of Shame–Guilt and remorse.

Implications for Effective Shaming

With the assumption that the resolution of shame is important, and that shaming plays an important role in achieving this, our results have practical implications for the facilitation of conferences. One factor which, as just discussed, appears to be important in determining whether Shame–Guilt or Unresolved Shame occurs is the degree to which shaming is reintegrative or stigmatic. This suggests that facilitators should, where reasonable, steer conferences away from stigmatization of the offender and provide the opportunity for reintegration. Indeed, a number of elements within the conference structure are aimed at achieving these objectives. Particularly important in conferences are the questions that facilitators ask the participants. A clear objective of these questions is to focus all participants at a

conference on the offense that has been committed and the consequences of that offense. For example, the victim is asked 'Now let's find out from (victim) in what way he/she has been affected? (Victim), would you tell us about that' (McDonald, Moore, O'Connell & Thorsborne, 1995: p. 62). Questions to victim supporters and others at the conference also focus upon the consequences of the offense and emotions arising from those consequences. This clear focus allows participants to express their emotions and disapproval but also helps divert attention from the offender's person, thus limiting stigmatization (McDonald et al., 1994). The importance of the way in which these issues are addressed, and the particular questions that are used in conferences, highlights the advantage of facilitators using questions or scripts developed with these specific aims in mind.

Other techniques important to achieving reintegrative outcomes are less easily scripted. For example the re-framing of angry, blaming outbursts into expressions of hurt are another way of refocusing conferences on the consequences of offenses rather than stigmatization (McDonald et al., 1994). The results in this book suggest that these techniques are an important, if not a crucial aspect, of the conferencing procedure. Enhancing the possibility for reintegration, and minimizing stigmatization, in this way appears to maximize the possibility of offenders feeling Shame–Guilt for the offense and minimizing Embarrassment–Exposure or Unresolved Shame. Qualitative observation suggests that one way such techniques impact upon conferences is by interrupting negative cycles of stigmatization, defiance and/or withdrawal by offenders: such cycles bring an increase in stigmatization as offenders communicate less and less remorse. By focusing conferences on the consequences, facilitators seem to reduce stigmatization and instead encourage reintegration and Shame–Guilt.

An important finding here was that the relationship between shaming and shame was moderated by the degree to which the offender respected those who effectively were the shamers. In those cases where there was high respect for the others present at the case, shaming increased the amount of Shame–Guilt felt. However, there was no significant relationship where respect was lower. This has important and fairly obvious implications for conferencing. Training of facilitators (McDonald et al., 1994) emphasizes the importance of having people who can best support the offender at the conference. A key method of determining this is by asking the offender whom they want present, whom they respect. In cases where the offender is not initially ashamed of their actions, disapproval by others would appear to play an important role in influencing them to see their actions as wrong. Perhaps even more importantly this type of shaming may help offenders who are uncertain to acknowledge Shame–Guilt. This suggests that the composition of conferences is important and that a particular emphasis

needs to be placed on identifying and inviting those whom the offender respects.

The importance that offender supporters play in conferences also has broader implications. A number of approaches to restorative justice, both theoretical and practical, have emphasized the importance of the interaction between victim and offender. A very good reason for this is that the basic philosophy behind restorative justice is that of reconciliation and restoration between the victim and offender. A second reason for this focus is the belief that it is having to actually face the victim which produces shame, remorse and empathy in offenders. While not arguing against the importance of these factors, the present results suggest that the offender's supporters may play a much more important role than is sometimes acknowledged and that this aspect should be given considerable emphasis in practice. The results might also be interpreted as supporting the use of conferencing in cases where there is no victim or where victims are unwilling to attend.

The importance of shamers being respected also has implications for the role facilitators or mediators play in criminal justice interventions. It is unlikely that a facilitator, whether a police officer or another official, will be highly respected by the offender. Even more certain is that the facilitator will not be respected as much or more than the offender's supporters. This suggests that shaming by the facilitator is unlikely to result in greater feelings of shame on the part of the offender, or at the very least will be less effective than shaming by others. Furthermore, if the facilitator is actually seen as an out-group member, dissimilar to the offender on relevant dimensions, some research (David & Turner, 1996) suggests that shaming by him or her may actually be counterproductive. Although not seen in the results presented in this book, this research suggests that shaming by disrespected others may result in the offender feeling less shame and perhaps even seeing the offense as less wrong. These results support training (McDonald et al., 1994) that encourages facilitators to avoid actively disapproving of the offense.

Unresolved Shame and Reintegrative Shaming Theory

Discussion of shaming within criminology, and particularly reintegrative shaming theory, has focused primarily upon the emotion of shame. However, the results presented in this book suggest that Unresolved Shame may be just as or even more important than Shame–Guilt in the prediction of recidivism. What is significant about these results for reintegrative shaming theory is that reintegration does not simply increase Shame–Guilt and stigmatization does not simply decrease Shame–Guilt. Reintegration also reduces Unresolved Shame while stigmatization increases it. Thus, predictions of recidivism may need to take into account both emotions.

One suggestion is that the ratio of the two emotions might provide a useful tool for understanding the emotional and motivational links between shaming and recidivism.

Table 12.1 illustrates predictions of recidivism that might be made if Shame–Guilt and Unresolved Shame are both taken into account. This model suggests that there are two situations in which clear predictions can be made. The first is where there are high feelings of Shame–Guilt and low Unresolved Shame. As the offender is primarily concerned with the 'wrongness' of what they have done it should be expected that recidivism will be low. In contrast, the low Shame–Guilt/high Unresolved Shame offender feels no Shame–Guilt during the case and is unsure about the fairness of their treatment and how wrong the offense actually was. The correlation between stigmatization and Unresolved Shame also suggests that bonds between the offender and their community may be weakened as a result of the case. This seems the condition most likely to result in recidivism. The future behavior of an offender feeling low Shame–Guilt and low Unresolved Shame is less easy to predict. It would appear that the offender is not emotionally affected by feelings that what they did was wrong. However, it is also evident that they do not feel unfairly treated by the intervention. It seems possible that this low level of emotionality may result in offenders behaving as rational actors: weighing up the desire to offend against deterrents. Makkai and Braithwaite's (1994) study of corporate deterrence found that managers with low emotionality perceived deterrent threats and were more likely to comply, while those high on emotionality were less likely to be deterred. This latter ideology of the highly emotional may be similar to the offender who feels both high Shame–Guilt and Unresolved Shame. These offenders feel remorse for what has occurred, but despite this, do not feel that important issues were resolved. These offenders may well have the hardest time due to this conflict of emotions. Re-offending in this group may hinge upon how this conflict is resolved, which suggests that re-offending is possible.

Table 12.1 Predicting Recidivism from Shame–Guilt and Unresolved Shame

	Low Shame–Guilt	High Shame–Guilt
Low Unresolved Shame	*Lower recidivism* – rationally calculated action.	*Lowest recidivism* – remorseful for offense
High Unresolved Shame	*Highest recidivism* – resentful at treatment, alienated from values and community	*Higher recidivism* – remorseful but also alienated from values and community

Summary

The results presented throughout this book show that the process of shaming and its emotional consequences are complex. The research implies that shaming should be thought of more broadly than as behavior intended to produce shame. The concept as defined by Braithwaite (1989) embodies a variety of ways in which disapproval is communicated intentionally and unintentionally. It is also true that communities engage in shaming of offenders through a variety of formal, non-formal, organized and non-organized mediums. This shaming seems to play an important role in whether offenders acknowledge that what they have done is wrong, whether they are able to repair the damage they caused, how they are treated by the community, and how they come to feel about themselves and the offense. Shaming and its role in the resolution of shame is also important because feelings of guilt and shame, whether acknowledged or not, are often connected with criminal offenses. Thus, it is argued that an important aspect of shaming in restorative justice procedures, such as restorative justice conferences or healing circles, is how it facilitates this process of resolution, what Ahmed calls 'shame management'. In the drink-driving component of the reintegrative shaming experiments it was evident that those participants who perceived that they were reintegratively shamed were much more likely to feel Shame–Guilt during the case and less Unresolved Shame afterwards. Notwithstanding the revisions to the theory of reintegrative shaming commended by these results, they provide strong support for the central tenets of the theory.

PART III

Shame Management: Regulating Bullying

Eliza Ahmed

CHAPTER 13

The Bullying Problem

> Shame is a thermostat; if it fails to function, regulation of
> relationships becomes impossible.
>
> *(Retzinger, 1996: p. 17)*

School bullying is widely regarded as a serious personal, social and educational problem which affects a substantial portion of school children. Not only does it cause harm and distress to the children who are bullied at the time (Besag, 1989; Callaghan & Joseph, 1995; Olweus, 1978, 1993; Rigby, 1996; Slee, 1994; Smith, 1991; Tattum & Lane, 1989), it also inflicts emotional and developmental scars that can persist into adolescence and beyond (Kochenderfer & Ladd, 1996a, 1996b; Olweus, 1993). Victims of bullying are not the only ones who are adversely affected. Children who bully others experience enjoyment in exercising power and status over victims (Besag, 1989; Rigby, 1996) and fail to develop empathy for others (Olweus, 1978; Smith, 1991). In this way, bullying eases the way for children who are drawn to a path of delinquency and criminality (Farrington, 1993; Junger, 1990). To the extent that schools carry responsibility for teaching children to contribute productively to society, effective containment of the bullying problem is a high priority.

While the severity of the bullying problem has resulted in widespread use of intervention programs, much remains to be understood about the antecedents of bullying: Why are some children more at risk of engaging in bullying than others? What makes them become involved in bullying? Why are some children victims of bullies while others are not? And most importantly, from the perspective of this book, does the emotion of shame have a role to play in the etiology of bullying/victimization?

A body of empirical work has produced information that profiles prototypical bullies and victims. Studies have adopted a number of different perspectives, with the result that the field lacks an overarching theoretical framework which accommodates the diverse set of empirical findings. Part III of this book develops an integrated model of bullying that incorporates

past theoretical and empirical work, and assigns a role to how children who bully others and are victimized by others manage the emotion of shame.

The present chapter briefly reviews research on bullying. Chapter 14 begins the work of integrating the bullying and shame literatures. Two consistent themes emerge: when shame is acknowledged it is adaptive; when shame is not acknowledged it is maladaptive. This chapter proposes a theoretical framework of shame management (SASD; Shame Acknowledgment and Shame Displacement) and presents a measuring instrument, the Management Of Shame State: Shame Acknowledgment and Shame Displacement (MOSS–SASD). Chapter 15 develops an integrated model of bullying which draws on the reintegrative shaming theory of crime (Braithwaite, 1989). The integrated shame management model incorporates an array of important variables to explain the underlying processes in the development of bullying, with a particular focus on feelings of shame. Chapter 16 tests the model outlined in Chapter 15 and demonstrates the way in which shame management is associated with bullying. Support is found for a partial mediational model. The data show that other variables identified in the bullying literature continue to play important roles. Chapter 17 relates shame management as measured by MOSS–SASD scales to bullying showing that different groups of children (bully, victim, bully/victim and non-bully/non-victim) exhibit different patterns of response to a shameful event.

What the Literature says about Bullying

What is Bullying?

Following Olweus (1991) and Rigby (1996), bullying is defined as:

(a) a repetitive aggressive act, either physical or non-physical, that causes distress to the victim(s);
(b) the dominance of the powerful over the powerless; and
(c) an act carried out without provocation.

As such, the term bullying is not a synonym for aggression or antisocial behavior, rather it refers to a type of aggression or antisocial behavior. Bullying refers to a variety of harmful actions, including name-calling, social exclusion, taking money or damaging belongings, as well as more obvious physical actions such as hitting and kicking (Smith, 1991). There is no age limit on bullying; a child or a parent or even a boss can be a bully if the act fulfils the above criteria.

Prevalence and Nature of Bullying

Most of the pioneering research on school bullying took place in the Scandinavian countries in the late 1960s and early 1970s (Heinmann, 1972; Olweus, 1973). In a very short period of time, the field has flourished with detailed documentation of the worldwide prevalence and nature of bullying among school children (e.g., Ahmad & Smith, 1989; Bjorkqvist, Ekman, & Lagerspetz, 1982; Boulton & Underwood, 1992; Chazan, 1989; Hazler, Hoover, & Oliver, 1991; Kikkawa, 1987; Lane, 1989; Olweus, 1978, 1991; O'Moore & Hillery, 1991; Rigby, 1996; Roland, 1989; Sharp & Smith, 1992; Stephenson & Smith, 1987; Tattum, 1989; Ziegler & Rosenstein-Manner, 1991).

In spite of the quantity of research undertaken, little consensus has emerged on the prevalence rate of bullying which appears to vary a great deal across studies. For example, based on teacher reports, Olweus (1978) identified five per cent of children as pronounced bullies and 5.3 per cent as less pronounced bullies. Stephenson and Smith (1989) identified 16 per cent of children as bullies. With a stricter criterion for bullying, Lowenstein (1978) identified only 1.4 per cent of children as bullies.

Prevalence rates of bullying have also been estimated from anonymous self-report questionnaires. Using a modified questionnaire of Olweus (1987), the estimated rate of primary school bullying was 10 per cent (Ahmad & Smith, 1989, 1990) and of secondary school bullying 12 per cent (Yates & Smith, 1989), using a cut-off point of bullying others 'now and then' or 'more often'.

When the cut-off point was set at 'sometimes' or 'more often', a number of studies have indicated that some countries have higher prevalence rates of bullying than others. For example, Mellor (1990) reported about 4 per cent of children as bullies in Scotland, whereas 17 per cent were identified in Sheffield, England (Boulton & Underwood, 1992). From Australian studies, the percentage of those who bully 'sometimes' or 'more often' was estimated as about 10 per cent (Rigby & Slee, 1990).

What becomes apparent from the above picture, apart from the variability in the prevalence of school bullying, is that bullying occurs in all cultures and countries. Differences in prevalence rates across studies are difficult to interpret because of variability in questionnaires and methodologies. Some researchers gathered prevalence data through self-report questionnaires (Ahmad & Smith, 1989, 1990; Olweus, 1990; O'Moore & Hillery, 1989; Rigby & Slee, 1991b; Yates & Smith, 1989), some used teacher and/or peer nominations (Bjorkqvist et al., 1982; Lagerspetz et al., 1982; Lowenstein, 1978; Stephenson & Smith, 1989) and some employed one-to-one interviews (Junger, 1990; Moran, Smith, Thompson, & Whitney, 1993). In

addition, some researchers preferred to use stringent criteria (Lowenstein, 1978) while others relied on broader criteria to measure bullying (Ahmad & Smith, 1989; Olweus, 1990; Rigby & Slee, 1991b). Equally, the prevalence rates of bullying have varied due to the differential selection of the cut-off points to determine the frequency of bullying. All these factors make it difficult to draw strong conclusions about the exact percentage of children involved in bullying. However, one conclusion that has been drawn from the diverse research is that around 10 per cent of school-aged children engage in behavior that fits a widely accepted understanding of bullying (Besag, 1989).

As for the nature of bullying activities, researchers agree that bullying may be physical (e.g., hitting, pushing, kicking), psychological (e.g., ignoring, excluding), and/or verbal (e.g., name-calling, teasing). Bullying seems to be greater among younger children compared with older children (Boulton & Underwood, 1992; Olweus, 1987; O'Moore & Hillery, 1989, 1991). The proportion of students victimized by peers in primary school is greater than in secondary schools (Kochenderfer & Ladd, 1996a, 1996b; Olweus, 1991).

Girls are more likely to use non-physical ways of bullying (e.g., spreading of rumors, exclusion from play) whereas boys engage in both physical and non-physical bullying (Bjorkvist et al., 1982; Boulton & Underwood, 1992; Hoover, Oliver & Hazler, 1992; Lowenstein, 1978; Olweus, 1978, 1993; Whitney & Smith, 1993). This gender difference also applies to children who are bullied. Sharp and Smith (1992) found that boys were more often the victims of physical bullying whereas girls were the victims of verbal and social bullying. It was also noted that boys bullied both girls and boys, while girls generally bullied other girls.

While this body of research has advanced our understanding of the prevalence and nature of bullying, another has focused on distinguishing the factors that are responsible for bullying. We consider first studies which look at family aspects as precursors of bullying, followed by studies examining the link between child characteristics and bullying.

Family Variables and Bullying

The importance of family variables in predicting bullying has emerged from a number of studies (e.g., Manning, Heron & Marshall, 1978; Olweus, 1978, 1980, 1984; Rican, 1995; Webb, 1969). Family aspects that have been examined as independent variables can be grouped into the following categories: (a) child-rearing styles; (b) parent–child bonds; and (c) family environment. Each of these will be reviewed in turn.

Child-rearing Styles and Bullying

A number of studies have explored the effects of parental child-rearing styles and parental values on their child's bullying behavior. Parental permissiveness which includes an inability to set limits and provide guidelines for acceptable behavior has a powerful influence on children's bullying behavior (Lowenstein, 1978; Olweus, 1980, 1984; Rican, 1995). Rican (1995) found that parents' tolerance of their child's aggressive behavior was linked to bullying. Based on child self-reports, Rican noted that parental encouragement of child aggression in the absence of limit-setting served to legitimize aggression as a means of solving problems. Lowenstein (1978) reported similar findings. From discussions with parents, he noted that the parents of bullies had an overly permissive approach to child-rearing.

Similar results have been reported by those investigations that link parents' permissiveness and the broader concept of child aggression. Olweus (1980, 1984) found that parents who adopted a permissive disciplinary style had boys with high levels of interpersonal aggressive behavior. According to Olweus, mothers who adopted a lax attitude and failed to set limits on their boys' aggressive behavior towards peers, siblings and adults, contributed greatly to the development of an aggressive reaction pattern in those boys. The concept of aggressive reaction pattern gives rise to the question of whether aggression should really be termed bullying. As Farrington (1993) says,

> Bullying is only one element of aggression, just as aggression is only one element of a larger syndrome of antisocial behavior.

Children's perceptions of inconsistency in their parents' disciplinary practices have also been regarded as an important determinant of bullying (Bowers, Smith & Binney, 1992, 1994; Olweus, 1980, 1984). Bowers et al. (1992, 1994) found that children who bully others perceived their parents as being poor on accurate monitoring of behavior, low on warmth, high on neglect, but also high on over-protection. Parents of aggressive boys were more likely to combine permissive child-rearing with power assertion strategies (Olweus, 1980, 1984).

These findings are similar to a number of earlier works (Lowenstein, 1978; Webb, 1969). Drawing from school records, Webb analyzed case histories of children who were the leaders of gangs. Common to these case histories was the children's experience of parental inconsistency, aggression or rejection, or a combination of these. Webb concluded that bullies tended to be exposed to disciplinary inconsistency along with parental rejection and aggression.

Significant findings have also emerged linking a child's bullying activities to the parent's use of an authoritarian strategy. Power assertion, the most

important component of an authoritarian strategy, was found to be associated with the boys' higher level of interpersonal aggressive behavior (Olweus, 1980, 1984). The pattern that emerges in Olweus' studies is that boys of parents who frequently used physical punishment and expressed threats as well as violent outbursts were more likely to become aggressive.

Likewise, a relationship between parental use of an authoritarian style at home, such as overcontrolling and dominating strategies, and children's bullying behavior at school has been documented by Manning et al. (1978). Consistent with these findings, Rican, Klicperova, and Koucka (1993) investigated the obverse of parental authoritarian control and dominance, encouragement of children's autonomy. Children who perceived their parents as supporting their independence were less likely to engage in bullying behavior.

An enormous literature surrounds the relationship between parental aggression and child aggression. A number of studies have examined how aggressiveness in parents can have a modeling effect on their children's bullying behavior (Farrington, 1993; Rican et al., 1993; Strassberg, Dodge, Pettit & Bates, 1994).

A central theoretical perspective for understanding this relationship has been offered by Bandura (1973, 1977, 1986). Bandura stressed the importance of observational learning processes as a frame of reference for aggressive and antisocial behavior in children. Children who observe their parents behaving aggressively begin to behave aggressively, as they come to believe that aggression is the norm, in the home and outside (Bandura, 1986).

Strassberg et al. (1994) examined the effect of the parental use of physical punishment on children's bullying aggression, defined as 'an unprovoked attack on a peer'. The findings indicated that children who were spanked and received other sorts of violent punishment exhibited higher rates of bullying aggression than other children. The authors concluded that violence at home placed children at risk of engaging in unprovoked coercive domination of peers. Rican et al. (1993) have also provided support for understanding bullying as modeling of parental aggression, particularly fathers' hostile expressions at home.

Evidence bearing on the intergenerational link surrounding bullying has also emerged from a number of longitudinal studies (e.g., Eron, 1987; Farrington, 1993; Lowenstein, 1978). The notion that parents who bully produce a generation of children who bully their peers has been supported by the work of Eron (1987). The Cambridge Study in Delinquent Development has also provided evidence of intergenerational transmission and continuity of bullying. This longitudinal survey of adolescents over a period of 24 years revealed that adolescent bullies tend to grow up to be adult bullies and also tend to have children who are bullies (Farrington, 1993).

Continuity of bullying in childhood and adolescence which extends into later violent crime has been supported by other studies (Greenbaum et al., 1989; Pulkkinen, 1996; Tattum, Tattum, & Herbert, 1993). Tattum et al. (1993) described the cyclic progression from pre-teen bullying to juvenile delinquency to violent adult criminality and family abuse as a 'Cycle of Violence'.

Parent–Child Bonds and Bullying
While a substantial body of research has documented the negative effects of parental disciplinary inconsistency, physical punishment and aggression, other research points to the protection afforded by the quality of the parent–child relationship, particularly warmth and early attachment (Junger, 1990; Olweus, 1980, 1984; Rican et al., 1993; Rigby, 1993; Stephenson & Smith, 1989; Troy & Sroufe, 1987).

The impact of a negative parent–child relationship was demonstrated by Olweus (1980, 1984). He found that when mothers showed negativism in relation to their sons, aggressive behavior was more likely to be evident in these boys. Negativism was defined as a lack of warmth and interest in involvement with the child (Olweus, 1978, 1980, 1984). The work of Junger (1990) also suggested that boys who bully tended to have a bad relationship with their parents. Rigby (1993) reported that children who perceived less positive relationships (e.g., less close relations and warmth) with their parents, especially with fathers, were more likely to have a tendency to bully their peers. It is of note that the measure of tendency to bully peers is one of proneness to bully rather than actual behavior that has occurred. It is possible that children who have a tendency to bully never actually bully others.

Apart from the warmth and affection shown to children, the quality of the attachment between parents and children has been associated with bullying. In this regard, Troy and Sroufe's (1987) work, which is based on Bowlby's attachment theory (1969, 1973), is noteworthy. According to Bowlby, attachment refers to a child's internal representational model based upon the history of interactions between the child and his/her attachment figure(s). The quality of an attachment can either be secure or insecure depending upon the emotional bond between the parties. Three major types of attachment relationships have been documented: secure, insecure anxious-avoidant and insecure anxious-resistant (Ainsworth, Blehar, Waters & Wall, 1978).

Troy and Sroufe (1987) have drawn predominantly upon this attachment theory in clarifying the nature of the parent–child bond in relation to bullying. In this experimental work, preschool children were paired with each other, according to their attachment histories (e.g., secure child was paired with insecure avoidant child, etc). It was found that children who

Table 13.1 Summary of Studies Linking Family Variables to Bullying

Researcher(s)	Source(s) of information	Dependent variable	Main findings
Webb (1969)	School records and discussion with parents of 80 children Boys (n = 60), Girls (n = 20)	Various types of behavioral problems including bullying	Parents of children with problems reported being aggressive, inconsistent in discipline and rejecting with their children.
Lowenstein (1978)	Parents, teachers and children (n = 166)	Bullying (teacher and peer nominated)	From a discussion, parents of bullies were found to have been bullies themselves, employ overstrict or overpermissive child-rearing and have a lack of sensitivity to others.
Olweus (1978)	Parents and boys (n = 1000)	Aggressive reaction pattern in boys	Aggressive reaction in boys was related to parental reports of less warmth and inconsistent discipline (e.g., overly lax or overly punitive).
Manning et al. (1978)	Mothers and children (n = 17)	Hostility including bullying	Interviews with mothers reveal that mothers of hostile children were more likely to be overcontrolling.
Troy & Sroufe (1987)	Children (n = 38)	Bullying was observed in experimental context	Children who bullied others exhibited insecure avoidant attachment with parents.
Stephenson & Smith Teachers (1989)		Teacher nominated bullying	Teachers rated bullies as having a difficult relationship with parents and as coming from homes where disciplinary practices were less firm and consistent.
Junger (1990)	Boys (n = 200)	Bullying	Boys who bully reported less warmth with parents and a lack of adequate supervision from parents.
Bowers et al. (1992)	Children (n = 80)	Peer nominated bullying	Bullies reported a disengaged and less cohesive family structure.
Bowers et al. (1994)	Children (n = 80)	Peer nominated bullying	Bullies reported family members as powerful, saw their families as less cohesive and had ambivalent involvement with siblings and others.

Table 13.1 Summary of Studies Linking Family Variables to Bullying (*cont.*)

Farrington (1993)	Boys (n = 411)	Bullying-delinquency-crime	This longitudinal study links bullying - delinquency - crime across the lifespan and across generations.
Rican et al. (1993)	Children (n = 471)	Peer nominated bullying	Children who did not bully reported parents' positive attitudes toward them and encouragement of the child's autonomy. Children who bullied reported parents as being hostile and controlling in their socialization techniques.
Rigby (1993)	Children n = (1012)	Tendency to bully others	Children who tended to bully reported less family cohesion, unclear communication between family members, negative attitudes to parents and a poor parent-child relationship.
Strassberg et al. (1994)	Parents and children (n = 273)	Types of aggressive behavior including bullying	Parents who reported child spanking and other physical punishment had children who bullied and were aggressive.
Rican (1995)	Children (n = 374)	Peer nominated bullying score and self-report of bullying	Bullies reported their families as low in selfless care.
Pulkkinen (1996)	Children (n = 369)	Proactive aggression	This longitudinal study showed proactively aggressive boys were prone to criminality in adulthood.
Berdondini & Smith (1996)	Children (n = 60)	Peer nominated bullying	Bullies reported father absence and lower cohesion with and between parents.

were not 'securely attached' to their mothers were involved in more bullying incidents. Specifically, children with an insecure avoidant attachment history were found to be negative and hostile in their interactions with peers, taking the role of bullies (Troy & Sroufe, 1987).

Family Environment and Bullying

The family environment has also emerged as an important predictor of bullying. The most extensively investigated dimensions have been family cohesiveness, power relationships, conflicts and care among family members (Berdondini & Smith, 1996; Bowers et al., 1992, 1994; Lowenstein, 1978; Rican, 1995; Rigby, 1993).

Gathering data from discussions with parents, Lowenstein reported higher amounts of conflict among the family members of bullies. In addition, parents who were observed as lacking sensitivity to other people were more likely to have children involved in bullying activities (Lowenstein, 1978).

Focusing on children's perceptions of family cohesiveness, Bowers et al. (1992, 1994) found that bullies were significantly more likely than others to perceive their family as lacking cohesion and warmth. Further to this, bullies were more likely not to have a father at home. Additional support for the role of family cohesiveness was provided by Berdondini and Smith (1996) who found that bullying children expressed lower cohesiveness with their parents and reported lower cohesiveness between their parents. Children who bully also perceived their families as having more structured hierarchical power relations (Bowers et al., 1992). In addition, these children showed ambivalent involvement with family members, including siblings who were viewed as more powerful than themselves.

Children's views of their families as functioning poorly on a number of criteria have been shown to play a significant part in bullying (e.g., Rican, 1995; Rigby, 1993). The tendency to bully peers at school has been linked with poorer psycho-social health of families (Rigby, 1993). These children perceived their families as low in cohesion and having unclear as well as indirect communications among members. Rican (1995) has stressed the importance of the care that a family can provide for children. On the basis of his findings, Rican concluded that bullies perceived their families as very weak in selfless care for each other.

These studies together point to the following family aspects as significant in the development of bullying: (a) permissive child-rearing; (b) punitiveness, in particular, parental use of physical punishment; (c) inconsistent and lax disciplining style; (d) low levels of parental affection and sensitivity; (e) high levels of family conflict, and (f) low family cohesion and care.

The family is undoubtedly the pre-eminent social system in which children are embedded. However, there is also substantial evidence that

child characteristics make some children more prone to bullying and victimization than others. In the next section, child characteristics that have been linked with bullying are reviewed.

Child Characteristics and Bullying

Considerable evidence has accumulated to show that children who bully others have a weak inhibition against aggression (Bjorkvist et al., 1982; Lagerspetz et.al., 1982; Olweus, 1978). Olweus (1978) reported that boys who bully others had an aggressive personality with a favorable attitude toward aggression and a strong need to dominate others. It was also noted that they achieved pleasure from acting aggressively against peers and they encouraged other boys to do it.

Consistent with these findings, Bentley and Li (1995) found that bullies were more likely to endorse aggression-supporting beliefs. Bullies have been reported as being physically strong, active and easily provoked and enjoying aggression (Stephenson & Smith, 1989). They have also been noted as consistently trying to control their peers through physical or verbal aggression (Elkind & Weiner, 1978).

In a later work by Olweus (1984), boys who bully were found as slightly below average in school attainment and having a negative attitude toward school work and teachers. These findings have been replicated in other studies. Children who bully others have been found to be below average in intelligence and reading ability (Lowenstein, 1978; O'Moore & Hillery, 1991). Moreover, they are likely to exhibit poor concentration in school work resulting in poor scholastic attainment (Stephenson & Smith, 1989).

Social competency also tends to be lower among children who bully. Bullies are lower than average in popularity among their peers (Boulton & Smith, 1994; Lagerspetz et al., 1982; O'Moore & Hillery, 1991; Rican, 1995), in some cases being regarded as controversial, in other cases being rejected outright (Boulton & Smith, 1994; Lagerspetz et al., 1982; Perry, Kusel & Perry, 1988; Rican, 1995; Smith & Boulton, 1991). Not surprisingly, they tend to be nominated more often as 'starting fights' and 'disrupting' others (Boulton & Smith, 1994; Whitney, Nabuzoka, & Smith, 1992).

Evidence of low empathy toward victims and low remorse about bullying has been documented by Olweus (1984). Bullies tend more often to feel positive or neutral about observing bullying incidents, whereas most children say they feel sad or unhappy about them (Smith, 1991). Children who bully others view little wrong in their behavior and show little awareness of the victim's feelings (Smith, Bowers, Binney, & Cowie, 1993).

A number of additional characteristics have been reported as distinctive of bullies: they tend to be unusually low in anxiety, prone to noncompliance

and unruliness as well as externalization (Pulkkinen, 1996), and likely to be uncooperative (Rigby, Cox & Black, 1997), hyperactive, impulsive and disruptive (Bjorkqvist et al., 1982; Lowenstein, 1978; Olweus, 1980, 1991, 1995).

Taking Eysenck and Eysenck's (1975) factors of psychoticism, extroversion and neuroticism, Slee and Rigby (1993) explored the relevance of personality traits to children's tendency to bully others. Children who showed a tendency to bully had significantly higher scores on psychoticism and extroversion (Slee & Rigby, 1993). They were identified as impulsive, hostile, lacking cooperation, socially insensitive and anxious with feelings of inferiority. However, somewhat different findings were produced by Lowenstein (1978) who reported bullies having higher scores on neuroticism, suggesting that bullies are fearful, obsessive, guilt-prone and lacking in self-esteem and autonomy.

The attributions that children made in explaining their own aggressive behavior were also investigated by Slee (1993). Children who expressed an external locus of control were significantly more likely to be involved in bullying others. Bullies stated that causes outside themselves, e.g., peer pressure, were responsible for shaping their behavior in such an aggressive manner. Bullying children also differed in how they perceived the consequences of their actions. While bullies focused on how aggression would get them into trouble with others (e.g., teachers), non-bullies focused on the way in which aggressive responses encouraged retaliatory action by escalating the conflict. In a study by Dodge, Pettit, McClaskey and Brown (1986), boys who bullied others tended to encode and perceive a range of situations as hostile.

Lack of social skills has been found as a factor in bullying in a number of studies (Dodge et al., 1986; Slee, 1993; Smith et al., 1993). Bullies demonstrated deficits in interpreting social signals correctly (Dodge et al., 1986). Findings in relation to leadership suggest that bullies, in spite of their capacity to influence others, had limited leadership ability. Trawick-Smith (1988) observed that bullies were unwilling to accept others' ideas, to negotiate with others, and to suggest changes in activities rather than demand them. In studying social problem-solving skills, Slee (1993) investigated the link between the tendency to bully others and social cognition. Children who tended to bully produced fewer solutions to hypothetical aggressive behavior against themselves. The solutions that they offered when faced with bullying conducted by other children were more aggressive compared to those of the victims and non-involved children (Slee, 1993).

A handful of studies have sought to understand bullying from a clinical perspective, examining the relationship between bullying, depression, self-esteem and happiness. A child's self-esteem is an important aspect of

his/her psychological development and well-being, but data linking self-esteem to bullying have produced conflicting findings. Some researchers have reported that bullies have levels of self-esteem that are comparable to those of non-involved children (Olweus, 1978), while others have found that bullies suffer from low self-esteem (O'Moore & Hillery, 1991; Rigby & Cox, 1996; Smith et al., 1993). When the dependent variable has been changed from bullying behavior to the tendency to bully others, no relationship has been found between self-esteem and bullying (Rigby & Slee, 1993b; Slee & Rigby, 1993). Possibly the inconsistencies can be explained in terms of whether or not bullying serves the purpose of enabling children to feel powerful and good about themselves. Presumably not all children who bully attain the status and esteem that they want when they engage in bullying activities.

An important aspect of children's well-being is depression. Severe depression has been related to the tendency to bully peers (Slee, 1995). According to Slee, depression in such children sits comfortably alongside the well-replicated finding that children who report a tendency to bully also report being unhappy at school and disliking school (O'Moore & Hillery, 1991; Rigby & Slee, 1993b; Slee, 1995; Slee & Rigby, 1993).

In the developmental literature, a substantial number of studies have shown how children's emotions are linked to their problem-solving skills (e.g., Cicchetti, 1996; Denham, McKinley, Couchoud, & Holt, 1990; Eisenberg, Cialdini, McCreath & Shell, 1987; Fox, 1994; Garber & Dodge, 1991; Saarni, 1990; see Eisenberg & Mussen, 1989, for a review). The importance of emotions in shaping behavioral outcomes has also been emphasized by Lazarus (1991). In describing a relational theory of emotion, Lazarus, Frijda and other functionalist theorists have noted a relationship between emotional states and behavioral manifestations. According to these scholars, emotion is a person–environment relationship which is characterized by different appraisal patterns as well as by different action tendencies. For example, Barrett (1995) has noted that shame is associated with particular appraisals and action tendencies regarding self and others; for example, 'I am useless' or 'someone thinks that I am useless' has been linked with avoidance of others. Given the importance of emotions as a necessary precursor of behavior, it appears very likely that at least some emotional states are more desirable than others in order to achieve competent interaction with peers.

In the clinical as well as developmental literatures, a frequently cited and important emotional state in relation to wrongdoing is shame. Shame has been viewed as a master emotion (Scheff, 1996a, 1996b), playing an important part in healthy social development (Ferguson, Stegge & Damahuis, 1990), psychological well-being (Bretherton, Fritz, Zahn-Waxler & Ridgeway, 1986; Zahn-Waxler, Kochanska, Krupnick & McKnew, 1990)

Table 13.2 Summary of Studies Linking Child Characteristics to Bullying

Researcher(s)	Source(s) of information	Dependent variable	Main findings
Lowenstein (1978)	Children (n = 166)	Bullying (teacher and peer nominated)	Bullies were more likely to be hyperactive and disruptive. They were also more likely to have lower intellectual and reading abilities.
Olweus (1978)	Boys (n = 1000)	Aggressive reaction pattern in boys	Aggressive boys were more likely to have strong aggressive tendencies, positive attitudes toward violence, low school attainment, a lack of empathy and remorse. They were physically strong. Boys with aggressive reaction patterns did not differ from the non-involved children in their self-esteem.
Bjorkqvist et al. (1982)	Children (n = 430)	Peer nominated bully	Bullies were dominant and impulsive. They were found to lack self-control and to have an acting-out personality.
Lagerspetz et al. (1982)	Children (n = 434)	Peer nominated bullying	Bullies had more positive attitudes toward aggression, more negative attitudes toward teachers and peers. They were also physically strong and unpopular among peers.
Perry et al. (1988)	Children (n = 165)	Aggression	Aggressive children were more likely to be rejected by their peers.
Stephenson & Smith (1989)	School teachers	Teacher nominated bullying	Teachers reported that bullies had positive attitudes toward violence; they were also unpopular among peers, physically strong and insecure and seemed to enjoy aggression.
O'Moore & Hillery (1991)	Children (n = 783)	Bullying	Bullies were found to have low self-esteem and low intellectual status; they were also less well-behaved, less happy and less popular among peers. Children who bullied obtained lower scores on self-esteem, happiness and satisfaction.

Table 13.2 Summary of Studies Linking Child Characteristics to Bullying *(cont.)*

Rigby & Slee (1993b)	Children (n = 1162)	Tendency to bully others	Children who tended to bully others showed less happiness and less liking for school. No relationship was found between self-esteem and tendency to bully.
Slee (1993)	Children (n = 76)	Tendency to bully others	Children who tended to bully were more likely to rely on situational factors than dispositional factors in providing the reasons for bullying; they chose more aggressive-oriented solutions in response to bullying done by others.
Slee & Rigby (1993)	Boys (n = 87)	Tendency to bully others	Children who tended to bully obtained high scores on psychoticism (impulsive, hostile, non-cooperative, socially insensitive, lacking in anxiety and inferiority). No relationship was found between self-esteem and tendency to bully others.
Boulton & Smith (1994)	Children (n = 158)	Peer nominated bullying	Children who bullied others were socially rejected by peers.
Rican (1995)	Children (n = 469)	Peer nominated bullying	Bullies received lower sociometric status than others.
Slee (1995)	Children (n = 353)	Tendency to bully others	Children's tendency to bully peers was linked with their depression.
Rigby & Cox (1996)	Children (n = 763)	Tendency to bully others	Children's tendency to bully peers was associated with low levels of self-esteem.
Pulkkinen (1996)	Children (n = 369)	Proactive aggression	Proactively aggressive children scored lower on self-control, anxiety and compliance; such boys scored higher on externalizing problems than proactively aggressive girls.
Rigby et al. (1997)	Children (n = 939)	Tendency to bully others and self-report of bullying	Children who bullied and tended to bully others obtained lower scores on cooperation.

and as a motivator of future behavior (Ferguson et al., 1990). At the same time, some psychologists have been concerned about the consequences of feeling too much shame too much of the time, arguing that heightened shame-proneness will adversely affect individual functioning (Tangney, 1991; Tangney et al., 1992a, 1992b). It seems that too little shame and too much shame both may result in adjustment difficulties for individuals.

Shame has rich theoretical roots in the clinical literature. Many theorists have been interested in explaining the co-occurrence of shame and anger (Katz, 1988; Kohut, 1971; Lansky, 1987; H. B. Lewis, 1971; M. Lewis, 1992; Retzinger, 1985, 1987, 1989; Scheff, 1989, 1990a). Both H. B. Lewis (1971, 1987b) and Scheff (1989, 1990a) put forward the view that shame is the critical instigator of anger and violence. Empirical evidence of a link between shame and anger has been reported in a number of studies. Tangney and associates have examined the way in which children's proneness to feel shame is linked with anger and hostile responses (Tangney, 1990; Tangney et al., 1996a). All these findings suggest that if bullying is the expression of anger, and anger is the expression of shame, bullying may also be an expression of a child's shame, particularly when shame is unacknowledged.

Extending Existing Research

The literature reviewed in this chapter points in two directions. First, it confirms that family variables play an important role in the development of bullying behavior in a child. Second, many child attributes have been associated with bullying, which may or may not be related to family factors. The review also provides a basis for identifying the work that remains to be done. We now consider the limitations of the bullying research to date so that we can find a way to contribute to this body of literature.

(a) Lack of information on child-rearing styles in specific contexts: Past research consistently shows that child-rearing styles are related to bullying behavior in children. When these parenting strategies have been investigated, the focus has tended to be on very broad categories of child-rearing styles across contexts, that is, general predispositions of permissiveness, punitiveness and/or disciplinary inconsistency. Self-reported context free parenting styles may not correspond to child-rearing strategies which are employed in specific contexts (e.g., Goodnow, 1988) such as when asked to deal with bullying in the school context. Consideration of parents' child-rearing responses to children's bullying behavior may provide a more fine-grained analysis of parenting influences on bullying.

(b) Paucity of child-rearing data on assisting children to refrain from bullying: Existing research explains that some children engage in bullying behavior

primarily because of difficulties in their family situation, such as dominating parents and negative parent–child relationships. A related but less closely scrutinized area for research involves parenting strategies that constrain or discourage children from engaging in bullying. When trying to provide a more enriched understanding of bullying, exploring only one side of child-rearing may not suffice. Therefore, in addition to asking which child-rearing strategies encourage bullying, there is a need to explore the factors that assist children to self-regulate and refrain from bullying. Such a change in focus may assist in answering the question posed in Part II of this book: How do we learn to manage shame well?

(c) Lack of data linking parent-reports of their child-rearing styles and child reports of bullying: The majority of the studies cited in Table 13.1 rely on child-reports of their parents' child-rearing strategies. Children who find themselves in trouble or feel unworthy and discontented with their lives might be inclined to see their value to parents more negatively than they might otherwise (Smetana, 1994). Also, it has been shown that parents' and children's perceptions of parenting styles differ markedly (Murphey, 1992; Smetana, 1994). More research, therefore, is required which relies on parents' own views of their child-rearing practices in conjunction with child-reports in explaining bullying.

(d) Lack of a process-oriented view: The extant literature has concentrated on identifying factors for bullying without seeking to explain the process by which parental child-rearing styles shape bullying behavior in children. Most studies leave open the question of intervening variables that may mediate or moderate relationships. An inadequate understanding of these processes results in difficulties in predicting how certain combinations of diverse categories of variables affect bullying behavior. For instance, it is possible that non-extreme punitive actions by parents may not be so destructive of children if they are employed within a loving atmosphere, as in the finding of Simons et al. (2000) that corporal punishment by high-warmth Taiwanese mothers did not increase delinquency. A process-oriented perspective would aid our understanding of how a variety of family variables work together to produce a certain outcome.

The above review demonstrates that bullying is a complex phenomenon and cannot be explained by only one or two constructs or measures. The most fruitful approach to inquiry would sustain a focus on a variety of constructs as well as multiple measures of those constructs. Research that is driven by interest in a particular category of variables (e.g., parent attributes or child attributes or school attributes) has little likelihood of capturing the complexity of bullying behavior and the richness of individual and contextual variation. This is a significant limitation in past research, since no framework has been offered that conceptualizes bullying as a

consequence of a combination of parent and child cognitions and behaviors. Without systematic and simultaneous consideration of these variables within the same sample, it becomes difficult to integrate findings and, therefore, to fully understand the bullying phenomenon.

Part of the problem is that much of the early work which sought to establish prevalence rates and identify predictors did not have a cohesive theoretical framework to guide the research. This case has been articulated most strongly by Farrington (1993):

> ... and while a great deal is known about characteristics of bullies, victims, and environments, no comprehensive theory of bullying that connects the disparate results has yet been developed. Researchers should attempt to develop such an all-embracing theory to guide future research and preventive efforts. (p. 404)

From the foregoing review of the bullying literature, a theoretical framework is required that recognizes a range of both family factors and child attributes, and explains their interrelationships in terms of risks and protections. Rather than attempting new theorizing in this area, researchers interested in bullying may benefit from the explorations, conceptualizations and theoretical developments that have occurred in other relevant fields. As Farrington stated (1993):

> Just as criminological researchers might learn from findings on bullying, bullying researchers would gain by taking account of criminological findings. The explosion of recent research on bullying has led to quick advances in knowledge but has been carried out ahistorically, failing to benefit from research in related fields such as criminology. (p. 383)

In accordance with this view and as an initial step toward addressing the above limitations, Part III of this book uses the theory of reintegrative shaming (Braithwaite, 1989) to forge links among the variables that have consistently been associated with bullying. Part III attempts to reinterpret many of the findings from the bullying literature in terms of the acknowledgment, management, and expression of the emotion of shame. Before elaborating further on this theoretical model, an analysis of the concept of shame management is warranted. This is the topic of the next chapter, along with the development of the MOSS–SASD scales that will be used as key explanatory variables in this research.

CHAPTER 14

The Concept of Shame Management

In Part II, Nathan Harris offers an ethical identity conception of shame. Shame involves a threat to identity as the individual confronts and acknowledges wrongdoing. Respected others can reinforce the individual's belief in norms, but at the same time provide a supportive environment where social bonds with the offender might be strengthened, and remorse and forgiveness expressed over the harm done. Providing the social context is right, Harris argues that shame can be managed well. In the daily lives of individuals, however, control of the situation may be more problematic, and shame management may pose a greater challenge. This part of the book examines children's shame management styles in the context of school bullying and their implications for children's behavior.

The Different Sides of Shame Management

Across a diverse literature, shame has been seen as an emotion exerting significant influence on personal and social development (Bretherton et al., 1986; Ferguson et al., 1990; Scheff, 1996a; Tangney, 1990, 1991). Shame serves to establish a moral direction for human behavior (Scheff, 1995). In addition, an ability to feel shame represents a particular evolutionary development which has an important role in maintaining standards in human societies (English, 1994).

Shame has also been recognized as a state encompassing feelings of inadequacy, inferiority, humiliation and dishonor, a sense of despair and deep suffering (Broucek, 1991; Gilbert, 1989, 1992; Lewis, 1971; Lindsay-Hartz, 1984; Nathanson, 1987; Tangney, 1990, 1993). Not surprisingly, therefore, individuals have developed defenses against feelings of shame. Considerable consensus surrounds the defensive role of anger in response

to feelings of shame (Katz, 1988; Kaufman, 1989, 1996; Lansky, 1992; Lewis, 1971; Nathanson, 1992; Potter-Efron, 1989; Retzinger, 1987, 1991a, 1991b; Scheff, 1987, 1990a). Feelings of shame are averted by anger and angry actions which can dominate, hurt and/or intimidate others. Researchers refer to this kind of shame as unacknowledged shame (Lewis, 1971, 1987b, 1995; Nathanson, 1992; Retzinger, 1985, 1987, 1991a, 1991b, 1996; Scheff, 1987, 1990a, 1996b).

Almost three decades ago, Lewis (1971) pioneered an elaborate theory of shame that gave voice to other clinicians' shared clinical observations of an interplay between unacknowledged shame and angry responses. Lewis described shame, when unacknowledged, as a reduction in self-worth felt by both the self and others resulting in humiliated fury or anger that functions to regain a sense of being valued. In describing her own clinical experiences, Lewis (1987b) stated that when she made patients aware that they were in a state of shame, they responded with emotional relief, as they came to accept that their behaviors might have become hostile due to the lack of its recognition.

In Lewis's clinical sessions, most shame episodes were unacknowledged and undischarged. She found it useful to distinguish between two types of unacknowledged shame experiences: overt-unidentified and by-passed. In overt-unidentified shame, the patient felt shame but denied owning the painful feelings of shame. They did not even label their own state as shame (Lewis, 1987b, 1995); they mislabeled to mask the shameful experience by using a variety of related terms, such as feeling helpless, stupid or foolish (Lewis, 1995).

In cases of by-passed shame, the individual remained aware of the cognitive substance of shame-eliciting events but lacked awareness of the affective elements of shameful experiences (Lewis, 1971). As described by Lewis, the patient experienced only a 'wince' or slight 'blow' at the time when the shameful event occurred (Lewis, 1971, 1995). In this form of unacknowledged shame, the individual attempts to distract the self from the painful feelings of shame. Lewis states that when shame is evoked, hostility is initially directed at self. But as shame involves real or imaginary others' condemnation, this hostility at self is redirected at others who may or may not be responsible for the shameful event. Through this process, shame is successfully by-passed.

Lewis's theorizing and its clinical support have been an important milestone in understanding both the adaptive and maladaptive functions of shame. Sociologists, Scheff and Retzinger, have followed Lewis's lead in their own theorizing.

In developing a theory of social action, Scheff (1987, 1988) states that shame arises from a lack of deference (disrespect). Scheff (1988) associates

shame with a threat to the bond with significant other(s). If shame occurs in a secure relationship, it is acknowledged and the bond will be repaired. In contrast, if shame occurs in an insecure relationship, it remains unacknowledged and damages the bond resulting in alienation. Unacknowledged shame was seen as a sufficient condition for the escalation of interpersonal conflict and destructive behavior (Retzinger, 1991a, 1991b, 1996; Scheff, 1988).

The prominence of shame and its role in violent crime and homicide is especially evident in Katz's (1988) analyses of criminal acts. Katz (1988) claims that insults and humiliation experienced by the perpetrators seemed to give rise to unacknowledged shame, which then led them to criminal acts, such as burglary, robbery or murder. According to Katz, 'He [the killer] must transform what he initially senses as an eternally humiliating situation into a blinding rage' (Katz, 1988). In studies of family violence, Lansky (1981, 1987, 1992) has shown that married couples in violent relationships are furious because of their unacknowledged shame experiences. From his clinical and theoretical works, Lansky concluded that family violence results from the disrespectful and insulting manner that partners adopted in their interactions with each other. For both parties, the relationship becomes emotionally distant through mutual shaming, especially shaming that hits its mark but remains unacknowledged (Lansky, 1995).

The role of shame in triggering anger and hostility has also been of interest to psychologists in explaining interpersonal conflict. Tangney and her colleagues have researched shame-proneness, a personality characteristic associated with feelings of threat to the whole self, as a correlate of anger and hostility (Tangney, 1991, 1993; Tangney et al., 1992a, 1992b). According to these researchers, individuals who are prone to feelings of shame are also more likely to express other-directed anger and hostility (Tangney, 1995b; Tangney et al., 1992a, 1992b). Tangney and her colleagues paint a picture of a shame-prone individual who experiences global attacks on the self, externalizes blame and displays direct and indirect anger in response to any negative outcome. Since such experiences are highly aversive and make it difficult to function, shame-prone individuals attempt to ward the shame affect off through externalizing the cause and expressing hostility to something or to nothing in particular. As a result, shame-proneness is constructed as an antisocial and debilitating affective personality characteristic.

Unlike most theories of crime, Braithwaite's (1989) reintegrative shaming theory places a prominent etiological role on shame in explaining crime. Braithwaite claims that individuals who do not feel shame readily commit crime. They neither have a 'fear of shame in the eyes of intimates' nor, more importantly, in their own eyes, and hence, they can contemplate criminal activities. While recognizing shame's maladaptive function, Braithwaite asserts that shame also has an adaptive self-regulatory function.

Shame helps individuals refrain from criminal behavior even in the absence of an external authority that has the power to impose sanctions over wrongdoing (Braithwaite, 1989). What remains to be done is to define and develop the characteristic features underpinning both the adaptive and maladaptive forms of shame.

The importance of acknowledged shame in regulating interpersonal relationships has been recognized in the literature. According to Retzinger (1996), shame acknowledgment brings a state of interpersonal closeness. She views shame acknowledgment as a process leading to greater awareness of both self and the social world. This is an integral part of healthy functioning for both individuals and communities. Retzinger's perspective on the connection between self and shame has a close affinity with Lynd (1958). In emphasizing the constructive role of acknowledged shame, Lynd states:

> Experiences of shame . . . are unrecognized aspects of one's personality as well as unrecognized aspects of one's society and of the world. If it is possible to face them, instead of seeking protection from what they reveal, they may throw light on who one is . . . (p. 183)

Turner (1995) also emphasizes that when shame is accepted and acknowledged, it can be the most positive experience in the world. It can originate and maintain healthy relationships between individuals and groups. Others view shame, that is acknowledged shame, as an integral part of a person's moral development (Braithwaite, 1989; Hultberg, 1988; Kaufman, 1989; Schneider, 1977; Wurmser, 1981). This group of researchers have provided an account of the theoretical importance of acknowledging shame but less research has been conducted to empirically demonstrate the benefits of shame acknowledgment to social living.

In this review we have identified two kinds of shame experiences, acknowledged and unacknowledged shame. In the former case, one accepts shame over wrongdoing and discharges the feelings of shame through engaging in some kind of reparative behavior. In the case of unacknowledged shame, the feeling remains undischarged, and interpersonal conflict can result. The foregoing review demonstrates that the consequences of acknowledging or not acknowledging shame are of enormous importance. We now move on to considering what constitutes unacknowledged and acknowledged shame, and how they might be measured.

Acknowledged versus Unacknowledged Shame: A Theoretical Clarification

In Part II, Harris concludes that shame is not an experience isolated from social context, but rather is part of a set of dynamic intrapersonal and

interpersonal processes which are sequentially bound up with one another. These processes can shape the degree to which an individual responds to a shameful event with acknowledgment or without it.

Acknowledged Shame

In acknowledged shame, individuals accept feelings of shame and believe that the way they behaved was morally wrong or socially undesirable. Consequently, acceptance of personal responsibility for the unacceptable behavior is likely to emerge, together with a desire for reparation (Lewis, 1971). Wicker, Payne and Morgan (1983) have also noted this relationship: '. . . the greater personal responsibility with shame may reflect a desire for reparation'.

Acknowledging shame thus involves: (a) admission of feelings of shame over a wrongdoing; (b) willingness to take responsibility for the wrongdoing; and (c) a desire for making amends for what happened.

It is proposed that the acceptance of feeling shame, with responsibility and reparative intent, is indicative of 'internal sanctioning' by an individual. The term 'internal sanctioning' is used here as a mechanism by which desirable behavior of an individual is facilitated, and unethical behavior prevented. Apart from a self-regulatory role, felt shame combined with personal responsibility and making amends together create a positive avenue for discharging shame. Acknowledging shame thereby provides an opportunity for wrongdoers to put the shameful event behind them, to mend relationships and be restored to a state of psychological well-being. Lewis's clinical observations support this contention, but questions still remain: Is the internal sanctioning mechanism sufficient to restore a state of psychological well-being? Are there other factors involved here?

It seems likely that the mere presence of this internal sanctioning mechanism is not sufficient to account for the process of discharging shame. In order to be appropriately discharged, internal sanctioning may have to be accompanied by the following two strategies:

(a) Escape from immersion in the state of confusion connected with blameworthiness, as discussed with Harris's Unresolved Shame factor (Part II). This confusion can be understood as oscillation between blaming self and blaming others. Perseveration is one way in which this is characterized in the literature. Past research has shown that the most frequent responses to a pathological state of shame are confusion, loss of esteem and fear of others' rejection (Kinston, 1984; Lewis, 1971, 1995; Scheff, 1987).

(b) Escape from anger that is destructive to either self or others. In response to a shameful event, an individual may feel anger at the situation to alleviate some of the distress. But a substantial amount of research

suggests that destructive and retaliatory anger does not reduce feelings of shame (Lewis, 1971; Retzinger, 1991a, 1991b, Scheff, 1987; Tangney, 1990; Tangney et al., 1992a, 1992b, 1996a).

Taken together, the absence of internalizing others' rejection, externalizing blame, blame-perseveration (not knowing who is to blame), and outward anger will assist the individual to maintain an integrated self. Importantly, the absence of these responses provides the utmost opportunity for the appropriate discharge of shame. In fact, we define discharged shame as shame that is dealt with in the absence of these pathologies. For shame to be appropriately discharged, the internal sanctioning mechanism must function but there must also be a mechanism for restoring social relationships, such that feelings of rejection towards self and others do not arise and anger is not triggered. Through these strategies, shame can not only be acknowledged but it can also be discharged adequately, and positive social relationships maintained. From the clinical literature, these strategies together establish the surest pathway to discharging shame adaptively (see Figure 14.1).

The concept of discharged shame is similar to moral shame as described by Green and Lawrenz (1994). According to these researchers, moral shame is the response to a transgression when the individual's moral sensitivity or conscience has been brought into play. Schneider (1977) calls it a 'mature sense of shame' or 'a sense of modesty'.

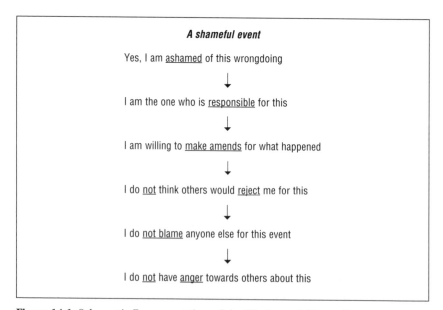

A shameful event

Yes, I am <u>ashamed</u> of this wrongdoing

↓

I am the one who is <u>responsible</u> for this

↓

I am willing to <u>make amends</u> for what happened

↓

I do <u>not</u> think others would <u>reject</u> me for this

↓

I do <u>not blame</u> anyone else for this event

↓

I do <u>not</u> have <u>anger</u> towards others about this

Figure 14.1 Schematic Representation of the Discharged Shame State

Tangney's (1990) guilt-proneness (as opposed to her shame-proneness) can be aligned with the concept of discharged shame in the present model. Guilt-proneness is associated with constructive intentions and behaviors, such as a tendency to accept responsibility for the negative event (Tangney et al., 1996a). In addition, guilt-proneness is less threatening to self and, hence, it is less likely to be linked to externalizing blame and destructive anger (Tangney et al., 1992a, 1996a). Thus, the current model proposes that discharged shame serves healthy adjustment in two related ways. On the one hand, it promotes strategies that have a constructive effect on interpersonal relationships, and on the other hand, it inhibits strategies which have destructive effects.

The next question is whether shame is always discharged when shame is acknowledged? What happens if an acknowledged shame state is not appropriately discharged for some reason; for example, because of unresolved self-threatening issues or blocking of an individual's capacity to use the last three strategies presented in Figure 14.1.

The presence of an internal sanctioning mechanism is a necessary requirement for acknowledging shame, but not sufficient for discharging shame. In experiencing a shameful event, there may remain an intense focus on feelings of inadequacy, incompetence, or real/imaginary others' condemnation and rejection (Elias, 1994; Gilbert, 1989, 1992; Lewis, 1971; Nathanson, 1987; Tangney, 1990, 1993). In such cases, despite acknowledging shame, individuals become fragile as a consequence of the self's real or imaginary (Lewis, 1987b) negative evaluation by the 'other' who is a valued social sanctioning agent(s).

The critical factor in releasing acknowledged shame, therefore, is whether the rejection of others has become internalized, even when the internal sanctioning mechanism favors its discharging. The individual becomes unable to free the self from the internalization of excessively self-critical evaluations. Therefore, self-threatening thoughts remain unresolved for the individual and shame persists. This will be called persistent shame in the proposed framework.

Individuals with persistent shame possess a feeling of others' rejection which is likely to become unbearable to them. Part of the self is then likely to resist feelings of blameworthiness, and perseveration over blameworthiness takes place. Such individuals move toward some sort of resentment, or 'impotent rage' (Goldberg, 1991), to seek some relief from such distressing feelings. This movement or displacement of shame to anger is an inward-going deflection in which anger is directed to self and relationships with others are avoided. The strategies involved in persistent shame are presented in Figure 14.2.

Persistent shame has parallels in the clinical literature. For example,

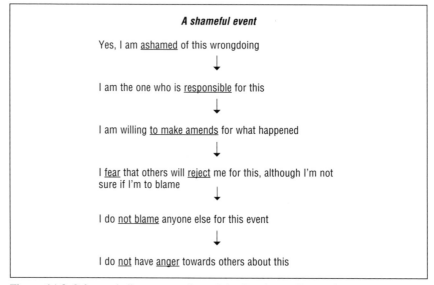

Figure 14.2 Schematic Representation of the Persistent Shame State

Morrison (1987, 1989) calls it narcissistic vulnerability, or the underside of narcissism, in which an individual feels inferior, inadequate and defective in comparison with others. In addition, persistent shame seems to have a close affinity with imposed shame which is the disgrace or devaluation inflicted by another (Green & Lawrenz, 1994). The notion of persistent shame is also consistent with Schneider's (1977) disgrace-shame which he describes as 'fear of rejection'. Fear of rejection is aroused by the consciousness of a disvalued or an undesirable quality of the self. It is characterized as the painful experience of the disintegration of one's world (Schneider, 1977).

In summary, current research points to two types of acknowledged shame: discharged and persistent. Discharged shame is thought to serve an adaptive function by releasing shame appropriately, whereas persistent shame is characterized by interference in the process of releasing shame. In cases of persistent shame, the obstacle that prevents individuals from releasing shame adequately is their belief that others are rejecting or condemning them.

Unacknowledged Shame

Two types of unacknowledged shame have been explicitly cited in the literature: by-passed and overt-unidentified (Lewis, 1971, 1987b; Scheff, 1989). When shame goes unacknowledged, the individual rejects the idea that he/she has done anything to be ashamed of. As a consequence, the individual is likely to resist taking personal responsibility and making

amends. In the absence of an internal sanctioning mechanism, individuals with unacknowledged shame have no options for the release of that feeling of shame.

Both by-passed and overt-unidentified shame have the common feature of the absence of internal sanctioning (e.g., absence of feeling shame, taking responsibility and making amends). They differ, however, in whether self-threatening feelings of shame are resolved.

According to the clinical literature, by-passed shame attempts to dissociate self from the unpleasant feelings of shame (Lewis, 1971; Scheff, 1990a). Based upon this, by-passed shame is purported to involve the following unique combination of strategies.

In the absence of an internal sanctioning mechanism, individuals experiencing by-passed shame will be unable to feel ashamed, take responsibility and make amends. Untouched by feelings of shame, such individuals are not likely to be bothered by either the exposure of their wrongdoing to social sanctioning agents or those agents' criticisms of the event. For those experiencing by-passed shame, such criticisms are considered to be unfair, and hence, the self-threatening thoughts become resolved. Yet at some level of social consciousness, the shameful event is not resolved since it remains unacknowledged. Thus, a displacement occurs and a general feeling of anger may ensue in such individuals in a bid to sedate the distress caused by the event. In this state of unacknowledged shame, individuals do not address the need for restoring relationships, rather they externalize blame for what happened and direct anger toward others. They begin to experience more disconnection with others and a state of blame-perseveration sets in. As a result, they may demand explanation and reparation from others in some quarter. The self is protected by finding or creating a 'scapegoat' in the external environment. Figure 14.3 shows the sequence of non-recognition of shame and the direction of blame and anger to others.

Major theoretical frameworks on shame indicate that individuals are most likely to generate anger in a shameful situation if it is by-passed (Lansky, 1992; Lewis, 1971, 1987b, 1995; Retzinger, 1991a, 1991b; Scheff, 1987, 1988, 1990a, 1991). In by-passed shame, individuals clearly deal with shameful events without being caught up in a shame state (Lewis, 1987b). Retzinger (1996) calls this a low-visibility state and Scheff (1990a) an overdistanced state. While experiencing by-passed shame, an individual creates a defense against shame through not recognizing its painful aspects, 'as if the pain were not happening' (Scheff, 1990a). A similar description can be seen in Schneider's (1977) work in which he places importance on the ethical element of shame. He contrasts the concept of 'a sense of shame' with 'shamelessness', suggesting that shamelessness is a moral deficiency which is demonic and destructive.

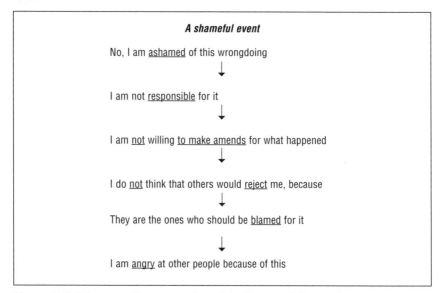

Figure 14.3 Schematic Representation of the By-passed Shame State

Overt–unidentified shame will be referred to as denied–by-passed shame in the framework we develop here. This category involves individuals justifying themselves by denying the unpleasant feelings of shame as well as denying that anything shameful has occurred. In this case, the individual initially denies the experience of shame. However, the context of the shameful event may make it impossible to suppress unpleasant feelings in the long term. As a consequence, the individual seeks relief through distorting portions of reality, e.g., 'It didn't happen that way.' Individuals can thereby offer explanations which distance them from blame and allow them to take on a victim role. Because it is difficult to distort the reality of what happened or the way it happened, this strategy is likely to collapse at some point, and by-passing begins through placing the blame on another person. Thus, whereas the by-passing of the painful aspects of shame is an immediate reaction in the case of by-passed shame, it is delayed and contingent upon exposure in the case of denied–by-passed shame.

In the framework being proposed here, it seems very likely that the 'process of denying in addition to by-passing' would constitute the essential aspect of overt-unidentified shame. For this reason, throughout the remainder of the book, overt-unidentified shame (Lewis, 1971) will be called denied–by-passed shame as this highlights the process involved.

When the denial of reality fails to save the threatened self from a humiliating experience, letting go of negative feelings can be difficult. Humiliation results in a destruction of the self as we view others criticizing us for wrong-

doing. At this point, we may adapt through self-righteous anger which is accusatory in nature. Therefore, internalizing others' rejection combined with by-passing characteristics (e.g., externalizing blame) produces this category of denied–by-passed shame in which blame-perseveration is a critical factor. The proposed strategies accompanying the denied–by-passed shame state are presented in Figure 14.4.

Denied–by-passed shame is conceptually similar to Lewis's (1971) overt–unidentified shame and Scheff's (1990a) underdistanced shame. Lewis (1971, 1987b, 1995) described overt-unidentified shame as a state which is not recognized as shame by the individual; rather it is viewed as feeling helpless, stupid, foolish, ridiculous, inadequate and having no control over events. Scheff (1979, 1990a) calls it underdistanced shame because the individual feels emotional pain but denies the painful aspects of shame from self and others. When shame is denied by the individual at a cognitive level, emotional indicators of shame (e.g., hiding self from others) nevertheless are often evident in the individual's behavior (Lewis, 1971, 1987b, 1995; Scheff & Retzinger, 1991). The individual has been touched by shame. Generally, once caught in shameful events, the individual is bothered by self-threatening thoughts that remain unresolved. These events threaten to humiliate the individual and communicate that the individual is no longer worthy of admiration or respect from the social sanctioning agent(s). This is likely to elicit feelings of anger in such an individual to minimize the distress.

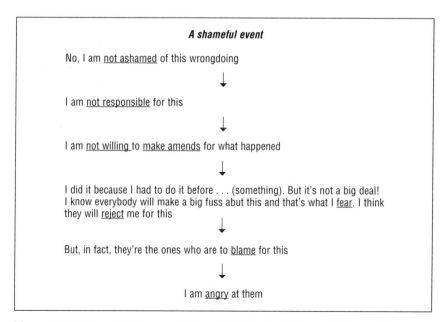

Figure 14.4 Schematic Representation of the Denied–By-passed Shame State

Figures 14.1 to 14.4 seek to clarify the conceptual issues surrounding the shame construct in order to demonstrate that shame has both an adaptive and maladaptive face. Acknowledging shame provides an opportunity for rebuilding interpersonal relationships, at the cost of confronting shame affect at the personal level. Whether or not acknowledged shame is adaptive (discharged) or maladaptive (persistent) depends on one's capacity to release the shame by putting it behind oneself and believing that one still has respect and value in one's social group.

Unacknowledged shame (by-passed shame and denied–by-passed shame), on the other hand, is adaptive in the short term in protecting the self from being humiliated as a result of wrongdoing, but is maladaptive from the perspective of good interpersonal relationships. Unacknowledged shame prevents the individual from repairing the damage done to his/her relationships with others.

The following sections focus on the development and evaluation of a scale to measure both adaptive and maladaptive aspects of shame based on this framework. The typology presented in Figures 14.1 to 14.4 has seven important elements:

1 acknowledging shame over the wrongdoing
2 taking responsibility for the wrongdoing
3 making amends for the harm done
4 internalizing others' rejection
5 blaming others
6 perseverating on who, if anyone, should be blamed
7 feeling angry

Development of an Instrument to Measure Shame

The 'Management Of Shame State–Shame Acknowledgment and Shame Displacement' (MOSS–SASD) scales were designed to assess strategies for dealing with shame state, particularly in the context of bullying (Ahmed, V. Braithwaite & J. Braithwaite, 1996).

Original Items and Format of the MOSS–SASD Scales

The MOSS–SASD scales use eight bullying scenarios as stimuli, covering a wide range of frequently occurring bullying acts experienced by Australian school children. Following each scenario, respondents are asked to give their views about how they would feel and what they would do if they were the actor in the story. Ten questions were formulated to represent the strategies of dealing with shame we have outlined. Thus 80 (eight scenarios x 10 questions) questions make up the MOSS–SASD instrument.

The bullying scenarios incorporated in the MOSS–SASD instrument were selected with four criteria in mind. The bullying acts had to be (a) representative of the experiences of both boys and girls; (b) illustrative of both physical and psychological bullying; (c) ecologically valid or common enough to be familiar to children; and (d) events likely to arouse feelings of shame.

In order to obtain a selection of scenarios that met the criteria, 17 scenarios describing bullying activities among school aged children were generated from a group of children and their parents. Bullying was defined for them in the following way: 'We call it bullying when someone repeatedly hurts or frightens someone weaker than themselves on purpose. Remember it is not bullying when two of you about the same strength have the odd fight or quarrel. Bullying can be done in different ways:[1] by hurtful teasing, threatening actions, name-calling or hitting or kicking.'

At the next stage, the 17 scenarios were rated by another group of children and parents in terms of the likelihood of their occurrence, keeping in mind their applicability to the above four criteria. On the basis of this second set of ratings, eight bullying scenarios were chosen for use in the final MOSS–SASD scales (see Table 14.1). The scenarios chosen described acts of tripping, grabbing, excluding, teasing, knocking things out of hands, and making rude comments.

For each bullying scenario, questions were generated to represent the elements of shame management discussed previously. An initial pool of 13 questions was evaluated independently by two researchers familiar with the guiding framework and with principles of scale development. Each question was evaluated in terms of its perceived relevance to the proposed dimensions. Questions judged as being less relevant to these dimensions or less clearly representative were discarded, while other questions were reworded to remove ambiguities. This process resulted in the selection of 10 questions to be used in relation to each bullying scenario. These questions together with their theoretical relevance are presented in Table 14.2.

The instructions for the MOSS–SASD scales asked participants to imagine themselves doing the bullying in each scenario, and then to indicate how likely it was that they would react in the way described in the shame management questions. For each question, respondents were asked to tick either 'yes' or 'no'. Piloting suggested it was preferable that the response format not provide a 'don't know' option.

Looking at the distributions of the MOSS–SASD scales, we found that they were highly skewed in some cases. This was consistent with the theoretical formulation of shame management. Most people in a society should know the adaptive ways of managing shame, even if they sometimes fail to act on this knowledge. Hence, the skewed distributions that accompany the measurement of compliance with social norms are to be expected.

Table 14.1 Bullying Scenarios Used in the MOSS–SASD Scales

1   Imagine that you are walking along the corridor at school and you see another student. You put your foot out and trip the student. Then you realize that the class teacher has just come into the corridor and saw what you did.

2   Imagine that this is lunchtime at school and you see a younger student. You grab the sweets from his/her hand. Then you realize that the class teacher saw what you did.

3   Imagine that you are in the school playground and you get your friends to ignore another student from your class. You then realize that the teacher on duty has been watching you.

4   Imagine that you are on the way home from school and see a younger student carrying something important that he/she has made at school. You knock the thing out of the child's hands. Then you realize that one of your teachers saw what you did.

5   Imagine that you have been making rude comments about a student's family. You find out that your class teacher heard what you said.

6   Imagine that a younger student is going to the canteen to buy something. You grab his/her money. You warn the student not to tell or else. Then you realize that your class teacher saw you and heard what you said.

7   Imagine that you started an argument in class with another student. Then you exclude the student from doing the class project with you. Suddenly the teacher comes in and is told what you did.

8   Imagine that you are left in the classroom alone with a student. You think that the teacher has gone and so you start teasing the student. Then you realize that the teacher is still in the classroom.

The 'Life at School Survey'

Participants

The sample consisted of 1401 students and their parents/guardians. Participation was voluntary. Data were collected between August and November 1996 from both public and private schools in the Australian Capital Territory (ACT). Of the 68 public schools in the ACT, 22 agreed to participate in the current study. Of the 28 private schools, 10 agreed to take part. All schools were co-educational.

Letters were sent home through schools asking students and their parents to take part in the "Life at School Survey" (Ahmed, 1996). Parents had to return a signed consent form to the school before children were allowed to take part in the study. The overall rate of participation was 47.3 per cent. It should be emphasized that obtaining both parent and child consent in this research involved ethically stringent participation criteria.

Table 14.2 MOSS–SASD Scale Items, Their Theoretical Concepts and Theoretical Relevances

Items	Theoretical concepts	Theoretical relevances
Would you feel ashamed of yourself?	Indicator of admission of feelings of shame.	Lewis, 1971; Retzinger, 1996; Scheff 1987; Schneider, 1977.
Would you wish you could just hide?	Indicator of being touched by shame, a desire to avoid others and escape from interpersonal domain.	Lewis, 1971; Lindsay-Hartz, 1984; Lindsay-Hartz, de-Riverra & Mascolo, 1994.
Would you feel like blaming yourself for what happened?	Indicator of willingness to take responsibility for a wrongdoing.	Lewis, 1971; Morrison, 1986; Janoff-Bulman 1979.
Do you think that others would reject you?	Indicator of an individual being bothered by others' rejecting thoughts.	Lewis, 1971, 1987b; Elias, 1994; Wurmser, 1981.
Would you feel like making the situation better?	Indicator of willingness to repair the harm done.	Lewis, 1971; Wicker et al, 1983.
Would you feel like blaming others for what happened?	Indicator of externalizing blame for the harm done.	Lewis, 1971, 1987b; Scheff, 1987; Tangney, 1990.
Would you be unable to decide if you were to blame?	Indicator of an unpleasant state of confusion or uncertainty about blameworthiness.	Lindsay-Hartz et al., 1994.
Would you feel angry at this situation?	Indicator of anger at the situation felt by the ashamed individual.	Lewis,1971; Miller, 1985.
Would you feel like getting back at [that student]?	Indicator of retaliatory anger and hostility toward others.	Lewis, 1971, 1987b; Scheff, 1987; Retzinger, 1987; Nathanson, 1987, 1992; Tangney et al., 1992a, 1992b.
Would you feel like throwing or kicking something?	Indicator of displacement of anger on someone or something which is not related to the source of anger.	Lewis, 1971.

This is consistent with previous research of this kind, where active consent from parents typically resulted in response rates ranging between 40 per cent and 60 per cent of the target group (Donovan, Jessor, & Costa, 1988; Josephson & Rosen, 1978; Lueptow, Muller, Hammes, & Master, 1977; Severson & Biglan, 1989).

Completed questionnaires were collected from 748 girls and 630 boys. The sample was drawn from students in grades four to seven: 209 children were in fourth grade (Mean age = 9.5 years); 555 in fifth grade (Mean age = 10.5 years); 572 in sixth grade (Mean age = 11.5 years); and 42 in seventh grade (Mean age = 12.5 years). The mean age of the sample was 10.9 years.

The parent/guardian who most frequently engaged with the student in everyday interaction was the one invited to participate in this research. Of the original sample of 1401 students, 978 parents returned the completed questionnaires, a 70 per cent return rate. The sample comprised 845 mothers (86.4 per cent), 132 fathers (13.5 per cent) and one guardian.

The self-reported ethnic composition of the sample was 79 per cent Australian and English, and 21 per cent non-Australian and/or non-English. According to records held by the ACT School Systems (ACTDET, 1996), 24.4 per cent of students are born either in a non-English-speaking country or in an English-speaking country with one or both parents born in a non-English-speaking country. The present sample, therefore, appears to represent a representative amount of ethnic diversity.

The 'Life at School Survey' for students was completed during school hours. Participating students were brought to an unoccupied and quiet classroom, hall or library room in the school separate from the non-participating students. The students sat apart from one another to complete the questionnaire in privacy. At the beginning of the survey, the purpose of the research was explained and students were reassured of the anonymity and confidentiality of their responses.

The students were encouraged to respond honestly and were asked not to discuss their responses with each other either during or after the survey session. To eliminate any probable discomfort for the participants, several precautions were undertaken. First, the participants were not asked to write their names on their questionnaire. Only an identification number appeared at the top of each questionnaire in order to match it with their parents' questionnaires. Second, peer nominations of bullies and victims were not sought from the students. Third, the participating students were separated from those not participating (those who did not return a consent form to the school). Finally, to ensure the confidentiality of responses, the session was administered by the researchers and the participants were assured that teachers would not have access to the findings.

All students were administered two questionnaire booklets: one was for them to answer, the other a packet containing a questionnaire for their parents. The survey was completed by students in the school setting and took approximately 25 to 40 minutes for the older groups, and 35 to 65 minutes for the younger groups. To ensure that students who finished early did not distract others, activities were included in the questionnaire booklet, for example, doing dot-to-dots or coloring in.

In completing their questionnaire, parents were explicitly asked to think of the son or daughter who also participated in the survey, and not any other child.

Psychometric Properties of the MOSS–SASD Scales

Dealing with the responses to 80 questions was somewhat challenging, and therefore, the following strategy was derived to collapse the data.

First, responses to each shame management question were compared across the bullying scenarios. The issue being addressed in this first set of analyses was the consistency of shame management responses across the scenarios. For example, was the child who accepted responsibility in one bullying situation likely to be the child who accepted responsibility in another bullying situation? The answer to this question was yes for each shame management question. The alpha reliability coefficients for each question asked in eight different contexts ranged from .88 to .95 with a median of .92. On this basis, responses were summed across the eight scenarios for each of the shame management questions. Total scores were divided by eight to bring scores back to the original 1–2 scale.

The next step in reducing the data involved asking whether the 10 shame management questions (with scores summed across scenarios) could be reduced to a smaller set of questions. In other words, were some questions so highly correlated that they appeared to be measuring the same underlying construct?

From the shame literature reviewed earlier in this chapter, positive correlations are expected among the MOSS–SASD questions about feeling shame, hiding self from others, taking responsibility, internalizing others' rejection, and making amends, as these were developed with a view to capturing the spirit of owning shame. Another set of positive correlations were expected among the MOSS–SASD questions about blaming others, perseverating over who should be blamed, feeling anger, wanting to retaliate, and displacing anger onto other things. These items were designed to capture the defenses employed to disown shame.

The shame literature also suggests that the acknowledgment variables of feeling shame, accepting responsibility and making amends should be

negatively correlated with externalizing blame, retaliatory anger and displaced anger. The former three measures are internal sanctioning or guilt-like measures, whereas the latter three measures represent distractions or diversions from activating the internal sanctioning mechanism.

The intercorrelations for the five MOSS–SASD scales, feeling shame, hiding self, taking responsibility, internalizing others' rejection and making amends, indicate strong positive intercorrelations, as expected. Similarly, the other five scales, externalizing blame, blame-perseveration, felt anger, retaliatory anger and displaced anger, were also strongly and positively intercorrelated. As can be seen from Table 14.3, feeling shame, taking responsibility and making amends were negatively correlated with externalizing blame, retaliatory anger and displaced anger. The correlations, however, were somewhat lower than one might have expected. The implication of this observation will be taken up later in the chapter.

The types of shame management that are most obviously represented by the intercorrelations among the MOSS–SASD questions are discharged shame and by-passed shame. The four shame measures that did not fit tightly with the Shame Acknowledgment cluster or the Shame Displacement cluster were hiding self, internalizing others' rejection, blame-perseveration and felt anger. These items reflect aspects of persistent shame and denied–by-passed shame. Further analyses are needed to understand the operations of these variables.

As a final step in reducing these data, a principal component analysis was conducted on the data for the 10 MOSS–SASD questions (averaged across the eight scenarios) to determine the major dimensions along which responses varied. The selection of the number of components was based on three criteria: (a) accepting components with eigenvalues greater than unity (Kaiser's criterion); (b) examination of the scree test (Cattell, 1966); and (c) replicability of the structure across the eight bullying scenarios.

A two factor solution was extracted, accounting for 50 per cent of the total variance, and was rotated using the Varimax procedure (see Table 14.4).

The first factor brought together the variables of feeling shame, hiding self, taking responsibility, internalizing others' rejection and making amends – all of which share a common concern with owning shame or accepting the shame for wrongdoing. Therefore, the first factor was labeled 'Shame Acknowledgment'.

Table 14.3 Intercorrelations Among the MOSS–SASD Scales

MOSS–SASD scales	1	2	3	4	5	6	7	8	9	10
1 Feeling shame	–									
2 Hiding self	.39	–								
3 Taking responsibility	.61	.30	–							
4 Internalizing others' rejection	.22	.32	.22	–						
5 Making amends	.52	.26	.51	.18	–					
6 Externalizing blame	-.17	.04(ns)	-.28	.12	-.22	–				
7 Blame-perseveration	.01(ns)	.12	-.04(ns)	.16	.04(ns)	.33	–			
8 Feeling anger	.11	.20	.05(ns)	.16	.09	.24	.29	–		
9 Retaliatory anger	-.24	.00 (ns)	-.27	.02(ns)	-.24	.50	.26	.26	–	
10 Displaced anger	-.18	-.02 (ns)	-.13	.05*	-.14	.33	.22	.24	.48	–

Note: All correlations reached .001 level of significance unless reported.

* p<.05

Table 14.4 Rotated (Varimax) Factor Loadings for the MOSS–SASD Scales After Principal Component Analysis (n = 1386)

MOSS–SASD scales	Factor 1	Factor 2
Shame Acknowledgment		
Feeling shame	.81	−.16
Hiding self	.63	.20
Taking responsibility	.76	−.23
Internalizing others' rejection	.49	.30
Making amends	.74	−.16
Shame Displacement		
Externalizing blame	−.17	.74
Blame-perseveration	.17	.60
Feeling anger	.29	.57
Retaliatory anger	−.24	.74
Displaced anger	−.14	.64
Eigenvalues (before rotation)	2.83	2.24

The second factor brings together variables that tap defensive strategies in response to shame: externalizing blame, blame-perseveration, felt anger, retaliatory anger and displaced anger. All these variables represent attempts to deflect shame through displacing the felt shame into other-directed anger or self-directed anger. Therefore, the second factor was labeled 'Shame Displacement'.

It is of note that the first factor, Shame Acknowledgment, has emerged as being independent of the second factor, Shame Displacement.[2] This finding is important because it allows for individuals to simultaneously acknowledge and displace shame, to acknowledge shame without displacement, to displace shame without acknowledging it, and to neither acknowledge nor displace shame.

What do the MOSS–SASD Scales measure?

A criticism that can be made of the MOSS–SASD scales is that they measure what children think they would do in a situation, not what they actually do. In other words, the MOSS–SASD scales do not measure how children actually manage shame when they confront it in real life. We cannot answer this question completely satisfactorily in this book, but we can address the criticism by asking children who had bullied others to report on how they felt at that time. By correlating imagined responses with real-life responses among this group of children, we can find out

if the MOSS–SASD scales reflect real world experiences. In the MOSS–SASD (real) version, children who had admitted to bullying another child were asked to remember such an incident and answer the 10 MOSS–SASD questions.

When MOSS–SASD (real) and (imaginary) questions were correlated with each other, all product-moment correlation coefficients were positive and significant. They ranged from .25 to .44 with a median of .34 (see Table 14.5). Given that the real-situation MOSS–SASD comprised single item measures, these correlations are considered to be quite strong and supportive of the construct validity of the MOSS–SASD (imaginary).

Test–Retest Reliability

The MOSS–SASD scales were critically scrutinized in a number of ways. First, we examined the degree to which responses to the 10 shame management questions were stable over time. In other words, would individuals respond in the same way if they completed the MOSS–SASD scales again two to three weeks later? The question of the stability of responses was addressed using a small sample of 14 children. Scores for each question (averaged over the eight scenarios) on the first occasion were correlated with the corresponding scores on the second occasion. The test-retest correlation coefficients were high ranging from .75 to .97 with a median of .86.

Table 14.5 Product-moment correlations between the MOSS–SASD Scales (Imaginary Situations) and the MOSS–SASD Question Items (Real Situation) for Children Who Had Experienced Bullying Another (N = 792)

MOSS–SASD scales	r
Feeling shame	.41***
Hiding self	.31***
Taking responsibility	.28***
Internalizing others' rejection	.41***
Making amends	.34***
Externalizing blame	.34***
Blame-perseveration	.25***
Feeling anger	.35***
Retaliatory anger	.32***
Displaced anger	.44***

*** p<.001

Internal Consistency

In order to measure the internal consistency in children's responses across scenarios, Cronbach's (1951) alpha reliability was calculated for each MOSS–SASD scale (10 in total). The alpha coefficients for each scale were high, ranging from .89 to .96 with a median of .92.

Not only did we wish to use the MOSS–SASD scales individually, but also we wanted to make use of the Shame Acknowledgment and Shame Displacement composites in later chapters. The alpha reliability for Shame Acknowledgment (based on the MOSS–SASD scores averaged across scenarios) was .70 with a sample mean of 1.72 (SD =.22). For Shame Displacement, the alpha reliability was .66 with a sample mean of 1.22 (SD = .21). Both scales had distributions that were notably skewed. Skewness was not considered a substantive problem because responding in a manner that is socially desirable is an essential part of feeling shame.

Construct Validity

The two factors extracted from the principal component analysis, Shame Acknowledgment and Shame Displacement, were developed independently of Harris's work on shame in Part II. Yet Shame Acknowledgment resembles Harris's Shame–Guilt dimension and Shame Displacement resembles Harris's Unresolved Shame dimension. No counterpart was found for Embarrassment–Exposure in Part III. Such items were not considered within scope when shame management was conceptualized as in the early sections of this chapter.

The extent to which Harris's dimensions overlap with those identified in this chapter cannot be empirically tested directly. The degree of overlap can be examined indirectly, however, through looking at whether Shame Acknowledgment and Shame Displacement are related to empathy and other measures from Tangney (shame-proneness, guilt-proneness and externalization) in the same way as the dimensions used in Part III relate to these measures.

The first set of hypotheses relate to Shame Acknowledgment. Shame Acknowledgment, like Shame–Guilt, involves feelings of shame accompanied by remorse, responsibility and a desire to make things right. It also involves a feeling of others' rejection which acts as a threat to self. Our prediction, therefore, is that Shame Acknowledgment will be correlated positively with Tangney et al.'s (1989) measures of shame-proneness and guilt-proneness, and Rigby's (Rigby & Slee, 1991a) measure of empathy for the victims of bullying.

The second set of hypotheses relate to Shame Displacement. Shame

Displacement explicitly recognizes aggressive feelings and differs from Harris's factor, Unresolved Shame, in this respect. Although Unresolved Shame was positively correlated with hostility when Harris did a validity test, it is notable that Unresolved Shame was also positively correlated with empathy. A positive correlation is not expected between Shame Displacement and empathy. Instead Shame Displacement is hypothesized as correlating positively with Tangney's scale of shame-proneness and externalization.

Our data support these hypotheses (see Table 14.6). Shame Acknowledgment correlated most strongly with guilt-proneness followed by shame-proneness and empathy as predicted. Shame Displacement correlated most highly with externalization, and to a lesser extent with shame-proneness. These findings support the validity of the MOSS–SASD scales and suggest that Shame Acknowledgment has elements of the shame- and guilt-proneness articulated by Tangney as does Harris's Shame–Guilt dimension. Shame Displacement shares an angry component with Harris's Unresolved Shame, but does not correlate positively with empathy. Instead, Shame Displacement and empathy are inversely related. Shame Displacement predominantly taps the extent to which others are blamed and feelings associated with wrongdoing are externalized.

Summary

The aim of this chapter was to point to the significance of acknowledged shame alongside unacknowledged shame and to develop a more sophisticated understanding of the concept of 'shame management'. Acknowledged shame is seen as being functional for constructing and maintaining social relationships, while unacknowledged shame has the potential to be destructive of social relationships.

An understanding of the impediments to acknowledging or not acknowledging shame was gained through conceptualizing shame as a threat to self. Threat to self can be resolved through taking responsibility and making

Table 14.6 Product-moment Correlations between MOSS–SASD Scales, Tangney's Shame-, Guilt-proneness and Externalization, and Rigby's Empathy Scale

Variables	Shame-proneness	Guilt-proneness	Externalization	Empathy
Shame Acknowledgment	.39***	.53***	−.11***	.30***
Shame Displacement	.15***	−.14***	.31***	−.08**

**p<.01

***p<.001

things right, thereby restoring a sense of worth in one's own eyes and others. Alternatively, threat to self can be unresolved through deflection, blaming others and feeling angry.

In order to provide a quantitative measure of different shame responses, the MOSS–SASD scales were developed and tested. Children are presented with hypothetical situations and are asked a series of questions that represent 10 shame reactions that tap both domains of acknowledged and unacknowledged shame.

This chapter also examined the psychometric properties of the MOSS–SASD scales, providing support for both the reliability and validity of the instrument. Principal component analysis produced two factors, Shame Acknowledgment and Shame Displacement. Shame Acknowledgment brought together subsets of questions concerned with feeling shame, taking responsibility and making amends. This dimension fits the ethical identity conception of shame developed by Harris in Part II because it involves recognition of having acted in a way which is not only seen as unacceptable by others, but also contradicts one's own standard of right and wrong.

The second dimension, Shame Displacement, focused on deflecting blame onto others and turning shame into anger. While it bears some resemblance to Harris's dimension of Unresolved Shame (particularly in its relationship with hostility), the match is not as compelling as it is in the case of Shame Acknowledgment. Part of the explanation is likely to stem from differences in social context. In Part II, adults reflect on wrongdoing with explicit reference to the reactions of others. In Part III, children were asked to imagine how they would feel doing something wrong and getting caught by an authority figure. Engagement with the significant other is not the center of attention.

Having established psychometric support for the MOSS–SASD scales, the next chapter uses Shame Acknowledgment and Shame Displacement to develop an integrated shame management model of bullying behavior.

Notes

1 Note that this defines bullying as a threat to freedom as non-domination, as developed by Braithwaite and Pettit (1990) and Pettit (1997). This is of methodological significance because one of the objectives of Braithwaite's theoretical program is to develop concepts that enable an interaction of the explanatory theory (ordered sets of propositions about the way the world is) and normative theory (ordered sets of propositions about the way the world ought to be) (Braithwaite & Parker, 1998; Braithwaite and Pettit, 2000). If the explanatory theory proves useful in the present research, defining bullying in this way leaves open the option of integration with Braithwaite and Pettit's republican normative theory.

2 An oblique rotation yielded a negligible inter-factor correlation.

CHAPTER 15

The Integrated Model of Shame Management and Bullying

Overview

The objective of this chapter is to use reintegrative shaming theory to draw together a number of different strands of research, each of which has addressed the problem of school bullying. The central theme of Part III is that bullying can be understood in terms of shame and shame management skills, acquired primarily through socialization experiences, first via the institution of the family and then via the institution of the school. While family and school provide the context for shaming and teaching shame management skills, individuals are considered to be active participants in how they interpret and use their experiences. Which shame management approaches are used by individuals will not be shaped by the environment alone, but by the personalities of those enmeshed in shame-producing encounters.

The model that will be developed in this chapter and tested in Chapter 16 is represented in Figure 15.1. The relevance of each of the variables in the integrated model is discussed, and scales that were used to assess these variables are described. Before considering each component of the model, however, we need to argue the case for how reintegrative shaming theory extends the understanding of bullying behavior offered by traditional social-developmental research.

The Relevance of Reintegrative Shaming Theory

As we have seen in Parts I and II, the means by which reintegrative shaming leads to effective crime control is through inducing and activating conscience in individuals. In effect, it sanctions the expression of love and respect from significant others to the wrongdoer, at the same time as

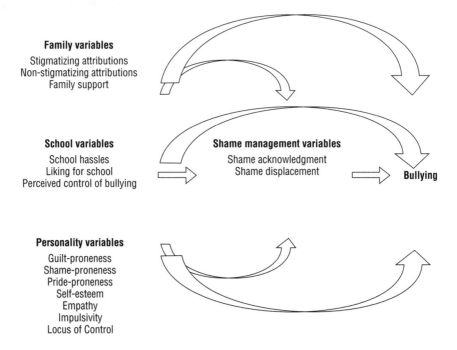

Family variables

Stigmatizing attributions
Non-stigmatizing attributions
Family support

School variables

School hassles
Liking for school
Perceived control of bullying

Shame management variables

Shame acknowledgment
Shame displacement

Bullying

Personality variables

Guilt-proneness
Shame-proneness
Pride-proneness
Self-esteem
Empathy
Impulsivity
Locus of Control

Figure 15.1 The Integrated Model of Shame Management and Bullying

condemning the wrongdoing. Reintegrative shaming involves disapproval of the wrongdoing, while re-accepting the wrongdoer in spite of the un-desirable act. Through this process, the wrongdoer is less likely to feel unworthy and detached from significant others, more likely to feel remorse-ful and apologetic for the offenses committed, and less likely to drift toward criminal subcultures in the future.

On the other hand, disintegrative shaming or stigmatization refers to disapproval of the wrongdoer's self, in addition to the act of wrongdoing. Disintegrative shaming damages the emotional bond between the shaming agent and the person who has committed the crime, as disapproval and rejection are directed at the wrongdoer's self. It thus becomes difficult for this 'rejected self' to activate conscience in response to wrongdoing. This purportedly results in a higher rate of subsequent criminal behavior.

In Part II of this book, Harris demonstrated that the core concepts of reintegration and stigmatization can co-exist in the real world. In other words, a person can shame another in a reintegrative and stigmatizing way within the space of a few seconds, that is, one kind of shaming does not rule out the other kind of shaming in real life. As in Part II, however, the starting model in Part III construed reintegration and stigmatization as polar oppo-sites. Shaming is depicted as a second independent dimension.

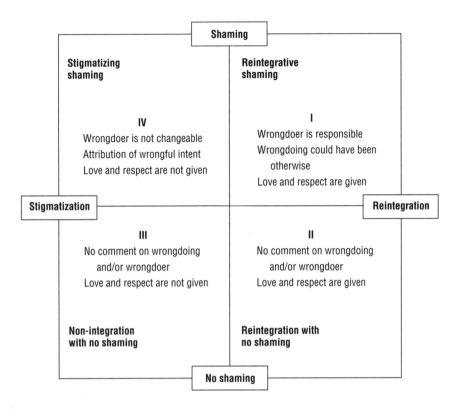

Figure 15.2 Two-dimensional Model of Shaming and Reintegration

From Figure 15.2, it can be seen that the 'shaming' region includes reintegrative shaming (Quadrant I) and stigmatizing shaming (Quadrant IV). Both involve shaming the wrongdoer, but they differ in how the shaming occurs. According to the model, reintegrative shaming gives the message that the act is wrong, but the person is worthy and can avoid future wrongdoing. This disapproval is terminated by significant other(s) showing love and respect for the wrongdoer. In contrast, stigmatizing shaming is directed towards the dispositional qualities of the wrongdoer, conveying, for instance, that he/she will repeat the wrongdoing because it was purposely performed. Love and respect are not offered to wrongdoers and accordingly, they feel detached from those persons who matter to them.

The 'no shaming' region in Figure 15.2 consists of reintegration without shaming (Quadrant II) and stigmatization without shaming (Quadrant III). Both show an absence of shaming, but they differ in terms of whether love and respect are offered to the wrongdoer. According to the model, individuals in the stigmatization without shaming quadrant receive neither a

message that the act is wrong nor love and respect from significant others. In contrast, individuals in the reintegration without shaming quadrant show love and respect to the wrongdoer without any sort of disapproval of the wrongdoing.

In this chapter, reintegration is conceived as an extended process through which the individual acquires self-regulatory strategies in the form of conscience. Conscience involves the internalization of communally shared moral standards, and the parent–child relationship is important for the transmission of this knowledge (Hoffman, 1970, 1983). Such a relationship might be expected to offer love and respect to the wrongdoer. Thus, Quadrants I and II should provide the base on which to build conscience.

While Quadrants I and II share the common feature of reintegration, they should not be equally effective in building conscience. In the absence of shaming from significant other(s) (Quadrant II), individuals are less certain about what is appropriate behavior in the eyes of significant other(s). Without a clear message, reintegration is not sufficient in the development of conscience. There will be a risk of unresolved shame, with its anger-inducing consequences. Quadrant I, therefore, is hypothesized as capturing the critical components for conscience development. Wrongdoers have the opportunity of knowing that the act is wrong which, in turn, enables them to interact more competently in future. In addition, they are made to feel a valued member of the group, in spite of their wrongdoing, through affirmation from significant other(s).

In contrast, Quadrants III and IV are unlikely to produce adequate conscience in individuals, primarily because they involve stigmatizing from significant other(s). Stigmatization fails to provide the resources for the development of conscience in individuals. Negative and disrespectful relationships between the shaming agent(s) and the wrongdoer lead wrongdoers to dissociate themselves from shamers and their norms or values (Quadrant IV). In addition, individuals in Quadrant III fail to receive messages of disapproval for wrongdoing. With the absence of shaming, such individuals neither understand the causes of significant others' dissociation from them nor can they learn norms of desirable behavior. The result is an ambivalent orientation to others based on ignorance of norms and a failure to feel part of the group.

Taken together, these considerations suggest that compared to other quadrants, individuals whose socializing experiences in the family fit the pattern described in Quadrant I (reintegrative shaming) should be the best prepared for coming to terms with their own wrongdoing and making amends. Parents who behave towards their children in the way described in Quadrant I will believe the child is capable of controlling future wrongdoing and therefore can be held responsible for the harm done. Having

disapproved of the child's wrongdoing in this manner, such parents will engage in loving and respectful communication with the child, bringing forth a sense of self-worth, and a desire to make up for the wrongdoing. These children should be least likely to be involved in bullying.

In contrast, it is proposed that parents who shame or disapprove of a child's wrongdoing in a disrespectful way are more likely to have children who have an insecure or dissociated relationship with their primary caregiver and a sense of themselves as unworthy through their parents' eyes. This idea has been captured in Quadrant IV (stigmatizing shaming). These children are expected to be the ones most likely to bully other children. These two hypotheses relating to the socialization experiences described in Quadrants I and IV will be put to the test through the integrated model of bullying.

Links with the Developmental Literature

This view of the effects of reintegrative and stigmatizing shaming on wrongdoing corresponds to the orientations of a number of social and developmental psychologists (e.g., Baumrind, 1967, 1991a, 1991b; Grusec, 1982; Grusec & Kuczynski, 1997; Hoffman, 1970, 1983; Kuczynski & Kochanska, 1990; Kuczynski, Zahn-Waxler & Radke-Yarrow, 1987; Leahy, 1981; Maccoby & Martin, 1983; Smetana, 1988). Parents who use an authoritative disciplinary style are known to facilitate the development of internalized moral values in their children because they combine strategies of explaining wrongdoing and communicating love and support (e.g., Leahy, 1981; Lytton, 1979; Power & Chapieski, 1986). Authoritative parenting has been found more generally to foster children's prosocial behavior (Baumrind, 1967, 1973, 1989, 1991a, 1991b; Feshbach, 1974; Hoffman, 1975; Grusec, 1982; Janssens & Dekovic, 1997). In contrast, an authoritarian disciplinary style which incorporates punishment after wrongdoing and shows disrespect for the child has been related to antisocial behavior in children (Bandura, 1977; Baumrind, 1993; Buss, 1961; Eron, Huesmann & Zelli, 1991; Farrington, 1978; Feldman, Rosenthal, Mon-Reynaud, Leung & Lau, 1991; Fletcher, Darling, Steinberg, & Dornbusch, 1995; Hetherington & Parke, 1979; Olweus, 1980; Patterson, 1982; Patterson, Reid & Dishion, 1992; Petit & Bates, 1989; Sears, Maccoby, & Levin, 1957; Steinberg, Mounts, Lamborn & Dornbusch, 1991; Trickett & Kuczynski, 1986).

A further link can be made between the model presented in Figure 15.2 and Weiner's (1980) attribution theory. Attribution research draws a distinction between explaining another's actions in terms of global and stable characteristics that are intentional (e.g. He has always been a bully and does it deliberately) and characteristics that recognize an ability to control and

change offending behavior (e.g. He is responsible for the bullying, but he is capable of controlling his behavior). Stigmatizing shaming in Figure 15.2 involves making attributions about wrongdoing being the result of a stable characteristic of the person and as being intentional. In the social-developmental literature, attributions of stability and intentionality in the context of wrongdoing have been associated with maladaptive outcomes (e.g., shame, anxiety, despair). In contrast, attributions that connote expectations of change for the better in the wrongdoer (e.g., controllability and responsibility) and avoid labeling individuals as possessing global personality deficits have been associated with positive outcomes (e.g., pro-social behavior, empathy, self-esteem).

From Shaming to Shame

In Part II, Harris demonstrated that the link between shaming (reintegrative or stigmatizing) and shame was not as straightforward as we initially expected. Most significantly from the perspective of this chapter, reintegrative shaming appears to be effective in eliciting Shame–Guilt only when those doing the shaming are respected by the wrongdoer. How then are the shaming attributions outlined in Figure 15.2 likely to impact on shame feelings?

In the context of the present study, we make the assumption that parents are considered as "significant others" by their primary school-age children. This is not always going to be the case, but it is likely to be the case for most of the children and parents who jointly consented to be part of this study. The children in this study are likely to be both emotionally and physically dependent on their parents. As such, parents at least can be thought of as significant others, if not always highly respected others.

The reintegrative and stigmatizing shaming styles represented in Figure 15.2, and used by parents in dealing with wrongdoing in their children, have been theoretically linked to the development of conscience. Shame feelings that involve acknowledgment of wrongdoing in combination with restraint from blaming others or the whole self are taken as our operational definition of an effective self-regulating conscience. Thus, the hypothesis tested in Part III of this book is in keeping with our initial formulation: Reintegrative shaming which disapproves of wrongdoing at the same time as conveying to the child a sense of being valued can be expected to lead to acknowledgment of shame (feeling shame, taking responsibility, making amends), without any displacement of shame. Stigmatizing shaming by parents, in contrast, will lead to low Shame Acknowledgment but high Shame Displacement (e.g., externalizing blame, feeling retaliatory anger).

A further point of difference between this study and that of Harris that should be noted is that Harris focused on a real-life incident and on how

individuals dealt with and perceived each other at this time. The shaming was real not imagined, as were the shame feelings. The present study is contextually different, and therefore may produce different insights into the shaming–shame relationship. The focus of shaming in Part III is on parents' attributions, made while completing a questionnaire about the hypothetical incidents described in the MOSS–SASD instrument. In other words, parents were required to indicate the attributions that they would be most likely to make if they were to catch their child being the offender in the bullying scenarios in the MOSS–SASD instrument. This means that in Part III the data reflect parents' and children's beliefs about their shaming strategies and their shame feelings should wrongdoing occur. The previous chapter demonstrated the connection between children's hypothetical responses and real-life bullying; parents' hypothetical responses, however, have been less well validated. This study advances on most other research in this field simply through seeking responses from parents. In most past research, children are asked to report on their perceptions of their parents' behavior. Previous research has shown that children's attributions and parents' attributions differ substantially (Huntley, 1995).

The bullying literature that was reviewed in Chapter 13 sits comfortably alongside the theory of reintegrative shaming as it is being applied in this chapter. Children who bully others were more likely to have parents who adopted a punitive approach to child-rearing (Manning et al., 1978; Olweus, 1980, 1984; Strassberg et al., 1994). They were also likely to come from a less cohesive family environment (Berdondini & Smith, 1996; Bowers et al., 1992, 1994; Rican, 1995). Bullying was found among those children with low self-esteem (O'Moore & Hillery, 1991; Rigby & Cox, 1996) as well as among those who externalize the causes of bullying (Slee, 1993). Deficiencies in impulse control and empathy were also found among children who bully others (Besag, 1989; Olweus, 1978). Deficiencies in empathy have been associated with shame-proneness as well as externalizing blame (Tangney, 1991). Interestingly, empathy has also been proposed as crucial to the healing of pathological shame (Jordan, 1997). Other individual characteristics associated with bullying are also implicated as correlates of poor shame management. For example, both impulsivity and internal locus of control were found to be high in individuals who had deficiencies in managing shame (Kipnis, 1968; Sanftner, Barlow, Marschall & Tangney, 1995; Wang, Wang & Zhang, 1992).

From Figure 15.2, adaptive shame management (Quadrant I) involving acknowledgment should come about when parents deal with their child's wrongdoing in a reintegrative manner; that is parents show love and support, while recognizing the harm done. Such parents are likely to communicate to the child about his/her capacity for change in the future.

They are also likely to provide the explanation that the wrongdoing is under the control of the child and will not happen again. In this way, messages of impulse control, empathy and self-worth are reinforced for the child.

In contrast, maladaptive shame management (Quadrant IV) involving denial of responsibility and anger at others is likely to arise when parents deal with wrongdoing in a stigmatizing and uncaring way. When parents fail to provide support and dismiss their child's capacity to do the right thing in the future (perhaps because of an impulsive personality), the child is less likely to learn and have the confidence to get it right next time. In particular, such children are unlikely to learn impulse control, believe that they can positively influence the direction that their life is taking and to feel that anyone cares about their well-being. Empathy is unlikely to be nurtured in this socializing context.

The next section uses the principles of reintegrative shaming theory to bring together feelings of shame and other personality variables that are known to influence bullying. Furthermore, because school experiences have been so consistently implicated in understanding bullying, a set of school-related variables have been included.

The Integrated Shame Management Model of Bullying

The integrated shame management model of bullying incorporates four major sets of variables hypothesized as influencing bullying behavior. The predictors are classified as: family variables, school variables, personality variables and, finally, shame management variables. It is proposed that each set of variables affects developmental outcomes that lead some children down the path of bullying behavior.

Focusing first on the role of families, the model emphasizes the importance of parental child-rearing beliefs in a developmental context. It postulates that child-rearing beliefs reflecting the practice of stigmatizing shaming attributions will increase the likelihood of bullying, and give children little opportunity to develop adaptive shame management skills. This situation is likely to be particularly destructive when stigmatizing shaming take place against a backdrop of family conflict and disharmony. In contrast, non-stigmatizing shaming attributions should be effective in developing adaptive shame management skills and reducing bullying, particularly when accompanied by family support.

The integrated shame management model also recognizes the role of school-related variables (e.g. liking for school, school hassles, school-level tolerance of bullying), all of which have been associated with bullying in past research. Children who do not like school and who have problems at school are more likely to have feelings of shame associated with personal

frustration and failure. School variables may be linked with family variables, since parental warmth and affection have been associated positively with indices of school adjustment and negatively with adjustment problems (Chen, Dong & Zhou, 1997; Scott & Scott, 1998).

Also incorporated into the integrated shame management model are a number of individual characteristics that fall under the general rubric of personality. These variables comprise empathy, self-esteem, locus of control, and impulsivity, and Tangney et al.'s (1989) measures of guilt-, shame- and pride-proneness. These variables, some of which may be shaped by shaming experiences in the family, have been linked with bullying behavior and discussed in the preceding chapters.

The integrated shame management model of bullying acknowledges previous findings that propose direct links between family, school and personality variables on the one hand, and bullying behavior on the other. It also proposes a special role for shame management skills. The shame management skills identified in the SASD framework are proposed as also having a direct effect on bullying, and as at least partially mediating the established relationships recognized above and discussed in more detail below.

Family Variables

Parental responses to wrongdoing are likely to influence the child's future perceptions and actions (e.g., Goodnow, 1988, 1992; Goodnow & Collins, 1990; Sigel, 1985; Sigel, McGillicuddy-DeLisi & Goodnow, 1992). Two kinds of parental responses were examined in this study. The first were the attributions that parents made about their child's wrongdoing. When a parent observes a child's transgression, he/she is likely to disapprove of the act and to explain it in certain ways. According to Weiner (1979, 1980), individuals are constantly searching for the causes behind behaviors or events they observe. These explanations can be seen as expressing disapproval with and without a stigmatizing quality. In addition to the way parents make sense of their child's wrongdoing, reintegrative shaming theory reminds us of the importance of communicating love and respect. Thus, in accordance with Figure 15.2, family support was measured along with stigmatizing and non-stigmatizing attributions. Critically important in respect of Figure 15.2 was to identify children who perceived their home environment as disintegrative and unsafe.

Stigmatizing Shaming Attributions
Child-rearing beliefs which disapprove of wrongdoing by sending the message that the child purposefully performed the transgression, and is likely to do the same thing in future, are 'stigmatizing' in nature. This sort

of parental belief reflects the child's fixed incapacity and/or insight deficits, and is likely to deliver a stigmatizing message from parents to the child. The stigma takes the form of implying to the child some dispositional characteristic which is not alterable, that is an enduring facet of the child. Such evaluations signal global unworthiness in the context of wrongdoing which the child is likely to internalize as a negative description of his/her self.

Thus, a merging of the attribution and reintegrative shaming literatures leads to the following proposed sequence in parent–child interactions:

Transgression ⇒ perceived stability and intentionality ⇒ stigmatizing shaming attributions ⇒ ineffective shame management skills ⇒ higher chance of bullying

The link between attributions and outcomes receives support from previous research: When harm is perceived as stable and intentional, the intensity of aggressive responses and interpersonal conflict is likely to increase (Averill, 1983; Bandura, 1973, 1986; Betancourt & Blair, 1992; Dodge & Crick, 1990; Ferguson & Rule, 1983; Feshbach, 1964).

Non-Stigmatizing Shaming Attributions

On the basis of reintegrative shaming theory, child-rearing beliefs which disapprove of the child's misdeed, without giving him/her the impression that the parent labels him/her as a deviant person are 'non-stigmatizing' in nature. This sort of parental belief conveys to the child that he/she is responsible for the undesirable act which 'could have been otherwise'. That is, child-rearing beliefs that result in non-stigmatizing attributions impart the impression that the child possesses necessary skills to control wrongdoing (controllability) and that the child is held responsible for his actions (responsibility) which need not occur again. This non-stigmatizing attribution ensures that the child is not branded with a deviant label. Instead disapproval is applied to a misdeed which is transient since the child is believed to have sufficient self-control to refrain from repeating it.

From an attributional perspective, controllability and responsibility are helpful in understanding how non-stigmatizing attribution works effectively in response to a transgression. Parents who conclude that the wrongdoing was under the control of the child and that the child should be held responsible are, in effect, disapproving of the act while affirming confidence in the child and his/her future capacities.

Transgression ⇒ perceived controllability and responsibility ⇒ non-stigmatizing shaming attribution ⇒ effective shame management skills ⇒ less chance of bullying

The adaptive nature of assigning responsibility and controlability can be found in the attribution literature. These two dimensions can evoke greater empathy for and guilt toward others, heighten a sense of worthiness, add to

the individual's self concept as a 'helpful person' (Eisenberg & Mussen, 1989; Weiner, 1993), lead to a more active problem solving approach (Anderson, Lytton & Romney, 1986; Sujan, 1986), and produce prosocial behaviors (Baumrind, 1971, 1989; Eisenberg et al., 1987; Staub, 1979; Whiting & Whiting, 1975).

On the basis of the theoretical considerations above, the current research suggests a link between child-rearing beliefs as expressions of shaming practices and a child's bullying behavior.

Measures of Stigmatizing and Non-stigmatizing Attributions

The Attributional Shaming Instrument (ASI; Ahmed, 1996) was developed to measure child-rearing beliefs that reflected stigmatizing and non-stigmatizing shaming attributions (for details see Table 15.1).

The ASI presents parents with stories describing hypothetical incidents in which their own child transgressed in a peer group situation. The ASI comprises eight scenarios of bullying at school (see Ahmed, 1999: Appendix 4.2)[1] that are used in the MOSS–SASD instrument. Following each scenario, parents answered four questions on a five-point scale ranging from (1) 'strongly disagree' to (5) 'strongly agree'. Attributions expressing stigmatizing shaming was assessed through two measures: stability (I would say my child will never repeat this behavior in future (reverse score)[2]) and intentionality (I would say that my child meant to do what he/she did). The correlation coefficients among the ratings for the eight scenarios ranged from .73 to .89 (median = .82) for stability and from .54 to .82 (median = .72) for intentionality. The stability and intentionality scales correlated positively ($r = .16$, $p<.001$) and were combined for future analyses to represent stigmatizing shaming attributions ($M = 3.44$; $SD = .72$).[3]

To assess parental expression of non-stigmatizing shaming, responses over the 8 scenarios were summed to produce two measures: responsibility (I would say that my child should not be blamed for the behavior (reverse score)[4]) and controllability (I would say that the behavior was under my child's control). Responses on responsibility correlated quite highly across the eight scenarios, ranging from .39 to .66 (median = .61). For controllability, the correlations were even higher, ranging from .65 to .90 (median = .80). The responsibility and controllability scales correlated positively ($r = .22$, $p<.001$) and were combined for the purposes of the analyses in Part III into an index representing non-stigmatizing shaming attributions ($M = 4.35$; $SD = .57$).[5]

Family Support

An essential feature of reintegrative shaming is the communication by significant others that the wrongdoer is loved, respected and valued as a

member of the family or the community. The attributional concepts discussed above do not capture this important facet of reintegrative shaming. Conversely, the emotional distancing that accompanies disrespect and lack of concern for the wrongdoer is an essential part of stigmatizing shaming. These variables, therefore, need to be measured separately to fully test the impact of parental shaming of a reintegrative or stigmatizing kind on the development of shame management skills.

In order to do this, the present study takes account of two constructs from the social developmental literatures that have been linked with bullying. The first is the warmth and love communicated to the child by the parent, more specifically the degree of positive affect present in the parent–child relationship. The second is the degree to which the family provides a supportive and harmonious environment for the child.

It is important to note that these are background variables in the context of the parental task of dealing with wrongdoing. Love, affection and supportiveness are not being measured in the context of wrongdoing but rather are being measured in relation to parent–child interaction more generally. If the aim is to test reintegrative shaming theory, it would appear that Harris's measure of reintegration in the context of drink-driving provides the stronger test of the effect of reintegrative and stigmatizing shaming on shame feelings. Our present objective, however, is to try to forge links between reintegrative shaming theory and social developmental explanations of bullying.

Thus, the integrated shame management model draws on reintegrative shaming theory to propose that reintegrative shaming in a family involves the use of non-stigmatizing attributions that communicate responsibility for the wrongdoing and controllability over the outcome, against a background of social relationships where the child has had a history of experiencing love and care at the hands of his/her parent and family.

In contrast, stigmatizing shaming in the parent role involves the use of attributions for wrongdoing whereby the parent states that his/her child intended the wrongdoing (intentionality) and will do it again (stability). These stigmatizing attributions are communicated against a background where the child has a history of conflict with the parent and feels unsupported in the family.

On the basis of past research, the family support variables are expected to have a main effect on bullying. They are also expected to have a direct link with shame management variables. Socialization research has shown that certain parental practices (such as, warmth, affection and democratic child-rearing) stimulate the child's feelings of worth (Baumrind, 1971; Radke-Yarrow, Zahn-Waxler & Chapman, 1983; Stipek, 1983) and pro-social behavior (Baumrind, 1971; Zhan-Waxler, Radke-Yarrow & King,

1979). Other studies have examined family functioning in general and found that greater family dysfunction was reflected in lower self-esteem (Werner & Broida, 1991). For this reason, one might expect that children from a disharmonious family, where care and support are in short supply, will have feelings of unworthiness and of being held in low regard. Non-supportive family environments are likely to leave children vulnerable to developing poor shame management skills and to adopt bullying behavior.

Measures of Family Support

Family support was measured with two scales. The first was based on parents' perceptions of positive parent–child affect assessed through seven items: (a) My child and I have warm, intimate times together; (b) I express affection by hugging, kissing and holding my child; (c) I find some of my greatest satisfactions in my child; (d) I joke and play with my child; (e) I am easy-going and relaxed with my child; (f) I often feel angry with my child (reverse score); and (g) There is a good deal of conflict between my child and me (reverse score). Parents' responses to these items were averaged to produce a score representing positive affect between parent and child ($M = 4.89$; $SD = .59$; $\alpha = .75$).

The second scale was based on children's perceptions of family harmony. Because the measure used in this study assesses whether a family is plagued by conflict and ignorance of needs and well-being, the term family disharmony is used. It comprised four items asking students: How often do you experience (1) parents ignoring you; (2) parents checking up on you; (3) difficulties among family members; and (4) arguments or disagreements in the family. Responses were averaged to produce a score representing the degree to which the family is perceived as unsupportive neither addressing the concerns of the child nor the respectful resolution of problems ($M = 1.75$; $SD = .43$; $\alpha = .65$).

Table 15.1 Summary of the Measures for Family Variables

Measure	Source and description	Response category
Child-rearing belief (Stigmatizing and Non-stigmatizing Shaming Attributions)	Attributional Shaming Instrument (Ahmed, 1996)	5-point ('Strongly disagree' to 'Strongly Agree')
Positive parent-child affect	Child-Rearing Practices Report (CRPR; Block, 1965)[6]	6-point rating scale ('Strongly disagree' to 'Strongly Agree')
Family disharmony	Groube (1987)	3-point ('never' to 'a lot of time')

School Variables

School Hassles

In a review of the literature, Aurora and Fimian (1988) concluded that perceived personal academic abilities and functioning, peer relationships, and teacher interactions were common sources of stress in children. For the purposes of the present research, school hassles are defined as disruptions and demands in the everyday lives of children that are frustrating and annoying, and that have the potential to pile up over time (Kanner, Coyne, Schaefer & Lazarus, 1981).

The stress paradigm has forged a strong empirical link between daily hassles and adjustment. Prospective research has revealed that daily hassles for school children lead them toward a range of behavioral problems (Compas, Howell, Phares, Williams & Ledoux, 1989; DuBois, Felner, Brand, Adan & Evans, 1992; Dubow, Tisak, Causey, Hryshko & Reid, 1991; Hastings, Anderson & Kelly, 1996). Creasey, Mitts and Catanzaro (1995) reported that children experiencing daily hassles may communicate problems through externalizing behaviors, or 'acting out' behaviors. Spicer and Franklin (1994) found that individuals' verbal aggression and violent acts were related to a high frequency of daily hassles. Sterling, Cowen, Weissberg, Lotyezewski and Boike (1985) found that stressful life events were associated with the presence of more serious school adjustment problems.

With these links between children's stress, school adjustment and behavioral problems, a child's experience of school hassles is expected to be positively related to bullying behavior. Furthermore, stressors at school may threaten the child's sense of self at a fundamental level, weakening a child's capacity to acknowledge shame, and increasing the tendency to displace shame onto others.

Measure of School Hassles

Eight items from Groube's (1987) Daily Hassles scale were used to examine school hassles (for details see Table 15.2). These are: (1) failing a test or exam; (2) feeling unsure about what is expected of me at school [e.g., schoolwork]; (3) doing worse in schoolwork than I expected; (4) failing to do my homework; (5) having no friends; (6) having things go wrong in my relationships with friends; (7) having to make new friends; and (8) disagreements or misunderstanding with friends. A school hassles score was computed for each child by averaging across children's responses to the eight items ($M = 1.79$; $SD = .32$; $\alpha = .71$). The higher the score, the more hassles at school.

Liking for School

A considerable body of research suggests a relationship between deviant behavior and disliking school (Agnew, 1985; Jensen & Eve, 1976; Johnson, 1979; Kaplan, Robbins & Martin, 1983; Koh, 1997; Slee, 1993, 1995; Thomas & Hyman, 1978; Wiatrowski, Griswald & Roberts, 1981). Research has shown that delinquents and/or bullies have lower academic achievement (Farrington, 1973; O'Moore & Hillery, 1991; Phillips & Kelly, 1979) and are less accomplished in peer relationships at school (Boulton & Smith, 1994; O'Moore & Hillery, 1991; Smith & Boulton, 1991), both of which are important factors for school satisfaction. Based on this evidence, it is hypothesized that children who bully others would have low scores on liking for school.

Furthermore, children who do not like school are unlikely to be sufficiently well connected to the school to feel safe enough to engage in shame acknowledgment. Dislike for school and the resulting emotional distance between the child and the school will also make the response of Shame Displacement much easier.

Measures of Liking for School

Liking for school was measured through two sets of drawings (for details see Table 15.2). The first was a pictorial representation of five faces along with thought bubbles containing words expressing different levels of satisfaction at school. The second was a newly developed measure featuring a series of five drawings of a boy and a girl bearing the postures of children exhibiting different levels of belongingness to their school. The two scales were positively correlated ($r = .46$, $p<.001$), and therefore, were averaged to construct the index of liking for school ($M = 3.90$; $SD = .79$; $\alpha = .63$), with a high score indicating greater liking and belongingness.

Perceived Control of Bullying

The literature on school bullying has suggested that teachers' messages to the students that they will not tolerate bullying and that they will take actions to build a safe school environment are an effective strategy for lowering rates of school bullying (Greenbaum, 1987; Hoover & Hazler, 1991).

Intraschool differences have also been investigated with bullying and aggression occurring more frequently in schools with low staff morale, unclear standards of behavior, inadequate supervision, and poor organization (Arora & Thompson, 1987; Elliott, 1991; Lane, 1989). In Stephenson and Smith's (1989) study, teachers in the low bullying schools expressed considered and purposeful views on bullying, and emphasized the

importance of controlling and preventing its occurrence. The action taken by schools is known to be a key factor in determining levels of bullying (Lane, 1989; Olweus, 1993; Rigby, 1996).

It is therefore hypothesized that the more a child views his/her school as able to handle bullying problems, the less likely he/she is to engage in bullying activities. When children see opportunities to bully others without imposition of sanctions, they may be more likely to believe that bullying is acceptable. In this way, school policies that are laissez-faire with regard to bullying may be undermining the development of prosocial shame management strategies.

Measure of Perceived Control of Bullying

This measure consisted of seven items (for details see Table 15.2). The respondents answered the following two questions on a four-point rating scale: (1) In your view, is this school a safe place for young people who find it hard to defend themselves from attack from other students? (2) Do you think that teachers at this school are interested in trying to stop bullying?

Five additional questions with a three-point response format were presented to the students as follows: (1) How often would you say that bullying happens at this school? (2) Have you noticed bullying going on in this school in any of these places? (a) in the classroom (b) at recess/lunch (c) on the way to school (d) on the way home from school. Items were scored so that a high score meant effective control against bullying at the school level. All these seven items were standardized before being averaged to form a composite variable ($M = .00$; $SD = .57$; $\alpha = .66$).

Table 15.2 Summary of the Measures for School Variables

Measure	Source and description	Response format
School Hassles	Groube (1987)	3-point ('never' to 'a lot of time')
Liking for School	(a) Smiley Face Scale (Mooney, Creeser, & Blatchford, 1991)	(a) 5-point ('Ugh, I hate it' to 'Great, I love it')
	(b) School Engagement-Withdrawal Scale (B. Braithwaite, 1996)	(b) 5-point (pictorial representation)
Perceived Control of Bullying	Peer Relations Questionnaire (Rigby & Slee, 1993a)	4-point rating scale ('never' to 'always'; 2 items) and 3-point scale ('never' to 'always'; 5 items)

Personality Variables

While experiences at home and at school are likely to shape shame management strategies and explain bullying, the following personality characteristics are likely to play a role as well.

Guilt-proneness, Shame-proneness and Pride-proneness

Guilt-proneness is a personality attribute describing individuals who are dealing with negative affective experience associated with negatively evaluated behavior, and who implicitly accept responsibility for that behavior (Tangney, 1990, 1992). As we have seen, guilt-proneness has much in common with the shame management constructs described in Chapter 14. The common features are taking responsibility and making amends along with the absence of externalizing or internalizing blame. Guilt-proneness may be regarded as an enduring tendency to show high Shame Acknowledgment and low Shame Displacement when confronted with wrongdoing.

Tangney (1990, 1991) has contrasted guilt-proneness with shame-proneness, arguing that guilt-proneness is less threatening to the self. Shame-proneness involves negative evaluation of the global self rather than the specific behaviors, and is, therefore more likely to invoke defensive maneuvers (e.g., externalizing blame and hostility). Recent work has differentiated guilt- and shame-prone individuals in terms of the way they deal with anger (Tangney et al., 1996). Guilt-prone individuals engage in constructive and rational strategies for managing their anger whereas shame-prone individuals express their anger destructively. It was hypothesized, therefore, that guilt-proneness, in contrast to shame-proneness, would be negatively related to bullying.

In addition to guilt- and shame-proneness, we incorporated pride-proneness in the model. Pride-proneness refers to a stable tendency to experience pride in performance in response to a positively evaluated behavior (Tangney, 1990). This sort of pride was labeled as beta pride in Tangney's research. Tangney found that pride-proneness is negatively related to shame-proneness and positively related to guilt-proneness. Evidence of the adaptive function of pride has been discussed in the developmental literature. Ornstein (1997) has demonstrated an inverse relation between pride and destructive aggression in children.

In view of these findings, we can hypothesize that pride-proneness would be positively related to Shame Acknowledgment which has much common with guilt-proneness, and negatively related to Shame Displacement and bullying.

Measures of Guilt-proneness, Shame-proneness and Pride-proneness
These personality variables were measured using the Test Of Self-Conscious Affect for Children (for details see Table 15.3). The TOSCA–C measures consist of 15 brief scenarios (10 negative and five positive in valence) which are relevant to the everyday contexts of respondents. Some wording and some pictures[7] that make up the TOSCA–C were modified to suit Australian children. The sample means were 2.88 for shame-proneness (SD = .65; α = .82), 3.72 for guilt-proneness (SD = .60; α = .83), and 3.62 for pride-proneness (SD = .67; α =.77).

Four additional personality variables are included in the integrated shame management model predicting bullying, because of their central importance in bullying research.

Self-esteem

Self-esteem refers to a person's general evaluations of self-worth whereby high self-esteem is characterized by positive feelings and liking for oneself (Rosenberg, 1965, 1979, 1986). Scheff (1996a) has put forward the view that individuals with low self-esteem are usually overwhelmed by unacknowledged and unresolved feelings of shame. Support was found for an inverse relationship between self-esteem and externalizing blame and anger (Abalakina, Stephan, Craig & Gregory, 1999). Along with this proposition, we must consider the history of inconsistent empirical findings regarding the relationship between self-esteem and bullying. Some researchers have found bullying to be positively related to self-esteem (Olweus, 1978), some have failed to document any significant relationship between them (Rigby & Slee, 1993b; Slee & Rigby, 1993), while others report an inverse link between bullying and self-esteem (O'Moore & Hillery, 1991; Rigby & Cox, 1996).

The inconsistency in findings may be due to how much self-esteem bullies derive from their bullying activities. Some may bully and be rewarded socially for their dominance. Others may bully and be ostracized for their behavior. Another explanation for the inconsistency may lie with the shame management variables. Bullies are expected to have low scores on Shame Acknowledgment and high scores on Shame Displacement. On the basis of past research, high Shame Displacement can be expected to correlate with low self-esteem. Low Shame Acknowledgment, however, is a response that may work well to protect self-esteem. If a child does not acknowledge wrongdoing, the child can avoid dealing with self-criticism. The present study, therefore, provides an opportunity to examine the role of self-esteem in bullying after taking account of the individual's shame management skills.

Measure of Self-esteem

The Short Form of the Rosenberg self-esteem scale (for details see Table 15.3) was used to measure self-esteem. Children indicated level of agreement with the following items: (1) I feel I have a number of good qualities; (2) I feel I do not have much to be proud of (reverse score); (3) I wish I could have more respect for myself (reverse score); (4) On the whole, I am satisfied with myself; (5) At times I think I am no good at all (reverse score); and, (6) I certainly feel useless at times (reverse score). Individual scores were averaged over these items so that the higher the score, the higher the self-esteem of the child (M = 2.86; SD = .56; α = .70).

Empathy

Empathy refers to the sharing of an emotional response between the observer and the victim, and has three components: (a) the cognitive ability to accurately read cues regarding the victim's emotional experience; (b) the affective capacity to personally experience the victim's perspective; and (c) the affective reaction to assist the victim (Hoffman, 1975).

Empathy increases the likelihood of prosocial behavior (Aronfreed, 1968; Eisenberg & Miller, 1987; Eisenberg & Strayer, 1987; Hoffman, 1982), reduces different forms of antisocial behavior (Miller & Eisenberg, 1988), and has frequently been shown to have a negative relationship with aggression and bullying (Miller & Eisenberg, 1988; Rigby & Slee, 1991b). Empathy has also been associated with shame-related variables. High empathy is found in those who are guilt-prone whereas low empathy is found in those who are prone to feel shame (Tangney, 1991, 1995a, 1995b) and to externalize blame (Wingrove & Bond, 1998).

On the basis of past findings, empathy is expected to be positively linked with Shame Acknowledgment and negatively with Shame Displacement. Empathy should also reduce the likelihood of bullying.

Measure of Empathy

Children's empathic concern for victimized children was assessed using three items (for details see Table 15.3): (1) I feel like standing up for kids who are being bullied; (2) I feel like helping kids who can't defend themselves; and (3) I feel like being angry when a kid is picked on without reason. Higher scores reflected a greater amount of empathy in children (M = 3.35; SD = .62; α =.73).

Impulsivity

Impulsivity is widely regarded as a temperament which describes a personality disposition to act on sudden urges without any thought or self-control

(Buss & Plomin, 1975; Eysenck, 1977). Impulsive behaviors tend to be characterized by a maladaptive sense of immediacy and spontaneity without consideration, foresight and adequate planning or regard for possible consequences. Those who score high on impulsivity tend to show a lack of regard for the harmful consequences of their actions to others.

Previous studies have shown that impulsivity is positively linked to shame-proneness and negatively linked to guilt-proneness (e.g., Milan, 1990; Sanftner et al., 1995). It has also been shown that impulsivity is an important contributor to externalizing blame (Archer, Kilpatrick, & Bramwell, 1995) and antisocial behavior (Barratt & Patton 1983; Bjorkqvist et al., 1982; Block, Block & Keyes, 1988; Buss, 1966; Eysenck & McGurk, 1980; Eysenck, 1977; 1981; Loeber, 1990; Magnusson, 1987; Moffitt, 1993; Olweus, 1978; Schalling, Edman, Asberg & Oreland, 1988; Whalen, Henker, Hinshaw & Granger (1989).

With the establishment of these links, impulsivity is expected to be negatively associated with Shame Acknowledgment and positively associated with Shame Displacement and bullying.

Measure of Impulsivity

This measure used selected items from two scales (for details see Table 15.3). Items taken from the first scale, the Junior Impulsiveness Scale, were: (1) I often get involved in things I later wish I could get out of, (2) I often get into trouble because I do things without thinking, and, (3) I often do and say things without stopping to think. Two items were taken from Buss and Plomin's EASI–III Temperament Survey: (1) I tend to hop from interest to interest quickly and (2) I get bored easily. Higher scores reflected a greater deficiency in impulse control ($M = 2.73$; $SD = .61$; $\alpha = .65$).

Internal Locus of Control

Relatively stable beliefs about the causes of one's actions are broadly referred to as locus of control beliefs (Rotter, 1966). An internal locus of control is defined as the belief that outcomes are contingent upon one's actions; an external locus of control refers to the belief that outcomes are not related to one's personal efforts. Previous work has linked an internal locus of control with high guilt (Graham, 1988; Graham, Doubleday, & Guarino, 1984) and low shame-proneness (Tangney, 1990). Furthermore, the greater one's internal locus of control, the less the likelihood of being involved in bullying others (Dodge & Frame, 1982; Pulkkinen, 1996; Slee, 1993).

On the basis of past findings, internal locus of control is expected to be positively linked with Shame Acknowledgment and negatively with Shame Displacement and bullying.

Measure of Internal Locus of Control

Selected items from the Multidimensional Measure of Children's Perceptions of Control (for details see Table 15.3) were used to examine children's locus of control in the 'Life at School Survey'. Three domains were used: cognitive, social and physical. Unfortunately, the internal consistencies of these scales were too low to be used in subsequent analysis. In view of the importance of the construct in past work, two items capturing belief in control over academic achievement were selected to at least partially represent the construct: (1) If I want to do well in school, it's up to me to do it; and (2) If I don't do well in school, it's my own fault. These two items were positively correlated ($r = .20$, $p<.001$) and showed a similar pattern of relationships to the outcome variables.[8] Scores were therefore averaged so that a higher score on this scale represented a greater sense of internal control in relation to school achievement ($M = 3.47$; $SD = .58$).

Shame Management Variables

Finally, the integrated shame management model of bullying in Figure 15.2 includes the Shame Acknowledgment and Shame Displacement scales as measures of adaptive and maladaptive shame management.

Shame Acknowledgment and Shame Displacement were measured using the Management Of Shame State–Shame Acknowledgment and Shame Displacement (MOSS–SASD) instrument. A detailed description of the MOSS–SASD scales and their psychometric properties have been provided in Chapter 14.

Outcome Measures

Three dependent variables were measured in this study: general bullying, self-initiated bullying, and victimization[9] (for details see Table 15.4). Following Olweus (1987), the method adopted to measure bullying and victimization was self-reports in which respondents remained anonymous. Among bullying researchers, the self-report procedure is accepted as an efficient measure of children's bullying involvement (Rigby, 1996). Self-reports produce sufficiently reliable and valid data for identifying young bullies and victims (Kochenderfer & Ladd, 1996a, 1996b; Olweus, 1990; Perry et al., 1988; Rigby, 1996). Ahmad and Smith (1990) compared anonymous questionnaires with individual interviews and found 90 per cent agreement for bullying and 95 per cent for victimization. There was also considerable agreement between self-reports and peer ratings on bullying ($r = .68$) and victimization ($r = .62$) (Ahmad & Smith, 1990). High agreement has also been observed in the percentages of bullies and victims

Table 15.3 Summary of the Measures for Personality Variables[10]

Measures	Source and description	Response format
Guilt-proneness	Test Of Self-Conscious Affect for Children (TOSCA–C; Tangney et al., 1989)	5-point ('very unlikely' to 'very likely')
Shame-proneness	Test Of Self-Conscious Affect for Children (TOSCA–C; Tangney et al., 1989)	5-point ('very unlikely' to 'very likely')
Pride-proneness	Test Of Self-Conscious Affect for Children (TOSCA–C; Tangney et al., 1989)	5-point ('very unlikely' to 'very likely')
Self-esteem	Rosenberg Self-esteem Scale (Rosenberg & Simmons; 1971)	4-point ('disagree a lot' to 'agree a lot')
Empathy	Selected items from the Attitudes towards Victims (Rigby & Slee, 1991a)	4-point ('disagree a lot' to 'agree a lot')
Impulsivity	Selected items from (a) Junior Impulsiveness Scale (Eysenck & Eysenck, 1977); and (b) EASI–III instrument (Emotionality, activity, sociability and impulsivity; Buss & Plomin, 1975)	4-point ('disagree a lot' to 'agree a lot')
Locus of control	Selected items from the Multidimensional Measure of Children's Perceptions of Control (MMCPC; Connell, 1985)	4-point ('disagree a lot' to 'agree a lot')

identified through self-reports from children compared to teacher reports (Olweus, 1987).

General bullying was measured by two questions: (a) 'How often have you been a part of a group that bullied someone during the last year?' and (b) 'How often have you, on your own, bullied someone during the last year?' To construct the bullying measure, responses of these two items were averaged ($r = .52$, $p<.001$) with a high score indicating high frequency of bullying ($M = 1.59$; $SD = .69$; $\alpha = .68$).

Previous work has drawn a distinction between children who bully others in a one-to-one situation and children who bully in groups in terms of their underlying motivations (Rigby, 1996). To assess self-initiated bullying where the perpetrator is a single individual, one item from the general bullying measure was used: 'How often have you, on your own, bullied someone during the last year?' ($M = 1.43$; $SD = .72$). The majority of the students (66.3%) reported not being involved in bullying in a one-to-one situation.

In order to provide a validity check on these two bullying measures, child self-reports were correlated with parent self-reports ('How often has your child been accused of being a bully?'). The correlation coefficients between child and parent self-reports of bullying were positive and significant ($r = .21$, $p<.001$ for general bullying and $r = .22$, $p<.001$ for self-initiated bullying). Considering that children often do not report bullying incidents to their parents (Rigby, 1996), these findings produce encouraging support for the validity of the child self-report measure used in this research.

Victimization represents children's experiences of being bullied either by a single individual or by a group. This was measured by asking students to indicate how often they had been the victims of bullying during the last year. Responses were made on a six-point scale ranging from 'most days' (1) to 'never' (6). This index was reverse scored such that a high score indicated high frequency of experiencing victimization ($M = 2.37$; $SD = 1.46$). To check the validity of the index, parents were asked: 'How often has your child been bullied by another student or group of students in the last year?' The response options matched those used in the child-report. The inter-correlation coefficient between child self-report and parent reports on children's victimization was .40 ($p<.001$), a strong degree of concordance between child-reports and parent-reports. It is interesting to note that positive correlations were found between child-reports of victimization and child-reports of self-initiated bullying ($r = .12$, $p<.001$) and general bullying ($r = .10$, $p<.001$). This is consistent with prior research (Besag, 1989; Olweus, 1978) and illustrates the way in which children take a bully/victim role by bullying others sometimes and being victimized at other times. This issue of the bully/victim role in relation to the shame management variables will be dealt with in Chapter 17.

Hypotheses

The following working hypotheses guided the investigation:

Family 1: *Family factors would be related to shame management skills in children.*
(a) Stigmatizing shaming attributions and family disharmony would be negatively related to Shame Acknowledgment and positively related to Shame Displacement;

Table 15.4 Summary of the Measures for Outcome Variables

Measure	Source and description	Response format
General bullying	Selected questions from Peer Relations Questionnaire (PRQ; Rigby & Slee, 1993a)	5-point ('never' to 'several times a week')
Self-initiated bullying	Selected questions from Peer Relations Questionnaire (PRQ; Rigby & Slee, 1993a)	5-point ('never' to 'several times a week')
Victimization	Peer Relations Questionnaire (PRQ; Rigby & Slee, 1993a)	6-point ('most days' to 'never')

(b) Non-stigmatizing shaming attributions and positive parent–child affect would be positively related to Shame Acknowledgment and negatively related to Shame Displacement.

Family 2: *Family factors would be related to bullying in children.*
(a) Stigmatizing shaming attributions and family disharmony would be positively related to bullying;
(b) Non-stigmatizing shaming attributions and positive parent–child affect would be negatively related to bullying.

School 1: *School factors would be related to shame management variables.*
(a) Liking for school and perceived control of bullying would be positively related to Shame Acknowledgment and negatively related to Shame Displacement;
(b) School hassles would be negatively related to Shame Acknowledgment and positively related to Shame Displacement.

School 2: *School factors would be related to bullying.*
(a) Liking for school and perceived control of bullying would be negatively related to bullying.
(b) School hassles would be positively related to bullying.

Personality 1: *Personality variables would be related to shame management variables.*
(a) Impulsivity would be negatively related to Shame Acknowledgment and positively related to Shame Displacement;
(b) Pride-proneness and internal locus of control would be positively related to Shame Acknowledgment and negatively related to Shame Displacement.

In Chapter 14, other personality variables were correlated with the shame management variables. Shame-proneness was positively related to both Shame Acknowledgment and Shame Displacement, suggesting that

shame-prone individuals both internalize and externalize their shame. Consistent with Tangney's theorizing, guilt-proneness was associated with the adaptive shame management pattern of high Shame Acknowledgment and low Shame Displacement. This pattern was also evident for those high on empathy.

Personality 2: *Personality variables would be related to bullying.*
(a) Shame-proneness and impulsivity would be positively related to bullying;
(b) Guilt-proneness, pride-proneness, empathy and internal locus of control would be negatively related to bullying.

Because recent theorization and empirical findings on the nature of the bullying–self-esteem relationship are unclear, no predictions were made regarding the relationships of self-esteem to shame management and bullying.

Shame Management 1: *Shame management variables would be related to bullying.*
(a) Shame Acknowledgment would be negatively related to bullying;
(b) Shame Displacement would be positively related to bullying.

Shame Management 2: *Shame management variables would mediate, partially if not fully, the relationships between other sets of predictor variables (e.g., family, school and personality variables) and bullying.* This hypothesis is based on the assumption that shame management variables can integrate the disparate empirical findings in bullying research.

Shame Management 3: *Bullying status (non-bully/non-victim, bully, victim and bully/victim) in children would be related to their shame management strategies.* This hypothesis is examined in Chapter 17.

Notes

1 The ASI was labeled as ESNS.
2 This item across eight scenarios was reverse scored so that a high score represented stability rather than changeability.
3 Combining measures usually require a stronger correlation between the components than occurs with these measures. A further series of analyses demonstrated that stability and intentionality behaved in the same way in predicting other variables. Because of their theoretical coherence, stability and intentionality were therefore combined into a stigmatizing shaming attributions index for the purposes of the analyses in Part III.
4 This item across eight scenarios was reverse scored so that a high score represented responsibility for the behavior rather than release from responsibility.
5 Aggregating measures usually require a stronger correlation between the

components than occurs with these measures. A further series of analyses demonstrated that responsibility and controllability behaved in the same way in predicting other variables. Because of their theoretical coherence, responsibility and controllability were therefore aggregated into a non-stigmatizing shaming attributions index for the purposes of the analyses in Part III.

6 This scale was a modified version of the CRPR based on the work by Kochanska, Kuczynski, & Radke-Yarrow (1989) and Huntley (1995).

7 For example, in a pilot study, it became apparent that the children understood 'I'm a dobber' and not 'I'm a tattle-tale". In addition, pictures accompanying each scenario were redrawn to make the characters gender-neutral.

8 Both items were positively correlated with shame acknowledgment and negatively correlated with shame displacement, general bullying and self-initiated bullying.

9 The victimization index is used in Chapter 17 to categorize children into different bullying status groups.

10 For self-esteem, empathy and impulsivity measures, minor modifications were made to frame original questions as statements in the questionnaire.

CHAPTER 16

Explaining Bullying

This chapter tests the hypotheses derived in the previous chapter using data collected from 978[1] children and their primary caregiver in the 'Life at School Survey". In the first section, each of the predictors representing family, school and personality is correlated with the shame management variables of Shame Acknowledgment and Shame Displacement. The second section presents the correlations of the family, school, personality and shame management variables with the outcome of bullying behavior. The third section integrates the findings of the previous sections, testing the importance of one set of predictors against another. Finally, the question of how well shame management mediates the relationship between family, school and personality variables, and bullying is addressed. Intercorrelations among all variables (family variables, school variables, personality variables, shame management variables and bullying measures) are presented in Appendix 16A.

I Are Family, School and Personality Variables Associated with Shame Management Variables?

Correlation coefficients were calculated between the family, school and personality variables and the shame management scales of acknowledgment and displacement. All analyses in this chapter control for child's sex and age. On the basis of past research, both variables are known to account for variation in bullying behavior. Furthermore, preliminary analyses confirmed that child's sex and age were related to a number of the independent and dependent variables in the 'Life at School Survey'. The coefficients presented in Table 16.1 are therefore partial correlation coefficients where sex and age have been controlled. The gender effects in this

study are consistent with the findings of previous research. Boys were more likely to engage in both kinds of bullying measured here with boys also being more likely than girls to say that they engaged in bullying to show others who is powerful. Girls were significantly more likely to acknowledge shame, boys significantly more likely to displace shame.

Five variables in Table 16.1 are associated with high Shame Acknowledgment and low Shame Displacement in the manner hypothesized. Positive parent–child affect, perceived control of bullying, guilt-proneness, empathy and internal locus of control were associated with what we have called adaptive shame management skills, that is high Shame Acknowledgment and low Shame Displacement. For two of the remaining variables, links were established with one shame management variable but not the other. Pride-proneness was positively related to Shame Acknowledgment, while liking for school was negatively related with Shame Displacement. Stigmatizing and non-stigmatizing shaming attributions were related to neither Shame Acknowledgment nor Shame Displacement in these analyses.

The variables hypothesized as being associated with low scores on Shame Acknowledgment and high scores on Shame Displacement behaved in a more complex manner than anticipated. Most notably, stigmatizing shaming attributions were not related to the shame management variables. Family disharmony and impulsivity were associated with higher Shame Displacement but were not significantly correlated with Shame Acknowledgment. School hassles and shame-proneness were positively linked with both Shame Acknowledgment and Shame Displacement, such that increases in hassles and shame-proneness were accompanied by greater acknowledgment and greater displacement.

No hypothesis had been put forward in relation to self-esteem, but this variable emerged as having a negative relationship with both Shame Acknowledgment and Shame Displacement. Those with high self-esteem not only had lower scores on Shame Displacement, but also had lower scores on Shame Acknowledgment.

These findings show that the shame management variables of acknowledgment and displacement relate to the more well-known correlates of bullying in very different ways. The guiding hypotheses proposed a set of relations that are clearly far too simplified to adequately capture the complexity of the interrelationships. These results confirm the important role that both Shame Acknowledgment and Shame Displacement have to play in the integrative shame management model of bullying, but further work is required to understand the nature of these connections. The findings presented in this section confirm the conclusions reached in Chapter 14. The principal components analysis indicated that children's willingness to

Table 16.1 Partial Correlation Coefficients of the Family, School and Personality Variables with Shame Management Controlling for Child's Sex and Age

Variables	Shame Acknowledgment (minimum n = 889)	Shame Displacement (minimum n = 871)
Family		
Stigmatizing shaming attributions	.00 (ns)	–.04 (ns)
Non-stigmatizing attributions	–.01 (ns)	–.03 (ns)
Positive parent–child affect	.09**	–.08*
Family disharmony	.02 (ns)	.15***
School		
School hassles	.15***	.14***
Liking for school	.04 (ns)	–.09**
Perceived control of bullying	.12***	–.18***
Personality		
Guilt-proneness	.47***	–.11***
Shame-proneness	.37***	.15***
Pride-proneness	.23***	–.03 (ns)
Self-esteem	–.12***	–.14***
Empathy	.26***	–.06*
Impulsivity	–.04 (ns)	.19***
Internal locus of control	.06*	–.09**

*p<.05   **p<.01   ***p<.001

acknowledge shame could exist, side by side, with a desire to displace shame. In other words, one shame state (Shame Acknowledgment) did not preclude the possibility of the other (Shame Displacement) occurring as well. The findings of this section show that different combinations of Shame Acknowledgment and Shame Displacement characterize different kinds of children. Children with low self-esteem, who are shame-prone and troubled at school both acknowledge their shame and displace it. Children who are impulsive, who experience family disharmony and dislike school are more likely to displace their feelings of shame. Children who are prone to experience pride are more likely to acknowledge shame. And what has been called an adaptive shame response, that is low displacement along with high acknowledgment, is more prevalent among children who have positive parent–child affect, who have high empathy, who have an internal locus of control, who are guilt-prone, and who perceive bullying as behavior that is well controlled at their school.

II Are Family, School and Personality Variables Associated with Bullying?

Table 16.2 presents partial correlation coefficients, controlling for child's age and sex, between the family, school, personality and shame management variables and both general and self-initiated bullying. As expected, general bullying was related to children's reports of family disharmony, not liking school, having hassles at school and not seeing control over bullying at school. Children who bullied others were more likely to be impulsive, to lack an internal locus of control, and to lack empathy. All these findings are consistent with previous research. What is new, and consistent with ur predictions, is the relationship of shame acknowledgment and shame displacement with bullying. Children who bullied others were less likely to acknowledge shame and more likely to displace shame. At this level of the analysis, however, there is no relationship between either stigmatizing or non-stigmatizing shaming attributions and bullying.

Table 16.2 Partial Correlation Coefficients of the Family, School, Personality and Shame Management Variables with Two Kinds of Bullying Measures Controlling for Child's Sex and Age

Correlates	General bullying (minimum n = 925)	Self-initiated bullying (minimum n = 925)
Family		
Stigmatizing shaming attributions	.05 (ns)	.05 (ns)
Non-stigmatizing shaming attributions	−.01 (ns)	−.04 (ns)
Positive parent-child affect	−.06 (ns)	−.06 (ns)
Family disharmony	.20***	.18***
School		
School hassles	.19***	.17***
Liking for school	−.13***	−.14***
Perceived control of bullying	−.29***	−.25***
Personality		
Guilt-proneness	−.14***	−.13***
Shame-proneness	.03 (ns)	.04 (ns)
Pride-proneness	−.09**	−.09**
Self-esteem	−.13***	−.14***
Empathy	−.10**	−.08**
Impulsivity	.25***	.22***
Internal locus of control	−.07*	−.07*
Shame management		
Shame acknowledgment	−.14***	−.14***
Shame displacement	.23***	.24***

*p<.05   **p<.01   ***p<.001

Tangney's measures of guilt-proneness and pride-proneness also correlated with bullying in theoretically meaningful ways. Guilt-proneness, a concept that has been aligned with Shame Acknowledgment in Chapter 14, is negatively correlated with bullying. Children who bullied peers were less likely to experience guilt when they did something wrong, and were also less likely to experience pride when they did something right.

The absence of a significant relationship between bullying and shame-proneness is of interest and is likely to be explained by the previously reported association of shame-proneness with high acknowledgment (a protector against bullying) and high displacement (a trigger towards bullying). Consistent with this argument, other analyses have revealed a positive relationship between shame-proneness and bullying when guilt-proneness (a proxy for Shame Acknowledgment) is controlled. Shame-proneness, it will be recalled, was similar to self-esteem in its relationships with the shame management variables. In the 'Life at School Survey', self-esteem was negatively correlated with bullying.

So far the discussion has focused on the first column of Table 16.2. The second column shows the relationship between the predictors and self-initiated bullying, where bullies initiate bullying acting on their own. Interestingly, the bivariate correlations change very little with a change in the dependent variable. This is not to say, however, that the explanatory model that works best in the general bullying context will be the model that works best in the more serious bullying context.

III Do Shame Management Variables Mediate the Relationships of Family, School and Personality Predictors with Bullying?

The correlations reported in this chapter reveal a complex pattern of relationships among the newly developed shame management variables and the traditional predictors of bullying. While these correlations suggest that it is reasonable to expect the shame management variables to play some kind of mediating role, it is also reasonable to ask whether the shame management variables add anything to the prediction of bullying above and beyond the predictors that have proven themselves to be useful over many years of research?

In order to answer this question, two hierarchical regression analyses[2] were performed in which age, sex, and all the family, school and personality variables were entered in Step 1, and the shame management variables were entered in Step 2. The results of the analyses are reported in Table 16.3 for general bullying and in Table 16.4 for self-initiated bullying. For both samples, shame management had a contribution to make above and beyond that of other traditional predictors.

While for general bullying, none of the shaming variables are significant, for self-initiated bullying, both shaming variables have significant effects in the predicted directions. Stigmatized shaming increases self-initiated bullying and non-stigmatized shaming reduces it (see Table 16.4). Caution is warranted, however. It may be that parents whose children have been involved in bullying on their own initiative resort to greater use of stigmatizing shaming attributions and less use of non-stigmatizing shaming attributions because of the severity of the problem. The behavior of the child may be leading the attribution process, rather than the attribution process leading the behavior of the child as we have theoretically postulated.

Table 16.3 Beta Coefficients and Adjusted R^2 for the Effects of All Variables in Predicting General Bullying in a Hierarchical Regression Analysis (n = 768)

Variables	Model 1	Model 2
Control variables		
Child's sex	−.12***	−.10***
Child's age	.12***	.12***
Family variables		
Stigmatizing shaming	.05 (ns)	.06 (ns)
Non-stigmatizing shaming	−.04 (ns)	−.04 (ns)
Positive parent-child affect	.02 (ns)	.02 (ns)
Family disharmony	.10**	.09**
School variables		
School hassles	.06 (ns)	.06 (ns)
Liking for school	.05 (ns)	.04 (ns)
Perceived control of bullying	−.22***	−.20***
Personality variable		
Guilt-proneness	−.13**	−.07 (ns)
Shame-proneness	.01 (ns)	.00 (ns)
Pride-proneness	−.01 (ns)	−.01 (ns)
Self-esteem	.01 (ns)	.01 (ns)
Empathy	−.07*	−.05 (ns)
Impulsivity	.18***	.16***
Internal locus of control	−.03 (ns)	−.02 (ns)
Shame management variables		
Shame acknowledgment	na	−.08*
Shame displacement	na	.14***
Multiple R	.46	.48
Adjusted R^2	.20***	.21***
R^2 change		.01

*p<.05   **p<.01   ***p<.001

Table 16.4 Beta Coefficients and Adjusted R^2 for the Effects of All Variables in Predicting Self-initiated Bullying in a Hierarchical Regression Analysis (n = 768)

Variables	Model 1	Model 2
Control variables		
Child's sex	–.17**	–.15**
Child's age	.10**	.11**
Family variables		
Stigmatizing shaming	.07*	.08*
Non-stigmatizing shaming	–.09**	–.09**
Positive parent-child affect	–.01 (ns)	.00 (ns)
Family disharmony	.09*	.07
School variables		
School hassles	.05 (ns)	.06 (ns)
Liking for school	.00 (ns)	.01
Perceived control of bullying	–.19***	–.16***
Personality variables		
Guilt-proneness	–.11*	–.05 (ns)
Shame-proneness	.04	.03
Pride-proneness	.01	.01
Self-esteem	.02	.00
Empathy	–.05	–.04
Impulsivity	.15***	.12**
Internal locus of control	–.03	–.03 (ns)
Shame management variables		
Shame acknowledgment	na	–.11**
Shame displacement	na	.15***
Multiple R	.45	.47
Adjusted R^2	.18***	.21***
R^2 change		.03

*p<.05   **p<.01   ***p<.001

The next task was to explore the way the shame management variables mediated the relationship between family, school and personality variables on the one hand, and bullying on the other. This task was exploratory, in view of the fact that some of our earlier hypotheses explaining how this mediation should take place were rejected. Nevertheless, other proposed relationships were supported, and with this in mind, it is worthwhile trying to make sense of these data in the hope that they deliver a further set of hypotheses that can be tested more exhaustively on a future occasion.

Initially, we had to choose a set of variables that would lend themselves to the relatively parsimonious modeling exercise we had in mind for this stage of the research. Variables were included if they satisfied the following criteria: (1) had theoretical salience in the context of bullying research; (2) appeared as significant correlates and/or predictors in the earlier analyses; and (3) did not overlap either theoretically or empirically with other measures. On this basis, 10 variables were selected for modeling general bullying. In addition to Shame Acknowledgment and Shame Displacement, the chosen variables were: (a) family disharmony from the family variables, (b) school hassles, liking for school and perceived control of bullying from the school variables, and (c) self-esteem, impulsivity, empathy and internal locus of control from the personality variables. For self-initiated bullying, 12 variables were also chosen for the modeling exercise. Apart from Shame Acknowledgment and Shame Displacement, they included (a) family disharmony, stigmatizing shaming attributions, and non-stigmatizing shaming attributions from the family variables; (b) school hassles, liking for school and perceived control of bullying from the school variables; and (c) self-esteem, impulsivity, empathy and internal locus of control from the personality variables.

The notable omissions from the above lists of variables were Tangney's scales of shame-, guilt- and pride-proneness. In the 'Life at School Survey', these variables appeared as significant correlates of shame management variables. At this stage, however, they are being conceptualized as covariates rather than as part of a mediating chain that leads to school bullying. This is not to suggest that they will not be considered as part of such a chain in the future after their relationship with the shame management variables is explored a little more fully. Shame-, guilt- and pride-proneness ultimately may provide a more useful personality base for this work than self-esteem, impulsivity, empathy and internal locus of control.

Testing the Mediational Model of Shame Management Variables on Bullying

Below we test a mediational model of school bullying. The regression analyses in the previous section provide support for a partial mediational model in which the shame management variables mediate the relationships between family, school and personality variables, and bullying. Earlier, we hypothesized (**Shame Management 2**) that shame management variables (Shame Acknowledgment and Shame Displacement) would mediate, partially if not fully, the relationships between explanatory variables (e.g., family, school and personality variables) and bullying. In order to evaluate the hypothesis, a path analysis was carried out using maximum likelihood

estimation (Arbuckle & Wothke, 1999; AMOS: Analysis of Moment Structures, Version 4).

Three models were effectively estimated: (1) a saturated model that included all direct and indirect paths to bullying (df = 0); (2) the mediational model that included only paths from explanatory variables to bullying through the shame management variables; and (3) the non-mediational model that included all paths from explanatory variables and shame management variables to bullying. The mediational model (Model 2) and the non-mediational model (Model 3) are nested in the saturated model (each set of path coefficients is a subset of the paths in the saturated model).

The difference between the saturated model (Model 1) and the mediational model (Model 2) was tested using the likelihood ratio test (the difference in the $-2 \times \log$ likelihood of the two nested models) which follows a chi-square distribution with degrees of freedom equal to the difference in the number of coefficients between the two models (Byrne, 1994; Hoyle & Panter, 1995). Since the difference between these two models consists of all non-mediational paths from explanatory variables to bullying, this test is equivalent to testing if any non-mediational paths are required in addition to the mediational paths. Similarly, a likelihood ratio test between the saturated model (Model 1) and the non-mediational model (Model 3) was carried out. Since the difference between these two models consists of all mediating paths (i.e., paths from explanatory variables to bullying through shame management variables), this test is equivalent to testing if the mediational paths are required in addition to the non-mediational paths.

Mediational Model with General Bullying[3]

When the saturated model was compared with the mediational model, the chi-square difference was significant ($\chi^2_8 = 134.12$, $p<.001$; N = 1166), indicating that the mediational model was not sufficient (i.e., at least some non-mediational paths from explanatory variables to bullying are required) to describe the correlational structure of the data. Again, when the saturated model was compared with the non-mediational model, the chi-square difference was also significant ($\chi^2_{16} = 315.99$, $p<.001$; N = 1166), indicating that at least some mediational paths from explanatory variables to shame management variables are required to adequately represent the data.

Therefore, as found earlier, a partial mediational model is supported in the prediction of general bullying. In order to estimate a parsimonious model, we started from the saturated model (Model 1). We started to eliminate direct paths from the explanatory variables to bullying. As a first step, paths which appeared non-significant in our earlier analyses were eliminated. These included school hassles, liking for school, self-esteem and

internal locus of control. As a second step, a diagnostic examination was performed to ensure that the remaining direct paths from the explanatory variables to bullying were statistically significant ($p<.05$), and no other paths were required to represent the data well.

A similar procedure was used to eliminate the non-significant mediational paths from the explanatory variables to the shame management variables. At first, the variables which remained significant after the shame management variables were added in the regression analysis were considered. These were family disharmony, perceived control of bullying and impulsivity. Paths from these explanatory variables to the shame management variables were eliminated in a test run. Diagnostic examination showed that paths from perceived control of bullying and impulsivity to both shame management variables were required, and therefore they were put back into the model. Further diagnostics showed non-significant paths from school hassles and liking for school to Shame Displacement, and therefore they were eliminated. The remaining mediational paths from explanatory variables to shame management variables were statistically significant ($p<.05$).

Following this procedure, a final model for general bullying was obtained. The goodness-of-fit indices[4] of this final model are presented in Table 16.5 (see last column). Figure 16.1 shows the diagrammatic representation of the final model with standardized beta coefficients. Covariances between the explanatory variables are not included in the diagram, though all covariances between the explanatory variables are included in the analysis. In other words, the explanatory variables were not treated as independent. The covariance matrix for all explanatory variables can be seen in Appendix 16B.

Figure 16.1 shows that Shame Acknowledgment and Shame Displacement have paths predicting general bullying, as expected. Shame Acknowledgment decreased bullying whereas Shame Displacement increased bullying.

Non-mediational effects were found for family disharmony, perceived control of bullying, impulsivity and empathy. Family disharmony and impulsivity increased bullying whereas perceived control of bullying and empathy decreased bullying.

In addition to having direct effects on bullying, four of these explanatory variables had further effects on bullying mediated through the shame management variables. Both perceived control of bullying and empathy increased Shame Acknowledgment and decreased Shame Displacement. In contrast, impulsivity decreased Shame Acknowledgment and increased Shame Displacement.

Four variables – school hassles, liking for school, self-esteem and internal locus of control – had no direct paths to bullying, having indirect paths to

Table 16.5 Chi-square Statistics and the Goodness of Fit Indices of the Mediational Model, the Non-mediational model and the Final Model for General Bullying

Goodness-of-Fit statistics	Mediational model	Non-mediational model	Final model
χ^2	134.12, p<.001	315.99, p<.001	12.82, p<.12
df	8	16	8
GFI = Goodness of Fit Index	.981	.956	.998
CFI = Comparative Fit Index	.930	.834	.997
RMSEA = Root Mean Square Error of Approximation	.12	.13	.02

bullying through either or both shame management variables. School hassles and liking for school acted only through Shame Acknowledgment. More hassles and liking for school were associated with greater Shame Acknowledgment. Internal locus of control increased Shame Acknowledgment and decreased Shame Displacement. Self-esteem decreased both Shame Acknowledgment and Shame Displacement.

Mediational Model with Self-initiated Bullying[5]

When the saturated model was compared with the mediational model for self-initiated bullying, the chi-square difference was significant ($\chi^2_{10} = 85.11$, p<.001; N = 785), indicating that the mediational model was not sufficient (i.e., at least some non-mediational paths from explanatory variables to self-initiated bullying are required) to describe the correlational structure of the data. Again, when the saturated model was compared with the non-mediational model, the chi-square difference was also significant ($\chi^2_{20} = 222.04$, p<.001; N = 785), indicating that at least some mediational paths from explanatory variables to shame management variables are required to adequately represent the data.

Therefore, as with general bullying, a partial mediational model is supported to explain self-initiated bullying. In order to estimate a parsimonious model, we started from the saturated model (Model 1). We started to eliminate direct paths from explanatory variables to self-initiated bullying. As a first step, paths which appeared non-significant in our earlier analyses were eliminated. These included school hassles, liking for school, self-esteem, empathy and internal locus of control. In the second step, diagnostic tests revealed that the remaining direct paths from explanatory to self-initiated bullying were statistically significant (p<.05), and no other direct paths were required to represent the data well.

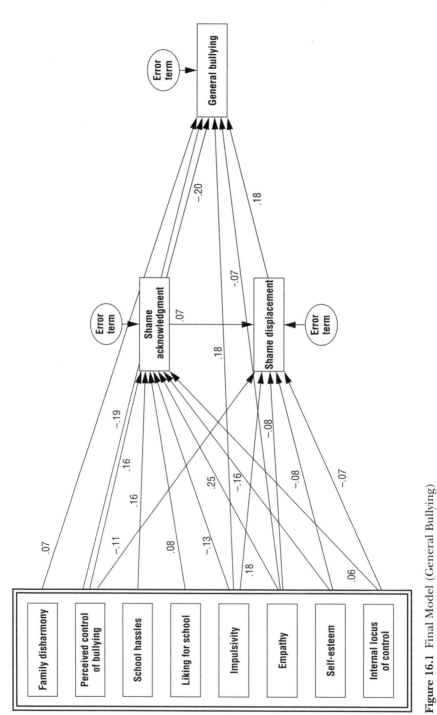

Figure 16.1 Final Model (General Bullying)

Note: The notation of the double-edged box indicates that all the covariances between explanatory variables were included in the analyses.

A similar procedure was used to eliminate the non-significant mediational paths from the explanatory variables to the shame management variables. At first, variables that remained significant even when shame management variables were added in the regression analysis were considered. These were stigmatizing shaming attributions, non-stigmatizing attributions, perceived control of bullying and impulsivity. Paths from these explanatory variables to shame management variables were eliminated to see if they were unnecessary. Diagnostic examination showed that paths from perceived control of bullying and impulsivity to both shame management variables were necessary, and therefore they were included. Other mediational paths that were shown to be non-significant were eliminated.

Following this procedure, a final model for self-initiated bullying was obtained. The goodness-of-fit indices[6] of this final model are presented in Table 16.6 (see last column). Figure 16.2 shows the diagrammatic representation of the final model with standardized beta coefficients. As with Figure 16.2, the covariances between the explanatory variables are not shown in the diagram, even though all covariances between the explanatory variables are included in the model. The covariance matrix for all explanatory variables can be seen in Appendix 16C.

Figure 16.2 shows that Shame Acknowledgment and Shame Displacement again predict self-initiated bullying, as expected. Shame Acknowledgment decreased bullying whereas Shame Displacement increased it. Non-mediational effects were found for family disharmony, stigmatizing shaming attributions, non-stigmatizing shaming attributions, perceived control of bullying and impulsivity. Family disharmony, stigmatizing shaming attributions and impulsivity increased bullying whereas non-stigmatizing shaming attributions and perceived control of bullying by the school decreased bullying.

In addition to these direct effects on bullying, some of these explanatory variables also had effects mediated through the shame management variables. Both family disharmony and impulsivity increased Shame Displacement, while perceived control of bullying decreased Shame Displacement. Perceived control of bullying increased Shame Acknowledgment, while impulsivity decreased Shame Acknowledgment.

Five variables – school hassles, liking for school, self-esteem, empathy and internal locus of control – had no direct paths to bullying, acting through either or both shame management variables. School hassles and liking for school were positively linked with Shame Acknowledgment while self-esteem was negatively correlated to Shame Acknowledgment. Empathy acted through both shame management variables, increasing Shame Acknowledgment and decreasing Shame Displacement. Finally, having an internal locus of control decreased Shame Displacement.

Table 16.6 Chi-square Statistics and the Goodness of Fit Indices of the Mediational Model, the Non-mediational Model and the Final Model for Self-initiated Bullying

Goodness-of-Fit statistics	Mediational model	Non-mediational model	Final model
χ^2	85.11, p<.001	222.04, p<.001	14.90, p<.38
df	10	20	14
GFI = Goodness of Fit Index	.984	.961	.997
CFI = Comparative Fit Index	.943	.847	.999
RMSEA = Root Mean Square Error of Approximation	.10	.11	.01

Summary of the Findings

Correlational findings presented in this chapter demonstrate that family, school, personality and shame management variables are useful in explaining bullying behavior, regardless of whether the population is serious bullies who are initiators or includes children who join others to bully their peers. Findings from the regression analyses demonstrated that the shame management variables had a notable contribution to make to explaining bullying, above and beyond the traditional predictors from the family, school and personality domains. Mediational model testing showed that shame management variables partially mediated the relationship between family, school and personality variables, and bullying. These findings alert us to the mix of protectors and triggers that surround children when they at risk of bullying encounters.

Table 16.7 provides a summary of findings alongside the hypotheses formulated at the end of Chapter 15. The following findings deserve detailed discussion, in turn: (1) the role of parental shaming attributions in explaining bullying; (2) the positive link between school hassles and Shame Acknowledgment; (3) the negative link between self-esteem and shame management variables; and (4) the positive link between Shame Acknowledgment and Shame Displacement.

Parental attributions of a stigmatizing and non-stigmatizing kind that were hypothesized to operate through the shame management variables instead had a direct effect on bullying, but only in the case of self-initiated bullying. These findings were partially supportive of reintegrative shaming theory, but questions remain as to the process by which the attributions affect behavior. The explanation that the labeling of a child as an intentional and stable bully increases bullying behavior requires more refined testing of the claimed direction of causality.

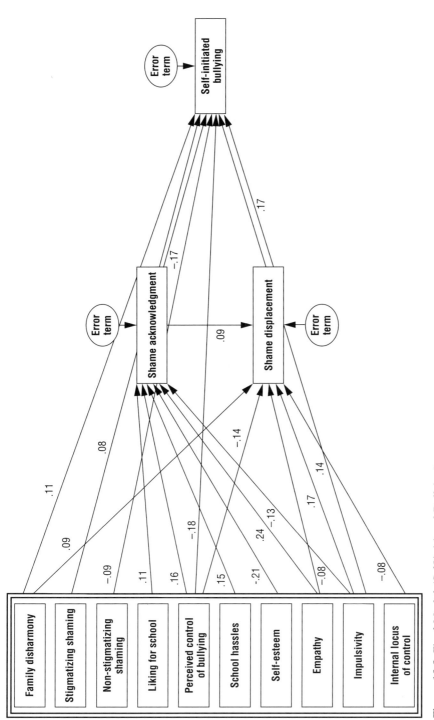

Figure 16.2 Final Model (Self-initiated Bullying)

Note: The notation of the double-edged box indicates that all the covariances between explanatory variables were included in the analyses.

Table 16.7 Summary of Outcomes for Hypotheses Tested

Hypotheses		Support for hypothesis
Family 1	(a) Stigmatizing shaming attributions and family disharmony would be negatively related to Shame Acknowledgment and positively related to Shame Displacement; (b) Non-stigmatizing shaming attributions and positive parent-child affect would be positively related to Shame Acknowledgment and negatively related to Shame Displacement.	*Partially supported.* Positive parent-child affect showed a positive association with Shame Acknowledgment and a negative association with Shame Displacement. Family disharmony showed a positive association with Shame Displacement.
Family 2	(a) Stigmatizing shaming attributions and family disharmony would be positively related to bullying; (b) Non-stigmatizing shaming attributions and positive parent-child affect would be negatively related to bullying.	*Partially supported.* Family disharmony showed a positive association with bullying.
School 1	(a) Liking for school and perceived control of bullying would be positively related to Shame Acknowledgment and negatively related to Shame Displacement; (b) School hassles would be negatively related to Shame Acknowledgment and positively related to Shame Displacement.	*Mostly supported.* Liking for school showed a negative association with Shame Displacement. Perceived control of bullying showed a positive association with Shame Acknowledgment and a negative association with Shame Displacement. School hassles showed a positive association with Shame Displacement. Unexpectedly, school hassles showed a positive association with Shame Acknowledgment.
School 2	(a) Liking for school and perceived control of bullying would be negatively related to bullying; (b) School hassles would be positively related to bullying.	*Supported.* Liking for school and perceived control of bullying showed a negative association with bullying. School hassles showed a positive association with bullying.

Table 16.7 Summary of Outcomes for Hypotheses Tested (*cont.*)

Personality 1	(a) Impulsivity would be negatively related to Shame Acknowledgment and positively related to Shame Displacement; (b) Pride-proneness and internal locus of control would be positively related to Shame Acknowledgment and negatively related to Shame Displacement.	*Partially supported.* Impulsivity showed a positive association with Shame Acknowledgment and a positive association with Shame Displacement. Pride-proneness and internal locus of control showed a positive association with Shame Acknowledgment. Internal locus of control showed a negative association with Shame Displacement.
Personality 2	(a) Shame-proneness and impulsivity would be positively related to bullying; (b) Guilt-proneness, pride-proneness, empathy and internal locus of control would be negatively related to bullying.	*Mostly supported.* Impulsivity showed a positive association with bullying. Guilt-proneness, pride-proneness, empathy and internal locus of control showed a negative association with bullying.
Shame management 1	(a) Shame Acknowledgment would be negatively related to bullying; (b) Shame Displacement would be positively related to bullying.	*Supported.* Shame Acknowledgment showed a negative association with bullying. Shame Displacement showed a positive association with bullying.
Shame management 2	Shame management variables would mediate, partially if not fully, the relationships between bullying and other sets of predictor variables.	*Supported.* Support was obtained for a partial mediational model.
Shame management 3	Bullying status (non-bully/non-victim, bully, victim and bully/victim) in children would be related to their shame management strategies.	To be tested in Chapter 17.

A surprising finding was the positive relationship between school hassles and Shame Acknowledgment. It comes as no surprise that children who are aware that they are having difficulties with their school work and peer relations would feel a sense of shame in terms of their poor performance, both academically and socially. The finding that they would be more likely to acknowledge that they have done wrong when caught in the act of bullying is more of a surprise and requires further investigation.

Related to this finding is that children with low self-esteem both acknowledge and displace shame more than other children. Recent work by Baumiester, Smart and Boden (1996) has suggested that self-esteem may not be as socially adaptive as has been assumed. Those with high self-esteem may have difficulty accepting failures that others point out and reject their critics as a consequence. While the findings reported here are not entirely consistent with Baumeister et al.'s (1996) formulation, they do reveal a dark side of high self-esteem. If high self-esteem precludes acknowledgment of wrongdoing, as our data suggest, high self-esteem has a socially destructive downside. On the other hand, there are social benefits when high self-esteem is a protective factor against Shame Displacement. The final chapter takes up the theme of how institutions can be designed to provide safe spaces for Shame Acknowledgment while minimizing Shame Displacement.

Notes

1 Total number of the participant children was 1401. To make our analyses comparable with child data and parent data, only students who have parent data available are included in this chapter.

2 Given that the measures of general bullying and self-initiated bullying were skewed, we adopted two strategies to verify the findings obtained from the hierarchical regression analyses. First, we reanalyzed the data with logarithmic and square-root transformations of the measures. Results were not substantially different from those obtained when the measure was not transformed. Second, we dichotomized the bullying measures and used logistic regression analyses. These analyses confirm that the findings reported using hierarchical regression analysis remained mostly the same although the strength of some associations changes slightly. It should be noted that in the case of self-initiated bullying, the measure was recoded from a five-point scale to a four-point scale, with the two extreme categories, 'about once a week' and 'several times a week', being collapsed into one category.

3 This analysis was performed with the full sample of 1166 students using listwise deletion of missing data.

4 (1) the chi-square statistic for which a significant value indicates that the model represented an inadequate fit; (2) Jöreskog and Sörbom's (1989) Goodness of Fit Index (GFI), for which values close to 1 indicate a very good fit (Arbuckle, 1997); (3) Bentler's (1990) Comparative Fit Index (CFI), for which values close to 1

suggest a very good fit (Arbuckle, 1997); and (4) Browne and Cudeck's (1993) Root Mean Square Error of Approximation (RMSEA), which is a direct measure of the discrepancy between the estimated correlation matrix and the matrix implied by the specified model (Arbuckle, 1997). This index explicitly takes the parsimony of the model into account (i.e., the number of parameters fixed vs. the number of parameters free to be estimated). Browne and Cudek (1993) suggested that a RMSEA of .05 or less indicates a close fit.

5 This analysis was performed with those children whose parent data were available to us (N = 785) using listwise deletion of missing data.

6 See note 4.

Appendix 16A

Intercorrelations (minimum n = 871) Among All Variables Included in the Integrated Model of Shame Management and Bullying (Family Variables, School Variables, Personality Variables, Shame Management Variables and Bullying Measures)

Variables	1	2	3	4	5	6	7	8	9	10	11	12	13	14	15	16	17	18
1. Stigmatizing shaming	-																	
2. Non-stigmatizing shaming	.40***	-																
3. Positive parent-child affect	-.02 (ns)	.10**	-															
4. Family disharmony	.06 (ns)	.06 (ns)	-.14***	-														
5. School hassles	.05 (ns)	.03 (ns)	-.07*	.49***	-													
6. Liking for school	-.02 (ns)	-.05 (ns)	.04 (ns)	-.23***	-.29***	-												
7. Perceived control of bullying	.03 (ns)	-.02 (ns)	.09**	-.20***	-.25***	.31***	-											
8. Guilt-proneness	-.06 (ns)	-.01 (ns)	.10**	.06*	.13***	.18***	.09**	-										
9. Shame-proneness	-.04 (ns)	.01 (ns)	.02 (ns)	.24***	.32***	-.15***	-.10***	.53***	-									
10. Pride-proneness	-.06 (ns)	-.04 (ns)	.07*	-.01 (ns)	-.03 (ns)	.17***	.06*	.41***	.11***	-								
11. Self-esteem	.03 (ns)	-.01 (ns)	.09**	-.31***	-.43***	.34***	.24***	-.07**	-.38***	.14***	-							
12. Empathy	-.03 (ns)	.06 (ns)	.08**	-.01 (ns)	.05*	.19***	-.03 (ns)	.40***	.17***	.28***	.02 (ns)	-						
13. Impulsivity	.02 (ns)	.03 (ns)	-.11***	.27***	.26***	-.18***	-.18***	-.03 (ns)	.14***	-.04 (ns)	-.33***	.01 (ns)	-					
14. Internal locus of control	-.04 (ns)	.05 (ns)	-.05 (ns)	-.03 (ns)	-.04 (ns)	.19***	.09***	.31***	.12***	.16***	.04 (ns)	.19***	.07**	-				
15. Shame acknowledgment	-.02 (ns)	-.01 (ns)	.11***	-.01 (ns)	.15***	.11***	.14***	.53***	.39***	.26***	-.10***	.30***	-.08**	.12***	-			
16. Shame displacement	-.03 (ns)	-.03 (ns)	-.08*	.15***	.16***	-.12***	-.15***	-.14***	.15***	-.04 (ns)	-.17***	-.08**	.22***	-.09**	.01 (ns)	-		
17. General bullying	.05 (ns)	.00	-.08*	.18***	.15***	-.19***	-.27***	-.24***	-.01 (ns)	-.15***	-.12***	-.15***	.28***	-.08**	-.23***	.26***	-	
18. Self-initiated bullying	.05 (ns)	-.03 (ns)	-.08*	.17***	.13***	-.19***	-.24***	-.22***	-.01 (ns)	-.12***	-.13***	-.12***	.22***	-.08**	-.22***	.25***	.84***	-

*p<.05   **p<.01   ***p<.001

Appendix 16B

Covariance Matrix (upper diagonal) and Correlation Matrix (lower diagonal) for the Explanatory Variables Used in Testing a Mediational Model for General Bullying

Variables	1	2	3	4	5	6	7	8
1. Family disharmony		-.04	.06	-.07	.07	.00	-.07	.00
2. Perceived control of bullying	-.18***		-.04	.14	-.05	.00	.07	.03
3. School hassles	.47***	-.24***		-.07	.04	.01	-.07	.00
4. Liking for school	-.22***	.31***	-.28***		-.09	.09	.15	.09
5. Impulsivity	.30***	-.17***	.26***	-.19***		.00	-.12	.01
6. Empathy	-.02 (ns)	-.02 (ns)	.05*	.19***	.00		.00	.06
7. Self-esteem	-.32***	.23***	-.44***	.33***	-.34***	.01 (ns)		.01
8. Internal locus of control	-.03 (ns)	.11***	-.05*	.20***	.04 (ns)	.18***	.05*	

*p<.05   ***p<.001

Appendix 16C

Covariance Matrix (upper diagonal) and Correlation Matrix (lower diagonal) for the Explanatory Variables Used in Testing a Mediational Model for Self-initiated Bullying

Variables	1	2	3	4	5	6	7	8	9	10
1. Family disharmony		.01	.01	-.08	-.04	.06	-.07	-.01	.07	.00
2. Stigmatizing shaming attributions	.04 (ns)		.16	-.01	.01	.01	.01	-.01	.00	-.01
3. Non-stigmatizing shaming attributions	.04 (ns)	.39***		-.02	-.01	.00	.00	.01	.00	.01
4. Liking for school	-.28***	-.03 (ns)	-.06 (ns)		.12	-.07	.15	.09	-.10	.07
5. Perceived control of bullying	-.19***	.03 (ns)	-.02 (ns)	.28***		-.04	.06	.00	-.07	.00
6. School hassles	.48***	.04 (ns)	.00	-.31***	-.27***		-.07	.00	.25	-.07
7. Self-esteem	-.31***	.04 (ns)	.00	.35***	.20***	-.44***		.00	-.12	.03
8. Empathy	-.04 (ns)	-.02 (ns)	.05 (ns)	.21***	-.02 (ns)	.04 (ns)	.02 (ns)		.00	.04
9. Impulsivity	.29***	.00 (ns)	.02 (ns)	-.21***	-.20***	.25***	-.35***	-.01 (ns)		.01
10. Internal locus of control	-.01 (ns)	-.04 (ns)	-.01 (ns)	.18***	.06 (ns)	-.07*	.03 (ns)	.14***	.03 (ns)	

*p<.05   ***p<.001

CHAPTER 17

Patterns of Shame: Bully, Victim, Bully/victim and Non-bully/Non-victim

Overview

In the previous chapter, we found that children's bullying behavior was related to their shame management skills. The data showed that children who do not acknowledge their shame, who displace their shame through externalizing blame and retaliatory anger are more likely to engage in bullying. The shame management variables had stronger effects on bullying than many of the traditional predictors of bullying, maintained strong effects net of the effects of the traditional predictors, and in addition mediated many of those effects of the traditional predictors.

The findings suggest there may be value in examining whether shame management skills are also important in understanding victimization by peers. A subsequent question is how do bully/victims manage their shame when they violate a social or moral standard of behavior? And what can their non-bully/non-victim peers tell us about the shame management strategies that may be of direct relevance to prevention and intervention efforts. This chapter partitions children into four bullying status groups – non-bully/non-victim, bully, victim and bully/victim. It then examines whether the shame management strategies of children explains whether they are bullies, victims, both or neither (**Shame Management 3**).

According to the findings presented in the previous chapter, it can be hypothesized that children in the bullying group will have lower scores on Shame Acknowledgment but higher scores on Shame Displacement. The hypothesis for the non-bully/non-victim group would be just the inverse. They would show higher scores on Shame Acknowledgment but lower scores on Shame Displacement. As for victims, it seems reasonable to expect that victims would show high scores on Shame Acknowledgment. Indeed, victims may be excessive in practices of Shame Acknowledgment

to the point of it being detrimental, particularly in internalizing others' rejection. Victims have been characterized as being prone to feeling ashamed (Olweus, 1992) and to engage in self-blame (DiLillo, Long & Russell, 1994; Graham & Juvonen, 1998; Janoff-Bulman, 1992). Following the clinical and developmental literature, individuals who feel shame following wrongdoing but have excessive self-rejecting thoughts are regarded as having poor skills in shame management. Finally, we hypothesize that the bully/victim group might show both the strategies adopted by bullies on one hand, and victims on the other.

Grouping Children According to their Involvement in Bullying

Self-reports of bullying and victimization were used to group children into four categories: (a) those who neither bullied nor were victimized (non-bully/non-victim); (b) those who were victims of bullies but did not bully others (victim); (c) those who bullied others, but were not victimized themselves (bully); and (d) those who both bullied and were victimized (bully/victim).

For the purposes of grouping, the frequency for bullying (group bullying and/or self-initiated bullying) was set at 'once or twice' or 'more often' in response to the bullying question(s) (described in Chapter 15). This follows the operational definition of Stephenson and Smith (1991) who argue that even a single incident of bullying is important to consider. Further to this, the act of bullying had to be unprovoked. In other words, the bullying classification did not apply to actions initiated in order to get even. If the intention behind the bullying act was to cause distress, and not to get even or to defend oneself, it was considered bullying.

Classifying children on whether or not they were victimized relied on responses to the question how often have you been bullied by another student or group of students? Children were classified as victims if they said it had happened 'every now and then' or 'more often'. As with bullying, the reason for being bullied had to be unprovoked. The victimization classification did not apply to those incidents which were provoked.

Following this strategy, four groups of children were identified as follows:

(1) the non-bully/non-victim group who neither bullied others nor were victims of bullying;
(2) the victim group who had been victimized without provocation and who had never bullied anyone;
(3) the bully group who had never been victimized; this means the bullying act, either general or self-initiated bullying, was performed without provocation; and

(4) the bully/victim group who both bullied others without provocation and were bullied themselves without provocation.

The children who did not fit the above categories comprised the 'left-over' group, primarily because their acts of bullying/victimization were provoked. It is important to remember that considerable attention was given to defining 'bullying' for the children who completed the survey. Children were told that bullying involves three criteria: (a) a repetitive aggressive act (e.g., teasing, threatening, name-calling, hitting/kicking) causing distress in the victim; (b) the dominance of the powerful over the powerless; and (c) an act carried out without provocation. However, a substantial number of children identified themselves as bully/victim even though provocation was a likely explanation for their behavior. These children comprise the less well-defined bully/victim category, described in Table 17.1 as 'provoked bully/victim'. It is most likely that these children's involvement in bullying/victimization took place in the course of routine daily activities, particularly when playground conflicts escalated.

By adopting the above criteria, it was possible to categorize 98.29 per cent of the children (n = 1377) into one of the five categories, with no child belonging to more than one group. The other one per cent of children could not be classified because of missing data on either the MOSS–SASD scales or on the bullying/victimization questions. The number and percentages of children in each group are presented in Table 17.1: 15 per cent of the sample were categorized as non-bully/non-victim, 13 per cent as bully, 21 per cent as victim and 11 per cent as bully/victim.

While estimates of the prevalence rate of bullying vary from study to study, reflecting respondents' age, sex, ethnicity and locality as well as methodology (Boulton, 1993), the prevalence results reported in Table 17.1 fall within the bounds suggested by past research.

Yates and Smith (1989) reported figures close to those reported in Table 17.1, about 12 per cent and 22 per cent for bullying and victimization, respectively. Boulton and Underwood (1992) identified 21 per cent of children as being victimized and Smith (1991) concluded that a prevalence rate of 20 per cent could be regarded as fairly typical in the school population.

When the cut-off for bullying or being victimized is made more stringent by requiring that incidents occur more than once, the percentages of bullies and victims drop substantially. Using the stricter criterion of bullying (that is, 'sometimes' or 'more often'), 8.6 per cent of children in the present data reported that they had bullied others. This is similar to the findings of Rigby and Slee (1993a) using the same question (see Rigby & Slee, 1993b). When the cut-off for victimization was set at 'once a week' or 'more', the prevalence rate was 11.2 per cent, which is much the same as that reported

Table 17.1 Percentages of Children Involved in Bullying Problems During the Last Year

Categories	Total	%
Children who neither bullied nor are bullied (non-bully/non-victim)	211	15.06
Children who are bullied (victim)	293	20.91
Children who bully others (bully)	179	12.78
Children who bully others and are bullied(bully/victim)	156	11.13
Children who bully others and are bullied (provoked bully/victim)	538	38.41
Total number of classified children	1377	98.29
Missing data	24	1.71
Total number of children participated	1401	100.00

by other researchers (Perry et al., 1988; Rigby & Slee, 1993b). When the frequency for being bullied is set at '1–2 days a week' or more, the prevalence of victimization decreases to 5.5 per cent which is in accord with the rate reported by Slee (1993).

In addition to the bully and victim groups, previous researchers (Besag, 1989; Bowers et al., 1992, 1994; Olweus, 1991) have identified the bully/victim subgroup. Only a few studies, however, have examined this group in any detail (e.g., Bowers et al., 1992, 1994; Olweus, 1991; Rican, 1995; Rican et al., 1993). Children who were identified as strictly defined bully/victims in the current sample comprised a relatively small number of children (11 per cent) which is quite consistent with prior research (e.g., Olweus, 1991; Stephenson & Smith, 1989).

Is Bullying Status Related to Shame Management?

In order to test the prediction that children's bullying status is related to their shame management skills (**Shame Management 3**), mean scores on the MOSS–SASD scales were compared for the four groups of children: non-bully/non-victim, victim, bully and bully/victim. It will be recalled that the MOSS–SASD scales comprised the 10 questions listed in Table 17.2. In order to make finer discriminations among the four groups, means were compared on each of the questions using scores averaged over the eight scenarios. Each score had a minimum value of 1 and a maximum of 2. The means and standard deviations of each of these variables are shown in Table 17.2. One way analyses of variance with post hoc tests (Scheffés) were performed to ascertain whether the mean differences were significant

for the MOSS–SASD scales among the four groups of children. At least two groups were significantly different for all 10 MOSS–SASD scales. Table 17.2 uses the first letter of the corresponded group (that is, N for non-bully/non-victim, V for victim, B for bully, and BV for bully/victim) to indicate which specific groups are significantly different from each other.

As Table 17.2 shows, the non-bully/non-victim children reported that they would feel shame if caught for the wrongdoing. They would also want to hide from others, be responsible for the wrong and make amends for the harm done. Importantly, these children neither reported a feeling of others' rejection nor a feeling of blaming someone else for what went wrong. They indicated that they would not feel like getting revenge with either the victim or someone/something else. Their pattern of responses suggested features that could mark them as successfully discharging their shame.

From Table 17.2, children who were victims had higher scores on all the Shame Acknowledgment variables, particularly on viewing others' rejection, as predicted. Children who were victims felt ashamed when they imagined doing something wrong, they wanted to hide, felt like blaming themselves, and wanted to do something to make the situation better. Interestingly, they were also more likely to feel confused about who was to blame. Children who were victims were less likely to displace their shame onto others. They were less likely to blame someone else and feel angry at others.

The bully status children reported lower scores on all Shame Acknowledgment variables, as expected. Bullies reported that they were less likely to feel shame when they did something wrong. They were also less likely to hide from others, to take responsibility for causing the harm, and for fixing things up afterwards. They did not report feeling rejected by others. Such children indicated higher scores on all the Shame Displacement variables. They were more likely to blame others for their wrongdoing and to feel anger at others (e.g., getting revenge).

Finally, the most interesting results come from the bully/victim group. The hypothesis that this group of children would share the shame patterns of both the bullies and victims was confirmed. These children felt shame when they did something wrong, wanted to hide, and showed a sense of being rejected by others almost as much as the victim status children did. Bully/victims also reported lower scores on taking responsibility and making amends higher scores on blaming others, feeling retaliatory anger at others as did bully status children. In this research, bully/victims emerged as a somewhat distinct subgroup of children plagued by the shame management problems of both bullies and victims. That is, they both internalize shame and displace shame.

Table 17.2 Mean Scores and SDs for the MOSS–SASD Scales for All Groups of Children with F Statistics from One-Way ANOVAs for the First Four Groups

MOSS–SASD scales[1]	Non-bully / non-victim (minimum n = 208)	Victim (minimum n = 286)	Bully (minimum n = 176)	Bully/victim (minimum n = 149)	Bully/victim (provoked)[2] (minimum n = 523)	F (3, 838)
Would you feel ashamed of yourself?						
Mean	1.94 B	1.91 B	1.80 N, V, BV	1.89 B	1.85	12.01***
SD	.18	.23	.22	.34	.28	
Would you wish you could just hide?						
Mean	1.66 B	1.65	1.55 N, BV	1.69 B	1.66	4.12**
SD	.39	.41	.43	.38	.39	
Would you feel like blaming yourself for what happened?						
Mean	1.89 B, BV	1.87 B	1.78 N, V	1.80 N	1.80	7.08***
SD	.24	.26	.31	.31	.30	
Do you think that others would reject you?						
Mean	1.32 V, BV	1.46 N, B	1.28 V, BV	1.51 N, B	1.42	15.05**
SD	.39	.42	.35	.41	.40	
Would you feel like making the situation better?						
Mean	1.92 B, BV	1.90 B	1.81 N, V	1.84 N	1.82	7.11***
SD	.21	.24	.31	.28	.30	
Would you feel like blaming others for what happened?						
Mean	1.05 B, BV	1.09	1.12 N	1.13 N	1.14	4.89***
SD	.15	.22	.25	.26	.26	

Table 17.2 Mean Scores and SDs for the MOSS–SASD Scales for All Groups of Children with F Statistics from One-Way ANOVAs for the First Four Groups *(cont.)*

MOSS–SASD scales[1]	Non-bully / non-victim (minimum n = 208)	Victim (minimum n = 286)	Bully (minimum n = 176)	Bully/victim (minimum n = 149)	Bully/victim[2] (provoked) (minimum n = 523)	F (3, 838)
Would you be unable to decide if you were to blame?						
Mean	1.18 BV	1.23 BV	1.27 N	1.35 N	1.29	7.66***
SD	.31	.36	.38	.38	.36	
Would you feel angry at this situation?						
Mean	1.36 BV	1.39 BV	1.41 BV	1.56 N, V, B	1.51	7.74***
SD	.43	.44	.42	.41	.41	
Would you feel like getting back at that student?						
Mean	1.07 B, BV	1.08 B, BV	1.19 N, V	1.19 N, V	1.17	12.37***
SD	.21	.22	.32	.33	.31	
Would you feel like throwing or kicking something?						
Mean	1.08 B	1.08 B	1.19 N, V	1.15	1.18	7.36***
SD	.26	.22	.35	.34	.33	

1 These scales represent reverse scores over eight scenarios ranging from 1 (no) to 2 (yes).
2 This group of children were involved in bullying and victimization episodes when they were getting even with someone or when they provoked someone. Because the current research restricts bullying to dominating behavior without provocation, this group has been excluded from this analysis.

Note. Significant differences in mean values among the groups are indicated by capital letters (N = non-bully/non-victim; V = victim; B = bully; BV = bully/victim)   **p<.01   ***p<.001.

Summary

The purpose of the above analyses was to relate the MOSS–SASD scales to children's bullying status in peer groups. It was based on the premise that children acquire behavioral orientations of bullying/victimization as a consequence of their shame management skills. In the MOSS–SASD, shame management skills are broken down into 10 components. While it must be acknowledged that the differences between the groups seem small in absolute terms on such a truncated 1–2 rating scale, the consistency, predictability and statistical significance of the differences are impressive. At this early stage, the SASD framework appears to offer promise to theorists and practitioners. Table 17.3 summarizes the obtained findings.

The findings demonstrate that the elements thought to be important for discharging shame were especially evident among non-bully/non-victim status children. Such children placed more emphasis on a style where they acknowledged their felt shame, made amends and took responsibility for their wrongdoing. Also, they were less inclined than other groups to displace their shame through blaming others and feeling angry with others. These data suggest that non-bully/non-victims are the most socially as well as emotionally competent children because they are capable of releasing their shame adequately. This idea of feeling and appropriately discharging shame complements Braithwaite's (1989) conception of conscience, and supports the view that shame enables an individual to monitor and self-regulate behavior in social situations to maintain positive interpersonal relationships (Schneider, 1977).

Victims followed the same general pattern of scores on the Shame Acknowledgment and Shame Displacement variables as was evident with the non-bully/non-victims with important exceptions. Victims were more likely to feel that others were rejecting them. This response combined with uncertainty about who should be blamed means that victims struggle to deal with shame which continuously lurks in the back of their minds. This finding is consistent with a study by Bijttebier and Vertommen (1998) who found evidence of victims using a coping strategy in which they blamed themselves for what went wrong. The profile for the victims suggests a depth of emotional pain, humiliation and rejection most other children do not experience.

The children in the bully status group followed a clear pattern of low Shame Acknowledgment and high Shame Displacement. When asked to imagine themselves getting caught for doing something wrong, such children were less likely to feel shame, and therefore, were less likely to take responsibility for what happened and to offer reparation. Because of their failure to own their shame, there is not much opportunity for shame to be

Table 17.3 Summary of the Results for Bullying Status, Shame Management and Theoretical Consequences

Bullying Status	Shame Management Skills	Consequences
Non-bully/non-victim (15%)	ACKNOWLEDGE SHAME (feel shame, take responsibility, make amends)	Shame is discharged
	RESIST DISPLACEMENT OF SHAME	
	(resist blaming others, feeling retaliatory anger and displaced anger)	
Victim (25%)	ACKNOWLEDGE SHAME (feel shame, take responsibility, make amends)	Shame is not discharged
	INTERNALIZE SHAME (internalizing others' rejection – self-blame)	
Bully (13%)	RESIST SHAME ACKNOWLEDGMENT	Shame is not discharged
	(resist feeling shame, taking responsibility, making amends)	
	DISPLACE SHAME	
	(blame others, feel retaliatory anger and displaced anger)	
Bully/victim (11%)	RESIST SHAME ACKNOWLEDGMENT	Shame is not discharged
	(resist taking responsibility and making amends)	
	INTERNALIZE SHAME	
	(internalizing others' rejection – self-blame)	
	DISPLACE SHAME	
	(blame others, feel retaliatory anger and displaced anger)	

discharged; rather there arises a need to defend the self from humiliation through directing the blame and anger towards others or toward revenge. These maladaptive efforts to manage shame among children who bully others mirror the concept of by-passed shame in the clinical literature (Lansky, 1987; 1995; Lewis, 1971; Nathanson, 1992; Retzinger, 1996; Scheff, 1991).

Finally, a mixed pattern of shame responses was found in the bully/victim group. This study has demonstrated that while bully/victims were more like victims in expressing shame acknowledgment (e.g., feeling shame, viewing others' rejection), they were also like bullies in displacing their shame (e.g., externalizing blame, retaliatory anger). When they acknowledged their shame, showing a sense of being exposed to others' criticism in particular, they took a victim role; when they displaced their shame, deflecting unreleased shame outside the self through anger and hostility toward others, they adopted a bully role. These children seem to experience the worst of both worlds when it comes to managing shame: They hurt inside and they hurt others as well.

Within the clinical literature, there is increasing evidence of 'comorbidity' or the co-occurrence of two or more distinct manifestations of poor adjustment in the same individual, such as the externalizing and internalizing of psychological problems (see Achenbach, 1991, 1993; Caron & Rutter, 1991; Kovacs, Paulauskas, Gatsonis & Richards, 1988; McBurnett, Lahey, Frick, Risch, Loeber, Hart, Christ & Hanson, 1991; Puig-Antich, 1982; Russo & Beidel, 1994; Walker, Lahey, Russo, Frick, Christ, McBurnett, Loeber, Stouthamer-Loeber & Green, 1991; Woolston, Rosenthal, Riddle, Sparrow, Cicchetti & Zimmerman, 1989; Zoccolillo, 1992). In the present research, Shame Displacement involving blaming others and taking retaliatory action, coupled with acknowledgment, particularly of others' rejection, is likely to lead bully/victims into inconsistent responses in relation to peers; bully at one moment, victim at another. Because bully/victims display both types of problems, they may have more serious difficulties in maintaining positive social relationships and a positive sense of self than other children.

All these findings suggest that it is worth investigating the role of shame management in greater depth in the future. Of particular importance is the distinction between anger directed at self and anger directed at others. If the MOSS–SASD scales are to be fully applied to victim problems as well as bullying problems, a separate measure is required for anger and the rejection of the self as opposed to anger toward others and feelings of rejection by others. Refinement of the MOSS–SASD instrument is now underway. Our follow-up 'Life at School Survey' shows that we are on the right track for refining and modifying the variables so as to capture more of the covert and overt aspects of shame state. There is, however, still a long way to travel before we reach our destination.

For the moment, the finding that non-bully/non-victims acknowledge and discharge shame while bullies resist acknowledgment and displace shame is an important one. So is the finding that victims feel ashamed and internalize the rejection of others while bully/victims struggle with both

the shame management problems of victims and those of bullies. Shame management research is left with many unsolved puzzles. Yet this research at least reveals that there is promise in seeking to unlock them.

PART IV

Conclusion

Valerie Braithwaite and *John Braithwaite*

CHAPTER 18

Creating Institutional Spaces for Shame Management

Comprehending the Enormity of Shame

Perhaps there are human beings who have never experienced shame. It is hard to imagine what such human beings would be like. At the end of the journey with this book, shame seems inevitable to the way we regulate ourselves and to our regulation by others. Since self- and social regulation are necessary to the just and peaceful co-existence of human communities, shame is to this extent desirable. At the same time, shame is revealed as a source of great suffering. Just as our capacity to be ashamed of ourselves when we are intolerant is important to the self-regulation of racism, so Shame Displacement (the externalization of anger onto the other) explains racism. Just as shame is part of how we self-regulate our violent side, so is it a cause of violence. Violence in the Middle East or the Balkans can be understood as a history of shame–rage spirals (Scheff, 1994), cycles of stigmatizing shaming followed by shame displaced into anger and violence, feeding back into more humiliation.

The interminability of the spiral is not only to do with cycles of hurt begetting hurt, but also with the fact that there is displacement. Writing of serial killers, Robert Hale (1993) finds that a humiliation is displaced as rage onto a murder victim. But since the murder is not removing the actual target, there is no release from shame, so the killings continue. Ted Bundy is a paradigm case, killing victims resembling a girlfriend who broke an engagement, brunettes with their hair parted down the middle. With serial rapists sometimes victims are substitutes for a specific woman who is a source of rage; in other cases the displacement is onto all women who need to be 'put in their place' (Scully & Marolla, 1985: p. 261).

Shame that is not discharged is not only harmful to others, more importantly it is harmful to the self. Shame sustains the subordination of the

315

oppressed. But some kinds of shame are more apt to do this than others. Janoff-Bulman (1979) distinguished behavioral self-blame, which is limited to a specific encounter, from characterological self-blame, which entails blaming an inadequate self. She found characterological self-blame was more common among depressed than non-depressed women and that among rape victims characterological self-blamers blamed themselves for the rape more than behavioral self-blamers.

The Morality of Shaming

While shame is an inevitable fact of the human condition, its form is not. While it is neither realistic nor desirable to seek to maximize cultural propensities to shame nor to minimize them, we can craft institutions that shape the form shame takes, in particular that create spaces for the kind of healthy shame management Ahmed finds in her non-bully/non-victims. Our final remarks in the conclusion to this chapter will be about how to do that. Before revisiting some of our main explanatory conclusions about the nature of shame, we must also return to the normative framework of shaming in Chapter 2, linking what has been revealed about shame management to the normative theory of shaming.

It is hard to see how we can ever have an obligation to shame the character of a person. If we are an educator we do have an obligation to shame the practice of cheating, in the sense of reasoning with our students about the unfairness it causes, confronting and disapproving specific instances of cheating when they occur. However, there is no moral obligation to shame cheats as persons, to name them as cheats, or to disapprove of their character. Unlike retributivists, we would also say there is no moral obligation to punish cheats.

When an injustice like cheating has been detected, it is morally wrong to walk away from the injustice, to ignore it. Our moral obligation extends to playing our part in confronting the injustice, in helping the perpetrator acknowledge their responsibility for the injustice, for putting it right, and in preventing blame from being passed on to any innocent party. Translating this normative argument into Ahmed's explanatory concepts, our obligation is to assist a Shame Acknowledgment that averts Shame Displacement. The empirical evidence of Parts II and III gives little reason to believe that there would be bad consequences from respectful behavioral disapproval of injustice. Disrespectful stigmatization of persons is another matter, however. Not only is that normatively wrong according to the philosophy outlined in Chapter 2, Harris's data suggest that it would increase Unresolved Shame (which is unhealthy for people) and Ahmed's data suggest it increases propensities to bully.

If there is some inevitability that shame acknowledgment will lead to at least some shame displacement, a concern we will return to, then perhaps we can learn from Shadd Maruna's (2001) finding that 'generative scripts' characterized desisters from crime. Desisters tended to see their former criminal self as someone who 'wasn't me"'; moreover, they had a desire to help others as part of defining a new pro-social identity for themselves. While this mostly took the form of wanting to help others like themselves who had fallen foul of the law, it also shows the wisdom of creating spaces where offenders have an opportunity to help victims. The support of loved ones seems crucial to the tricky process of flipping from the 'contamination sequences' that typify the narratives of persisters to the 'redemption sequences' that two blind independent raters found to be significantly more common in the narratives of desisters.

Shame, Ethics and Identity

In Part II of this book, Nathan Harris demonstrated that the link between shaming and shame was socially and psychologically complex. At the heart of his analysis is the notion of threat to self, and the role that respected others play in helping an individual deal with shame in a personally and socially constructive way. Harris concluded that how the individual manages shame is critical to understanding the outcomes of any shaming experience. Shame is found to be explained by a person's beliefs about the ethicality of what was done, others' beliefs about its wrongness (communicated through shaming), the nature of the relationship with those others (whether they are highly respected), and how those others communicate their views (reintegratively or stigmatically). The respect involved in communication from others gives us information about whether we share an identity with them. Stigmatization tells us that the stigmatizers do not see themselves as like us, so we will be reluctant to identify with their ethics. Obversely, those who disapprove of our unethical act while letting us know that they have a lot of respect for us as a person are more likely to be persuasive and to shape an identity we share with them. An interesting Taiwanese study which supports Harris's ethical conception is by Jou (1995) who found that family shame (not embarrassment) had a significant effect in reducing delinquency, but only for those kinds of delinquency most disapproved of by Taiwanese families. Examples of kinds of delinquency not disapproved by Taiwanese families were driving a motorcycle without a licence, cheating at school and illegal gambling.

Harris concludes that Unresolved Shame arises when we are uncertain about whether what we have done is right or wrong. Perhaps this is because we are unsure about whether shamers are on our side or not, whether we

buy their analysis of right and wrong, or whether they are the sort of people we would want to identify with. Such Unresolved Shame, according to Harris, is toxic, not only because the failure to lock in to a pro-social identity prevents us from acknowledging shame and moving on, but also because the uncertainty puts us at risk of remaining unattached to any kind of identity. When we are unclear about who we are the shame will keep coming back to trouble us. Psychologically, we will be better off if we reject our rejectors. The shame will be resolved by rejecting their ethical view; we have nothing to be ashamed about and thus our self-esteem can be preserved.

We see this in Ahmed's data where the bullies seem to be better off psychologically than the bully/victims. It is the bully/victims who don't know who to blame. They have the highest scores on 'Blame-perseveration'. Blame-perseveration in Part III correlates with both 'Internalizing others' rejection' and 'Externalizing blame'. One reason the bully/victims get the worst of both worlds is that they seem to endlessly replay thoughts about blaming themselves and thoughts about blaming others. They perseverate with unresolved shame instead of discharging it.

Deliberation, talking through that which is unresolved, is one remedy for Harris. Reintegration and the offender being convinced that the offence was wrong are the variables that reduce Unresolved Shame, stigmatization the variable that makes it worse. Hence, respectful dialogue among friends that helps the lawbreaker clarify their ethical position and see a way that they can reclaim respect by repairing the harm is in the interests of their psychological well-being. Inkpen's (1999) intensive observational study of Canberra drink-driving conferences found that quite often drinking mates and relatives in these conferences persuade offenders that they really have not done anything wrong, at least not seriously wrong. To that extent the conferences may be ineffective in preventing drink-driving. But at least they leave the offender unburdened from Unresolved Shame as a result of entanglement with the criminal process. For most kinds of criminal offences we can expect ethical uncertainty to be more likely to be resolved by family and friends persuading the offender that the offence was wrong. Drink-driving where there is no actual victim is a hard case in terms of community consensus in a heavy-drinking culture like Australia (Mugford & Inkpen, 1995).

For us, this is the most interesting aspect of Harris's results. While reintegration and shaming increase Shame–Guilt and stigmatization reduces it in a way that approximates the predictions of the theory of reintegrative shaming, their coefficients are reversed with Unresolved Shame. The new research and policy challenge therefore becomes how to design deliberative institutions that help us to acknowledge shame for injustices for which we wish to take some responsibility, but also how to end perseveration with shame. There are many ways of accomplishing the latter. One is by

concluding that the law is unjust and should be challenged (a position we have seen marijuana users and their families come to in conferences). Another of course is to come to terms with the fact that one was in the wrong.

Between these extremes, there are many more nuanced cognitive paths to ending shame. One is suggested by the Jesse Jackson slogan: 'You are not responsible for being down, but you are responsible for getting up' (Maruna, 2001: p. 148). In the all-too-common cases of children in poverty who have been physically or sexually abused, they do frequently feel that they are not responsible, that their life circumstances have condemned them to regular encounters with the criminal justice system. Criminal lawyers see moral peril in allowing the law to accept poverty as an excuse. An attraction of restorative justice is that it creates a space where it can be accepted as just for such victimized offenders to believe: 'I am the real victim in this room. While I am not responsible for the abused life that led me into a life of crime on the streets, I am responsible for getting out of it and I am also responsible for helping this victim who has been hurt by my act.' Maruna (2001) found empirically that desisters from crime moved from 'contamination scripts' to 'redemption scripts' through just this kind of refusal to take responsibility for being down while accepting responsibility for getting up. No kind of unresolved shame deserves our care more than that of the legions of homeless, sexually abused children who rob and sell drugs.

The beauty of the research program that is opened up by Harris's work is that it allows us to dissect this problem as, on the one hand acknowledging shame over a specific harm suffered by a victim who has been mugged, while more importantly, seeking to resolve shame about a bigger life situation in a way that might involve a just denial of blame. No less than 'justice with love' may be needed for this challenge. It is one quite beyond the justice of the courts.

In this research program, methods beyond those used here and data sources beyond schools and courts in Canberra are needed. Eliza Ahmed is collecting data on shame management in the poor Muslim country of Bangladesh to compare results with affluent, Christian Canberra. Tom Scheff made a telling comment about the limitations of our method for shame as a topic:

> . . . most shame is ego-threatening. Shame feels not only like rejection, but weakness and worthlessness to the point of the dissolution of the ego. For this reason, most people most of the time avoid awareness of shame. This is to say most shame is unacknowledged, and to a large extent outside of awareness. But if one emotion is largely conscious [guilt], the other mostly unconscious

[shame], what will happen if one conflates them? The subjects' responses concern mostly conscious feelings. It is true that in some subjects shame and guilt are correlated. But in others they are not. Most frequently, guilt is a defence against shame. So guilt responses hide shame more frequently in subjects' consciousness as well as revealing it.

Clinical and physiological data as well as data from conversational analysis and ethnography seem the correctives to this troubling methodological limitation. A lot of studies of this kind are already out there. Indeed, theories derived from such research informed the measures for the methods deployed here. Readers must make their own judgments as to whether the methods used in this book allow a different, complementary kind of insight. We think they do add value, though they can never supplant the value of what we learn from the other methods. Sadly we are a doomed research group for we work at the intersection of two phenomena that people have maximum reason to hide – shame and lawbreaking. That is one reason we believe ultimately in backing our theoretical judgments with interventions whose rather poorly understood effects can be tested through randomized controlled trials. But we do hope that the kind of work in this book is an important part of the getting of the wisdom to craft more promising and morally decent interventions.

Mapping Shame Management

Part III takes us further with the task of mapping how individuals manage shame. The setting for this analysis is the school, in many ways a microcosm of society. Within the school setting children learn to engage with a community of strangers and acquire skills that equip them for the dual social goals of competition and cooperation. Furthermore, school life revolves around change, be it in relation to knowledge, physical appearance, physical prowess, or social relationships. Within the school setting, children are bombarded with experiences that may threaten self, potentially leaving them feeling inadequate in their own eyes and in those of others. Within such an environment, children begin the task of learning to manage shame.

The analysis of Part III, however, does not sweep across the full gamut of shame-producing experiences. It focuses on one aspect of school life that involves both breaking rules and hurting others, school bullying. Significantly, the consequences of school bullying appear to be far-reaching, often affecting individuals in their adult life. Research findings suggest that this may be an arena where shame is not managed well either by those who victimize or those who are victimized.

The contribution of Part III to this book is threefold. First, the 'Life at School Survey' provided an opportunity to demonstrate the importance of shame management in explaining bullying and victimization behavior. Second, Part III sets out a basic strategy for the measurement of shame management, and more specifically, offers the MOSS–SASD as an instrument that may be used in the context of school bullying. The third contribution is that through the analyses presented in Chapter 16, insight is provided into the levers that may be important in building shame management capacity. The findings of Part III will be discussed in these terms, dealing first with the measurement of shame management.

The Measurement of Shame Management

The MOSS–SASD, developed in Chapter 14, has two distinctive features. The first concerns the sampling frame used to generate the shame management questions of the MOSS–SASD. The second involves the focus on social context.

The MOSS–SASD should be seen as an instrument that can be used in other schools to assess shame reactions to bullying. It should also be seen as a blue print for measuring shame management in a variety of social contexts. What this means is that users should feel free to create representative scenarios that suit their context, and then apply the questions regarding acknowledgment and displacement to these new scenarios. To date, we have had success with this strategy, although much more data from different populations are required to provide a more rigorous test of the robustness of the shame management dimensions identified in this work. New scenarios have been developed and tested by Eliza Ahmed in her work in Bangladesh, Valerie Braithwaite in her work on tax compliance, and Brenda Morrison in her work on children and bullying at home.

Measures of this type that explicitly recommend scenario re-construction to fit the social context are not usual in the social sciences. Concerns about generalizability underlie reluctance to recommend such a step, and such concerns are well-justified. However, proceeding with caution with a re-construction approach is recommended in any context where one is looking for institutional levers to promote change. As scenarios change, the degree to which individuals feel shame and believe they should feel shame also changes. The MOSS–SASD, while telling us something about the psychology of individuals, also tells us something about the legitimacy of authority and the social mores that surround the wrongdoing that is being placed under the microscope. As Harris has shown in Part II, an important part of feeling shame is believing that one's behavior is wrong. In our work, shame is not just an individual psychological variable that weighs more heavily on

the shoulders of some than others regardless of situation. Shame is conceived as a feeling associated with an ethical violation that must be understood in a social context where the individual is negotiating a relationship with others, be they imagined or real. Changing the social context changes the threat to ethical identity which, in turn, changes the feeling of shame and its management. This is a core assumption of the work in Part III and a core assumption of reintegrative shaming theory. It is also fundamentally important in designing restorative justice interventions within the justice system and within schools.

The sampling frame used for developing the items of the MOSS–SASD is worthy of comment because it was different to that used by Harris. The focus of Part III was on the measurement of what has been called adaptive shame management and maladaptive shame management. Descriptions in the sociological, psychological and clinical literatures of shame and its behavioral consequences led to the construction of vignettes of shame management. No attempt was made to measure the typicality of these responses. Rather the shame management sequences were used to identify facets of shame management. These facets formed the basis for the development of 10 shame management questions that factored into two dimensions, labeled Shame Acknowledgment and Shame Displacement. Adaptive shame management was defined as a combination of high acknowledgment and low displacement, whereas maladaptive shame management was defined as a combination of low acknowledgment and high displacement.

The Relevance of Shame Acknowledgment and Shame Displacement

These expectations about adaptive and maladaptive shame management strategies received some support, but the 'Life at School Survey' also presented us with some unexpected and very significant surprises. The adaptive shame management style was successfully linked with well established correlates of low aggression, low bullying and low delinquency: positive parent–child affect, perceived control of bullying in the school, internal locus of control, guilt-proneness and empathy. When a path model was developed to show how shame management and competing predictors might affect bullying of a general or self-initiated kind, three variables followed the expected path. Children who were low on impulsivity, high on empathy and who perceived control of bullying in the school were more likely to acknowledge shame without displacement. Other variables such as liking for school, school hassles and self-esteem displayed different patterns of association with acknowledgment on the one hand, and displacement on

the other. The path model reinforced the message that first appeared at the correlational level. Acknowledgment and displacement need to be conceptualized as distinct dimensions of shame management. In other words, children may acknowledge and displace shame almost simultaneously, and such children may be having as many difficulties, if not more difficulties than those with the predicted maladaptive response of low acknowledgment and high displacement. Indeed, bully/victims who typified this pattern of both acknowledging and displacing may be suffering more than any other group as they punish themselves, reject others, and thereby further invite external punishment. So may those children with low self-esteem and shame-proneness who also exhibit the pattern of acknowledgment accompanied by displacement. The two dimensions of acknowledgment and displacement should be uncoupled in future theorizing. The roles that they play in mediating relationships between family, school and personality on the one hand, and bullying on the other appear to be more distinct than we assumed previously.

Shame Acknowledgment decreases the likelihood of bullying and is related to liking school, perceiving control over bullying in the school, empathy, guilt- and pride- proneness, and low impulsivity. These findings are consistent with seeing acknowledgment as an adaptive shame management strategy. Interestingly, acknowledgment is also connected with high shame-proneness, having hassles at school and low self-esteem, all of which connote poor adaptation. Further work is underway to tease out the meaning of these relationships. One possibility is that the acknowledgment scale incorporates elements of being hard on oneself in terms of self-criticism. Another is that children who have high scores on acknowledgment tend to be more honest with themselves and others, and are less likely to respond to social demands for positive self-presentation. A third possibility is that high self-esteem, a hassle-free life and low shame-proneness may foster a degree of generalized pride (Tangney's alpha pride as distinct from beta pride) that is not always adaptive in terms of one's capacity to engage constructively with society. Baumeister et al. (1996) have suggested that individuals with high self-esteem may be unwilling to revise their self-esteem downward and therefore actively work at avoiding negative evaluation. While one option might be to reject the critics (Baumeister et al., 1996), another might be to transcend criticism with artful deflection of the negative evaluation. Successful deflection of blame for wrongdoing would be associated with low acknowledgment in the MOSS–SASD context, and if the deflection of blame were clever enough, the need to engage in displacement would not arise.

Of more concern, however, in the present research is the plight of children with low self-esteem, those who acknowledge their shame and

displace it as well. We saw in the path diagrams in Chapter 16 that acknowledgment can increase the likelihood of displacement. An important issue to address is how one handles the fact that high self-esteem children have the best of both worlds psychologically because they shield themselves from shame and maintain positive relationships with their peers. In contrast, low self-esteem children have the worst of both worlds psychologically, hurting inside as a result of acknowledgment, and damaging their relationships with others through displacement. Do we really want to rob high self-esteem children of their resiliency, and how do we, from our current theoretical perspective, ease the pain suffered by low self-esteem children? As we argue below, the answer lies in designing institutions that enable acknowledgment without displacement, that build individual wisdom and strengthen social ties. Putting the problem rather than the person in the centre of the circle may not only allow us to avert characterological shame, it may allow behavioral shame acknowledgment without displacement. Our current thinking is guided by an institutional hypothesis that outlines the circumstances in which acknowledgment is safe for the individual and the collective.

Putting the above reservations to one side, the findings of Part III support conceiving of acknowledgment as an adaptive shame management skill. From a psychological perspective, the strongest support comes from the significant level of overlap between guilt-proneness (Tangney et al., 1989) and the acknowledgment scale. The concepts of guilt-proneness, shame acknowledgment and Harris's conception of Shame–Guilt all reflect recognition of wrongdoing, acceptance of responsibility and a desire to make amends. The differences may lie in pedagogy rather than in the detail of construct definition and measurement. While Tangney is concerned about measuring an individual's general predisposition to respond to shame over socially inappropriate behavior in an adaptive way, the focus of this book is on measuring an individual's response to particular acts of wrongdoing that are confronted in the presence of significant others. We accept Tangney and her colleague's starting point that individuals differ in their capacities to handle emotions, as they differ in abilities, be they physical or mental. What we have tried to do in Part III is to change the focus to pick up on institutional and social parameters that can magnify or reduce the significance of the individual's capacities, for better or for worse. As our telescope focuses on social context and as Tangney and her colleagues focus on individual personality, it is not too surprising to find one group of researchers merging shame and guilt, while the other separates these constructs. Tangney is able to identify for us those individuals who persistently, regardless of context, become overwhelmed by their feelings of shame. We suspect that for such individuals, the social context is far less salient for shame management than what is going on in their minds as they

wrestle with a steady stream of threats to self from their social world. For those who are more socially secure in their knowledge of their positive social identities, self preoccupations about shame are likely to give way to an awareness of context, of the seriousness of the act, and its consequences. Thus, self and social context, guilt and shame come together in the mind of the wrongdoer in search of an explanation of what went wrong and a way of retrieving a sense of personal dignity.

In Part III, retrieval of personal dignity is assumed to be accomplished most effectively through acknowledgment without displacement. Underlying this assumption is an acceptance that bullying is a form of oppression of one individual by another that is individually and socially destructive and that should be resisted. But as Harris has pointed out in Part II, individuals may not always believe that what they have done is wrong, even if society labels it so. Acknowledgment therefore needs to be theorized in conjunction with another construct, personal belief that the act is wrong, or more broadly, acceptance of just rules and standards. Through measuring the belief that societal rules are just along with acknowledgment, we might provide a more complete measure of one aspect of what we have called an ethical conception of shame.

While acknowledgment represented recognizing the harm done and the need to repair a damaged social relationship, displacement increased the social rift between the wrongdoer and the victim. Shame was displaced by transforming it into anger and blaming others. Shame Displacement increased the likelihood of bullying and was associated with high impulsivity, externalization and shame-proneness, and low internal locus of control, self-esteem, guilt-proneness, and empathy. Displacement is likely to be higher when children report family conflict and perceive lack of control over bullying in the school. As noted above, displacement may also increase with acknowledgment.

Parallels have been drawn between shame displacement and Harris's dimension of Unresolved Shame in that both evoke images of avoidance of accepting responsibility for harm done. Harris's factor, however, incorporated more subtle strategies. Harris found that Unresolved Shame was related to empathy for others, uncertainty over wrongdoing and perhaps questions about fairness. In the case of children, such subtleties were not apparent. Shame Displacement put distance between oneself, the act and those affected. Social rift appeared to be high for children imagining themselves being caught by an authority figure. Shame Displacement involved responses of hitting back, without consideration for consequences. Whether or not the differences reflect the process of maturation as opposed to different styles of shame management remains a question for future research.

An important aspect of the research presented in Part III is that it allows us to compare the relative importance of personality and institutional factors in the prediction of bullying. While it is clear from the data in Chapter 16 that personality and institutional factors are not independent (e.g. impulsive children are more likely to report problems with school and family), the personality of the child is clearly not all that matters and is not the only point of leverage for interventions. Impulsivity is well established in the literature as a precursor of aggression, delinquency and criminal behavior. The data reported in Part III support these findings, and confirm the role of other personality variables such as locus of control and empathy. The data in Part III also show, however, that the institutions of the school and the family cannot be sidelined in an analysis of bullying and shame management. Perceptions of families being caring and supportive are important. So too are perceptions of schools being safe with effective control over bullying.

The path analyses reported in Chapter 16 must be seen as a beginning for understanding bullying in terms of shame management and as a source for deriving hypotheses rather than testing them. What appears clear from these results, however, is that shame management does not explain all the links between traditional predictors and bullying. Of the variables that have direct links to bullying, the most noteworthy from a reintegrative shaming perspective are the stigmatizing and non-stigmatizing shaming attributions. Parents who responded to the bullying scenarios by claiming that their child probably did it on purpose and would do it again (stable and intentional attributions) were more likely to have children who identified themselves as self-initiated bullies. In other words, the stigmatizing attributions of parents were accompanied by self-identification of serious bullying by their children. Shame management was not a mediator in this relationship. Perhaps these children did not feel much shame about their bullying status. Perhaps their parents did not see the need to feel shame either.

The other parental attribution, referred to as non-stigmatizing shaming, was negatively related to self-initiated bullying, again with no links to the shame management variables. In this case parents who held the child responsible for the behavior and believed that the behavior was under the child's control (controllable and responsible attributions) had children who did not report repeated involvement in self-initiated bullying. This finding suggests that communicating confidence in the child and expecting improved behavior is directly linked with less bullying. Here, the absence of links with the shame management variables is more puzzling. One might take the view that non-stigmatizing shaming was working in this context as a very effective preventive measure rather than as a corrective measure after a bullying incident. At this stage, however, it is best to reserve

judgment until further work is undertaken to flesh out the explanation for the absence of linkage to the shame management variables. Suffice it to say that the links between stigmatizing and non-stigmatizing shaming attributions and bullying are reassuring, and consistent with reintegrative shaming theory.

One of the most consistent and important predictors of school bullying was the degree to which children perceived the school as being serious in its attempts to control bullying behavior. This finding is well known in the bullying literature (Lane, 1989; Olweus, 1993; Rigby, 1996). Children's perceptions of control by the school also worked to reduce bullying through both acknowledgment and displacement. Children who perceived their school as having effective control over bullying reported greater acknowledgment of harm done, and were less likely to displace shame onto others. Our hypothesis for future research here is that schools which respond early to bullying before it gets out of hand are politically capable of confronting it in a non-punitive way. This means they create safe spaces where children can own responsibility for bullying and for failures to intervene to protect victims.

Shame Management and Institutional Design

The findings associated with parental expectations and school control of bullying convey the importance of setting and enforcing standards in relation to personal conduct in schools. Before taking this principle further into the arena of policy, however, there is another story that warrants consideration having to do with self-worth and the human need to protect the self. The path diagrams in Chapter 16 draw attention to the problem posed for all of us when we try to regain our self-esteem after we have had to confront our own wrongdoing. Acknowledgment involves facing up to our own wrongdoing. Acknowledgment decreases the likelihood of bullying. However, as we acknowledge, we are also likely to displace our shame, and shame displacement increases the likelihood of bullying. This poses a paradox for those wishing to advocate the importance of acknowledgment as a means to violence prevention.

The solution we offer is in the form of an institutional hypothesis. Children need to be provided with a carefully regulated and safe environment in which they can acknowledge and if necessary, displace shame without doing harm to others or themselves. Some have argued for a whole school approach to bullying where anti-bullying values and policies are strongly upheld and children are taught to deal with each other with respect, tolerance and empathy. Building a school culture of this kind would satisfy the requirements of our institutional hypothesis. The anger

that children are likely to express when they acknowledge their shame is likely to be met with understanding, without being accepted as desirable conduct. The cohesiveness and the care of the group envelop the child until shame is discharged and the incident is put in the past.

Sometimes, however, schools are structured in a way where a whole school approach is not completely feasible. The school may be particularly large and hierarchical, or the resources may not be available to initiate the cultural revolution that the whole school approach entails. In such cases we argue that something still can be done to make it safe for children to acknowledge wrongdoing and minimize the adverse impact of displacement. Peer groups can provide the safe space that children need as long as they understand the dynamics of shame management, the difficulty of acknowledgment, and the temptation of displacement.

On the basis of the research reported in Part III, an intervention program for school bullying was started in Canberra in 1999. It was called PRISM, Program for Reintegration and Individual Shame Management. The idea behind PRISM was to change the behavior of children who are bullied and who bully others by improving their capacity to build relationships of respect and trust with each other and with others in the school community. In its initial stages, the key to bringing about change in behavior was competency in shame management. PRISM rested on the premise that children became locked into hurtful relations with each other either because (a) they were unable to recognize their feelings of shame, and therefore, were unable to take the actions required to discharge shame in a positive way, or because (b) they became overwhelmed by shame, drowning in feelings of helplessness and an all encompassing loss of self-worth. The first response was prototypical of bullies in Part III, the second prototypical of victims.

Since the early stages of setting up PRISM, the program has evolved to take on another component, the development of a positive school identity. Under the directorship of Brenda Morrison, the new program called RCP (Responsible Citizenship Program) gives equal attention to building a positive school identity within peer groups and uses three important cornerstones of restorative justice – Respect, Consideration and Participation – to set the framework in which children can learn about shame management and feel safe in the process of acknowledging shame. After a period for team building and developing trust relationships, children are introduced to the REACTion keys for dealing with wrongdoing. Again drawing on restorative justice philosophy, children become familiar with five principles captured by REACT:

(a) Repair the harm done
(b) Expect the best from others
(c) Acknowledge feelings of self and others
(d) Care for others
(e) Take responsibility for actions and feelings.

Finally, children learn how their REACTion keys can help de-escalate conflict and allow forgiveness and reintegration into the peer group. The 10 workshops that make up this program have been discussed in detail elsewhere (Morrison, forthcoming). At this stage of evaluation, the program looks promising. What we can say with some certainty at this time arises out of the major lesson that we learnt from our early mistakes. Shame management can never be effectively taught on an individual basis, nor should it be. These skills have to be nurtured in social groups, where children feel supported and respected. Acknowledgment does hurt; it hurts our self-esteem. Under such circumstances, it may be easier for us to keep quiet, to deflect the blame, or to put social distance between ourselves and our accusers. The costs to society are high. As LaFree (1998) recently pointed out, social distance to protect self-respect, if carried out on a large scale, can ultimately delegitimize our social institutions. In contrast, shame acknowledgment with reintegration that affirms our self-worth, can build stronger institutions in the long term. But in order for individuals to acknowledge shame and to feel better for having done so, they must feel safe, they must be safe.

Safety to acknowledge shame is not on offer through traditional Western rule enforcing institutions. Indeed, one might argue that acknowledgment is the worst thing to do if you want to avoid punishment: Better to deny wrongdoing and displace shame onto others to avoid the immediate harm threatened by the court system. Harris's finding that court was more likely to be associated with embarrassment rather than Shame–Guilt is consistent with our analysis of how individuals step away from acknowledgment to protect themselves from further harm. They cannot learn from mistakes that have never been faced. What is more, the protection afforded by social distance means that the wrongdoer steps outside the reach of communal regulation, making future offenses more rather than less likely.

Conferencing and circles provide interesting alternatives for administering justice. They provide the opportunity for building adaptive shame management skills in the offender, rather than encouraging the adoption of maladaptive shame management skills. The care and support of those who are respected by the offender provide the safety required for the acknowledgment of shame, expressions of displacement that might be validated through deliberation as just, and ultimately the effective discharge of

shame. The wrongdoing is sanctioned, the ritual is terminated with forgiveness, and the individual has the opportunity to make amends and learn from mistakes that have been openly and honestly acknowledged.

All of this admittedly is a long way from where we started. The links that we have postulated are speculative. They are links, however, that signpost the way for our future research endeavors. We hope others feel inspired to take up the research challenge with us. It is no less than a research agenda on how to make deliberative democracy work so that it might confront injustice in a way that heals rather than damages people.

References

Abalakina, P. M., Stephan, W. G., Craig, T., & Gregory, W. L. (1999). Beliefs in conspiracies. *Political Psychology*, 20(3), 637–647.

Abrams, D., Wetherell, M., Cochrane, S., Hogg, M. A., & Turner, J. C. (1990). Knowing what to think by knowing who you are: Self-categorization and the nature of norm formation, conformity and group polarization. *British Journal of Social Psychology*, 29(2), 97–119.

Achenbach, T. M. (1991). Comorbidity in child and adolescent psychiatry: Categorical and quantitative perspectives. *Journal of Child and Adolescent Psychopharmacology*, 1, 271–278.

Achenbach, T. M. (1993). Taxonomy and comorbidity of conduct problems: Evidence of empirically based approaches. *Development and Psychopathology*, 5, 51–64.

ACTDET. (1996). *A datafile on ACT school systems*. Canberra: Australia.

Agnew, R. (1985). Social control theory and delinquency: A longitudinal test. *Criminology*, 23, 47–61.

Ahmad, Y., & Smith, P. K. (1989). Bully/victim problems among school children. Poster paper presented at Conference of the BPS, Guildford.

Ahmad, Y., & Smith, P. K. (1990). Behavioral measures review: Bullying in schools. *Newsletter of the Association for Child Psychology and Psychiatry*, 12, 26–27.

Ahmed, E. (1996). *Life at School Survey*. The Australian National University, Canberra.

Ahmed, E. (1996). Attributional Shaming Instrument (ASI). *Life at School Survey* (pp. 12–14). The Australian National University, Canberra.

Ahmed, E. (1999). Shame management and bullying. Unpublished Doctoral Dissertation, The Australian National University, Canberra.

Ahmed, E., Braithwaite, V. A., & Braithwaite, J. B. (1996). Management Of Shame State: Shame Acknowledgment and Shame Displacement (MOSS–SASD). *Life at School Survey: Child questionnaire* (pp. 28–32). Unpublished booklet.

Aiken, L. S., & West, S. G. (1991). *Multiple regression: Testing and interpreting interactions*. Newbury Park, CA, USA: Sage Publications.

Ainsworth, M., Blehar, M., Waters, E., & Wall, S. (1978). *Patterns of attachment*. Hillsdale, NJ: Erlbaum.

Alessandri, S. M., & Lewis, M. (1993). Parental evaluation and its relation to shame and pride in young children. *Sex Roles*, 29(5), 335–343.

Amato, P. R., & Keith, B. (1991). Parental divorce and the well-being of children: A meta-analysis. *Psychological Bulletin*, 110(1), 26–46.

Anastasi, A. (1968). *Psychological testing*. (3rd edn). New York: MacMillan.

Anderson, E. (1994). The codes of the streets. *Atlantic Monthly*, 273(5), 81–94.

Anderson, K. E., Lytton, H., Romney, D. M. (1986). Mothers' interactions with normal and conduct-disordered boys: Who affects whom? *Developmental Psychology*, 22(5), 604–609.

Andrews, D. (1995). The psychology of criminal conduct and effective treatment. In J. McGuire (ed.), *What works: Reducing reoffending – guidelines from research and practice*. West Sussex, UK: John Wiley.

Arbuckle, J. (1997). AMOS User's Guide. Version 3.6. Small-Waters Corporation.

Arbuckle, J. & Wothke, W. (1999). AMOS 4.0 User's Guide. Illinois: SPSS.

Archer, J., Kilpatrick, G., & Bramwell, R. (1995). Comparison of two aggression inventories. *Aggressive Behavior*, 21(5), 371–380.

Aronfreed, J. (1968). *Conduct and conscience: The socialization of internalized control over behavior.* New York: Academic Press.

Aronson, E. (1969). A theory of cognitive dissonance: A current perspective. In Berkowitz (ed.), *Advances in Experimental Social Psychology* (Vol. 4, pp. 1–34). N.Y.: Academic Press.

Aronson, E. (1997). The theory of cognitive dissonance: The evolution and vicissitudes of an idea. In C. McGarty, and Haslam, S. A. (ed.), *The message of social psychology* (pp. 20–35). Oxford, UK: Blackwell.

Arora, C. M., & Thompson, D. A. (1987). Defining bullying for a secondary school. *Educational and Child Psychology*, 4(3–4), 110–120.

Asch, S. E. (1956). Studies of independence and conformity: I. A minority of one against a unanimous majority. *Psychological Monographs*, 70(9), 70.

Aurora, D., & Fimian, M. J. (1988). Dimensions of life and school stress experienced by young people. *Psychology in the Schools*, 25, 44–53.

Ausubel, D. P. (1955). Relationships between shame and guilt in the socializing Process. *Psychological Review*, 62, 5, 378–390.

Averill, J. R. (1983). Studies on anger and aggression: Implications for theories of emotion. *American Psychologist*, 38(11), 1145–1160.

Ayres, I. & Braithwaite, J. (1992). Designing responsive regulatory institutions. *Responsive Community*, 2(3), 41–47.

Bachman, R., Paternoster, R., & Ward, S. (1992). The rationality of sexual offending: Testing a deterrence/rational choice conception of sexual assault. *Law and Society Review*, 26(2), 343–372.

Bagaric, M. & Amarasekara, K. (2000). The errors of retributivism. *Melbourne University Law Review*, 24(1): 124–189.

Bandura, A. (1973). *Aggression: A social learning analysis.* Englewood Cliffs, NJ: Prentice-Hall.

Bandura, A. (1977). *Social learning theory.* Englewood Cliffs, NJ: Prentice-Hall.

Bandura, A. (1986). *Social foundations of thought and action: A social cognition theory.* Englewood Cliffs, NJ: Prentice-Hall.

Bandura, A. (1999). Moral disengagement in the perpetration of inhumanities. *Personality and Social Psychology Review*, 3(3), 193–209.

Bandura, A., Barbaranelli, C., Caprara, G. V., & Pastorelli, C. (1996). Mechanisms of moral disengagement in the exercise of moral agency. *Journal of Personality and Social Psychology*, 71, 364–374.

Barbalet, J. M. (1998). *Emotion, social theory, and social structure: A macrosociological approach.* Cambridge: Cambridge University Press.

Barnes, G. (1999). *Procedural justice in two contexts: Testing the fairness of diversionary conferencing for intoxicated drivers.* Unpublished Doctoral Dissertation, Dept. of Criminal Justice and Criminology, University of Maryland, College Park.

Baron, R. M., & Kenny, D. A. (1986). The moderator-mediator variable distinction in social psychological research: Conceptual, strategic and statistical considerations. *Journal of Personality and Social Psychology*, 51, 1173–1182.

Barratt, E. S., & Patton, J. H. (1983). Impulsivity: cognitive, behavioral and psychophysiological correlates. In M. Zuckerman (ed.), *The biological bases of sensation seeking, impulsivity and anxiety* (pp. 77–116). Hillsdale, NJ: Erlbaum.

Barrett, K. C. (1995). A functionalist approach to shame and guilt. In J. P. Tangney & K. W. Fischer (eds.), *Self conscious emotions: The psychology of shame, guilt, embarrassment, and pride* (pp. 25–63). New York, NY: Guilford Press.

Barrett, K. C., & Campos, J. J. (1987). Perspectives on emotional development II: A functionalist approach to emotions. In J. D. Osofsky et al. (eds.), *Handbook of Infant Development* (2nd edn, pp. 555–578). New York, NY: John Wiley & Sons.

Barton, A. (1999). Breaking the crime/drugs cycle: The birth of a new approach? *Howard Journal of Criminal Justice*, 38(2), 144–157.

Batson, C. D. (1987). Prosocial motivation: Is it ever truly altruistic? In L. Berkowitz (ed.), *Advances in Experimental Social Psychology*. New York, NY: Academic Press.

Baum, S. (1999). Self-reported drink driving and deterrence. *Australian and New Zealand journal of Criminology*. 32(3), 247–262.

Baumeister, R. F., & Cairns, K. J. (1992). Repression and self-presentation: When audiences interfere with self-deceptive strategies. *Journal of Personality and Social Psychology*, 62(5), 851–862.

Baumeister, R. F., & Leary, M. R. (1995). The need to belong: Desire for interpersonal attachments as a fundamental human motivation. *Psychological Bulletin*, 117(3), 497–529.

Baumeister, R. F., Smart, L., & Boden, J. M. (1996). Relation of threatened egotism to violence and aggression: The dark side of high self-esteem. *Psychological Review*, 103(1), 5–33.

Baumeister, R. F., Stillwell, A. M., & Heatherton, T. F. (1994). Guilt: An interpersonal approach. *Psychological Bulletin*, 115, 243–267.

Baumeister, R. F., Stillwell, A. M., & Heatherton, T. F. (1995). Interpersonal aspects of guilt: Evidence from narrative studies. In J. P. Tangney & K. W. Fischer (eds.), *Self conscious emotions: The psychology of shame, guilt, embarrassment, and pride* (pp. 255–273). New York, NY: Guilford Press.

Baumrind, D. A. (1967). Child care practices anteceding three patterns of preschool behavior. *Genetic Psychology Monographs*, 75(1), 43–88.

Baumrind, D. A. (1971). Current patterns of parental authority. *Developmental Psychology*, 4(2), 1–103.

Baumrind, D. A. (1973). The development of instrumental competence through socialization. In A. Pick (ed.), *Minnesota symposium on child psychology*, 7, 3–46. Minneapolis: University of Minnesota Press.

Baumrind, D. A. (1978). Parental disciplinary patterns and social competence in children. *Youth and Society*, 9, 239–276.

Baumrind, D. A. (1989). Rearing competent children. In W. Damon (ed.), *Child development today and tomorrow* (pp. 349–378). San Francisco, CA: Jossey-Bass.

Baumrind, D. A. (1991a). Effective parenting during the early adolescent transition. In E. M. Hetherington, et al. (eds.), *Family transitions: Advances in family research series* (pp. 111–163). Hillsdale, NJ: Erlbaum.

Baumrind, D. A. (1991b). The influence of parenting style on adolescent competence and substance use. *Journal of Early Adolescence*, 11(1), 56–95.

Baumrind, D. A. (1993). The average expectable environment is not good enough: A response to Scarr. *Child Development*, 64(5), 1299–1317.

Bell, R. Q., & Chapman, M. (1986). Child effects in studies using experimental or brief longitudinal approaches to socialization. *Developmental Psychology*, 22, 595–603.

Benedict, R. (1946). *The chrysanthemum and the sword: Patterns of Japanese culture*. Boston: Houghton Mifflin.

Bentler, P. M. (1990). Comparative fit indexes in structural models. *Psychological Bulletin*, 107, 238–246.

Bentler, P. M. (1993). *Structural equations program manual*. Los Angeles: BMPD Statistical Software Inc.

Bentley, K. M., & Li, A. K. F. (1995). Bully and victim problems in elementary schools and students' beliefs about aggression. *Canadian Journal of School Psychology*, 11(2), 153–165.

Berdondini, L., & Smith, P. K. (1996). Cohesion and power in the families of children involved in bully/victim problems at school: An Italian replication. *Journal of Family Therapy*, 18, 99–102.

Besag, V. E. (1989). *Bullies and victims in schools*. Milton Keynes: Open University Press.

Betancourt, H., & Blair, I. (1992). A cognition (attribution)-emotion model of violence in conflict situations. *Personality and Social Psychology Bulletin*, 18(3), 343–350.

Biaggio, M. K., & Godwin, W. H. (1987). Relation of depression to anger and hostility constructs. *Psychological Reports*, 61, 87–90.

Bijttebier, P., & Vertommen, H. (1998). Coping with peer arguments in school-age children with bully–victim problems. *The British Journal of Educational Psychology*, 68(3), 387–394.

Bjorkqvist, K., Ekman, K. & Lagerspetz, K. (1982). Bullies and victims: Their ego picture, ideal ego picture and normative ego picture. *Scandinavian Journal of Psychology*, 23, 307–313.

Blasi, A., & Glodis, K. (1995). The development of identity: A critical analysis from the perspective of the self as subject. *Developmental Review*, 15, 404–433.

Block, J. H. (1965). *The child rearing practices report*. Institute of Human Development, University of California, Berkeley.

Block, J. H. (1981). *The child-rearing practices report (CRPR): A set of Q items for the description of parental socialization attitudes and values*. Unpublished manuscript. Institute of Human Development, University of California, Berkeley.

Block, J., Block, J. H., & Keyes, S. (1988). Longitudinally foretelling drug usage in adolescence: Early childhood personality and environmental precursors. *Child Development*, 59(2), 336–355.

Boggiano, A. K., Barrett, M., Weiher, A. W., McLelland, G. H. & Lusk, C. M. (1987). Use of the maximal operant principle to motivate children's intrinsic interest. *Journal of Personality and Social Psychology*, 53, 866–879.

Bollen, K. A. (1989). *Structural equations with latent variables*. New York, NY: John Wiley and Sons.

Bonnano, G. A., & Singer, J. L. (1995). Repression and dissociation: Implications for personality theory, psychopathology and health. *Mental health and development* (pp. 435–470). Chicago, IL: University of Chicago Press.

Bonta, J., Wallace-Capretta, S. & Rooney, J. (1998). *Restorative justice: an evaluation of the restorative resolutions project*. Ottawa: Solicitor-General Canada.

Boulton, M. J. (1993). Proximate causes of aggressive fighting in middle school children. British *Journal of Educational Psychology*, 63, 231–244.

Boulton, M. J., & Smith, P. K. (1994). Bully/victim problems among middle school children: Stability, self-perceived competence, and peer acceptance. *British Journal of Developmental Psychology*, 12, 315–329.

Boulton, M. J., & Underwood, K. (1992). Bully/victim problems among middle school children. *British Journal of Educational Psychology*, 62(1), 73–87.

Bowers, L., Smith, P. K., & Binney, V. (1992). Cohesion and power in the families of children involved in bully/victim problems at school. *Journal of Family Therapy*, 14, 371–87.

Bowers, L., Smith, P. K., & Binney, V. (1994). Perceived family relationships of bullies, victims and bully/victims in middle childhood. *Journal of Social and Personal Relationships*, 11, 215–232.

Bowlby, J. (1969). *Attachment and loss: Vol. 1. Attachment.* New York, NY: Basic Books.

Bowlby, J. (1973). *Attachment and loss: Vol. 2. Separation.* New York, NY: Basic Books.

Bradburn, N. M. (1969). *The structure of psychological well-being.* Chicago, IL: Aldine.

Bradshaw, J. (1988). *Healing the shame that binds you.* Deerfield Beach, FL Health Communications.

Braithwaite, B. (1996). *School Engagement–Withdrawal Scale. Life at School Survey: Child questionnaire* (p. 11). Unpublished booklet.

Braithwaite, J. (1989). *Crime, shame and reintegration.* Cambridge: Cambridge University Press.

Braithwaite, J. (1991). Poverty, power, white-collar crime and the paradoxes of criminological theory. *Australian and New Zealand Journal of Criminology*, 24, 40–58.

Braithwaite, J. (1993). Shame and modernity. *British Journal of Criminology*, 33(1), 1–18.

Braithwaite, J. (1995). Inequality and republican criminology. In J. Hagan & R. Peterson (eds.), *Crime and Inequality.* Palo Alto, CA: Stanford University Press.

Braithwaite, J. (1996a). Shame and modernity. In D. Parker, R. Dalziell, & I. Wright (eds.), *Shame and the modern self.* Australian Scholarly Publishing, Australia.

Braithwaite, J. (1996b). *Reintegrative shaming.* Abridged from *Crime, shame and reintegration* (1989, pp. 69–83). Cambridge: Cambridge University Press.

Braithwaite, J. (1996c). *Restorative justice and a better future.* Paper presented at the Dorothy J. Killam Memorial Lectures, Dalhousie University.

Braithwaite, J. (1997). Charles Tittle's control balance and criminological theory. *Theoretical Criminology* 1(1), 77–97.

Braithwaite, J. (1998). Linking crime prevention to restorative justice. In T. Wachtel (ed.), *Conferencing: A new response to wrongdoing.* Pipersville, PA: Real Justice (*www.realjustice.org*).

Braithwaite, J. (1999a). Restorative justice: Assessing optimistic and pessimistic accounts. In M. Tonry (ed.), *Crime and Justice: A Review of Research*, vol. 25. Chicago, IL: University of Chicago Press, 1–127.

Braithwaite, J. (1999b). Institutionalising distrust, enculturating trust. In V. Braithwaite and M. Levi (eds.), *Trust and governance.* New York, NY: Russell Sage.

Braithwaite, J. (1999c). A future where punishment is marginalized: realistic or utopian? UCLA *Law Review*, 46(6): 1727–1750.

Braithwaite, J. (2001) *Restorative justice and responsive regulation.* New York: Oxford University Press.

Braithwaite, J., & Makkai, T. (1994). Trust and compliance. *Policing and Society*, 4, 1–12.

Braithwaite, J., & Mugford, S. (1994). Conditions of successful reintegration ceremonies: Dealing with juvenile offenders. *British Journal of Criminology*, 34(2), 139–171.

Braithwaite, J., & Parker, C. (1998). Restorative justice is republican justice. In L. Walgrave & G. Bazemore (eds.), *Restoring juvenile justice: An exploration of the restorative justice paradigm for reforming juvenile justice.* Monsey, NY: Criminal Justice Press.

Braithwaite, J., & Pettit, P. (1990). *Not just deserts: A republican theory of criminal justice.* Oxford: Oxford University Press.

Braithwaite, J., & Pettit, P. (2000). Republican and restorative justice: An explanatory and normative connection. In H. Strang & J. Braithwaite (eds.), *Restorative justice: from philosophy to practice.* Aldershot: Dartmouth.

Braithwaite, J. & Roche, D. (2000). Responsibility and restorative justice. In M. Schiff & G. Bazemore (eds.), *Restorative Community Justice: Repairing Harm and Transforming Communities.* Anderson Publishing, Cincinnati.

Braithwaite, V. (1987). The scale of emotional arousability: Bridging the gap between the neuroticism construct and its measurement. *Psychological Medicine*, 17, 217–225.

Braithwaite, V. (1998). The value balance model of political evaluations. *British Journal of Psychology*, 89(2), 223–247.

Braithwaite, V., Braithwaite, J. Gibson, D., & Makkai, T. (1994). Regulatory styles, motivational postures and nursing home compliance. *Law and Policy*, 16, 363–394.

Brehm, J. W. (1966). *A theory of psychological reactance.* New York, NY: Academic Press.

Brehm, S. S., & Brehm, J. W. (1981). *Psychological reactance: A theory of freedom and control.* New York, NY: Academic Press.

Brennan, G. (1999). Esteem and the variety of regulatory regimes. Unpublished paper, Social and Political Theory Program Australian National University, Canberra.

Bretherton, J., Fritz, J., Zahn-Waxler, C., & Ridgeway, D. (1986). Learning to talk about emotions: A functionalist perspective. *Child Development*, 57, 529–548.

Brody, G. H., & Shaffer, D. R. (1982). Contributions of parents and peers to children's moral socialization. *Developmental Review*, 2(1), 31–75.

Broucek, F. J. (1991). *Shame and the self.* New York, NY: Guilford Press.

Brown, R. (1990). *Group processes: Dynamics within and between groups.* Oxford: Basil Blackwell.

Browne, M. W., & Cudeck, R. (1993). Alternative ways of assessing model fit. In K. A. Bollen & J. S. Long (eds.), *Testing structural equation models* (pp. 136–162). Newbury Park, CA: Sage.

Brownell, A., & Shumaker, S. A. (1984). Social support: An introduction to a complex phenomenon. *Journal of Social Issues*, 40(4), 1–9.

Bryant, F. B., & Veroff, J. (1982). The structure of psychological well-being: A sociohistorical analysis. *Journal of Personality and Social Psychology*, 43(4), 653–673.

Burford, G., &. Pennell, J. (1998). *Family group decision making project: Outcome report*, I. St. John's: Memorial University, Newfoundland.

Buss, A. H. (1961). Stimulus generalization and aggressive verbal stimuli. *Journal of Experimental Psychology*, 61, 469–473.

Buss, A. H. (1966). *Psychopathology.* New York, NY: Wiley.

Buss, A. H. (1980). *Self-consciousness and social anxiety.* San Francisco, CA: Freeman.

Buss, A. H. & Plomin, R. (1975). *A temperament theory of personality development.* New York, NY: Wiley.

Buss, D. M. (1981). Predicting parent–child interactions from children's activity level. *Developmental Psychology*, 17, 59–65.

Byrne, B. M. (1994). *Structural equation modeling with EQS: Windows.* Thousand Oaks, CA: Sage.

Cacioppo, J. T., & Gardner, W. L. (1993). What underlies medical donor attitudes and behavior? *Health Psychology*, 12(4), 269–271.

Cacioppo, J. T., Gardner, W. L., & Berntson, G. G. (1997). Beyond bipolar conceptualizations and measures: The case of attitudes and evaluative space. *Personality and Social Psychology Review*, 1(1), 3–25.

Callaghan, S., & Joseph, S. (1995). Self-concept and peer victimization among school children. *Personality and Individual Differences*, 18(1), 161–163.

Caron, C., & Rutter, M. (1991). Comorbidity in child psychopathology: Concepts, issues and research strategies. *Journal of Child Psychology and Psychiatry*, 32, 1063–1080.

Cattell, R. B. (1966). The scree test for the number of factors. *Multivariate Behavioral Research*, 1, 245–276.

Chamlin, M., & Cochran, J. (1997). Social altruism and crime. *Criminology*, 35, 203–228.

Chapman, W. R. (1985). Parental attachment to the child and delinquent behavior. Paper to American Society of Criminology Meeting, San Diego.

Chazan, M. (1989). Bullying in the infant school. In D.P. Tattum & D.A. Lane (eds.), *Bullying in Schools*. London: Trentham Books.

Cheek, J. M., & Hogan, R. (1983). Self-concepts, self-presentations, and moral judgements. In J. Suls & A. G. Greenwald (eds.), *Psychological perspectives on the self* (Vol. 2). Hillsdale NJ: Erlbaum.

Chen, X., Dong, Q., & Zhou, H. (1997). Authoritative and authoritarian parenting practices and social school performance in Chinese children. *International Journal of Behavioral Development*, 21(4), 855–873.

Chiles A., Miller, M. L., & Cox, G. B. (1980). Depression in an adolescent delinquent population. *Archives of General Psychiatry*, 37, 1179–1184.

Christie, Nils (1995). *Crime control as industry: Towards Gulags, Western style?* London: Routledge.

Cicchetti, D. (1996). Regulatory processes [Special issue]. *Development and Psychopathology*, 8, 1–305.

Clake, E., & Mak, S. (1997). A systematic counselling approach to the problem of bullying. *Elementary School Guidance and Counselling*, 31(4), 310–325.

Clark, F. C. (1995). Anger and its disavowal in shame-based people. *Transactional Analysis Journal*, 25(2), 129–132.

Cohen, A. K. (1955). *Delinquent boys: The culture of the gang*. Glencoe, IL: Free Press.

Cohen, S., & Wills, T. A. (1985). Stress, social support, and the buffering hypothesis. *Psychological Bulletin*, 98, 310–357.

Coker, D. (1999). Enhancing autonomy for battered women: lessons from Navajo peacemaking. *UCLA Law Review*, 47(1), 1–111.

Compas, B. E., Howell, D. C., Phares, V., Williams, R. A., & Ledoux, S. (1989). Risk factors for emotional/behavioral problems in young adolescents: A prospective analysis of adolescent and parental stress and symptoms. *Journal of Consulting and Clinical Psychology*, 57(6), 732–740.

Connell, J. P. (1985). A new multidimensional measure of children's perceptions of control. *Child Development*, 56, 1018–1041.

Conte, J., & Berliner, L. (1988). The impact of sexual abuse on children: Empirical findings. In L. E. A. Walker (ed.), *Handbook on Sexual Abuse of Children: Assessments and Treatment Issues* (pp. 72–93). New York, NY: Springer.

Cooley, C. H. (1922). *Human nature and the social order*. New York, NY: Scribner's.

Coopersmith, S. (1967). *The antecedents of self-esteem*. San Francisco, CA: W. H. Freeman.

Costanzo, M., & Costanzo, S. (1992). Jury decision making in the capital penalty phase: Legal assumptions, empirical findings, and a research agenda. *Law and Human Behavior*, 16(2), 185–201.

Costello, C. G. (1993). *Symptoms of depression*. Wiley series on personality processes. New York, NY: John Wiley & Sons.

Craig, W. M. (1998). The relationship among bullying, victimization, depression, anxiety, and aggression in elementary school children. *Personality and Individual Differences*, 24(1), 123–130.

Creasey, G., Mitts, N., & Catanzaro, S. (1995). Associations among daily hassles, coping and behavior problems in nonreferred kindergarteners. *Journal of Clinical Child Psychology*, 24(3), 311–319.

Crick, N. R., Bigbee, M. A., & Howes, C. (1996). Gender differences in children's normative beliefs about aggression: How do I hurt thee? Let me count the ways. *Child Development*, 67, 1003–1014.

Cronbach, L. S. (1951). Coefficient alpha and the internal structure of tests. *Psychometrika*, 16, 297–334.

Crozier, W. R. (1990). Social psychological perspectives on shyness, embarrassment and shame. In W. R. Crozier (ed.), *Shyness and embarrassment: Perspectives from Social Psychology*. Cambridge: Cambridge University Press.

Cullen, F. T. (1994). Social support as an organizing concept for criminology: Presidential address to the Academy of Criminal Justice Sciences. *Justice Quarterly* 11(4), 527–559.

Cullen, F. T & Gendreau, P. (2000). Assessing correctional rehabilitation: Policy, practice, and prospects. In J. Horney (ed.), *Criminal Justice 2000* (vol. 3). *Policies, processes, and decisions in the Criminal Justice System*, Washington, DC: U.S.

Daly, K. (1999). *Revisiting the relationship between restorative and retributive justice*. Paper presented at the Restorative Justice and Civil Society Conference, Canberra, Australia.

Daly, K. (2000). *Ideals meet reality: research results on youth justice conferences in South Australia*. Paper to Fourth International Conference on Restorative Justice for Juveniles, Tuebingen.

Damon, W. (1989). *Child development today and tomorrow*. San Francisco, CA: Jossey-Bass

David, B., & Turner, J. C. (1996). Studies in self-categorization and minority conversion: Is being a member of the out-group an advantage? *British Journal of Social Psychology*, 35(1), 179–199.

Dawkins, J. (1995). Bullying in schools: Doctors' responsibilities. *British Medical Journal*, 310, 274–275.

De Rivera, J. (1984). The structure of emotional relationships. In P. Shaver (ed.), *Review of Personality and Social Psychology* (vol. 5). Emotions, relationships and health. Beverly Hills, CA: Sage.

Deci, E. L., Nezlek, J., & Sheinman, L. (1981). Characteristics of the rewarder and intrinsic motivation of the rewardee. *Journal of Personality and Social Psychology*, 40(1), 1–10.

Deci, E. L. & Ryan, R. M. (1980). The empirical exploration of intrinsic motivational processes. In L. Berkowitz (ed.), *Advances in Experimental Social Psychology*, (vol. 13). N.Y.: Academic Press.

Deng, X. & Jou, S. (2000). Shame and the moral educative effects on deviant behavior in cross-cultural context. Proceedings of Criminology Theory and its Applications in the Year 2000. National Taipei University. Taipei, Taiwan.

Denham, S., McKinley, M., Couchoud, E., & Holt, R. (1990). Emotional and behavioral predictors of preschool peer ratings. *Child Development*, 61, 1145–1152.

Denzin, N. K. (1988). Triangulation. In J. P. Keeve (ed.), *Educational Research, Methodology, and Measurement: An International Handbook*. Oxford: Pergamon Press.

Deutsch, M., & Gerard, H. B. (1955). A study of normative and informational social influences upon individual judgment. *Journal of Abnormal and Social Psychology*, 51, 629–636.

De-Viney, S. (1995). Life course, private pension, and financial well-being. *American Behavioral Scientist*, 39(2), 172–185.

Diener, E. (1984). Subjective well-being. *Psychological Bulletin*, 95(3), 542–575.

Diener, E., & Emmons, R. A. (1984). The independence of positive and negative affect. *Journal of Personality and Social Psychology*, 47(5), 1105–1117.

DiLillo, D. K., Long, P. J., & Russell, L. M. (1994). Childhood coping strategies of intrafamilial and extrafamilial female sexual abuse victims. *Journal of Child Sexual Abuse*, 3(2), 45–65.

Dodge, K. A., & Crick, N. R. (1990). Social information-processing bases of aggressive behavior in children. *Personality and Social Psychology Bulletin*, 16, 8–22.

Dodge, K. A., & Frame, C. (1982). Social cognitive biases and deficits in aggressive boys. *Child Development*, 53, 620–635.

Dodge, K. A., Pettit, G. S., McClaskey, C. L., & Brown, M. M. (1986). Social competence in children. *Monographs of the Society for Research in Child Development*, 51(2), 1–85.

Donovan, J. E., Jessor, R., & Costa, F. M. (1988). Syndrome of problem behavior in adolescence: A replication. *Journal of Consulting and Clinical Psychology*, 56(5), 762–765.

Dowden, C. & Andrews, D. A. (1999). What works for female offenders: A meta-analytic review. *Crime and delinquency*, 45(4), 438–452.

Dresler-Hawker, E. (1999) Unpublished PhD Dissertation, Psychology, Victoria University, Wellington.

Drummond, S. G. (1999). *Incorporating the familiar: An investigation into legal sensibilities in Nunavik*. Montreal and Kingston: McGill-Queen's University Press.

DuBois, D. L., Felner, R. D., Brand, S., Adan, A. M., & Evans, S. (1992). A prospective study of life stress, social support, and adaptation in early adolescence. *Child Development*, 63(3), 542–557.

Dubow, E. F., Tisak, J., Causey, D., Hryshko, A., & Reid, D. (1991). A two-year longitudinal study of stressful life events, social support, and social problem-solving skills: Contributions to children's behavioral and academic adjustment. *Child Development*, 62(3), 583–599.

Duff, R. A.(1986). *Trials and punishments*. Cambridge: Cambridge University Press.

Duff, R. A. (1996). Penal communications: Recent work in the philosophy of punishment. In M. Tonry (ed.), *Crime and justice: A review of research* (pp. 1–97). Chicago, IL: University of Chicago Press.

Duke, M. P., & Fenhagen, E. (1975). Self-parental alienation and locus of control in delinquent girls. *Journal of Genetic Psychology*, 127(1), 103–107.

Duval, S., & Wicklund, R. A. (1972). *A theory of objective self-awareness*. New York, NY: Academic Press.

Edelmann, R. J. (1987). *The psychology of embarrassment*. Chichester, UK: John Wiley and Sons.

Efron, B. (1979). Bootstrap methods: Another look at the jacknife. *Annals of Statistics*, 7, 1–26.

Eisenberg, N., Cialdini, R. B., McCreath, H., & Shell, R. (1987). Consistency-based compliance: When and why do children become vulnerable? *Journal of Personality and Social Psychology*, 52(6), 1174–1181.

Eisenberg, N., Fabes, R. A., Shepard, S. A., Murphy, B. C., Guthrie, I. K., Jones, S., Friedman, J., Poulin, R., & Maszk, P. (1997). Contemporaneous and longitudinal prediction of children's social functioning from regulation and emotionality. *Child Development*, 68(4), 642–664.

Eisenberg, N., & Miller, P. A. (1987). Empathy, sympathy, and altruism: Empirical and conceptual links. In N. Eisenberg & J. Strayer (eds.), *Empathy and its development. Cambridge studies in social and emotional development* (pp. 292–316). New York, NY: Cambridge University Press.

Eisenberg, N., & Mussen, P. H. (1989). *The roots of prosocial behavior in children*. Cambridge: Cambridge University Press.

Eisenberg, N., & Strayer, J. (1987). Critical issues in the study of empathy. In N. Eisenberg, & J. Strayer, (eds.), *Empathy and its development. Cambridge Studies in Social and Emotional Development* (pp. 3–13). New York, NY: Cambridge University Press.

Elias, N. (1994). *The civilizing process: The history of manners, and state formation and civilization* (trans. E. Jephcoft). Oxford: Blackwell.

Elkind, D., & Weiner, I. B. (1978). *Development of the child*. New York, NY: Wiley.

Elliot, A. J., & Devine, P. G. (1994). On the motivational nature of cognitive dissonance: Dissonance as psychological discomfort. *Journal of Personality and Social Psychology*, 67(3), 382–394.

Elliott, D.S. & Rinehart, M. (1995). *Moral disengagement, delinquent peers and delinquent behavior.* Unpublished manuscript, University of Colorado, Institute of Behavioral Science.

Elliott, M. (1991). *Bullying: A practical guide to coping for schools.* London: Longman.

Emler, N. & Reicher, S. (1995). *Adolescence and delinquency: the collective management of reputation.* Cambridge, Mass.: Blackwell.

English, F. (1994). Shame and social control revisited. *Transactional Analysis Journal*, 24(2), 109–120.

Epstein, A. L. (1984). *The experience of shame in Melanesia.* London: Royal Anthropological Institute of Great Britain and Ireland.

Erikson, K. T. (1962). Notes on the sociology of deviance. *Social Problems*, 9, 307–314.

Eron, L. D. (1987). The development of aggressive behavior from the perspective of a developing behaviorism. *American Psychologist*, 42, 435–442.

Eron, L. D., Huesmann, L. R., & Zelli, A. (1991). The role of parental variables in the learning of aggression. In D. J. Pepler & K. H. Rubin (eds.), *The development and treatment of childhood aggression* (pp. 169–188). Hillsdale, NJ: Erlbaum.

Eysenck, H. J. (1977). *Crime and personality* (3rd edn). London: Routledge and Kegan Paul.

Eysenck, H. J., & Eysenck, S. B. J. (1975). *Manual of the Eysenck Personality Questionnaire.* New York, NY: Hodder & Stoughton.

Eysenck, S. B. J. (1981). Impulsiveness and anti-social behavior in children. *Current Psychological Research*, 1, 31–37.

Eysenck, S. B. J., & Eysenck, H. J. (1977). The place of impulsiveness in a dimensional system of personality description. *British Journal of Social and Clinical Psychology*, 2, 46–55.

Eysenck, S. B. G., & Eysenck, H. J. (1978). Impulsiveness and venturesomeness: Their position in a dimensional system of personality description. *Psychological Reports*, 43, 1247–1255.

Eysenck, S. B. J., & McGurk, B. J. (1980). Impulsiveness and venturesomeness in a detention center population. *Psychological Reports*, 47, 1299–1306.

Farella, J. R. (1993). *The wind in a jar.* Albuquerque: University of New Mexico Press.

Farrington, D. P. (1973). Self-reports of deviant behavior: Predictive and stable? *Journal of Criminal Law and Criminology*, 64(1), 99–110.

Farrington, D. P. (1978). The family backgrounds of aggressive youths. In L. Hersov, M. Berger, & D. Shaffer (eds.), *Aggression and antisocial behavior in childhood and adolescence* (pp. 73–93). Oxford: Pergamon.

Farrington, D. P. (1993). Understanding and Preventing Bullying. In M. Tonry & N. Morris (eds.), *Crime and Justice*: vol. 17. University of Chicago Press.

Feldman, S. S., & Gehring, T. M. (1988). Changing perceptions of family cohesion and power across adolescence. *Child Development*, 59, 1034–1045.

Feldman, S. S., & Weinberg, D. A. (1994). Self-restraint as a mediator of family influences on boys' delinquent behavior: A longitudinal study. *Child Development*, 65, 195–211.

Feldman, S. S., Rosenthal, D. A., Mon-Reynaud, R., Leung, K., & Lau, S. (1991). Ain't misbehavin': Adolescent values and family environment as correlates of misconduct in Australia, Hong Kong and the United States. *Journal of Research on Adolescence*, 1(2), 109–134.

Feldman, S. S., Wentzel, K. R., & Gehring, T. M. (1989). A comparison of the views of mothers, fathers and preadolescents about family cohesion and power. *Journal of Family Psychology*, 3, 39–61.

Ferguson, T. J., & Rule, B. G. (1983). An attributional perspective on anger and aggression. In R. Geen & E. Donnerstein (eds.), *Aggression: Theoretical and empirical reviews*, 1 (pp. 41–74). New York, NY: Academic Press.

Ferguson, T. J., Stegge, H., & Damahuis, I. (1990). Guilt and shame experiences in elementary school-age children. In R.J. Takens (ed.), *European perspectives in psychology*, 1 (pp. 195–218). New York, NY: Wiley.

Feshbach, N. D. (1969). Sex differences in children's modes of aggressive responses towards outsiders. *Merrill Palmer Quarterly*, 15, (249–258).

Feshbach, N. D. (1974). The relationship of child rearing factors to children's aggression, empathy and related positive and negative social behavior. In J. de-Wit & W. W. Hartup (eds.), *Determinants and Origins of Aggressive Behavior* (pp. 427–436). The Hague: Mouton, New Babylon.

Feshbach, N. D. (1975). Empathy in children: Some theoretical and empirical considerations. *Counseling Psychologist*, 5(2), 25–30.

Feshbach, N. D., & Feshbach, S. (1972). Children's aggression. In W. W. Hartup (ed.), *The Young Child: Review of Research*, 2 (pp. 284–304). Washington, DC: National Association for the Education of Young Children.

Feshbach, N. D., & Feshbach, S. (1987). Affective processes and academic achievement. *Child Development* [Special Issue: Schools and development], 58(5), 1335–1347.

Feshbach, S. (1964). The function of aggression and the regulation of aggressive drive. *Psychological Review*, 71, 257–272.

Festinger, L. (1950). Informal social communication. *Psychological Review*, 57, 271–282.

Festinger, L., & Carlsmith, J. M. (1959). Cognitive consequences of forced compliance. *Journal of Abnormal and Social Psychology*, 58, 203–210.

Fishbein, M., & Ajzen, I. (1975). *Belief, attitude, intention, and behaviour: An introduction to theory and research*. Reading, US: Addison-Wesley.

Fletcher, A. C., Darling, N. E., Steinberg, L., & Dornbusch, S. M. (1995). The company they keep: Relation of adolescents' adjustment and behavior to their friends' perceptions of authoritative parenting in the social network. *Developmental Psychology*, 31(2), 300–310.

Fossum, M. A., & Mason, M. J. (1986). *Facing shame: Families in recovery*. New York, NY: Norton.

Foster, P., & Thompson, D. (1991). Bullying: Towards a non-violent sanctions policy. In P. K. Smith & D. Thompson (eds.), *Practical approaches to bullying*. London: David Fulton.

Fox, N. A. (1994). Dynamic cerebral processes underlying emotion regulation. *Monographs of the Society for Research in Child Development*, 59 (2–3), 152–283.

Freud, S. (1949/1930). *Civilization and its discontents*. London: Hogarth Press and Institute of Psycho-analysis.

Garber, J., & Dodge, K. A. (1991). *The development of emotion regulation and dysregulation*. Cambridge: Cambridge University Press.

Garfinkel, H. (1956). Conditions of successful degradation ceremonies. *American Journal of Sociology*, 61, 420–424.

Gartin, P. R. (1995). Dealing with design failures in randomised field experiments: Analytical issues regarding the evaluation of treatment effects. *Journal of Research in Crime and Delinquency*, 32(4), 425–445.

Gehring, T. M., & Feldman, S. S. (1988). Adolescents' perceptions of family cohesion and power: a methodological study of the Family System Test. *Journal of Adolescent Research*, 3, 39–61.

Gendreau, P. (1998). Keynote speech: what works in community corrections: promising approaches in reducing criminal behavior. In B.J. Auerbach and T.C. Castellano (eds.), *Successful community sanctions and services for special offenders*. Lanham, MD: American Correctional Association.

Gendreau, P., Goggin, C., & Cullen, F. T. (1999). *The ettects of prison sencences on recidivism. A report to the Corrections Research and Development and Aboriginal Policy Branch,* Solicitor General of Canada, Ottawa.

Gibbons, F. X. (1990). The evolution and manifestation of social anxiety. In W. R. Crozier (ed.), *Shyness and embarrassment: Perspectives from social psychology.* Cambridge: Cambridge University Press.

Gibbs, J. C. (1991). Sociomoral developmental delay and cognitive distortion: Implications for the treatment of antisocial youth. In W. M. Kurtinies & J. L. Gewirtz (eds.), *Handbook of moral behavior and development,* 3, (pp. 95–110). Hillsdale, NJ: Erlbaum.

Gilbert, P. (1989). *Human nature and suffering.* London: Erlbaum.

Gilbert, P. (1992). *Depression: The evaluation of powerlessness.* Hove: Erlbaum/New York, NY: Guilford.

Gilbert, P. (1997). The evolution of social attractiveness and its role in shame, humiliation, guilt and therapy. *British Journal of Medical Psychology,* 70, 113–147.

Goffman, E. (1959). *The presentation of the self in everyday life.* New York, NY: Anchor.

Goldberg, C. (1991). *Understanding shame and healing shame.* London: Jason Aronson.

Goldstein, M. D., & Strube, M. J. (1994). Independence revisited: The relationship between positive and negative affect in a naturalistic setting. *Personality and Social Psychology Bulletin,* 20, 57–64.

Gondolf, E. W. (1985). *Men who batter.* Holmes Beach, FL: Learning Publications.

Goodnow, J. J. (1988). Parents' ideas, actions, and feelings: Models and methods from developmental and social psychology. *Child Development,* 59(2), 286–320.

Goodnow, J. J. (1992). Parents' ideas, children's ideas: Correspondence and divergence. In I. E. Sigel, D. McGillicuddy, & V. Ann (eds.), *Parental Belief Systems: The psychological consequences for children* (2nd edn) (pp. 293–317). Hillsdale, NJ: Erlbaum.

Goodnow, J. J., & Collins, W. A. (1990). *Development according to parents: The nature, sources, and consequences of parents' ideas.* Hove, UK: Erlbaum.

Gordon, D., Nowicki, S., & Wichern, F. (1981). Observed maternal and child behaviors in a dependency producing task as a function of children's locus of control orientation. *Merrill Palmer Quarterly,* 27(1), 43–51.

Gorsuch, R. L. (1983). *Factor analysis.* Hillsdale, NJ: Erlbaum.

Graham, S. (1988). Children's developing understanding of the motivational role of affect: An attributional analysis. *Cognitive Development,* 3(1), 71–88.

Graham, S., Doubleday, C., & Guarino, P. A. (1984). The development of relations between perceived controllability and the emotions pity, anger and guilt. *Child Development,* 55, 561–565.

Graham, S. & Juvonen, J. (1998). Self-blame and peer victimization in middle school: An attributional analysis. *Developmental Psychology,* 34(3), 587–538.

Graham, S., & Weiner, G. (1986). From an attributional theory of emotion to developmental psychology: A roundtrip ticket? *Social Cognition,* 4, 152–179.

Grasmick, H. G., & Bursik, R. J. (1990). Conscience, significant others, and rational choice: Extending the deterrence model. *Law and Society Review,* 24(3), 837–861.

Grasmick, H. G., Bursik, R. J. & Kinsey, K. A. (1991). Shame and embarrassment as deterrents to noncompliance with the law: The case of an antilittering campaign. *Environment and Behavior,* 23(2), 233–251.

Green, D. R., & Lawrenz, M. (1994). *Encountering shame and guilt: A short-term structured model.* Grand Rapids, USA: Baker Books.

Greenbaum, S. (1987). What can we do about schoolyard bullying? *Principal*, 67(2), 21–24.

Greenbaum, S., Brenda T., & Roland, D. S. (1989). *Set straight on bullies*. Mailbu, CA: National School Safety.

Greenberg, M. T., Siegel, J. M., & Leitch, C. J. (1983). The nature and importance of attachment relationships to parents and peers during adolescence. *Journal of Youth and Adolescence*, 12, 373–386.

Grolnick, W. S., Deci, E. L., & Ryan, R. M. (1991). Inner resources for school achievement: Motivational mediators of children's perceptions of their parents. *Journal of Educational Psychology*, 83, 508–517.

Groube, M. (1987). *Control in adolescent stress and coping*. Unpublished dissertation. The Australian National University, Canberra.

Grusec, J. E. (1982). *The socialization of altruism*. In N. Eisenberg (ed.), The development of prosocial behavior (pp. 139–165). New York, NY: Academic Press.

Grusec, J. E., & Goodnow, J. J. (1994). Impact of parental discipline methods on the child's internalization of values: A reconceptualization of current points of view. *Developmental Psychology*, 30(1), 4–19.

Grusec, J. E., & Kuczynski, L. (1980). Direction of effect in socialization: A comparison of the parent's versus the child's behavior as determinants of disciplinary techniques. *Developmental Psychology*, 16(1), 1–9.

Grusec, J. E., & Kuczynski, L. (1997). *Parenting and children's internalization of values: A Handbook of contemporary theory*. Toronto: John Wiley & Sons.

Hagan, J., & McCarthy, B. (1997). *Mean streets: Youth crime and homelessness*. Cambridge: Cambridge University Press.

Hale, R. (1993) The role of embarrassment in serial murder. Unpublished paper, Dept of Sociology, Mississippi State University.

Hamilton, V. L. & Sanders, J. (1992). *Everyday justice*. New Haven, CT: Yale University Press.

Harder, D. W. (1995). Shame and guilt assessment, and relationships of shame- and guilt-proneness to psychopathology. In J. P. Tangney & K. W. Fischer (eds.), *Self conscious emotions: The psychology of shame, guilt, embarrassment, and pride* (pp. 368–392). New York, NY: Guilford Press.

Harder, D. W., & Lewis, S. J. (1986). The assessment of shame and guilt. In J. N. Butcher & C. D. Spielberger (eds.), *Advances in personality assessment*, vol. 6 (pp. 89–114). Hillside, NJ: Erlbaum.

Harré, R. (1990). Embarrassment: A conceptual analysis. In W. R. Crozier (ed.), *Shyness and embarrassment: Perspectives from social psychology*. Cambridge: Cambridge University Press.

Harris, N. (1999). Shaming and shame: An empirical analysis. Unpublished PhD dissertation, RSSS, Australian National University, Canberra.

Harris, N., & Burton, J. B. (1997). *The reliability of observed reintegrative shaming, shame, defiance and other key concepts in diversionary conferences* (5). Canberra: Australian National University.

Harris, N., & Burton, J. B. (1998). Testing the reliability of observational measures of reintegrative shaming at community accountability conferences and at court. *Australian and New Zealand Journal of Criminology*, 31, 230–241.

Hastings, T. L., Anderson, S. J., & Kelly, M. L. (1996). Gender differences in coping and daily stress in conduct-disorder and non-conduct-disordered adolescents. *Journal of Psychopathology and Behavioral Assessment*, 18(3), 213–226.

Havlicek, L. L., & Peterson, N. L. (1977). Effects of the violation of assumptions upon significance levels of the Pearson r. *Psychological Bulletin*, 84, 373–377.

Hay, C. (2001). An exploratory test of Braithwaite's reintegrative shaming theory. *Journal of Research in Crime and Delinquency*, 38(2).

Hazler, R. J., Hoover, J. H., & Oliver, R. (1991). Student perceptions of victimization by bullies in *school. Journal of Humanistic Education and Development*, 29, 143–150.

Heckhausen, H. (1984). Emergent achievement behavior: Some early developments. In J. Nicholls (ed.), *The development of achievement motivation* (pp.1–32). Greenwich, CT: JAI Press.

Heinmann, P. P. (1972). *Mobbing*. Gruppvald bland barn ochvuxna. Stockholm: Natur och kultur.

Heller, A. (1982). *The power of shame*. London: Routledge and Kegan Paul.

Herman J. L. (1992) *Trauma and recovery: The aftermath of violence – from domestic abuse to political terror*. New York, NY: Basic Books.

Hetherington, E. M., & Martin, B. (1979). Family interaction. In H.C. Quay & J. C. Werry (eds.), *Psychopathological disorders* of childhood. New York, NY: Wiley.

Hetherington, E. M., & Parke, R. D. (1979). *Child psychology: A contemporary viewpoint* (2nd edn). New York, NY: McGraw-Hill.

Hinde, R. A., Tamplin, A., & Barrett, J. (1993). Home correlates of aggression in preschool. *Aggressive Behavior*, 19, 85–105.

Hirshfeld, R., & Blumenthal, S. (1986). Personality, life events and other psychological factors in adolescent depression and suicide. In G. Klerman (ed.), *Suicide and depression among adolescents and young adults* (pp. 215–255). Washington, DC: American Psychiatric Press.

Hoblitzelle, W. (1987). Differentiating and measuring shame and guilt: The relation between shame and depression. In H. B. Lewis (ed.), *The role of shame in symptom formation* (pp. 207–235). Hillsdale, NJ: Erlbaum.

Hobsbawm, E. J. (1996). *The age of extremes: a history of the world, 1914–1991*. New York, NY: Vintage.

Hodgens, J. B., & McCoy, J. F. (1989). Distinctions among rejected children on the basis of peer-nominated aggression. *Journal of Clinical Child Psychology*, 18, 121–128.

Hoffman, M. L. (1963a). Childrearing practices and moral development: Generalizations from empirical research. *Child Development*, 34(2), 295–318.

Hoffman, M. L. (1963b). Personality, family structure, and social class as antecedents of parental power assertion. *Child Development*, 34(4), 869–884.

Hoffman, M. L. (1970). Moral development. In P. H. Mussen (ed.), *Carmichael's manual of child psychology*, vol. 2. New York, NY: Wiley.

Hoffman, M. L. (1975). Altruistic behavior and the parent child relationship. *Journal of Personality and Social Psychology*, 11, 937–943.

Hoffman, M. L. (1982). Affect and moral development. *New Directions for Child Development*, 16, 83–103.

Hoffman, M. L. (1983). Affective and cognitive processes in moral internalization. In E. T. Higgins, D. N. Rubble & W. W. Hartup (eds.), *Social cognition and social development*. New York: Cambridge University Press.

Hoffman, M. L. (1994). Discipline and internalization. *Developmental Psychology*, 30(1), 26–28.

Hogg, M. A., & Turner, J. C. (1987). Social identity and conformity: A theory of referent information influence. In W. Doise, S. Moscovici et al. (eds.), *Current issues in European social psychology*, Vol. 2 (pp. 139–182). Cambridge: Cambridge University Press.

Hoglund, C. L., & Nicholas, K. B. (1995). Shame, guilt, and anger in college students exposed to abusive family environments. *Journal of Family Violence*, 10(2), 141–157.

Hoover, J. H., & Hazler, R. J. (1991). Bullies and victims. *Elementary School Guidance and Counseling*, 25(3), 212–219.

Hoover, J. H., Oliver, R., & Hazler, R. J. (1992). Bullying: Perceptions of adolescent victims in the Midwestern USA. *School Psychology International*, 13(1), 5–16.

Horne, A. M., & Socherman, R. (1996). Profile of a bully: Who would do such a thing? *Educational Horizons*, 7782.

Hoyle, R. H., & Panter, A. T. (1995). Writing about structural equation models. In R. H. Hoyle (ed.), *Structural Equation Modeling: Concepts, Issues, and Applications* (pp. 158–176). Thousand Oaks, CA: Sage.

Hultberg, P. (1988). Shame: A hidden emotion. *Journal of Analytical Psychology*, 33(2), 109–126.

Huntley, S. (1995). The socialization of pride, shame and guilt. Unpublished Honours thesis. The Australian National University, Canberra.

Hyndman, M., Thorsborne, M., & Wood, S. (1996). *Community accountability conferencing: Trial report*. Department of Education, Queensland.

Inkpen, N. (1999) Reintegrative shaming through collective conscience building. Unpublished PhD dissertation, Sociology, The Australian National University, Canberra.

Izard, C. E. (1977). *Human emotions*. New York: Plenum Press.

Jacobson, R. H., Lahey, B. B., & Strauss, C. C. (1983). Correlations of depressed mood in normal children. *Journal of Abnormal Child Psychology*, 11, 29–40.

Jankowski, M. S. (1991). *Islands in the street: Gangs and American urban society*. Berkeley, CA: University of California Press.

Janoff-Bulman, R. (1979). Characterological versus behavioral self-blame: Inquiries into depression and rape. *Journal of Personality and Social Psychology*, 37(10), 1798–1809.

Janoff-Bulman, R. (1992). Shattered assumptions: Towards a new psychology of trauma. New York, NY: The Free Press.

Janssens, J. M. A. M., & Dekovic, M. (1997). Child rearing, prosocial moral reasoning and prosocial behavior. *International Journal of Behavioral Development*, 20(3), 509–527.

Jenkins, A. (1990). *Invitations to responsibility: The therapeutic engagement of men who are violent and abusive*. Adelaide: Dulwich Centre Publications.

Jenkins, A. (1991). Intervention with violence and abuse in families: The inadvertent perpetuation of irresponsible behavior. *Australian and New Zealand Journal of Family Therapy*, 12(4), 186–195.

Jenkins, A. (1997). The role of managerial self-efficacy in corporate compliance with regulatory standards. Unpublished PhD dissertation, The Australian National University, Canberra.

Jenkins, P. H. (1997). School delinquency and the school social bond. *Journal of research in crime and delinquency*, 34(3), 337–367.

Jensen, G. F., & Eve, R. (1976). Sex differences in delinquency: An examination of popular sociological explanations. *Criminology*, 13, 427–448.

Johnson, R. E. (1979). *Juvenile delinquency and its origin*. Cambridge: Cambridge University Press.

Johnson, T. R. (1995). The significance of religion for aging well. *American Behavioral Scientist*, 39(2), 186–208.

Jones, W. H., Kugler, K., & Adams, P. (1995). You always hurt the one you love: Guilt and transgressions against relationship partners. In J. P. Tangney & K. W. Fischer (eds.), *Self conscious emotions: The psychology of shame, guilt, embarrassment, and pride* (pp. 301–321). New York, NY: Guilford Press.

Jordan, J. (1997). Relational development: Therapeutic implications of empathy and shame. In J. V. Jordan et al. (eds.), *Women's growth in diversity: More writings from the Stone Center* (pp. 138–161). New York, NY: Guilford Press.

Jöreskog, K. G., & Sörbom, D. (1989). *LISREL–7 user's reference guide*. Mooresville, Indiana: Scientific Software.

Josephson, E., & Rosen, M. (1978). Panel loss in a high school study. In D. Kandel (ed.), *Longitudinal research on drug use: empirical findings and empirical issues*. Washington, DC: Hemisphere-Wiley.

Jou, S. (1995) Deterrent effects of formal and informal social controls on delinquency. *Journal of Criminology* (Chinese Association of Criminology, Taipei). 1995(1): 31–50.

Junger, M. (1990). Intergroup bullying and racial harassment in the Netherlands. *Sociology and Social Research*, 74, 65–72.

Kahan, D. M. (1996). What do alternative sanctions mean? *University of Chicago Law Review*, 63, 591–653.

Kahan, D. M. (1998). The anatomy of disgust in criminal law. *Michigan Law Review*, 69(6), 1621–1657.

Kanner, A. D., Coyne, J. C., Schaefer, C., & Lazarus, R. S. (1981). Comparison of two modes of stress management: Daily hassles and uplifts versus major life events. *Journal of Behavioral Medicine*, 4, 1–10.

Kaplan, H. B., Robbins, C., & Martin, S. S. (1983). Toward the testing of a general theory of deviant behavior in longitudinal perspective: Patterns of psychopathology. *Research in Community and Mental Health*, 3, 27–65.

Katz, J. (1988). *Seductions to crime*. New York, NY: Basic Books.

Kaufman, G. (1989). *The psychology of shame: Theory and treatment of shame-based syndromes* (1st edn). New York, NY: Springer.

Kaufman, G. (1996). *The psychology of shame: Theory and treatment of shame-based syndromes* (2nd edn). New York, NY: Springer.

Kelley, H. H. (1952). The two functions of reference groups. In G. E. Swanson, T. M. Newcomb, & E. L. Hartley (eds.), *Readings in social psychology* (revised edn, pp. 410–414). New York, NY: Holt.

Kelman, H. C. (1958). Compliance, identification and internalization: Three processes of attitude change. *Journal of Conflict Resolution*, 2, 51–60.

Kiesler, C. A., & Pallak, M. S. (1976). Arousal properties of dissonance manipulations. *Psychological Bulletin*, 83(6), 1014–1025.

Kikkawa, M. (1987). Teachers' opinions and treatments for bully/victim problems among students in junior and senior high schools: Results of a fact-finding survey. *Journal of Human Development*, 23, 25–30.

Kinston, W. (1984). The shame of narcissism. In D. L. Nathanson et al. (eds.), *The Many Faces of Shame* (pp. 214–245). New York, NY: Guilford Press.

Kipnis, D. (1968). Studies in character structure. *Journal of Personality and Social Psychology*, 8(3), 217–227.

Kirk, R. E. (1982). *Experimental design: Procedures for the behavioral sciences* (2nd edn). Pacific Grove, CA: Brooks/Cole.

Kirschner, D. (1992). Understanding adoptees who kill: Dissociation, patricide, and the psychodynamics of adoption. *International Journal of Offender Therapy and Comparative Criminology*, 36, 323–333.

Kitayama, S., Markus, H. R., & Matsumoto, H. (1995). Culture, self, and emotion: A cultural perspective on 'self-conscious' emotions. In J. P. Tangney & K. W. Fischer (eds.), *Self-conscious emotions: The psychology of shame, guilt, embarrassment, and pride* (pp. 439–464). New York, NY: Guilford Press.

Kochanska G., & Murray, K. (1992). *Temperament and conscience development.* Paper presented at the Ninth Occasional Temperament Conference, Bloomington, Indiana, October 29–31.

Kochanska, G. (1991). Socialization and temperament in the development of guilt and conscience. *Child Development,* 62, 1379–1392.

Kochanska, G., Kuczynski, L., & Radke-Yarrow, M. (1989). Correspondence between mothers' self-reported and observed child-rearing practices. *Child Development,* 60, 56–63.

Kochenderfer, B. J., & Ladd, G. W. (1996a). Peer victimization: Cause or consequence of school maladjustment? *Child Development,* 67(4), 1305–1317.

Kochenderfer, B. J., & Ladd, G. W. (1996b). Peer victimization: Manifestations and relations to school adjustment in kindergarten. *Journal of School Psychology,* 34, 267–283.

Koh, A. C. E. (1997). *The delinquent peer group: Social identity and self-categorization perspectives.* Unpublished PhD dissertation, The Australian National University, Canberra.

Kohut, H. E. (1971). *Thoughts on narcissism and narcissistic rage: The search for the self.* New York, NY: International University Press.

Kovacs, M., Paulauskas, S., Gatsonis, C., & Richards, C. (1988). Depressive disorders in childhood: III. A longitudinal study of comorbidity with and risk for conduct disorders. *Journal of Affective Disorders,* 15, 205–217.

Krain, M. A. (1995). Policy implications for a society aging well: Employment, retirement, education, & leisure policies for the 21st century. *American Behavioral Scientist,* 39(2), 131–151.

Krohne, H. W. (1993). Attention and avoidance: Two central strategies in coping with aversiveness. In H. W. Krohne (ed.), *Attention and avoidance: Strategies in coping with aversiveness,* (pp. 3–50). Seattle, WA: Hogrefe & Huber.

Kuczynski, L., & Kochanska, G. (1990). Development of children's noncompliance strategies from toddlerhood to age 5. *Developmental Psychology,* 26(3), 398–408.

Kuczynski, L., Zahn-Waxler, C. & Radke-Yarrow, M. (1987). Development and content of imitation in the second and third years of life: A socialization perspective. *Developmental Psychology,* 23(2), 276–282.

Kwak, K. & Bandura, A. (1998). Role of perceived self-efficacy and moral disengagement in antisocial conduct. Unpublished manuscript, Osan College, Seoul, South Korea.

LaFree, G. (1998). *Losing legitimacy: Street crime and the decline of social institutions in America.* Westview Press, Cumnor Hill, Oxford.

Lagerspetz, K. M. J., Bjorkquist, K., Berts, M., & King, E. (1982). Group aggression among school children in three schools. *Scandinavian Journal of Psychology,* 23, 45–52.

Landman, J. (1993). *Regret: The persistence of the possible.* New York, NY: Oxford University Press.

Landy, S., & Peters, R. D. V. (1992). Toward an understanding of a developmental paradigm for aggressive conduct problems during the pre-school years. In R. DeV. Peters, R. J. McMahon & V. L. Quinsey (eds.), *Aggression and Violence Throughout the Lifespan* (pp. 1–30). Newbury Park, CA: Sage Publications.

Lane, D. A. (1989). Bullying in school: The need for an integrated approach. *School Psychology International,* 10, 211–215.

Lansky, M. R. (1981). Treatment of the narcissistically vulnerable couple. In M. R. Lansky (ed.), *Family therapy and major psychopathology.* New York, NY: Grune & Stratton.

Lansky, M. R. (1987). Shame and domestic violence. In D. Nathanson (ed.), *The Many Faces of Shame* (pp. 335–362). New York, NY: Guildford Press.

Lansky, M. R. (1992). *Fathers who fail: Shame and psychopathology in the family system.* London: Hillsdale/The Analytic Press.

Lansky, M. R. (1994). Shame: Contemporary psychoanalytic perspectives. *Journal of the American Academy of Psychoanalysis*, 22(3), 433–441.

Lansky, M. R. (1995). Shame and the scope of psychoanalytic understanding. *American Behavioral Scientist*, 38(8), 1076–1090.

Lau, S., & Leung, K. (1992). Self-concept, delinquency, relations with parents and school and chinese adolescents' perceptions of personal control. *Personality and Individual Differences*, 13(5), 615–622.

Lazarus, R. (1991). *Emotion and adaptation*. New York, NY: Oxford University Press.

Lazarus, R. S., DeLongis, A., Folkman, S., & Gruen, R. (1985). Stress and adaptational outcomes: The problem of confounded measures. *American Psychologist*, 40(7), 770.

Lazarus, R. S. (1993). Coping theory and research: Past, present and future. *Psychosomatic Medicine*, 55, 234–247.

Leahy, R. L. (1981). Parental practices and the development of moral judgment and self-image disparity during adolescence. *Developmental Psychology*, 17(5), 580–594.

Leary, M. R. (2000). Affect, cognition, and the social emotions. In J. P. Forgas (ed.), *Feeling and thinking: The role of affect in social cognition*. Cambridge: Cambridge University Press.

Leary, M. R., & Downs, D. L. (1995). Interpersonal functions of the self-esteem motive: The self-esteem system as a sociometer. In M. H. Kernis (ed.), *Efficacy, agency, and self esteem: Plenum series in social/clinical psychology* (pp. 123–144). New York, NY: Plenum Press.

Lebra, T. S. (1983). Shame and guilt: A psychocultural view of the Japanese self. *Ethos*, 11(3), 192–209.

Lee, R.G., & Wheeler, G. (1996). *The voice of shame: Silence and connection in psychotherapy*. San Francisco, CA: Jossey-Bass.

Lempers, J. D., Clark-Lampers, D., & Simons, R. D. (1989). Economic hardship, parenting and distress in adolescence. *Child Development*, 60, 25–39.

Lepper, M.R. & Greene, D. (1978). *The hidden costs of reward*. Hillsdale, NJ: Erlbaum.

Levi, M. (1988). *Of rule and revenue*. Berkeley, CA: University of California Press.

Levin, J., & McDevitt, J. (1993). *Hate crimes: The rising tide of bigotry and bloodshed*. New York, NY: Plenum Press.

Lewis, H. B. (1971). *Shame and guilt in neurosis*. New York, NY: International University Press.

Lewis, H. B. (1976). *Psychic war in men and women*. New York, NY: New York University Press.

Lewis, H. B. (1987a). Shame and the narcissistic personality. In D.L. Nathanson (ed.). *The many faces of shame* (pp. 93–132). New York, NY: Guilford Press.

Lewis, H. B. (1987b). *The role of shame in symptom formation*. Hillsdale, NJ: Erlbaum.

Lewis, H. B. (1995). Shame, repression, field dependence and psychopathology. In J. L. Singer (ed.), *Repression and dissociation: Implication for personality theory, psychopathology and health*. The John D. and Catherine T. MacArthur Foundation series on mental health and development. (pp. 233–257). Chicago, IL: University of Chicago Press.

Lewis, M. (1992). *Shame: The exposed self*. New York, NY: Free Press.

Lindsay-Hartz, J. (1984). Contrasting experiences of shame and guilt. *American Behavioral Scientist*, 27, 689–704.

Lindsay-Hartz, J., De Rivera, J., & Mascolo, M. F. (1995). Differentiating guilt and shame and their effects on motivation. In J. P. Tangney & K. W. Fischer (eds.), *Self-conscious emotions: The psychology of shame, guilt, embarrassment, and pride* (pp. 274–300). New York, NY: Guilford Press.

Lipsey, M. W. (1995) What do we learn from 400 research studies on the effectiveness of treatment with juvenile delinquents? In J. McGuire (ed.), *What works: reducing reoffending – guidelines from research and practice*. Chichester, UK: Wiley, pp. 63–78.

Loeber, R. (1990). Development and risk factors of juvenile antisocial behavior and delinquency. *Clinical Psychology Review*, 10, 1–41.

Losel, F. (1995). The efficacy of correctional treatment: a review and synthesis of meta-evaluations. In J. McGuire (ed.), *What works: reducing reoffending – guidelines from research and practice*. Chichester, UK: Wiley.

Lowenstein, L. F. (1978). Who is the bully? *Bulletin of the British Psychological Society*, 31, 147–149.

Lu, H. (1998). Community policing – rhetoric or reality? The contemporary Chinese community-based policing system in Shanghai. DAI, Humanities and Social Sciences, 59(3).

Lu, H. (1999). Sang jiao and reintegrative shaming in China's urban neighborhoods. *International Journal of Comparative and Applied Criminal Justice*. 23(1): 115–125.

Lueptow, L., Muller, S., Hammes, R., & Master, L. (1977). The impact of informed consent regulations on response rate and response bias. *Sociological Methods and Research*, 6, 183–204.

Lynd, H. M. (1958). *On shame and the search for identity*. New York, NY: Harcourt, Brace, and World.

Lytton, H. (1979). Disciplinary encounters between young boys and their mothers and fathers: Is there a contingency system? *Developmental Psychology*, 15, 256–268.

Lytton, H. (1990). Child and parent effects in boys' conduct disorder: A reinterpretation. *Developmental Psychology*, 26(5), 683–697.

Maccoby, E., & Martin, J. (1983). Socialization in the context of the family: Parent–child interaction. In E. M. Hetherington (ed.), *Handbook of Child Psychology: vol. 4. Socialization, Personality, and Social Development* (pp. 1–101). New York, NY: Wiley.

MacDonald, J. M. (1975). *Armed robbery: Offenders and their victims*. Springfield, IL: Charles C. Thomas.

McGarrell, E. F., Olivares, K., Crawford, K.& Kroovand, N. (2000). *Returning justice to the community: The Indianapolis juvenile restorative justice experiment*. Indianapolis, IN: Hudson Institute.

Mackay, R. E. (1992). The resuscitation of assythement? Reparation and the Scottish criminal. *Juridical Review*, 3, 242–255.

Mackie, D. M. (1986). Social identification effects in group polarization. *Journal of Personality and Social Psychology*, 50(4), 720–728.

Magnusson, D. (1987). Adult delinquency in the light of conduct and physiology at an early age: A longitudinal study. In D. Magnusson & A. Oehman (eds.), *Psychopathology: An interactional perspective. Personality, psychopathology, and psychotherapy* (pp. 221–234). Orlando, FL: Academic Press.

Maines, B., & Robinson, G. (1998). The no blame approach to bullying. In D. Shorrocks-Taylor (ed.), *Directions in educational psychology* (pp. 281–295). London: Whurr Publishers.

Makkai, T., & Braithwaite, J. (1994). Reintegrative shaming and compliance with regulatory standards. *Criminology*, 32, 361–385.

Makkai, T., & Braithwaite, J. (1996). Procedural justice and regulatory compliance. *Law and Human Behavior*, 20(1):83–98.

Makkai, T. & Braithwaite, J. (1991). Criminological theories and regulatory compliance. *Criminology*, 29(2), 191–220.

Makkai, T. & Braithwaite, J. (1993). Praise, pride and corporate compliance. *International Journal of the Sociology of Law*, 21, 73–91.

Malatesta, C. Z., & Wilson, A. (1988). Emotion cognition interaction in personality development: A discrete emotions, functionalist analysis. *British Journal of Social Psychology*, 27, 91–112.

Mann, D. W. (1997). Victims from a sense of shame. *Contemporary Psychoanalysis*, 33(1), 123–132.

Manning, M., Heron, J., & Marshall, T. (1978). Styles of hostility and socialinteractions at nursery, at school and at home: an extended study of children. In L. A. Hersov, M. Berger, & D. Shaffer (eds.), *Aggression and Antisocial Behavior in Childhood and Adolescence* (pp. 29–58). Oxford: Pergamon.

Maruna, S. (2001). *Making good: How ex-convicts reform and rebuild their lives*. Washington, DC: American Psychological Association.

Massaro, T. M. (1997). The meanings of shame: Implications for legal reform. *Psychology, Public Policy, and Law*, 3(4), 645–704.

Matza, D. (1964). *Delinquency and drift*. New York, NY: Wiley.

Maxwell, G. M. & Morris, A. (1993). *Family, victims and culture: Youth justice in New Zealand*. Wellington: Social Policy Agency and Institute of Criminology, Victoria University of Wellington.

Maxwell, G. M. & Morris, A. (1999). *Reducing reoffending*. Wellington: Institute of Criminology, Victoria University of Wellington.

Maxwell, G. M., Allison, M., & Anderson, T. (1999). *Community Panel Adult Pre-Trial Diversion: Supplementary Evaluation*. Research Report, Crime Prevention Unit, Department of Prime Minister and Cabinet and Institute of Criminology, Victoria University of Wellington, New Zealand.

McBurnett, K., Lahey, B. B., Frick, P. J., Risch, C., Loeber, R., Hart, E. L., Christ, M. A. G., & Hanson, K. S. (1991). Anxiety, inhibition, and conduct disorder in children: II. Relation to salivary cortisol. *Journal of the American Academy of Child and Adolescent Psychiatry*, 30, 197–201.

McCold, P. (1997). Restorative justice: Variations on a theme. Paper presented at the Restorative Justice for Juveniles – Potentialities, Risks and Problems for Research, Leuven, Belgium, 12–14 May.

McCormick, A. (1999). Restorative justice in a Northern Canadian community: The potential of sentencing circles to address issues associated with youth crime through community building. Paper presented to American Society of Criminology meeting, Toronto.

McCubbin, H. I., & Patterson, J. M. (1982). Family adaptation to crises. In H. I. McCubbin, A. E. Cauble & J. M. Patterson (eds.), *Family stress, coping and social support* (pp. 26–47). Springfield, IL: Charles C. Thomas.

McDonald, J. M., Moore, D. B., O'Connell, T. A., & Thorsborne, M. (1995). *Real Justice training manual: Coordinating family group conferences*. Pennsylvania, PA: Pipers Press.

McDonald, J. M., O'Connell, T. A., Moore, D. B., & Bransbury, E. (1994). *Convening family conferences: Training manual*. New South Wales Police Academy.

McFadden, J. (1986). Bullies and victims. *Primary Education*. Sept/Oct. 25–26.

Mead, M. (1937). *Cooperation and competition among primative peoples*. New York, NY: McGraw-Hill.

Mehrabian, A., & Epstein, N. (1972). A measure of emotional empathy. *Journal of Personality*, 40(4), 525–543.

Mellor, A. (1990). *Bullying in Scottish secondary schools*. Edinburgh: Scottish Council for Research in Education.

Melton, A. P. (1995). Indigenous justice systems and tribal society. *Judicature*, 79, 126–133.

Milan, M. A. (1990). Antisocial personality disorder in adulthood. In M. Hersen & C. Last

(eds.), *Handbook of child and adult psychopathology: A longitudinal perspective*. Pergamon general psychology series (vol. 161; pp. 307–321). New York, NY: Pergamon.

Miller, P. A., & Eisenberg, N. (1988). The relation of empathy to aggressive and externalizing/antisocial behavior. *Psychological Bulletin*, 103(3), 324–344.

Miller, R. S. (1995). Embarrassment and social behavior. In J. P. Tangney & K. W. Fischer (eds.), *Self-conscious emotions: The psychology of shame, guilt, embarrassment, and pride*. New York, NY: Guilford Press.

Miller, R. S., & Tangney, J. P. (1994). Differentiating embarrassment and shame. *Journal of Social and Clinical Psychology*, 13(3), 273–287.

Miller, S. (1985). *The shame experience*. Hillsdale, NJ: Erlbaum.

Miyake, K., & Yamazaki, K. (1995). Self-conscious emotions, child rearing, and child psychopathology in Japanese culture. In J. P. Tangney & K. W. Fischer (eds.), *Self-conscious emotions: The psychology of shame, guilt, embarrassment, and pride*. New York, NY: Guilford Press.

Moffitt, T. E. (1993). Adolescence-limited and life-course-persistent antisocial behavior: A developmental taxonomy. *Psychological Review*, 100, 674–701.

Mooney, A., Creeser, R., & Blatchford, P. (1991). Children's views on teasing and fighting in junior schools. *Educational Research*, 33, 103–12.

Moore, D., & Forsythe, L. (1995). *A new approach to juvenile justice: An evaluation of family conferencing in Wagga Wagga*. Wagga Wagga: Juvenile Justice, The Centre for Rural Research.

Moore, D. & McDonald, J. (2001). Community conferencing as a spiral case of conflict resolution. In H. Strang and J. Braithwaite (eds.). *Restorative Justice and Civil Society*. Melbourne: Cambridge University Press.

Moran, S., Smith, P. K., Thompson, D., & Whitney, I. (1993). Ethnic differences in experiences of bullying: Asian and white children. *British Journal of Educational Psychology*, 63, 431–440.

Morgan, A. (1995). Taking responsibility: Working with teasing and bullying in schools. *Schooling and Education* (Dulwich Centre Newsletter), 2–3, 16–27.

Morris, R. (1995). Not Enough! *Mediation-Quarterly*, 12(3), 285–291.

Morrison, A. P. (1986). Shame, ideal self, and narcissism. In A.P. Morrison (ed.), *Essential Papers on Narcissism* (pp. 348–371). New York, NY: New York University Press.

Morrison, A. P. (1987). The role of shame in schizophrenia. In H. B. Lewis (ed.), *The role of shame in symptom formation*. Hillsdale, NJ: Erlbaum.

Morrison, A. P. (1989). *Shame: The underside of narcissism*. Hillsdale, NJ: Analytic Press.

Morrison, B. (forthcoming). *Conflict resolution through restorative justice: A learning unit to address bullying in primary schools*.

Moscovici, S. (1976). *Social influence and social change*. London: Academic Press.

Mugford, S. & Inkpen, N. (1995). The implementation of conferences as a new policy strategy: the case of drink drivers. Paper to American Society of Criminology Conference, Boston.

Murphey, D. A. (1992). Constructing the child: Relations between parents' beliefs and child outcomes. *Developmental Review*, 12, 199–232.

Nagin, D. S. & Paternoster, R. (1993). Enduring individual differences and rational choice theories of crime. *Law and Society Review*, 27(3), 467–496.

Nathanson, D. L. (1987). The shame/pride axis. In H. B. Lewis (ed.), *The role of shame in symptom formation* (pp. 183–205). Hillsdale, NJ: Erlbaum.

Nathanson, D. L. (1992). *Shame and pride: Affect, sex and the birth of the self*. New York, NY: W. W. Norton.

Nathanson, D. L. (1997). Affect theory and the compass of shame. In M. R. Lansky (ed.), *The widening scope of shame* (pp. 339–354). Hillsdale, NJ: The Analytic Press.

Newcomb, T. M. (1943). *Personality and social change; attitude formation in a student community.* New York, NY: Dryden Press.

Newcomb, T. M., Koenig, L. E., Flacks, R., & Warwick, D. P. (1967). *Persistence and change: Bennington College and its students after twenty-five years.* New York, NY: John Wiley.

Niedenthal, P. M., Tangney, J. P., & Gavanski, I. (1994). 'If only I weren't' versus 'If only I hadn't'": Distinguishing shame and guilt in counterfactual thinking. *Journal of Personality and Social Psychology,* 67(4), 585–595.

O'Connell, T. & Thorsborne, M. (1995). *Student behavior outcomes: Choosing appropriate paths.* Paper presented at the Conference: A restorative approach to interventions for serious incidents of harm in the school setting.

Olson, S. L., Bates, J. E., & Bayles, K. (1989). Predicting long-term developmental outcomes from maternal perceptions of infant and toddler behavior. *Infant Behavior and Development,* 12(1), 77–92.

Olson, S. L., Bates, J. E., & Bayles, K. (1990). Early antecedents of childhood impulsivity: The role of parent–child interaction, cognitive competence and temperament. *Journal of Abnormal Child Psychology,* 18, 317–334.

Olweus, D. (1973). *Hackkycklingar och oversittare.* Kungalv: Almqvist & Wiksell.

Olweus, D. (1977). Aggression and peer acceptance in adolescent boys; two short-term longitudinal studies of ratings. *Child Development,* 48, 1301–1313.

Olweus, D. (1978). *Aggression in the schools: Bullies and the whipping boys.* New York, NY: John Wiley.

Olweus, D. (1980). Familial and temperamental determinants of aggressive behavior in adolescent boys: A causal analysis. *Developmental Psychology,* 16, 644–660.

Olweus, D. (1984). Aggressors and their victims: Bullying at school. In N. Frude & H. Gault (eds.), *Disruptive Behavior in the Schools* (pp. 57–76). New York, NY: John Wiley.

Olweus, D. (1987). Bully/victim problems among school children in Scandinavia. In J. P. Myklebust & R. Ommundsen (eds.), *Psykologprofesjonen mot ar* 2000, Universitetsforlaget, Oslo.

Olweus, D. (1990). Bullying among school children. In K. Hurrelmann & F. Loesel (eds.), *Health Hazards in Adolescence: Prevention and Intervention in Childhood and Adolescence,* (pp. 259–297). Berlin: Walter De Gruyter.

Olweus, D. (1991). Bully/victim problems among school children: Basic facts and effects of a school based intervention program. In K. Rubin & D. Pepler (eds.), *The Development and Treatment of Childhood Aggression* (pp. 45–102). Hillsdale, NJ: Erlbaum.

Olweus, D. (1992). Bullying among children: Intervention and prevention. In R. D. V. Peters, R. J. McMahon, & V. L. Quinsey (eds.), *Aggression and violence throughout the life span* (pp. 100–125). Newbury Park, CA: Sage.

Olweus, D. (1993). *Bullying at school: What we know and what we can do.* Oxford: Blackwell.

Olweus, D. (1995). Bullying or peer abuse in school: Intervention and prevention. In D. Graham., L. Sally (eds.), *Psychology, Law, and Criminal Justice: International Developments in Research and Practice.* (pp. 248–263). Berlin: Walter De Gruyter.

O'Moore, A. M., & Hillery, B. (1989). Bullying in Dublin schools. *The Irish Journal of Psychology,* 10, 426–441.

O'Moore, A. M., & Hillery, B. (1991). What do teachers need to know? In M. Elliott (ed.), *Bullying: A practical guide to coping for schools* (pp. 56–69). Harlow, UK: Longman.

Ornstein, A. (1997). A developmental perspective on the sense of power, self-esteem, and destructive aggression. *Annual of Psychoanalysis*, 25, 145–154.

Osofsky, J.D. (1987). *Handbook of infant development* (2nd edn). New York, NY, and New Orleans, LA: John Wiley.

Oyserman, D., & Markus, H. R. (1990). Possible selves and delinquency. *Journal of Personality and Social Psychology*, 59(1), 112–125.

Oyserman, D., & Saltz, E. (1993). Competence, delinquency, and attempts to attain possible selves. *Journal of Personality and Social Psychology*, 65(2), 360–374.

Papini, D. R., & Rogman, L. A. (1992). Adolescent perceived attachment to parents in relation to competence, depression and anxiety: A longitudnal study. *Journal of Early Adolescence*, 12, 420–440.

Parke, R. D., & Ladd, G. W. (1992). *Family-peer relationships: Modes of linkage*. Hillsdale, NJ: Erlbaum.

Paternoster, R., & Iovanni, L. (1986). The deterrent effect of perceived severity: A reexamination. *Social Forces*, 64(3), 751–777.

Patterson G. R., Reid, J. B., & Dishion, T. J. (1992). *Antisocial boys. A social interactional approach* (vol. 4). Eugene, Oregon: Castalia Publishing Company.

Patterson, G. R. (1982). *Coercive family process*. Eugene, Oregon: Castalia Publishing Company.

Patterson, G. R. (1992). Developmental changes in antisocial behavior. In R. D. V. Peters, R. J. McMahon, & V. L. Quinsey (eds.), *Aggression and Violence Throughout the Lifespan*. Newbury Park, CA: Sage Publications.

Pearce, J. (1991). What can be done about the bully? In M. Elliott (ed.), *Bullying: A Practical Guide to Coping for Schools* (pp. 70–89). Harlow, UK: Longman.

Pease, K. (1998). Crime, labour and the wisdom of Solomon, *Policy Studies*, 19, 257–259.

Perry, D. G. (1995). Researching the aging well process. *American Behavioral Scientist*, 39(2), 152–171.

Perry, D. G., Kusel, S. J., & Perry, L. C. (1988). Victims of peer aggression. *Developmental Psychology*, 24(6), 807–814.

Perry, D. G., Williard, J. C., & Perry, L. C. (1990). Peers' perceptions of the consequences that victimized children provide aggressors. *Child Development*, 61, 1289–1309.

Peto, R., Pike, M. C., Armitage, P., Breslow, N. E., Cox, D. R., Howard, S. V., Mantel, N., McPherson, K., Peto, J., & Smith, P. G. (1976). Design and analysis of randomized clinical trials requiring prolonged observation of each patient: Part I – introduction and design. *British Journal of Cancer*, 34, 585–612.

Petrunik, M. & Shearing, C. D. (1988). The 'I', the 'me' and the 'it': Moving beyond the Meadian conception of the self. *Canadian Journal of Sociology*, 13, 435–448.

Pettit, G. S. (1997). The developmental course of violence and aggression: Mechanisms of family and peer influence. *Psychiatric Clinics of North America*, 20(2), 283–299.

Pettit, G. S., & Bates, J. E. (1989). Family interaction pattern and children's behavior problems from infancy to four years. *Developmental Psychology*, 25, 413–420.

Phares, V., Compas, B. E., & Howell, D. C. (1989). Perspectives on child behavior problems: Comparisons of children's self-reports with parent and teacher reports. *Psychological-Assessment*, 1(1), 68–71.

Phillips, J. C., & Kelly, D. H. (1979). School failure and delinquency: Which causes which? *Criminology*, 17(2), 194–207.

Piers, G., & Singer, M. B. (1953). *Shame and guilt: A psychoanalytic and a cultural study*. New York, NY: Norton.

Pittelkow, Y. E. (1991). *Bootstrap Confidence Region in Regression Problems.* Unpublished Master's thesis, The Australian National University, Canberra.

Potter-Efron, R. T, & Potter-Efron, P. (1989). *Letting go of shame.* Centre City, MN: Hazelden.

Potter-Efron, R. T. (1989). Shame, guilt and alcoholism: *Treatment issues in clinical practice. Haworth Series in Addictions Treatment* (vol. 2). New York, NY: Haworth Press.

Power, T. G., & Chapieski, M. L. (1986). Childrearing and impulse control in toddlers: A naturalistic investigation. *Developmental Psychology,* 22(2), 271–275.

Presser, L. & Gaarder, E. (1999). Can restorative justice reduce battering? Some preliminary considerations. Paper to Annual Meeting of the Academy of Criminal Justice Sciences, Orlando, Florida.

Puig-Antich, J. (1982). Major depression and conduct disorder in pre-puberty. *Journal of the American Academy of Child Psychiatry,* 21, 118–128.

Pulakos, J. (1996). Family environment and shame: Is there a relationship? *Journal of Clinical Psychology,* 52(6), 617–623.

Pulkkinen, L. (1996). Proactive and reactive aggression in early adolescence as precursors to anti and prosocial behavior in young adults. *Aggressive Behavior,* 22, 241–257.

Punamaeki, R. L., Quota, S., & El-Sarraj, E. (1997). Models of traumatic experiences and children's psychological adjustment: The roles of perceived parenting and children's own resources and activity. *Child Development,* 68(4), 718–728.

Radke-Yarrow, M., & Zahn-Waxler, C. (1986). The role of familial factors in the development of prosocial behavior: Research findings and questions. In D. Olweus, J. Block, & M. Radke-Yarrow (eds.), *Development of Antisocial and Prosocial Behavior: Research, Theories and Issues.* New York, NY: Academic Press.

Radke-Yarrow, M., Zahn-Waxler, C., & Chapman, M. (1983). Children's prosocial dispositions and behavior. In P. H. Mussen (ed.), *Handbook of Child Psychology: Vol. 2* (pp. 469–545). New York, NY: Wiley.

Ransford, H. E. (1968). Isolation, powerlessness, and violence: A study of attitudes and participation in the Watts riot. *American Journal of Sociology,* 73(5), 581–591.

Reicher, S., & Hopkins, N. (1996). Seeking influence through characterizing self-categories: An analysis of anti-abortionist rhetoric. *British Journal of Social Psychology,* 35(2), 297–311.

Reid, K. (1982). The self-concept and persistent school absenteeism. *British Journal of Educational Psychology,* 52, 179–187.

Retzinger, S. M. (1985). The resentment process: Videotape studies. *Psychoanalytical Psychology,* 2, 129–153.

Retzinger, S. M. (1987). Resentment and laughter: video studies of the shame–rage spiral. In Lewis H.B. (ed.), *The role of shame in symptom formation* (pp. 151–181). Hillsdale, NJ: LEA.

Retzinger, S. M. (1989). A theory of mental illness: Integrating social and emotional aspects. *Psychiatry,* 152(3), 325–335.

Retzinger, S. M. (1991a). Shame, anger and conflict: Case study of emotional violence. *Journal of Family Violence,* 6(1).

Retzinger, S. M. (1991b). *Violent Emotions: Shame and Rage in Marital Quarrels.* Newbury Park, CA: Sage Publications.

Retzinger, S. M. (1996). Shame and the social bond. In D. Parker, R. Dalziel. & I. Wright (eds.), *Shame and the modern self* (pp. 6–20). Victoria: Australian Scholarly Publishing.

Retzinger, S. M., & Scheff, T. J. (1996). Strategy for community conferences: Emotions and social bonds. In B. Galaway & J. Hudson (eds.), *Restorative justice: International perspectives.* Monsey, NY: Criminal Justice Press.

Rican, P. (1995). Family values may be responsible for bullying. *Studia Psychologica*, 37(1), 31–36.

Rican, P., Klicperova, M., & Koucka, T. (1993). Families of Bullies and Their Victims: A Children's View. *Studia Psychologica*, 35(3), 261–266.

Rigby, K. (1993). School children's perceptions of their families and parents as a function of peer relations. *Journal of Genetic Psychology*, 154(4), 501–513.

Rigby, K. (1994). Psychosocial functioning in families of Australian adolescent school children involved in bully victim problems. *Journal of Family Therapy*, 16, 173–187.

Rigby, K. (1996). *Bullying in schools: What to do about it.* Melbourne: Australian Council for Education Research Limited.

Rigby, K., & Cox, I. (1996). The contribution of bullying at school and low self-esteem to acts of delinquency among Australian teenagers. *Personality and Individual Differences*, 21(4), 609–612.

Rigby, K., Cox, I., & Black, G. (1997). Cooperativeness and bully/victim problems among Australian school children. *The Journal of Social Psychology*, 137(3), 357–368.

Rigby, K., & Slee, P. T. (1990). Victims and bullies in school communities. *Journal of the Australasian Society of Victimology*, 1(2), 23–28.

Rigby, K., & Slee, P. T. (1991a). Victims in school communities. *Journal of the Australasian Society of Victimology*, 25–31.

Rigby, K., & Slee, P. T. (1991b). Bullying among Australian school children: Reported behavior and attitudes toward victims. *Journal of Social Psychology*, 131(13), 615–627.

Rigby, K., & Slee, P. T. (1993a). *The Peer Relations Questionnaire (PRQ).* Adelaide: University of South Australia.

Rigby, K., & Slee, P. T. (1993b). Dimensions of interpersonal relation among Australian children and implications for psychological well-being. *Journal of Social Psychology*, 133(1), 33–42.

Riley, W. T., Treiber, F. A., & Woods, M. G. (1989). Anger and hostility in depression. *Journal of Nervous and Mental Disease*, 177, 668–674.

Robinson, J. L., & Zahn-Waxler, C. (1994). Patterns of development in early empathic behavior: Environmental and child constitutional influences. *Social Development*, 3, 125–145.

Rogers, C. R., & Dymond, R. F. (1954). *Psychotherapy and personality change.* Chicago, IL: University of Chicago Press.

Rokeach, M. (1973). *The nature of human values.* New York, NY: Free Press.

Roland, E. (1989). Bullying: the Scandinavian research tradition. In D. P. Tattum & D. A. Lane (eds.), *Bullying in Schools.* London: Trentham Books.

Rollins, B. C., & Thomas, D. L. (1979). Parental support, power and control techniques in the socialization of children. In W. R. Burr, R. Hill, F. I. Nye, & I. L. Reiss (eds.), *Contemporary theories about the family: Research based theories.* Vol. 1. New York, NY: Free Press

Rosenberg, M. (1965). *Society and the adolescent self-image.* Princeton, NJ: Princeton University Press.

Rosenberg, M. (1979). Group rejection and self-rejection. *Research in Community and Mental Health*, 1, 3–20.

Rosenberg, M. (1986). *Concerning the self.* Malabar: Kreiger.

Rosenberg, M., & Simmons, R. G. (1971). *Black and white self-esteem: The urban school child.* Washington, DC: American Sociological Association.

Ross, D. M. (1996). *Childhood bullying and teasing: What school personnel, other professionals, and parents can do.* Alexandria, VA.

Ross, R. (1996). *Returning to the teachings. Exploring aboriginal justice.* London: Penguin Books.

Rotter, J. B. (1966). Generalized expectancies for internal versus external control of reinforcement. *Psychological Monographs: General and Applied*, 80(1), 1–28.

Rushton, J. P., Brainerd, C. J., & Pressley, M. (1983). Behavioral development and construct validity: The principal of aggregation. *Psychological Bulletin*, 94, 462–469.

Russo, M. F., & Beidel, D. C. (1994). Comorbidity of childhood anxiety and externalizing disorders: Prevalence, associated characteristics, and validation issues. *Clinical Psychology Review*, 14(3), 199–221.

Saarni, C. (1990). Emotional competence: How emotions and relationships become integrated. In R. A. Thompson (ed.), *Socioemotional Development* (pp. 115–182). Lincoln: University of Nebraska Press.

Sabini, J. & Silver, M. (1997). In defense of shame: Shame in the context of guilt and embarrassment. *Journal for the Theory of Social behavior*, 27(1), 1–15.

Sachdev, P. S. (1990). Whakama: Culturally determined behaviour in the New Zealand Maori. *Psychological Medicine*, 20(2), 433–444.

Sampson, R. J., & Laub, J. H. (1993). *Crime in the making: Pathways and turning points through life.* Cambridge, MA: Harvard University Press.

Sanftner, J. L., Barlow, D., Marschall, D. E. & Tangney, J. P. (1995). The relation of shame and guilt to eating disorder symptomatology. *Journal of Social and Clinical Psychology*, 14(4), 315–324.

Sartre, J. P. (1956). *Being and nothingness.* New York, NY: Philosophical Library.

Schachter, S., & Singer, J. (1962). Cognitive, social, and physiological determinants of emotional state. *Psychological Review*, 69, 379–399.

Schalling, D., Edman, G., Asberg, M., & Oreland, L. (1988). Platelet MAO activity associated with impulsivity and aggressivity. *Personality and Individual Differences*, 9(3), 597–605.

Scheff, T. J. (1979). *Catharsis in healing, ritual and drama.* Berkeley, CA: University of California Press.

Scheff, T. J. (1987). The shame–rage spiral: A case study of an interminable quarrel. In H. B. Lewis (ed.), *The role of shame in symptom formation.* (pp. 109–149). Hillsdale, NJ: Erlbaum.

Scheff, T. J. (1988). Shame and conformity: The deference-emotion system. *American Sociological Review*, 53(3), 395–406.

Scheff, T. J. (1989). Cognitive and emotional conflict in anorexia: Reanalysis of a classic case. *Psychiatry*, 52(2), 148–161.

Scheff, T. J. (1990a). *Microsociology: Discourse, emotion, and social structure.* Chicago, IL: University of Chicago Press.

Scheff, T. J. (1990b). Review essay: A new Durkheim. *American Journal of Sociology*, 96 (3), 741–746.

Scheff, T. J. (1991). The origins of World War I: A sociological theory. Paper presented at the Society for the Study of Social Problems (SSSP). Department of Sociology, University of California, Santa Barbara.

Scheff, T. J. (1994). *Bloody revenge: Emotions, nationalism, and war.* Boulder, CO: Westview Press.

Scheff, T. J. (1995). Shame and related emotions: Overview. *American Behavioral Scientist*, 38(8), 1053–1059.

Scheff, T. J. (1996a). Self-esteem and shame: Unlocking the puzzle. In R. Kwan (ed.), *Individuality and social control: Essays in honour of Tamotsu Shibutani.* Greenwich: JAI Press.

Scheff, T. J. (1996b). Shame and the origins of World War II: Hitler's appeal to German

people. In D. Parker, R. Dalziel, & I. Wright (eds.), *Shame and the modern self.* (pp. 97–115). Victoria: Australian Scholarly Publishing.

Scheff, T. J., & Retzinger, S. M. (1991). *Emotions and violence: Shame and rage in destructive conflicts.* Lexington, MA: Lexington Books/D. C. Heath and Company.

Schneider, C. D. (1977). *Shame, exposure, and privacy.* New York, NY: W. W. Norton.

Schur, E. M. (1973). *Radical non-intervention: Rethinking the delinquency problem.* Englewood Cliffs, NJ: Prentice-Hall.

Schwartz, D., Dodge, K. A., Pettit, G. S., & Bates, J. E. (1997). The early socialization of aggressive victims of bullying. *Child Development*, 68(4), 665–675.

Schwartz, S. H. (1977). Normative influences on altruism. In L. Berkowitz (ed.), *Advances in experimental social psychology* (Vol. 10). New York, NY: Academic Press.

Scott, R., & Scott, W. A. (1998). *Adjustment of adolescents: Cross-cultural similarities and differences.* New York, NY: Routledge.

Scully, D. and Marolla, J. (1985). 'Riding the bull at Gilley's': Convicted rapists describe the rewards of rape. *Social Problems*, 32: 251–263.

Sears, R. R., Maccoby, E. E., & Levin, H. (1957). *Patterns of child rearing.* New York, NY: Harper & Row.

Seligman, M. E. P. (1975). *Helplessness: On depression, development and death.* San Francisco, CA: W. H. Freeman.

Severson, H., & Biglan, A. (1989). Rationale for the use of passive consent in smoking prevention research: Politics, policy, and pragmatics. *Preventive Medicine*, 18, 267–279.

Sharp, S., & Smith, P. K. (1992). Bullying in UK schools: The DES Sheffield bullying project. *Early Childhood Development and Care*, 77, 47–55.

Sherif, M. (1936). *The psychology of social norms.* New York, NY: Harper.

Sherif, M., & Sherif, C. W. (1969). *Social psychology.* New York, NY: Harper and Row Publishers.

Sherman, L. W. (1992). *Policing domestic violence.* New York, NY: Free Press.

Sherman, L. W. (1993). Defiance, deterrence, and irrelevance: A theory of the criminal sanction. *Journal of Research in Crime and Delinquency*, 30(4), 445–473.

Sherman, L. W., Strang, H., Barnes, G., Braithwaite, J., Inkpen, N., & Teh, M. (1998). *Experiments in restorative policing: A progress report.* Canberra: Australian National University.

Sherman, L., Gottfredson, D., MacKenzie, D., Eck, J., Reuter, P., & Bushway, S. (1997). *Preventing crime: What works, what doesn't, what's promising: A report to the United States Congress.* Washington, DC: National Institute of Justice.

Sherman, L., Braithwaite, J., & Strang, H. (1994). *Reintegrative shaming of violence, drink driving and property crime: A randomised controlled trial.*

Sigel, I. E. (1985). *Parental belief systems: The psychological consequences for children.* (1st edn). Hillsdale, NJ: Erlbaum Associates.

Sigel, I. E., McGillicuddy-DeLisi, A. V., & Goodnow, J. J. (1992). *Parental belief systems: The psychological consequences for children* (2nd edn). Hillsdale, NJ: Erlbaum Associates.

Simons, R. L., Wu, C., Lin, K., Gordon, L. & Conger, R.D. (2000). A cross-cultural examination of the link between corporal punishment and adolescent antisocial behavior. *Criminology*, 38 (1), 47–79.

Simpson, S. S. (1998). *Shaming the corporate criminal.* Paper presented at the 12th International Congress on Criminology, Seoul, Korea.

Slee, P. T. (1993). Bullying: A preliminary investigation of its nature and the effects of social cognition. *Early Child Development and Care*, 87, 47–57.

Slee, P. T. (1994). Life at school used to be good. Victimization and health concerns of secondary students. *Youth Studies*, December.

Slee, P. T. (1995). Peer victimization and its relationship to depression among Australian primary school students. *Personality and Individual Differences*, 18(1), 57–62.

Slee, P. T., & Rigby, K. (1993). The relationship of Eysenck's personality factors and self-esteem to bully-victim behavior in Australian school boys. *Personality and Individual Differences*, 14(2), 371–373.

Smetana, J. G. (1988). Adolescents' and parents' conceptions of parental authority. *Child Development*, 59(2), 321–335.

Smetana, J. G. (1994). Beliefs about parenting: Origins and developmental implications. *New Directions for Child Development* (vol. 66, pp. 5–19). San Francisco, CA: Jossey-Bass.

Smith, D., & Stephenson, P. (1991). Why some schools don't have bullies. In M. Elliott (ed.), *Bullying: A practical guide to coping for schools* (pp. 133–145). Harlow, UK: Longman.

Smith, P. K. (1991). The silent nightmare: Bullying and victimization in school peer groups. *The Psychologist*, 4, 243–248.

Smith, P. K., & Boulton, M. J. (1991). Rough and tumble play. *Ethology and Sociobiology*, 10, 331–341.

Smith, P. K., Bowers, L., Binney, V., & Cowie, H. (1993). Relationships of children involved in bully/victim problems at school. In S. Duck (ed.), *Learning about relationships*, Vol. 2 (pp. 184–204). Newbury Park, CA: Sage.

Snyder, J. & Patterson, G. (1990). Family interaction and delinquent behavior. In H.C. Quay (ed.), *Handbook of Juvenile Delinquency* (pp. 216–243). New Yorl, NY: John Wiley and Sons.

Spicer, S. J., & Franklin, C. (1994). Exploratory effects of social support, stress and locus of control on the conflict tactics of parents at-risk for child maltreatment. *Journal of Social Service Research*, 19(3–4), 1–22.

Staub, E. (1979). *Positive social behavior and morality: Socialization and development* (Vol. 2). San Diego, CA: Academic Press.

Staub, E. (1989). *The roots of evil: The origins of genocide and other group violence.* Cambridge: Cambridge University Press.

Steele, C. M. (1988). The psychology of self-affirmation: Sustaining the integrity of the self. In L. Berkowitz & et al. (eds.), *Advances in experimental social psychology, Vol. 21: Social psychological studies of the self: Perspectives and programs* (pp. 261-302). San Diego, CA: Academic Press.

Steele, C. M., & Liu, T. J. (1983). Dissonance processes as self-affirmation. *Journal of Personality and Social Psychology*, 45, 5–19.

Stein, K. F., Roeser, R., & Markus, H. R. (1998). Self-schemas and possible selves as predictors and outcomes of risky behaviors in adolescents. *Nursing Research*, 47(2), 96–106.

Steinberg, L., Mounts, N. S., Lamborn, S. D., & Dornbusch, S. M. (1991). Authoritative parenting and adolescent adjustment across varied ecological niches. *Journal of Research on Adolescence*, 1(1), 19–36.

Stephenson, P., & Smith, D. (1987). Anatomy of a playground bully. *Education*, 18, 236–237.

Stephenson, P., & Smith, D. (1989). Bullying in the junior school. In D. P. Tattum & D. A. Lane (eds.), *Bullying in Schools* (pp. 45–57). Stoke-on-Trent: Trentham Books.

Sterling, S., Cowen, E. L., Weissberg, R. P., Lotyezewski, B. S., & Boike, M. (1985). Recent stressful life events and young children's school adjustment. *American Journal of Community Psychology*, 13(1), 87–98.

Stewart, T. (1993). The Youth Justice Co-Ordinator's role – A personal perspective of the new legislation in action. In B.J. Brown, & F.W.M. McElrea (eds.) *The Youth Court in New Zealand: A new model of justice*, Auckland: Legal Research Foundation.

Stewart, M. A., De-blois, S., Meardon, J., & Cummings, C. (1980). Aggressive conduct disorder of children: The clinical picture. *Journal of Nervous and Mental Disease*, 168, 604–610.

Stipek, D. J. (1983). A developmental analysis of pride and shame. *Human Development*, 26(1), 42–54.

Stipek, D. J., Recchia, S., & McClintic, S. (1992). Self-evaluation in young children. *Monographs of the Society for Research in Child Development*, 57(1), Mono 226: 100.

Strang, H. (2000). Victim participation in a restorative justice process: The Canberra Reintegrative Shaming Experiments. Unpublished PhD Dissertation, Australian National University, Canberra.

Strang, H., & Sherman, L. W. (1997). The victim's perspective. Paper 2, RISE Working Paper, Law Program, RSSS, Australian National University, Canberra.

Strassberg, Z., Dodge, K. A., Pettit, G. S., & Bates, J. E. (1994). Spanking at home and children's subsequent aggression toward kindergarten peers. *Development and Psychopathology*, 6(3), 445–461.

Sujan, H. (1986). Smarter versus harder: An exploratory attributional analysis of salespeople's motivation. *Journal of Marketing Research*, 23(1), 41–49.

Sykes, G., & Matza, D. (1957). Techniques of neutralization: a theory of delinquency. *American Sociological Review*. 22, 664–70.

Tabachnick, B. G., & Fidell, L. S. (1989). *Using mulitivariate statistics*. (2nd edn). New York, NY: Harper and Row Publishers.

Tajfel, H. (1972). La categorisation sociale. In S. Moscovichi (ed.), *Introduction a la psychologie sociale* (pp. 272–302). Paris: Larousse.

Tajfel, H., & Turner, J. C. (1979). An integrative theory of intergroup conflict. In W. G. Austin & S. Worchel (eds.), *The social psychology of intergroup relations*. Monterey, CA: Brooks/Cole.

Tangney, J. P. (1990). Assessing individual differences in proneness to shame and guilt: Development of the self-conscious affect and attribution inventory. *Journal of Personality and Social Psychology*, 59, 102–111.

Tangney, J. P. (1991). Moral affect: The good, the bad, and the ugly. *Journal of Personality and Social Psychology* 61(4), 598–607.

Tangney, J. P. (1992). Situational determinants of shame and guilt in young adulthood. *Personality and Social Psychology Bulletin*, 18(2), 199–206.

Tangney, J. P. (1993). Shame and guilt. In C.G. Costello (ed.), *Symptoms of depression*. (pp. 161–180). New York, NY: John Wiley & Sons.

Tangney, J. P. (1995a). Shame and guilt in interpersonal relationships. In J. P. Tangney & K.W. Fisher (eds.), *Self-conscious emotions:The psychology of shame, guilt, embarrassment and pride* (pp. 114–139). New York, NY: Guilford Press.

Tangney, J. P. (1995b). Recent advances in the empirical study of shame and guilt. *American Behavioral Scientist*, 38(8), 1132–1145.

Tangney, J. P., Burggraf, S. A., & Wagner, P. E. (1995). Shame-proneness, guilt-proneness, and psychological symptoms. In J. P. Tangney & K.W. Fischer (eds.), *Self-conscious emotions: The psychology of shame, guilt, embarrassment, and pride*. (pp. 343–367). New York, NY: Guilford Press.

Tangney, J. P., Hill-Barlow, D., Wagner, P. E., Marschall, D. E., Borenstein, J. K., Sanftner, J. M. T., & Gramzow, R. (1996a). Assessing individual differences in constructive versus destructive responses to anger across the lifespan. *Journal of Personality and Social Psychology*, 70(4), 780–796.

Tangney, J. P., Miller, R. S., Flicker, L., & Barlow, D. H. (1996b). Are shame, guilt, and embarrassment distinct emotions? *Journal of Personality and Social Psychology*, 70(6), 1256–1269.

Tangney, J. P., Wagner, P. E., Fletcher, C., & Gramzow, R. (1992a). Shamed into anger? The relation of shame and guilt to anger and self-reported aggression. *Journal of Personality and Social Psychology*, 62, 669–675.

Tangney, J. P., Wagner, P. E., & Gramzow, R. (1989). *The test of self-conscious affect*. Fairfax, VA: George Mason University.

Tangney, J. P., Wagner, P. E., & Gramzow, R. (1992b). Proneness to shame, proneness to guilt, and psychopathology. *Journal of Abnormal Psychology*, 101(3), 469–478.

Tangney, J. P., Wagner, P. E., Hill-Barlow, D., Marschall, D. E., & Gramzow, R. (1996c). Relation of shame and guilt to constructive versus destructive responses to anger across the lifespan. *Journal of Personality and Social Psychology*, 70(4), 797–809.

Taris, T. W., & Bok, I. A. (1996). Parenting environment and scholastic achievement during adolescence: A retrospective study. *Early Child Development and Care*, 121, 67–83.

Tattum, D. P. (1989). Violence and aggression in schools. In D. P. Tattum & D. A. Lane (eds.), *Bullying in Schools*. London: Trentham Books.

Tattum, D. P. (1993). *Understanding and managing bullying*. Oxford: Heinemann.

Tattum, D. P., & Lane, D. A. (1989). *Bullying in schools*. Stoke-on-Trent: Trentham Books.

Tattum, D. P., Tattum, E., & Herbert, G. (1993). *Bullying in secondary schools* (video and resource pack). Cardiff: Drake Educational Associates.

Tattum, D., & Herbert, G. (1990). *Bullying: A positive response*. Cardiff: Cardiff Institute of Higher Education.

Taylor, C., & Kleinke, C. L. (1992). Effects of severity of accident, history of drunk driving, intent, and remorse on judgments of a drunk driver. *Journal of Applied Social Psychology* 22(21), 1641–1655.

Taylor, G. (1985). *Pride, shame and guilt: Emotions of self-assessment*. Oxford: Oxford University Press.

Tellegen, A., Lykken, D. T., & Bouchard, T. J. (1988). Personality similarity in twins reared apart and together. *Journal of Personality and Social Psychology*, 54, 1031–1039.

Thomas, C. W., & Hyman, J. M. (1978). Compliance theory, Control theory and Juvenile delinquency. In M. D. Krohn & R. L. Akers (eds.), *Crime, Law and Sanctions*. London: Sage.

Tibbetts, S. G. (1997). Shame and rational choice in offending decisions. *Criminal Justice and Behavior*, 24(2), 234–255.

Tisak, M. S., & Jankowski, A. M. (1996). Societal rule evaluations: Adolescent offender' reasoning about moral, conventional, and personal rules. *Aggressive Behavior*, 22(3), 195–207.

Tittle, C. R. (1995). *Control balance: toward a general theory of deviance*. Boulder, CO: Westview Press.

Tomkins, S. S. (1962). *Affect, imagery, consciousness: Vol. I. The positive affects*. New York, NY: Springer.

Tomkins, S. S. (1963). *Affect, imagery, consciousness: Vol. II*. New York, NY: Springer.

Tomkins, S. S. (1981). The quest for primary motives: Biography and autobiography of an idea. *Journal of Personality and Social Psychology* 41(2), 306–329.

Tomkins, S. S. (1987). Shame. In D. L. Nathanson (ed.), *The many faces of shame* (pp. 133–161). New York, NY: Guilford Press.

Trasler, G. (1972). The context of social learning. In J. B. Mays (ed.). *Juvenile delinquency, the family and the social group.* London: Longman.

Trawick-Smith, J. (1988). Let's say you're the baby, ok? Play leadership and following behavior of young children. *Young Children*, 43(5), 51–59.

Trickett, P. K., & Kuczynski, L. (1986). Children's misbehaviors and parental discipline strategies in abusive and nonabusive families. *Developmental Psychology*, 22(1), 115–123.

Trotter, C. (1990). Probation can work: a research study using volunteers. *Australian Journal of Social Work*, 43(2),13–18.

Trotter, C. (1993). The effective supervision of offenders. Unpublished Doctoral Dissertation, La Trobe University, Melbourne.

Trotter, C. (1999). *Working with involuntary clients.* St. Leonards, Australia: Allen and Unwin.

Troy, M., & Sroufe, L. A. (1987). Victimization among preschoolers: Role of attachment relationship history. *Journal of the American Academy of Child and Adolescent Psychiatry*, 26, 166–172.

Turner, F. (1995). Shame, beauty, and the tragic view of history. *American Behavioral Scientist*, 38(8), 1060–1075.

Turner, J. C. (1991). *Social influence.* Pacific Grove, CA: Brooks/Cole.

Turner, J. C., & Onorato, R. S. (1999). Social identity, personality, and the self-concept: A self-categorizing perspective. In T. R. Tyler (ed.), *The psychology of the social self. Applied social research* (pp. 11–46). Mahwah, NJ: Erlbaum.

Turner, J. C., Hogg, M. A., Oakes, P. J., Reicher, S. D., & Wetherell, M. S. (1987). *Rediscovering the social group: A self-categorization theory.* New York, NY: Basil Blackwell.

Tutu, Desmond (1999). *No future without forgiveness.* London: Rider.

Tyler, T. R. (1990). *Why people obey the law.* New Haven, CT: Yale University Press.

Tyler, T. R. (1997). The psychology of legitimacy: A relational perspective on voluntary deference to authorities. *Social Psychology Review*, 4, 323–345.

Tyler, T. R. (1999). Trust and democratic governance. In V. Braithwaite and M. Levi (eds.), *Trust and governance.* New York, NY: Russell Sage.

Tyler, T. R. & Degoey, P. (1996). Trust in organizational authorities: the influence of motive attributions on willingness to accept decisions. In R. Kramer and T. R. Tyler (eds.), *Trust in organizations.* Thousand Oaks, CA: Sage.

Tyler, T. R., Degoey, P., & Smith, H. (1996). Understanding why the justice of group procedures matters: A test of the psychological dynamics of the group-value model. *Journal of Personality and Social Psychology*, 70(5), 913–930.

Umbreit, M. (1985). *Crime and reconciliation: Creative options for victims and offenders.* Nashville, TN: Abigton Press.

Van Ness, D. (1997). *Restoring justice.* Cincinnati: Anderson Publishing.

Von Hirsch, A. (1993). *Censure and sanctions.* Oxford: Oxford University Press.

Wachtel, T. & McCold, P. (2001). Restorative justice in everyday life. In H. Strang & J. Braithwaite (eds.), *Restorative Justice and Civil Society.* Cambridge: Cambridge University Press.

Wagatsuma, H. & Rosett, A. (1986). The Implications of Apology: Law and culture in Japan and the United States. *Law and Society Review*, 20 (4), 461–498.

Walker, J. L., Lahey, B. B., Russo, M. F., Frick, P. J., Christ, M. A. G., McBurnett, K., Loeber, R., Stouthamer-Loeber, M., & Green, S. M. (1991). Anxiety, inhibition, and conduct disorder in children: I. Relations to social impairment. *Journal of the American Academy of Child Psychiatry*, 30, 187–191.

Wallbott, H. G., & Scherer, K. R. (1995). Cultural determinants in experiencing shame and guilt. In J. P. Tangney & K. W. Fischer (eds.), *Self conscious emotions: The psychology of shame, guilt, embarrassment, and pride* (pp. 465–487). New York, NY: Guilford Press.

Wang, D., Wang, Y., & Zhang, Y. (1992). The relationship between locus of control, depression, shame, and self-esteem. *Child Mental Health Journal*, 6(5), 207–210.

Weatherburn, D. & Lind, B. (forthcoming). *The Economic and Social Antecedents of Delinquent-Prone Communities*. Cambridge: Cambridge University Press.

Webb, L. (1969). *Children with special needs in the infants' school*. London: Fontana Books.

Weiner, B. (1979). A theory of motivation for some classroom experiences. *Journal of Educational Psychology*, 71(1), 3–25.

Weiner, B. (1980). A cognition (attribution) -emotion-action model of motivated behavior: An analysis of judgments of help-giving. *Journal of Personality and Social Psychology*, 29, 186–200.

Weiner, B. (1985). An attributional theory of achievement motivation and emotion. *Psychological Review*, 92, 548–73.

Weiner, B. (1991). On perceiving others as responsible. In R. Dientsbier (ed.), *Nebraska symposium on motivation*, Vol. 38, (pp. 165–198). Lincoln: University of Nebraska Press.

Weiner, B. (1993). On sin versus sickness: A theory of perceived responsibility and social motivation. *American Psychologist*, 48, 957–965.

Weiner, B. (1995). *Judgements of responsibility: A foundation for a theory of social conduct*. New York, NY: Guilford Press.

Weiss, B., Dodge, K. A., Bates, J. E., & Pettit, G. S. (1992). Some consequences of early harsh discipline: Child aggression and a maladaptive social information processing style. *Child Development*, 63, 1321–1335.

Weitekamp, E. G. M. (1998). Continuity and Discontinuity in Criminal Careers. *American Journal of Sociology*, 103(4), 1145–1147.

Weitekamp, E. G. M. (1999). The history of restorative justice. In G. Bazemore & L. Walgrave (eds.), *Restorative Juvenile Justice: Repairing the Harm of the Youth Crime*. Monsey, NY: Criminal Justice Press.

Werner, L. J., & Broida, J. P. (1991). Adult self-esteem and locus of control as a function of family alcoholism and dysfunction. *Journal of Studies on Alcohol*, 52(3), 249–252.

Whalen, C. K., Henker, B., Hinshaw, S. P., & Granger, D. A. (1989). Externalizing behavior disorders, situational generality, and the type A behavior pattern. *Child Development*, 60(6), 1453–62.

Whiting, B. B., & Whiting, J. W. (1975). *Children of six cultures: A psycho-cultural analysis*. Cambridge, MA: Harvard University Press.

Whitney, I., & Smith, P. K. (1993). A survey of the nature and extent of bullying in junior/middle and secondary schools. *Educational Research*, 35, 3–25.

Whitney, I., Nabuzoka, D., & Smith, P. K. (1992). Bullying in schools: Mainstream and special needs. *Support for Learning*, 7(1), 3–7.

Wiatrowski, M. D., Griswald, D. B., & Roberts, M. R. (1981). Social control theory and delinquency. *American Sociological Review*, 46, 525–541.

Wicker, F. W., Payne, G. C., & Morgan, R. D. (1983). Participant descriptions of guilt and shame. *Motivation and Emotion*, 7, 25–39.

Wikstrom, P. H. (1998) Communities and crime. In M. Tonry (ed.), *The handbook of crime and punishment*. New York: Oxford University Press.

Wiehe, V. R. (1991). *Perilous rivalry: When siblings become abusive*. Lexington, MA: Health/Lexington Books.

Williams, B. (1993). *Shame and necessity*. Berkeley, CA: University of California Press.

Wingrove, Janet, & Bond, Alyson J. (1998). Angry reactions to failure on a cooperative computer game: The effect of trait hostility, behavioural inhibition, and behavioural activation. *Aggressive Behavior*, 24(1), 27–36.

Witkin, H. A. (1965). Psychological differentiation and forms of pathology. *Journal of Abnormal Psychology*, 70(5), 317–336.

Witkin, H. A., Lewis, H. B., Hertzman, M., Machover, K., Meissner, P. B., & Wapner, S. (1954). *Personality through perception: an experimental and clinical study*. New York, NY: Harper.

Woolston, J. L., Rosenthal, S. L., Riddle, M. A., Sparrow, S. S., Cicchetti, D., & Zimmerman, L. D. (1989). Childhood comorbidity of anxiety/affective disorders and behavior disorders. *Journal of the American Academy of Child Psychiatry*, 28, 707–713.

Wright, M. (1996). *Justice for victims and offenders: A restorative response to crime* (2nd edn). Winchester: Waterside Press.

Wurmser, L. (1981). *The mask of shame*. Baltimore: John Hopkins University Press.

Wurmser, L. (1994). *The mask of shame*. Northvale, NJ: Jason Aronson.

Wyatt G. E., & Mickey, M. R. (1988). The support of parents and others as it mediates the effects of child sexual abuse: An exploratory study. In G. E. Wyatt & G. J. Powell (eds.), *Lasting effects of child sexual abuse* (pp. 211–226). Newbury Park, CA: Sage Publications.

Yates, C., & Smith, P. K. (1989). Bullying in two English comprehensive schools. In E. Roland & E. Munthe (eds.), *Bullying: An international perspective*. London: David Fulton.

Zahn-Waxler, C., & Radke-Yarrow, M. (1990). The origins of empathic concern. *Motivation and Emotion*, 14, 107–130.

Zahn-Waxler, C., & Robinson, J. (1995). Empathy and guilt: Early origins of feelings of responsibilty. In J. P. Tangney & K. W. Fisher (eds.), *Self-conscious emotions: The Psychology of shame, guilt, embarrassment and pride* (pp. 143–173). New York, NY: Guilford Press.

Zahn-Waxler, C., Kochanska, G., Krupnick, J., & McKnew, D. (1990). Patterns of guilt and children of depressed and well mothers. *Developmental Psychology*, 26, 51–59.

Zahn-Waxler, C., Radke-Yarrow, M., & King, R. A. (1979). Child rearing and children's initiations toward victims of distress. *Child Development*, 50, 319–330.

Zehr, H. (1990). *Changing lenses: A new focus for criminal justice*. Scottsdale, PA: Herald Press.

Zehr, H. (1995). Rethinking criminal justice: Restorative justice. Unpublished paper.

Zehr, H. (2000). Journey of belonging. Paper to Fourth International Conference on Restorative Justice. Tuebingen.

Zevon, M. A., & Tellegen, A. (1982). The structure of mood change: An idiographic/nomothetic analysis. *Journal of Personality and Social Psychology*, 43, 111–122.

Zhang, L., & Zhang, S. (2000). Reintegrative shaming and delinquency. Unpublished paper. Saint Francis College, Loretto, PA.

Zhang, L., Zhou, D., Messner, S., Liska, A. E., Krohn, M. D., Liu, J., & Zhou, L. (1996). Crime prevention in a communitarian society: Bang-jiao and tiao-jie in the People's Republic of China. *Justice Quarterly*. 13, 199–222.

Zhang, S. X. (1995). Measuring shaming in an ethnic context. *British Journal of Criminology*, 35(2), 248–262.

Ziegler, S., & Rosenstein-Manner, M. (1991). *Bullying at school: Toronto in an international context.* Toronto: Board of Education.

Zoccolillo, M. (1992). Co-occurrence of conduct disorder and its adult outcomes with depressive and anxiety disorders: A review. *Journal of the American Academy of Child Psychiatry*, 31, 973–981.

Index

10

B-
108-

132

182

262